SOLVING PROBABILITY

Solutions to Problems Suggested by Grimmett and Welsh

Huy Bui

BS in Mathematics, Georgia Institute of Technology

Cover Designer: Huyen Truong / VINOEP JSC
Cover Illustration: : Pham Thi Meo / Instagram: pham.thi.meo
Compositor: VINOEP JSC

About the cover: A Mekong Delta farmer wearing a Non La and a Khan Ran.

Printed by Amazon.com Services LLC

Preface

The present volume contains hints or full solutions to many of the exercises in the first eight chapters of the text *Probability: An Introduction*, 2nd Edition by Geoffrey Grimmett, *Professor of Mathematical Statistics, University of Cambridge*, and Dominic Welsh, *Professor of Mathematics (retired), University of Oxford*. Solving problems being an essential part of the learning process, my goal is to provide those learning and teaching probability with a large number of worked out exercises. Grimmet and Welsh's textbook covers all the topics in probability that are usually taught at the undergraduate level for math students with calculus, but not measure theory: probabilities, random variables, discrete and continuous distributions, joint distributions, transformations, moments, conditioning, basic limit theorems, inequalities. Therefore this solutions manual can be helpful to anyone learning or teaching probability at the college level.

As Grimmett and Welsh's textbook appears simple until you try to do the exercises, I encourage the reader to work through all of the exercises. Many ideas are contained in a few words of typical probability problems such as dice, cards, coins, etc. To make the solutions concise, I have included only the necessary arguments; the reader may have to fill in the details to get complete proofs.

Comments and questions on possibly erroneous solutions, as well as suggestions for more elegant or more complete solutions will be greatly appreciated.

Huy Bui
Georgia Tech, 2019

Contents

Part 1

Basic Probability

CHAPTER 1

Events and probabilities

1.1. Experiments with chance

1.2. Outcomes and events

EXERCISE (1.8). If $A, B \in \mathcal{F}$, show that $A \cap B \in \mathcal{F}$.

SOLUTION. The complement of $A \cap B$ equals $(\Omega \backslash A) \cup (\Omega \backslash B)$, which is the union of events and is therefore an event. Hence $A \cap B$ is an event, by (1.3).

EXERCISE (1.9). The *difference* $A \backslash B$ of two subsets A and B of is the set $A \cap (\Omega \backslash B)$ of all points of Ω which are in A but not in B. Show that if $A, B \in \mathcal{F}$, then $A \backslash B \in \mathcal{F}$.

SOLUTION. The complement of $A \backslash B$ equals $(\Omega \backslash A) \cup B$, which is the union of events and is therefore an event. Hence $A \backslash B$ is an event, by (1.3).

EXERCISE (1.10). The *symmetric difference* $A \triangle B$ of two subsets A and B of is defined to be the set of points of which are in either A or B but not both. If $A, B \in \mathcal{F}$, show that $A \triangle B \in \mathcal{F}$.

SOLUTION. $A \triangle B$ equals $(A \backslash B) \cup (B \backslash A)$, which is the union of events (see Exercise 1.9) and is therefore an event. Hence $A \triangle B$ is an event, by (1.4).

EXERCISE (1.11). If $A_1, A_2, \ldots, A_m \in \mathcal{F}$ and k is positive integer, show that the set of points in which belong to exactly k of the A_i belongs to $\mathcal{F}$ (the previous exercise is the case when $m = 2$ and $k = 1$).

SOLUTION. First, we prove

$$\bigcap_{j=1}^{k} A_{i_j} \in \mathcal{F},$$

by induction on k, considering first the case $k = 2$ (obviously, the result if true for $k = 1$). Certainly the complement of $A_{i_1} \cap A_{i_2}$ equals $(\Omega \backslash A_{i_1}) \cup (\Omega \backslash A_{i_2})$, which is the union of events and is therefore an event. Hence $A_{i_1} \cap A_{i_2}$ is an event, by (1.3). Thus the result is true for $k = 2$. Let $h \geq 2$ and suppose that the result is true for $k \leq h$. Then

$$\bigcap_{j=1}^{h} A_{i_j} \in \mathcal{F},$$

so that

$$\bigcap_{j=1}^{h+1} A_{i_j} = (\bigcap_{j=1}^{h} A_{i_j}) \cap A_{i_{h+1}}.$$

Using the induction hypothesis, we obtain the result. Next, let A be the set of points in which belong to exactly k of the A_i belongs to $\mathcal{F}$. We have that

$$A = \bigcup_{\binom{m}{k} \text{ unions}} (\bigcap_{j=1}^{k} A_{i_j}),$$

which is the union of events and is therefore an event. Hence A is an event, by (1.4).

EXERCISE (1.12). Show that, if Ω is a finite set, then $\mathcal{F}$ contains an even number of subsets of Ω.

SOLUTION. Define a mapping $f \colon \mathcal{F} \to \mathcal{F}$ by $f(A) = \Omega \backslash A$ for any event $A \in \mathcal{F}$. The mapoing f is injective for if $A_1 = A_2$, then $\Omega \backslash A_1 = \Omega \backslash A_2$, so $f(A_1) = f(A_2)$. The mapping f is surjetive for if $B \in \mathcal{F}$, then $f(\Omega \backslash B) = B$. Thus f is a bijective. Hence for any element A in $\mathcal{F}$, there exists a unique $\Omega \backslash A \neq A$, so $\mathcal{F}$ contains an even number of subsets of Ω.

1.3. Probabilities

EXERCISE (1.17). Let $p_1, p_2, \ldots, p_N$ be non-negative numbers such that $p_1 + p_2 + \cdots + p_N = 1$, and let $\Omega = \{\omega_1, \omega_2, \ldots, \omega_N\}$, with $\mathcal{F}$ the power set of Ω, as in Example 1.16. Show that the function $\mathbb{Q}$ given by

$$\mathbb{Q}(A) = \sum_{i : \omega_i \in A} p_i \qquad \text{for } A \in \mathcal{F},$$

is a probability measure on $(\Omega, \mathcal{F})$. Is $\mathbb{Q}$ a probability measure on $(\Omega, \mathcal{F})$ if $\mathcal{F}$ is not the power set of but merely some event space of subsets of Ω?

SOLUTION. For the first part, it is not too difficult to check that a function is a probability measure on $(\Omega, \mathcal{F})$ if and only if it satisfies conditions (a), (b) and (c) of Defintion 1.13. Condition (a): $\mathbb{Q}(A) \geq 0$ for $A \in \mathcal{F}$ because

$$\mathbb{Q}(A) = \sum_{i : \omega_i \in A} p_i \geq 0 \qquad \text{for } A \in \mathcal{F},$$

since $p_i \geq 0$ for all i. Condition (b): $\mathbb{Q}(\Omega) = 1$ because

$$\mathbb{Q}(\Omega) = \sum_{i:\omega_i \in \Omega} p_i = \sum_{i=1}^{N} p_i = 1.$$

$\mathbb{Q}(\varnothing) = 0$ by its defintion. Condition (c): We first prove

$$\mathbb{Q}(\bigcup_{i=1}^{n} A_i) = \sum_{i=1}^{n} \mathbb{Q}(A_i),$$

where $A_1, A_2, \ldots, A_n$ are disjoint events in $\mathcal{F}$ (in that $A_i \cap A_j = \emptyset$ whenever $i \neq j$), by induction on n, considering first the case $n = 2$. Then

$$\mathbb{Q}(A_1 \cup A_2) = \sum_{i:\omega_i \in A_1 \cup A_2} p_i$$

$$= \sum_{i:\omega_i \in A_1} p_i + \sum_{i:\omega_i \in A_2} p_i$$

$$= \mathbb{Q}(A_1) + \mathbb{Q}(A_2).$$

Hence the result is true for $n = 2$. Let $m \geq 2$ and suppose that the result is true for $n \leq m$. Then

$$\mathbb{Q}\left(\bigcup_{i=1}^{m} A_i\right) = \sum_{i=1}^{m} \mathbb{Q}(A_i),$$

so that

$$\mathbb{Q}(\bigcup_{i=1}^{m+1} A_i) = \mathbb{Q}((\bigcup_{i=1}^{m} A_i) \cup A_{m+1})$$

$$= \mathbb{Q}(\bigcup_{i=1}^{m} A_i) + \mathbb{Q}(A_{m+1}) \qquad \text{since } (\bigcup_{i=1}^{m} A_i) \cap A_{m+1} = \varnothing$$

$$= \sum_{i=1}^{m} \mathbb{Q}(A_m) + \mathbb{Q}(A_{m+1}) \qquad \text{using the induction hypothesis}$$

$$= \sum_{i=1}^{m+1} \mathbb{Q}(A_i),$$

and the induction step is complete. Also, since n is an arbitrary constant, it follows that

$$\mathbb{Q}(\bigcup_{i=1}^{\infty} A_i) = \sum_{i=1}^{\infty} \mathbb{Q}(A_i),$$

as desired.

For the scond part, the answer to this question is yes.

1.4. Probability spaces

EXERCISE (1.19). If $A, B \in F$, show that $\mathbb{P}(A \backslash B) = \mathbb{P}(A) - \mathbb{P}(A \cap B)$.

SOLUTION. The set A is union of the disjoint sets $A \backslash B$ and $A \cap B$, and hence

$$\mathbb{P}(A) = \mathbb{P}(A \backslash B) + \mathbb{P}(A \cap B) \qquad\qquad \text{by (1.14),}$$

giving that

$$\mathbb{P}(A \backslash B) = \mathbb{P}(A) - \mathbb{P}(A \cap B).$$

EXERCISE (1.20). If $A, B, C \in \mathcal{F}$, show that

$$\mathbb{P}(A \cup B \cup C) = \mathbb{P}(A) + \mathbb{P}(B) + \mathbb{P}(C) - \mathbb{P}(A \cap B) - \mathbb{P}(B \cap C) - \mathbb{P}(A \cap C) - \mathbb{P}(A \cap B \cap C).$$

SOLUTION. We have (using the property that if $A, B \in \mathcal{F}$ then $\mathbb{P}(A \cup B) = \mathbb{P}(A) + \mathbb{P}(B) - \mathbb{P}(A \cap B)$) that

$$\begin{aligned}
\mathbb{P}(A \cup B \cup C) &= \mathbb{P}((A \cup B) \cup C) \\
&= \mathbb{P}(A \cup B) + \mathbb{P}(C) - \mathbb{P}((A \cup B) \cap C) \\
&= \mathbb{P}(A) + \mathbb{P}(B) - \mathbb{P}(A \cap B) + \mathbb{P}(C) - \mathbb{P}((A \cap C) \cup (B \cap C)) \\
&= \mathbb{P}(A) + \mathbb{P}(B) + \mathbb{P}(A \cap B) + \mathbb{P}(C) - [\mathbb{P}(A \cap C) + \mathbb{P}(B \cap C) - \mathbb{P}((A \cap B) \cap (B \cap C))] \\
&= \mathbb{P}(A) + \mathbb{P}(B) + \mathbb{P}(C) - \mathbb{P}(A \cap B) - \mathbb{P}(B \cap C) - \mathbb{P}(A \cap C) - \mathbb{P}(A \cap B \cap C).
\end{aligned}$$

EXERCISE (1.21). Let A, B, C be three events such that

$$\mathbb{P}(A) = \frac{5}{10}, \qquad\qquad \mathbb{P}(B) = \frac{7}{10}, \qquad\qquad \mathbb{P}(C) = \frac{6}{10},$$
$$\mathbb{P}(A \cap B) = \frac{3}{10}, \qquad\qquad \mathbb{P}(B \cap C) = \frac{4}{10}, \qquad\qquad \mathbb{P}(A \cap C) = \frac{2}{10},$$
$$\mathbb{P}(A \cap B \cap C) = \frac{1}{10}.$$

By drawing a Venn diagram or otherwise, find the probability that exactly two of the events A, B, C occur.

SOLUTION. Let D be the event that exactly two of the events A, B, C occur. Then

$$D = [(A \cap B) \backslash (A \cap B \cap C)] \cup [(A \cap C) \backslash (A \cap B \cap C)] \cup [(B \cap C) \backslash (A \cap B \cap C)].$$

The events $[(A \cap B) \backslash (A \cap B \cap C)]$, $[(A \cap C) \backslash (A \cap B \cap C)]$ and $[(B \cap C) \backslash (A \cap B \cap C)]$ are disjoint events, and so

$$\begin{aligned}
\mathbb{P}(D) &= \mathbb{P}((A \cap B) \backslash (A \cap B \cap C)) + \mathbb{P}((A \cap C) \backslash (A \cap B \cap C)) + \mathbb{P}((B \cap C) \backslash (A \cap B \cap C)) \\
&= \mathbb{P}(A \cap B) - \mathbb{P}(A \cap B \cap C) + \mathbb{P}(A \cap C) - \mathbb{P}(A \cap B \cap C) + \mathbb{P}(B \cap C) - \mathbb{P}(A \cap B \cap C) \\
&= \frac{3}{10} - \frac{1}{10} + \frac{4}{10} - \frac{1}{10} + \frac{2}{10} - \frac{1}{10} \\
&= \frac{6}{10}.
\end{aligned}$$

EXERCISE (1.22). A fair coin is tossed 10 times (so that heads appears with probability $\frac{1}{2}$ at each toss). Describe the appropriate probability space in detail for the two cases when

(a) the outcome of every toss is of interest,

(b) only the total number of tails is of interest.

In the first case your event space should have $2^{2^{10}}$ events, but in the second case it need have only 2^{11} events.

SOLUTION. (a) Representing heads by H and tails by T. The probability space of this experiment is the triple $(\Omega, \mathcal{F}, \mathbb{P})$, where

(i) Ω is the set of all ordered sequences of length 10 containing the letters H and T, where the kth entry of such a sequence represents the result of the kth toss,

(ii) $\mathcal{F}$ to be the set of all subsets of Ω,

(iii) each point ω in Ω has equal probability, so that

$$\mathbb{P}(\omega) = \frac{1}{2^{2^{10}}},$$

and, more generally,

$$\mathbb{P}(A) = \frac{1}{2^{2^{10}}} |A| \qquad \text{for each } A \subseteq \mathcal{F}.$$

for $A \in \mathcal{F}$.

(b) The probability space of this experiment is the triple $(\Omega, \mathcal{F}, \mathbb{P})$, where

(i) $\Omega = \{i \colon i = 0, 1, \ldots, 10\}$, the set of all integers between 0 and 10,

(ii) $\mathcal{F}$ to be the set of all subsets of Ω,

(iii) for each $i \in \Omega$, we define the probability that i is the actual outcome

by

$$\mathbb{P}(i) = \frac{\binom{10}{i}}{2^{10}} \qquad \text{for } i = 0, 1, \ldots, 10,$$

and, more generally,

$$\mathbb{P}(A) = \sum_{i \in A} \mathbb{P}(i) \qquad \text{for each } A \subseteq \mathcal{F}.$$

for $A \in \mathcal{F}$.

1.5. Discrete sample spaces

EXERCISE (1.25). Show that if a coin is tossed n times, then there are exactly

$$\binom{n}{k} = \frac{n!}{k!(n-k)!}$$

sequences of possible outcomes in which exactly k heads are obtained. If the coin is fair (so heads an tails are equally likely on each toss), show that the probability of getting at least k heads is

$$\frac{1}{2^n} \sum_{r=k}^{n} \binom{n}{r}.$$

SOLUTION. For the first part, representing heads by H and tails by T, the sample space is the set of all ordered sequences of length n containing the letters H and T, where the ith entry of such a sequence represents the result of the lth toss. When we choose k entries in order from n entries, the first entry can be chosen in n ways, leaving $n-1$ choices for the second entry, and so on. After $k-1$ entries have been chosen there remain $n - (k-1) - n - k + 1$ entries from which to make the kth choice. Hence, the total number of ways of making these choices is $n(n-1)\cdots(n-k+1)$. This number can be rewritten as

$$\frac{n(n-1)\cdots(n-k+1)(n-k)(n-k-1)\cdots 2 \cdot 1}{(n-k)(n-k-1)\cdots 2 \cdot 1},$$

and using the factorial notation, we can write this expression succinctly as

$$\frac{n!}{(n-k)!}.$$

However there are $k!$ different sequences that have exactly k heads. Thus $\dfrac{n!}{(n-k)!}$ gives the number of sequences having exactly k heads, when each sequence is counted $k!$ times. Hence the number of sequences of possible outcomes in which exactly k heads are obtained is

$$\binom{n}{k} = \frac{n!}{k!(n-k)!}.$$

For the last part, the sample space is the set of possible outcomes. It has 2^n elements, each of which is equally likely. Let A be the event that getting at least k heads. Then

$$\mathbb{P}(A) = \sum_{r=k}^{n} \mathbb{P}(\omega_r).$$

where ω_r, for $r = k, k+1, \ldots, n$, is the event of getting exactly i heads. By the above,

$$\mathbb{P}(\omega_i) = \frac{1}{2^n} \binom{n}{i},$$

giving that

$$\mathbb{P}(A) = \sum_{r=k}^{n} \frac{\binom{n}{i}}{2^n}.$$

EXERCISE (1.26). We distribute r distinguishable balls into n cells at random, multiple occupancy being permitted. Show that
(a) there are n^r possible arrangements,
(b) there are $\binom{r}{k}(n-1)^{r-k}$ arrangements in which the first cell contains exactly k balls,
(c) the probability that the first cell contains exactly k balls is

$$\binom{r}{k}\left(\frac{1}{n}\right)^k \left(1 - \frac{1}{n}\right)^{r-k}.$$

SOLUTION. (a) If there are r successive choices to be made in order to put r distinguishable balls into n cells at random and, for $1 \le i \le r$, the ith choice can be made in n ways since multiple occupancy being permitted, the the total number of ways of making these choices is n^r.

(b) There are $\binom{r}{k}$ ways to arrange r balls into the first cell. The number of ways to arrange $r - k$ balls into $n - 1$ remain cells is $(n-1)^{r-k}$ by part (a). Thus there are $\binom{r}{k}(n-1)^{r-k}$ possible arrangements which the first cell containing k balls.

(c) The sample space is the set of possible outcomes. It has n^r elements, each of which is equally likely. Let A be the event that the first cell contains exactly k balls. Then A has $\binom{r}{k}(n-1)^{r-k}$ elements. The probability of A is

$$\frac{\binom{r}{k}(n-1)^{r-k}}{n^r} = \binom{r}{k}\left(\frac{1}{n}\right)^k \left(\frac{n-1}{n}\right)^{r-k}$$

$$= \binom{r}{k}\left(\frac{1}{n}\right)^k \left(1 - \frac{1}{n}\right)^{r-k}.$$

EXERCISE (1.27). In a game of bridge, the 52 cards of a conventional pack are distributed at random between the four players in such a way that each player receives 13 cards. Show that the probability that each player receives one ace is

$$\frac{24 \cdot 48! \cdot 13^4}{52!} = 0.105 \ldots.$$

SOLUTION. The sample space is the set of possible outcomes. It has

$$\binom{52}{13}\binom{39}{13}\binom{26}{13}$$

elements, each of which is equally likely. There are

$$4!\binom{48}{11}\binom{36}{12}\binom{24}{12}$$

ways that each player receives one ace. Therefore, the answer is

$$\frac{4!\binom{48}{11}\binom{36}{12}\binom{24}{12}}{\binom{52}{13}\binom{39}{13}\binom{26}{13}} = \frac{24 \cdot 48! \cdot 13^4}{52!}$$

$$= 0.105\ldots$$

EXERCISE (1.28). Show that the probability that two given hands in bridge contain k aces between them is

$$\binom{4}{k}\binom{48}{26-k}\Big/\binom{52}{26}.$$

SOLUTION. The sample space is the set of possible outcomes. It has $\binom{52}{26}$ elements, each of which is equally likely. There are $\binom{4}{k}\binom{48}{26-k}$ ways that one player receives k ace. Therefore, the answer is

$$\frac{\binom{4}{k}\binom{48}{26-k}}{\binom{52}{26}}.$$

EXERCISE (1.29). Show that the probability that a hand in bridge contains 6 spades, 3 hearts, 2 diamonds and 2 clubs is

$$\binom{13}{6}\binom{13}{3}\binom{13}{2}^2\Big/\binom{52}{13}.$$

SOLUTION. The sample space is the set of possible outcomes. It has $\binom{52}{13}$ elements, each of which is equally likely. There are $\binom{13}{6}\binom{13}{3}\binom{13}{2}^2$ ways that a hand in bridge contains 6 spades, 3 hearts, 2 diamonds and 2 clubs. Therefore, the answer is

$$\binom{13}{6}\binom{13}{3}\binom{13}{2}^2\Big/\binom{52}{13}.$$

EXERCISE (1.30). Which of the following is more probable:
(a) getting at least one six with 4 throws of a die,
(b) getting at least one double six with 24 throws of two dice?

This is sometimes called 'de Méré's paradox', after the professional gambler Chevalier de Méré, who believed these two events to have equal probability.

SOLUTION. The probability of getting at least one six with 4 throws of a die is

$$1 - \left(\frac{5}{6}\right)^4 = 0.5177\cdots,$$

which is slightly higher than the probability of getting at least one double six with 24 throws of two dice,

$$1 - \left(\frac{35}{36}\right)^{24} = 0.4914\cdots.$$

1.6. Conditional probabilities

EXERCISE (1.34). If $(\Omega, \mathcal{F}, \mathbb{P})$ is a probability space and A, B, C are events, show that

$$\mathbb{P}(A \cap B \cap C) = \mathbb{P}(A \mid B \cap C)\mathbb{P}(B \mid C)\mathbb{P}(C)$$

so long as $\mathbb{P}(B \bigcap C) > 0$.

SOLUTION. We have that

$$
\begin{aligned}
\mathbb{P}(A \cap B \cap C) &= \mathbb{P}(A \cap (B \cap C)) \\
&= \mathbb{P}(A \mid (B \cap C))\mathbb{P}(B \cap C) && \text{by (1.32)} \\
&= \mathbb{P}(A \mid (B \cap C))\mathbb{P}(B \mid C)\mathbb{P}(C)
\end{aligned}
$$

so long as $\mathbb{P}(B \bigcap C) > 0$.

EXERCISE (1.35). Show that

$$\mathbb{P}(B \mid A) = \mathbb{P}(A \mid B)\frac{\mathbb{P}(B)}{\mathbb{P}(A)}$$

if $\mathbb{P}(A) > 0$ and $\mathbb{P}(B) > 0$.

SOLUTION. We have that

$$\mathbb{P}(B \mid A) = \frac{\mathbb{P}(B \cap A)}{\mathbb{P}(A)} \qquad \text{by (1.32)}$$

$$= \frac{\mathbb{P}(A \cap B)}{\mathbb{P}(A)}$$

$$= \frac{\mathbb{P}(A \mid B)\mathbb{P}(B)}{P(A)} \qquad \text{by (1.32)}$$

$$= \mathbb{P}(A \mid B)\frac{\mathbb{P}(B)}{\mathbb{P}(A)}$$

if $\mathbb{P}(A) > 0$ and $\mathbb{P}(B) > 0$.

EXERCISE (1.36). Consider the experiment of tossing a fair coin 7 times. Find the probability of getting a prime number of heads given that heads occurs on at least 6 of the tosses.

SOLUTION. The probability space of this experiement is the triple $(\Omega, \mathcal{F}, \mathbb{P})$, where

(i) $\Omega = \{H_i : 0 \leq i \leq 7\}$, ($H_i$ is the event that heads occur i times)
(ii) $\mathcal{F}$ is the set of all subsets of Ω,
(iii) each point in Ω has

$$\mathbb{P}(H_i) = \binom{7}{i}\left(\frac{1}{2}\right)^i\left(\frac{1}{2}\right)^{7-i}$$

$$= \binom{7}{i}\left(\frac{1}{2}\right)^7.$$

Let A be the event that we get 2, 3, 5, or 7 heads and B be the event that heads occur 6 or 7 times. We neet to find $\mathbb{P}(A \mid B)$. The events A and B are subsets of Ω given by

$$A = \{H_2, H_3, H_5, H_7\},$$
$$B = \{H_6, H_7\}.$$

The event B has

$$\mathbb{P}(B) = \mathbb{P}(H_6) + \mathbb{P}(H_7)$$

$$= \binom{7}{1}\left(\frac{1}{2}\right)\left(\frac{1}{2}\right)^6 + \left(\frac{1}{2}\right)^7$$

Finally, $A \cap B$ is given by

$$A \cap B = \{H_7\},$$

so that

$$\mathbb{P}(A \cap B) = \left(\frac{1}{2}\right)^7$$

and

$$\mathbb{P}(A \mid B) = \frac{\mathbb{P}(A \cap B)}{\mathbb{P}(B)}$$

$$= \frac{\left(\frac{1}{2}\right)^7}{\binom{7}{1}\left(\frac{1}{2}\right)\left(\frac{1}{2}\right)^6 + \left(\frac{1}{2}\right)^7}.$$

1.7. Independent events

EXERCISE (1.42). Let A and B be events satisfying $\mathbb{P}(A), \mathbb{P}(B) > 0$, and such that $\mathbb{P}(A \mid B) = \mathbb{P}(A)$. Show that $\mathbb{P}(B \mid A) = \mathbb{P}(B)$.

SOLUTION. We have that

$$
\begin{aligned}
\mathbb{P}(B \mid A) &= \frac{\mathbb{P}(B \cap A)}{\mathbb{P}(A)} && \text{by (1.32)} \\
&= \frac{\mathbb{P}(A \cap B)}{\mathbb{P}(A)} \\
&= \frac{\mathbb{P}(A \mid B)\mathbb{P}(B)}{P(A)} && \text{by (1.32)} \\
&= \mathbb{P}(A \mid B)\frac{\mathbb{P}(B)}{\mathbb{P}(A)} \\
&= \mathbb{P}(A)\frac{\mathbb{P}(B)}{\mathbb{P}(A)} && \text{since } \mathbb{P}(A \mid B) = \mathbb{P}(A) \\
&= \mathbb{P}(B),
\end{aligned}
$$

as required.

EXERCISE (1.43). If A and B are events which are disjoint and independent, what can be said about the probabilities of A and B?

SOLUTION. By the definition of independence events,

$$\mathbb{P}(A)\mathbb{P}(B) = \mathbb{P}(A \cap B)$$
$$= 0$$

since A and B are disjoint. Thus, either A or B must have zero probability.

EXERCISE (1.44). Show that events A and B are independent if and only if A and $\Omega \backslash B$ are independent.

SOLUTION. Suppose that A and B are independent. Writing $P(A \cap (\Omega \backslash B)) = P(A \backslash B)$ (see Exercise 1.9). The set A is union of the disjoint sets $A \backslash B$ and $A \cap B$, and hence

$$\mathbb{P}(A) = \mathbb{P}(A \backslash B) + \mathbb{P}(A \cap B) \qquad \text{by (1.14)},$$

giving that

$$\begin{aligned} \mathbb{P}(A \backslash B) &= \mathbb{P}(A) - \mathbb{P}(A \cap B) \\ &= \mathbb{P}(A) - \mathbb{P}(A)\mathbb{P}(B) \qquad \text{since } A \text{ and } B \text{ are independent} \\ &= \mathbb{P}(A)(1 - \mathbb{P}(B)) \\ &= \mathbb{P}(A)\mathbb{P}(\Omega \backslash B). \end{aligned}$$

Thus

$$P(A \cap (\Omega \backslash B)) = \mathbb{P}(A)\mathbb{P}(\Omega \backslash B),$$

so A and $\Omega \backslash B$ are independent.

Conversely, suppose that A and $\Omega \backslash B$ are independent. By the above, A and $B = \Omega \backslash (\Omega \backslash B)$ are independent

EXERCISE (1.46). If $A_1, A_2, \ldots, A_m$ are independent and $\mathbb{P}(A_i) = p$ for $i = 1, 2, \ldots, m$, find the probability that
(a) none of the A_i occur,
(b) an even number of the A_i occur.

SOLUTION. (a) Since $A_1, A_2, \ldots, A_m$ are independent, $\Omega \backslash A_1, \Omega \backslash A_2, \ldots, \Omega \backslash A_m$ are also independent (see Exercise 1.45). Thus

$$\begin{aligned} \mathbb{P}((\Omega \backslash A_1) \cap (\Omega \backslash A_2) \cap \cdots \cap (\Omega \backslash A_m)) &= \mathbb{P}(\Omega \backslash A_1)\mathbb{P}(\Omega \backslash A_2) \cdots \mathbb{P}(\Omega \backslash A_m) \\ &= (1 - p)^m. \end{aligned}$$

(b) Let B be the event that there is an even number of the A_i occur. Then

$$\mathbb{P}(B) = \sum_{o \leq 2i \leq m} \binom{m}{2i} p^{2i} q^{m-2i},$$

where $p + q = 1$. Note that

$$(q-p)^m = \sum_{i=0}^{m} (-1)^i \binom{m}{i} q^{m-i} p^i$$

$$= \sum_{0 \le 2i \le m} \binom{m}{2i} p^{2i} q^{m-2i} - \sum_{0 \le 2i+1 \le m} \binom{m}{2i+1} p^{2i+1} q^{m-2i-1}, \quad (1)$$

and

$$1 = (q+p)^m$$

$$= \sum_{0 \le 2i \le m} \binom{m}{2i} p^{2i} q^{m-2i} + \sum_{0 \le 2i+1 \le m} \binom{m}{2i+1} p^{2i+1} q^{m-2i-1}. \quad (2)$$

Adding equations (1) and (2) to obtain

$$1 + (q-p)^m = 2 \sum_{0 \le 2i \le m} \binom{m}{2i} p^{2i} q^{m-2i}$$

$$= 2\mathbb{P}(B),$$

giving that

$$\mathbb{P}(B) = \frac{1}{2}[1 + (q-p)^m],$$

where $p + q = 1$.

EXERCISE (1.47). On your desk, there is a very special die with a prime number p of faces, and you throw this die once. Show that no two events A and B can be independent unless either A or B is the whole sample space or the empty set.

SOLUTION. We may take $\Omega = \{1, 2, \ldots, p\}$. Consider two events A and B. If $A \cap B = \varnothing$, $A \ne \varnothing$ and $B \ne \varnothing$, then $\mathbb{P}(A)\mathbb{P}(B) > 0 = \mathbb{P}(A \cap B)$, so A and B are dependent. If $A \cap B \ne \varnothing$ and A and B are independent, then

$$\mathbb{P}(A \cap B) = \frac{|A \cap B|}{p} = \frac{|A|}{p} \cdot \frac{|B|}{p},$$

implying

$$|A \cap B| = \frac{|A| \, |B|}{p}.$$

Since $|A \cap B|$ is an integer, it follows that $p \mid |A| \, |B|$, giving that $p \mid |A|$ or $p \mid |B|$. This implies that $|A| = p$ or $|B| = p$ since $|A|, |B| \le p$. Hence, $A = \Omega$ or $B = \Omega$.

If $A = \varnothing$ or $B = \varnothing$, then the result is trivial. Therefore no two events A and B can be independent unless either A or B is the whole sample space or the empty set.

1.8. The partition theorem

EXERCISE (1.52). Here are two routine problems about balls in urns. You are presented with two urns. Urn I contains 3 white and 4 black balls, and Urn II contains 2 white and 6 black balls.

(a) You pick a ball randomly from Urn I and place it in Urn II. Next you pick a ball randomly from Urn II. What is the probability that the ball is black?

(b) This time, you pick an urn at random, each of the two urns being picked with probability $\frac{1}{2}$, and you pick a ball at random from the chosen urn. Given the ball is black, what is the probability you picked Urn I?

SOLUTION. Let A be the event that I pick a white ball from Urn I and place it in Urn II and B be the event that I pick a black ball from Urn II. The pair A, A^c is a partition of the sample space (since exactly one of them must occur)

EXERCISE (1.53). A biased coin shows heads with probability $p = 1 - q$ whenever it is tossed. Let u_n be the probability that, in n tosses, no two heads occur successively. Show that, for $n \geq 1$,

$$u_{n+2} = qu_{n+1} + pqu_n,$$

and find u_n by the usual method (described in Appendix B) when $p = \frac{2}{3}$.

SOLUTION. For the first part, let A be the event be the event that no two heads occur successively in $n + 2$ tosses and B be the event that the final toss shows tails. The pair B, B^c is a partition of the sample space (since exactly one of them must occur). Then

$$\mathbb{P}(A \mid B^c) = pqu_n,$$

and

$$\mathbb{P}(A \mid B) = qu_{n+1}.$$

By Theorem 1.48,

$$\mathbb{P}(B) = \mathbb{P}(A)\mathbb{P}(B \mid A) + \mathbb{P}(A^c)\mathbb{P}(B \mid A^c),$$

which is to say that

$$u_{n+2} = qu_{n+1} + pqu_n,$$

as required.

For the last part, we shall find the solution of the difference equation

$$u_{n+2} - qu_{n+1} - pqu_n = 0$$

subject to the boundary conditions $u_1 = 1$, $u_2 = 1 - \frac{2}{3} \cdot \frac{2}{3} = \frac{5}{9}$. The auxiliary equation is

$$\theta^2 - \frac{1}{3}\theta - \frac{2}{9} = 0$$

with roots $\theta = \frac{2}{3}, -\frac{1}{3}$. The general solution is therefore

$$u_n = a(\frac{2}{3})^n + b(-\frac{1}{3})^n,$$

where the constants a, b are found from the boundary conditions to be given by $a = \frac{4}{3}, b = -\frac{1}{3}$.

1.9. Probability measures are continuous

1.10. Worked problems

1.11. Problems

PROBLEM (1.11.1). A fair die is thrown n times. Show that the probability that there are an even number of sixes is $\frac{1}{2}\left[1 + \left(\frac{2}{3}\right)^n\right]$. For the purpose of this question, 0 is an even number.

SOLUTION. We prove this by induction on n, considering first the case $n = 0$. Certainly the probability that there are an even number of sixes is 1 which is agreement with $\frac{1}{2}\left[1 + \left(\frac{2}{3}\right)^0\right]$; roughly speaking, this is because since if the fair die is thrown 0 times, then there is 0 (an even number) sixes. Hence the result is true for $n = 0$. Let $m \geq 0$ and suppose that the result is true for $n \leq m$. Then consider the case that a fair die is thrown $m + 1$ times. Let A be the event that there are an even number of sixes among $m + 1$ throws and B be the event that there are an even number of sixes among the first m throws. The pair B, B^c is a partition of the sample space (since exactly one of them must occur). It is easy to see that

$$\mathbb{P}(A \mid B) = \frac{5}{6}$$

since if B occurs, then A occurs if and only if the result of the $(n+1)$th throw is a number other than six. Similarly,

$$\mathbb{P}(A \mid B^c) = \frac{1}{6}.$$

By Theorem 1.48,

$$
\begin{aligned}
\mathbb{P}(A) &= \mathbb{P}(A \mid B)\mathbb{P}(B) + \mathbb{P}(A \mid B^c)\mathbb{P}(B^c) \\
&= \frac{5}{6} \cdot \frac{1}{2}[1 + (\frac{2}{3})^m] + \frac{1}{6} \cdot \{1 - \frac{1}{2}[1 + (\frac{2}{3})^m]\} \quad \text{by the induction hypothesis} \\
&= \frac{1}{2}[1 + (\frac{2}{3})^{m+1}]
\end{aligned}
$$

The result follows by induction.

PROBLEM (1.11.2). Does there exist an event space containing just six events?

SOLUTION. The answer to this question is no. We prove this by contradiction. Assume there exists an event space $\mathcal{F}$ containing just six events. The event space $\mathcal{F}$ must contain the empty set $\varnothing$ and the whole set Ω. Since the event space $\mathcal{F}$ has six events, it follows that $\{\varnothing, \Omega, A, A^c, B, B^c\}$ where $A, B \neq \Omega$ with $A \neq B$ and $B \neq A^c$. Since $A, B \in \mathcal{F}$, so $A \cap B = (A^c \cup B^c)^c \in \mathcal{F}$ by (1.4). If $A \cap B = \Omega$, then $A = \Omega$ and $B = \Omega$, which contradicts the fact that $A, B \neq \Omega$. If $A \cap B = B$, then $B \subseteq A$, and so $A \backslash B = A \cap B^c \in \mathcal{F}$. This is a contradiction since $A \backslash B \neq A$, $A \backslash B \neq B$, $A \backslash B \neq \varnothing$, $A \backslash B \neq \Omega$, $A \backslash B \neq A^c$, $A \backslash B \neq B^c$. Similarly, $A \cap B = A$ will yeild a contradiction. Thus

$$A \cap B = \varnothing. \qquad\qquad (1)$$

Since $A, B \in \mathcal{F}$, it follows that $A \cup B \in \mathcal{F}$. If $A \cup B \neq \Omega$, then $\Omega \backslash (A \cup B) = (A \cup B)^c \in \mathcal{F}$. But $(A \cup B)^c \neq A$, $(A \cup B)^c \neq B$, $(A \cup B)^c \neq A^c$, $(A \cup B)^c \neq B^c$, $(A \cup B)^c \neq \varnothing$, $(A \cup B)^c \neq \Omega$, so $(A \cup B)^c \notin \mathcal{F}$, a contradiction. Thus

$$A \cup B = \Omega. \qquad\qquad (2).$$

From (1) and (2) we obtain that $B = A^c$, which contradicts the fact that $B \neq A^c$. Therefore there does not exist an event space containing just six events.

PROBLEM (1.11.3). Prove *Boole's Inequality*:

$$\mathbb{P}\left(\bigcup_{i=1}^{n} A_i\right) \leq \sum_{i=1}^{n} \mathbb{P}(A_i).$$

SOLUTION (1). Let $B_1 = A_1$ and $B_i = A_i \backslash (\bigcup_{k=1}^{i-1} A_k)$ for $i = 2, 3, \ldots, n$. Then

$$\bigcup_{i=1}^{n} A_i = \bigcup_{i=1}^{n} B_i$$

is the union of disjoint events in $\mathcal{F}$. By (1.14),

$$\mathbb{P}\left(\bigcup_{i=1}^{n} A_i\right) = \mathbb{P}\left(\bigcup_{i=1}^{n} B_i\right)$$
$$= \sum_{i=1}^{n} \mathbb{P}(B_i).$$

However, by construction $B_i \subseteq A_i$ for $i = 1, 2, \ldots, n$, so

$$\mathbb{P}(B_i) \leq \mathbb{P}(A_i) \qquad \text{for } i = 1, 2, \ldots, n$$

and so

$$\mathbb{P}\left(\bigcup_{i=1}^{n} A_i\right) \leq \sum_{i=1}^{n} \mathbb{P}(A_i),$$

as required.

Note that this proof requires to show that $\bigcup_{i=1}^{n} B_i$ is the union of disjoint events in $\mathcal{F}$ such that

$$\bigcup_{i=1}^{n} B_i = \bigcup_{i=1}^{n} A_i$$

where

$$B_1 = A_1$$
$$B_i = A_i \backslash (\bigcup_{k=1}^{i-1} A_k) \qquad \text{for } i = 2, 3, \ldots, n.$$

We first show that $B_r \cap B_s = \emptyset$ for $r \neq s$. Without loss of generality, assume that $r < s$, then for any $x \in B_s$, $x \in A_s \backslash \bigcup_{j=1}^{s-1} A_j$ so that $x \in A_s$ and $x \notin \bigcup_{j=1}^{s-1} A_j$. Thus $x \notin A_r$ and hence $x \notin B_r$. We next show that

$$\bigcup_{i=1}^{n} B_i = \bigcup_{i=1}^{n} A_i.$$

Indeed, for any $x \in \bigcup_{i=1}^{n} B_i$ then $x \in B_h$ for some $h \in \{1, 2, \ldots n\}$, so that $x \in A_k \setminus \bigcup_{j=1}^{k-1} A_j$. Thus $x \in A_k \subset \bigcup_{i=1}^{n} A_i$. So

$$\bigcup_{i=1}^{n} B_i \subset \bigcup_{i=1}^{n} A_i. \tag{1}$$

Conversely, for any $x \in \bigcup_{i=1}^{n} A_i$, then $x \in A_k$ for some $k \in \{1, 2, \ldots, n\}$. If $x \in A_k$ and $x \in \bigcup_{j=1}^{k-1} A_j$. then $x \in A_1 = B_1$. So $x \in c$. If $x \in A_k$ and $x \notin \bigcup_{j=1}^{k-1} A_j$, then $x \in A_k \setminus \bigcup_{j=1}^{k-1} A_j = B_k$. So $x \in \bigcup_{i=1}^{n} B_i$. Hence

$$\bigcup_{i=1}^{n} A_i \subset \bigcup_{i=1}^{n} B_i. \tag{2}$$

By (1) and (2),

$$\bigcup_{i=1}^{n} A_i = \bigcup_{i=1}^{n} B_i,$$

as required.

SOLUTION (2). The first inequality is trivially true if $n = 1$. Let $m \geq 1$ and assume that the inequality holds for $n \leq m$. Then

$$\mathbb{P}(\bigcup_{i=1}^{m+1} A_i) = \mathbb{P}(\bigcup_{i=1}^{m} A_i) + \mathbb{P}(A_{m+1}) - \mathbb{P}(\bigcup_{i=1}^{m}(A_i \cap A_{m+1}))$$

$$\leq \mathbb{P}(\bigcup_{i=1}^{m} A_i) + \mathbb{P}(A_{m+1}) \leq \sum_{i=1}^{m+1} \mathbb{P}(A_i),$$

by the hypothesis. The result follows by induction.

PROBLEM (1.11.4). Prove that

$$\mathbb{P}(\bigcap_{i=1}^{n} A_i) \geq 1 - n + \sum_{i=1}^{n} \mathbb{P}(A_i).$$

This is sometimes called *Bonferroni's inequality*, but the term is not recommended since it has multiple uses.

SOLUTION. We have that

$$\mathbb{P}(\bigcap_{i=1}^{n} A_i) = \mathbb{P}(\bigcap_{i=1}^{n}(A_i^c)^c) \qquad \text{using } (A_i^c)^c$$

$$= \mathbb{P}((\bigcup_{i=1}^{n} A_i^c)^c) \qquad \text{using De Morgan's Laws}$$

$$= 1 - \mathbb{P}(\bigcup_{i=1}^{n} A_i^c)$$

$$\geq 1 - \sum_{1}^{n} \mathbb{P}(A_i^c) \qquad \text{using Boole's inequality } \mathbb{P}(\bigcup_{i=1}^{n} B_i) \leq \sum_{i=1}^{n} \mathbb{P}(B_i)$$

$$= 1 - \sum_{1}^{n}(1 - P(A_i))$$

$$= 1 - n + \sum_{i=1}^{n} \mathbb{P}(A_i),$$

as required.

PROBLEM (1.11.5). Two fair dice are thrown. Let A be the event that the first shows an odd number, B be the event that the second shows an even number, and C be the event that either both are odd or both are even. Show that A, B, C are pairwise independent but not independent.

SOLUTION. The probability space of this experiment is the triple $(\Omega, \mathcal{F}, \mathbb{P})$, where
(i) $\Omega = \{(i,j) : i,j = 1, 2, \ldots, 6\}$, the set of all ordered pairs of integers between 1 and 6,
(ii) $\mathcal{F}$ is the set of all subsets of Ω,
(iii) each point in Ω has equal probability, so that

$$P((i,j)) = \frac{1}{36} \qquad \text{for } i,j = 1, 2, \ldots, 6,$$

and, more generally,

$$\mathbb{P}\left(S\right) = \frac{1}{36}\left|S\right| \qquad\qquad \text{for each } S \subseteq \Omega.$$

The events A,B and C are subset of Ω given by

$$
\begin{aligned}
A &= \left\{(i,j) : i = 1,3,5 \text{ and } j = 1,2,\ldots,6\right\}, \\
B &= \left\{(i,j) : i = 1,2,\ldots,6 \text{ and } j = 2,4,6\right\}, \\
C &= \left\{(i,j) : i \text{ and } j \text{ are either both are odd or both are even}\right\}.
\end{aligned}
$$

The event A contains $3 \times 6 = 18$ ordered pairs, B contains $6 \times 3 = 18$ ordered pairs, and C contains $3 \times 3 + 3 \times 3 = 18$ ordered pairs, giving that

$$\mathbb{P}\left(A\right) = \frac{18}{36} = \frac{1}{2}, \qquad \mathbb{P}\left(B\right) = \frac{18}{36} = \frac{1}{2}, \qquad \mathbb{P}\left(C\right) = \frac{18}{36} = \frac{1}{2}.$$

Finally,

$$
\begin{aligned}
A \cap B &= \left\{(i,j) : i = 1,3,5 \text{ and } j = 2,4,6\right\}, \\
A \cap C &= \left\{(i,j) : i = 1,3,5 \text{ and } j = 1,3,5\right\}, \\
B \cap C &= \left\{(i,j) : i = 2,4,6 \text{ and } j = 2,4,6\right\}, \\
A \cap B \cap C &= \varnothing.
\end{aligned}
$$

The event $A \cap B$ contains $3 \times 3 = 9$ ordered pairs, $A \cap C$ contains $3 \times 3 = 9$ ordered pairs, $B \cap C$ contains $3 \times 3 = 9$ ordered pairs, and $A \cap B \cap C$ contains no ordered pair, so that

$$
\begin{aligned}
\mathbb{P}\left(A \cap B\right) &= \frac{9}{36} = \frac{1}{4} = \frac{1}{2} \cdot \frac{1}{2} = \mathbb{P}\left(A\right)\mathbb{P}\left(B\right), \\
\mathbb{P}\left(A \cap C\right) &= \frac{9}{36} = \frac{1}{4} = \frac{1}{2} \cdot \frac{1}{2} = \mathbb{P}\left(A\right)\mathbb{P}\left(C\right), \\
\mathbb{P}\left(B \cap C\right) &= \frac{9}{36} = \frac{1}{4} = \frac{1}{2} \cdot \frac{1}{2} = \mathbb{P}\left(B\right)\mathbb{P}\left(C\right), \\
\mathbb{P}\left(A \cap B \cap C\right) &= 0 \neq \frac{1}{8} = \frac{1}{2} \cdot \frac{1}{2} \cdot \frac{1}{2} = \mathbb{P}\left(A\right)\mathbb{P}\left(B\right)\mathbb{P}\left(C\right).
\end{aligned}
$$

Therefore the events A, B, C are pairwise independent but not independent.

PROBLEM (1.11.6). Urn I contains 4 white and 3 black balls, and Urn II contains 3 white and 7 black balls. An urn is selected at random, and a ball is picked from it. What is the probability that this ball is black? If this ball is white, what is the probability that Urn I was selected?

SOLUTION. Let A be the event that a black ball is picked and let B be the event that the first urn is selected. The pair B, B^c is a partition of the sample space (since exactly one of them must occur). We have

$$\mathbb{P}(A \mid B) = \frac{3}{7}, \mathbb{P}(A \mid B^c) = \frac{7}{10},$$

$$\mathbb{P}(B) = \frac{1}{2}, \mathbb{P}(B^c) = \frac{1}{2}.$$

By Partition theorem, Theorem 1.48,

$$
\begin{aligned}
\mathbb{P}(A) &= \mathbb{P}(A \mid B)\mathbb{P}(B) + \mathbb{P}(A \mid B^c)\mathbb{P}(B^c) \\
&= \frac{3}{7} \cdot \frac{1}{2} + \frac{7}{10} \cdot \frac{1}{2} \\
&= \frac{79}{140}.
\end{aligned}
$$

We shall calculate $\mathbb{P}(B \mid A^c)$. We have $\mathbb{P}(A^c) = 1 - \mathbb{P}(A) = 1 - 79/140 = 61/140$. By Bayes's theorem, Theorem 1.50,

$$
\begin{aligned}
\mathbb{P}(B \mid A^c) &= \frac{\mathbb{P}(A^c \mid B)\mathbb{P}(B)}{\mathbb{P}(A^c)} \\
&= \frac{\frac{4}{7} \cdot \frac{1}{2}}{\frac{61}{140}} = \frac{61}{490}.
\end{aligned}
$$

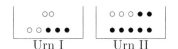

Urn I   Urn II

PROBLEM (1.11.7). A single card is removed at random from a deck of 52 cards. From the remainder we draw two cards at random and find that they are both spades. What is the probability that the first card removed was also a spade?

SOLUTION. Let A be the event that the first card removed was a spade and B be the event that from the remainder we draw two cards at random and find that they are both spades. The pair A, A^c is a partition of the sample space (since exactly one of them must occur). It is easy to see that

$$\mathbb{P}\left(B \mid A\right) = \frac{12}{51},$$

$$\mathbb{P}\left(B \mid A^c\right) = \frac{13}{51},$$

$$\mathbb{P}\left(A\right) = \frac{13}{52},$$

$$\mathbb{P}\left(A^c\right) = \frac{39}{52}.$$

By Partition theorem, Theorem 1.48,

$$
\begin{aligned}
\mathbb{P}\left(B\right) &= \mathbb{P}\left(B \mid A\right)\mathbb{P}\left(A\right) + \mathbb{P}\left(B \mid A^c\right)\mathbb{P}\left(A^c\right) \\
&= \frac{12}{51} \cdot \frac{13}{52} + \frac{13}{51} \cdot \frac{39}{52} \\
&= \frac{1}{4} \quad .
\end{aligned}
$$

We shall calculate $\mathbb{P}\left(A \mid B\right)$. By Bayes's theorem, Theorem 1.50,

$$
\begin{aligned}
\mathbb{P}\left(A \mid B\right) &= \frac{\mathbb{P}\left(B \mid A\right)\mathbb{P}\left(A\right)}{\mathbb{P}\left(B\right)} \\
&= \frac{\frac{12}{51} \cdot \frac{13}{54}}{\frac{1}{4}} = \frac{104}{459}.
\end{aligned}
$$

PROBLEM (1.11.8). A fair coin is tossed $3n$ times. Find the probability that the number of heads is twice the number of tails. Expand your answer using Stirling's formula.

SOLUTION. The sample space is the set of possible outcomes. It has 2^{3n} elements, each of which is equally likely. There are $\binom{3n}{2n}$ ways to throw so that that the number of heads is twice the number of tails. Therefore, the answer is

$$\frac{1}{2^{3n}} \binom{3n}{2n}. \tag{1}$$

To understand how this behaves for large n, we need to expand the binomial coefficient in terms of polynomials and exponentials. The relevant asymptotic formula is called *Stirling's formula*,

$$n! \sim (n/e)^n \sqrt{2\pi n} \qquad \text{as } n \to \infty, \tag{2}$$

where $a_n \sim b_n$ means $a_n/b_n \to 1$ as $n \to \infty$. See Theorem A.4 for a partial proof of this.

Applying Stirling's formula to (1), we obtain

$$
\begin{aligned}
\frac{1}{2^{3n}}\binom{3n}{2n} &= 2^{-3n}\frac{(3n)!}{(2n)!n!} \\
&\sim 2^{-3n}\frac{(3n/3)^{3n}\sqrt{2\pi 2n}}{(2n/e)^{2n}\sqrt{2\pi 2n}(n/e)^{n}\sqrt{2\pi n}} \\
&\sim 2^{-3n}\frac{(3n)^{3n}}{(2n)^{2n}n^{n}}\frac{\sqrt{3}}{2\sqrt{n}} \\
&= 2^{-3n}\frac{3^{3n}\sqrt{3}}{2^{2n}2\sqrt{n}} \\
&= \left(\frac{27}{32}\right)^{n}\frac{\sqrt{3}}{2\sqrt{n}}.
\end{aligned}
$$

The factorials and exponentials are gigantic but they cancel out.

PROBLEM (1.11.9). Two people toss a fair coin n times each. Show that the probability they throw equal numbers of heads is

$$
\binom{2n}{n}\left(\frac{1}{2}\right)^{2n}.
$$

SOLUTION. Firstly, we shall show that

$$
\binom{n}{0}^{2} + \binom{n}{1}^{2} + \binom{n}{2}^{2} + \cdots + \binom{n}{n}^{2} = \binom{2n}{n}.
$$

Indeed,

$$
(1+x)^{2n} = 1 + \binom{2n}{1}x - \binom{2n}{2}x^{2} + \cdots + \binom{2n}{n}x^{n} + \cdots + \binom{2n}{2n}x^{2n}
$$

and

$$
\begin{aligned}
(1+x)^{n}(1+x)^{n} &= \left[1 + \binom{n}{1}x + \binom{n}{2}x^{2} + \cdots + \binom{n}{n}x^{n}\right]\left[1 + \binom{n}{1}x + \binom{n}{2}x^{2} + \cdots + \binom{n}{n}x^{n}\right] \\
&= 1 + \left[\binom{n}{1} + \binom{n}{1}\right]x + \left[\binom{n}{2} + \binom{n}{1}^{2} + \binom{n}{2}\right]x^{2} + \cdots \\
&\quad + \left[\binom{n}{n} + \binom{n}{n-1}\binom{n}{1} + \binom{n}{n-2}\binom{n}{2} + \cdots + \binom{n}{n}\right]x^{n} + \cdots.
\end{aligned}
$$

Thus the coefficient of x^{n} in the expansion of $(1+x)^{2n}$ is $\binom{2n}{n}$. The coefficient of x^{n} in the expansion of $(1+x)^{n}(1+x)^{n}$ is

$$\binom{n}{n} + \binom{n}{n-1}\binom{n}{1} + \binom{n}{n-2}\binom{n}{2} + \cdots + \binom{n}{n} = \binom{n}{0}^2 + \binom{n}{1}^2 + \cdots + \binom{n}{n}^2$$

since $\binom{n}{k} = \binom{n}{n-k}$. Thus

$$\binom{n}{0}^2 + \binom{n}{1}^2 + \cdots + \binom{n}{n}^2 = \binom{2n}{n}.$$

There are $\binom{n}{k}$ where $k \in \{0, 1, \ldots n\}$ ways for first person or the second person toss k heads. So there are $\binom{n}{k}^2$ ways for both people have the number of heads equal k. The number of cases both people throw equal numbers of heads is

$$\sum_{k=0}^{n} \binom{n}{k}^2 = \binom{n}{0}^2 + \binom{n}{1}^2 + \cdots + \binom{n}{n}^2 = \binom{2n}{n}.$$

Thus the probability they throw equal numbers of heads is

$$\binom{2n}{n}\left(\frac{1}{2}\right)^{2n}.$$

PROBLEM (1.11.10). In the circuits in Figure 1.2, each switch is closed with probability p, independently of all other switches. For each circuit, find the probability that a flow of current is possible between A and B.

SOLUTION. For the first circuit in Figure 1.2, let C be the event that a flow of current is impossible between A and B, and D, E, F be the events that the middle, top, bottom paths are discnnected, respectively. Then

$$\mathbb{P}(C) = \mathbb{P}(D)\mathbb{P}(E)\mathbb{P}(F).$$

Note that $\mathbb{P}(D) = 1 - p$, and $\mathbb{P}(E) = \mathbb{P}(F) = (1 - p^2)$. Thus

$$\mathbb{P}(C) = (1-p)(1-p^2)^2.$$

Hence

$$\mathbb{P}(C^c) = 1 - \mathbb{P}(C)$$
$$= 1 - (1-p)(1-p^2)^2.$$

For the second circuit in Figure 1.2, let C be the event that a flow of current is impossible between A and B, and D be the event that the middle vertical switch is open. The pair D, D^c is a partition of the sample space (since exactly one of them must occur). By Theorem 1.48,

$$\mathbb{P}(C) = \mathbb{P}(C \mid D)\mathbb{P}(D) + \mathbb{P}(C \mid D)\mathbb{P}(D^c).$$

Note that $\mathbb{P}(C \mid D)\mathbb{P}(D) = (1 - p)(1 - p^2)$. In order to calculate $\mathbb{P}(C \mid D)\mathbb{P}(D^c)$, notice that impossble current flows given that the middle vertical switch is closed if and only if the two switches on the left are both open or the the two switches on the right are both open. This equivant to the fact that possible currents flows if and only if the two swiches on the left are not both open and the two switches on the right are not both open; this situation happens with probability $[1 - (1 - p)^2]^2$, hence $\mathbb{P}(C \mid D)\mathbb{P}(D^c) = p\{1 - [1 - (1 - p)^2]\}^2$. Thus $\mathbb{P}(C) = (1 - p)(1 - p^2) + p\{1 - [1 - (1 - p)^2]\}^2$. Therefore,

$$\begin{aligned}\mathbb{P}(C^c) &= 1 - \mathbb{P}(C) \\ &= 1 - (1 - p)(1 - p^2) + p\{1 - [1 - (1 - p)^2]\}^2.\end{aligned}$$

PROBLEM (1.11.11). Show that if u_n is the probability that n tosses of a fair coin contain no run of 4 heads, then for $n \geq 4$

$$u_n = \frac{1}{2}u_{n-1} + \frac{1}{4}u_{n-2} + \frac{1}{8}u_{n-3} + \frac{1}{16}u_{n-4}.$$

Use this difference equation to show that $u_8 = \dfrac{208}{256}$.

SOLUTION. For the first part, let A be the event that n tosses of a fair coin contain no run of 4 heads, B_i, $i = 1, 2, 3, 4$ be the event that $n - i$ tosses of a fair coin contain no run of 4 heads. $\{B_1, B_2, B_3, B_4\}$ is a partition of the sample space (since exactly one of them must occur). It is easy to see that

$$\mathbb{P}(A \mid B_1) = \frac{1}{2}$$
$$\mathbb{P}(A \mid B_2) = \frac{1}{4}$$
$$\mathbb{P}(A \mid B_3) = \frac{1}{8}$$
$$\mathbb{P}(A \mid B_4) = \frac{1}{16}$$

By Theorem 1.48,

$$\mathbb{P}(A) = \mathbb{P}(A \mid B_i)\mathbb{P}(B_i), \qquad\qquad \text{for } i = 1, 2, 3, 4$$

which is to say that

$$u_n = \frac{1}{2}u_{n-1} + \frac{1}{4}u_{n-2} + \frac{1}{8}u_{n-3} + \frac{1}{16}u_{n-4},$$

as required.

For the last part, note that $u_1 = 1$, $u_2 = 1$, $u_3 = 1$, $u_4 = (\frac{1}{2})^4 = \frac{1}{16}$. Thus

$$
\begin{aligned}
u_5 &= \frac{1}{2}u_4 + \frac{1}{4}u_3 + \frac{1}{8}u_2 + \frac{1}{16}u_1 \\
&= \frac{1}{2}\cdot\frac{1}{16} + \frac{1}{4}\cdot 1 + \frac{1}{8}\cdot 1 + \frac{1}{16}\cdot 1 = \frac{15}{32} \\
u_6 &= \frac{1}{2}u_5 + \frac{1}{4}u_4 + \frac{1}{8}u_3 + \frac{1}{16}u_2 \\
&= \frac{1}{2}\cdot\frac{15}{32} + \frac{1}{4}\cdot\frac{1}{16} + \frac{1}{8}\cdot 1 + \frac{1}{16}\cdot 1 = \frac{7}{16} \\
u_7 &= \frac{1}{2}u_6 + \frac{1}{4}u_5 + \frac{1}{8}u_4 + \frac{1}{16}u_3 \\
&= \frac{1}{2}\cdot\frac{7}{16} + \frac{1}{4}\cdot\frac{15}{32} + \frac{1}{8}\cdot\frac{1}{16} + \frac{1}{16}\cdot 1 = \frac{13}{32} \\
u_8 &= \frac{1}{2}u_7 + \frac{1}{4}u_6 + \frac{1}{8}u_5 + \frac{1}{16}u_4 \\
&= \frac{1}{2}\cdot\frac{13}{32} + \frac{1}{4}\cdot\frac{7}{16} + \frac{1}{8}\cdot\frac{15}{32} + \frac{1}{16}\cdot\frac{1}{16} = \frac{3}{8}
\end{aligned}
$$

PROBLEM (*1.11.12). Any number $\omega \in [0, 1]$ has a decimal expansion

$$\omega = 0.x_1 x_2 \ldots,$$

and we write $f_k(\omega, n)$ for the proportion of times that the integer k appears in the first n digits in this expansion. We call ω a *normal number* if

$$f_k(\omega, n) \to \frac{1}{10} \qquad\qquad \text{as } n \to \infty$$

for $k = 0, 1, 2, \ldots, 9$. On intuitive grounds we may expect that most numbers $\omega \in [0, 1]$ are normal numbers, and Borel proved that this is indeed true. It is quite another matter to exhibit specific normal numbers. Prove the number

$$0.1234567891011121314\ldots$$

is normal. It is an unsolved problem of mathematics to show that $e - 2$ and $\pi - 3$ are normal numbers also.

PROBLEM (1.11.14). (a) Let $\mathbb{P}(A)$ denote the probability of the occurrence of an event A. Prove carefully, for events $A_1, A_2, \ldots, A_n$, that

$$P(\bigcup_{i=1}^{n} A_i) = \sum_{i} \mathbb{P}(A_i) - \sum_{i<j} \mathbb{P}(A_i \cap A_j) + \sum_{i<j<k} \mathbb{P}(A_i \cap A_j \cap A_k) - \cdots$$
$$+ (-1)^{n+1} \mathbb{P}(\bigcap_{i} A_i).$$

(b) One evening, a bemused lodge-porter tried to hang n keys on their n hooks, but only managed to hang them independently and at random. There was no limit to the number of keys which could be hung on any hook. Otherwise, or by using (a), find an expression for the probability that at least one key was hung on its own hook.

The following morning, the porter was rebuked by the Bursar, so that in the evening she was careful to hang only one key on each hook. But she still only managed to hang them independently and at random. Find an expression for the probability that no key was then hung on its own hook.

Find the limits of both expressions as n tends to infinity.

You may assume that, for real x,

$$e^x = \sum_{r=0}^{\infty} \frac{x^r}{r!} = \lim_{N \to \infty} (1 + \frac{x}{N})^N.$$

(Oxford 1978M)

SOLUTION. (a) We prove this by induction on n, considering first the case $n = 2$. Certainly, $A_1 \cup A_2 = A_1 \cup (A_2 \backslash A_1)$ is a disjoint union, so that

$$\mathbb{P}(A_1 \cup A_2) = \mathbb{P}(A_1) + \mathbb{P}(A_2 \backslash A_1)$$
$$= \mathbb{P}(A_1) + \mathbb{P}(A_2 \backslash (A_1 \cap A_2))$$
$$= \mathbb{P}(A_1) + \mathbb{P}(A_2) - \mathbb{P}(A_1 \cap A_2).$$

Hence the result is true for $n = 2$. Let $m \geq 2$ and suppose that the result is true for $n \leq m$. Then it is true for m events. That is to say

$$\mathbb{P}\left(\bigcup_{i=1}^{m} A_i\right) = \sum_{i=1}^{m} \mathbb{P}(A_i) - \sum_{i<j} \mathbb{P}(A_i \cap A_j) + \sum_{i<j<k} \mathbb{P}(A_i \cap A_j \cap A_k) - \cdots + (-1)^{m+1} \mathbb{P}\left(\bigcap_{i=1}^{m} A_i\right),$$

so that

$$\mathbb{P}\left(\bigcup_{i=1}^{m+1} A_i\right) = \mathbb{P}\left(\left(\bigcup_{i-1}^{m} A_i\right) \cup A_{m+1}\right)$$

$$= \mathbb{P}\left(\bigcup_{i=1}^{m} A_i\right) + \mathbb{P}(A_{m+1}) - \mathbb{P}\left(\left(\bigcup_{i=1}^{m} A_i\right) \cap A_{m+1}\right)$$

$$= \sum_{i=1}^{m} \mathbb{P}(A_i) - \sum_{i<j\leq m} \mathbb{P}(A_i \cap A_j) + \sum_{i<j<k\leq m} \mathbb{P}(A_i \cap A_j \cap A_k) - \cdots$$

$$+ (-1)^{m+1}\mathbb{P}\left(\bigcap_{i=1}^{m} A_i\right) + \mathbb{P}(A_{m+1}) - \mathbb{P}\left(\left(\bigcup_{i=1}^{m} A_i\right) \cap A_{m+1}\right)$$

$$= \sum_{i=1}^{m} \mathbb{P}(A_i) + P(A_{m+1}) - \mathbb{P}\left(\left(\bigcup_{i=1}^{m} A_i\right) \cap A_{m+1}\right) - \sum_{i<j\leq m} \mathbb{P}(A_i \cap A_j)$$

$$+ \sum_{i<j<k} \mathbb{P}(A_i \cap A_j \cap A_k) - \cdots + (-1)^{m+1}\mathbb{P}\left(\bigcap_{i=1}^{m} A_i\right)$$

$$= \sum_{i=1}^{m+1} \mathbb{P}(A_i) - \mathbb{P}\left(\bigcup_{i=1}^{m} (A_i \cap A_{m+1})\right) - \sum_{i<j\leq m} \mathbb{P}(A_i \cap A_j)$$

$$+ \sum_{i<j<k\leq m} \mathbb{P}(A_i \cap A_j \cap A_k) - \cdots + (-1)^{m+1}\mathbb{P}\left(\bigcap_{i=1}^{m} A_i\right)$$

$$= \sum_{i=1}^{m+1} \mathbb{P}(A_i) - [\sum_{i=1}^{m} \mathbb{P}(A_i \cap A_{m+1}) - \sum_{i<j\leq m} \mathbb{P}(A_i \cap A_j \cap A_{m+1})$$

$$+ \sum_{i<j<k\leq m} \mathbb{P}(A_i \cap A_j \cap A_k \cap A_{m+1}) - \cdots + (-1)^{m+1}\mathbb{P}\left(\bigcap_{i=1}^{m+1} A_i\right)]$$

$$- \sum_{i<j\leq m} \mathbb{P}(A_i \cap A_j) + \sum_{i<j<k\leq m} \mathbb{P}(A_i \cap A_j \cap A_k) - \cdots + (-1)^{m+1}\mathbb{P}\left(\bigcap_{i=1}^{m} A_i\right)$$

$$= \sum_{i=1}^{m+1} \mathbb{P}(A_i) - \sum_{i<j\leq m+1} \mathbb{P}(A_i \cap A_j) + \sum_{i<j<k\leq m+1} \mathbb{P}(A_i \cap A_j \cap A_k) - \cdots$$

$$+ (-1)^{m+2}\mathbb{P}\left(\bigcap_{i=1}^{m+1} A_i\right).$$

The result follows by induction.

(b) Consider n keys was hung on their n hooks. Let A_i be the event that the ith key hung on its own hook, where $i \in \{1, 2, \ldots, n\}$. Then

$$\mathbb{P}(A_i) = \frac{(n-1)!}{n!} = \frac{1}{n},$$

$$\mathbb{P}(A_i \cap A_j) = \frac{(n-2)!}{n!}, \qquad \text{for } i < j$$

$$\mathbb{P}(A_{i_1} \cap A_{i_2} \cap \cdots \cap A_{i_k}) = \frac{(n-k)!}{n!}. \qquad \text{for } i_1 < i_2 < \cdots < i_k$$

Let A be the event that ther is at least one key hung on its own hook. Then

$$\mathbb{P}(A) = \mathbb{P}\left(\bigcup_{i=1}^{n} A_i\right)$$

$$= \sum_{i=1}^{n}(A_i) - \sum_{i<j}\mathbb{P}(A_i \cap A_j) + \sum_{i<j<k}\mathbb{P}(A_i \cap A_j \cap A_k) - \cdots$$

$$+ (-1)^{n+1}\mathbb{P}\left(\bigcap_{i=1}^{n} A_i\right)$$

$$= n\frac{1}{n} - \binom{n}{2}\frac{1}{2!} + \binom{n}{3}\frac{1}{3!} - \cdots + (-1)^{n+1}\binom{n}{n}\frac{1}{n!}$$

$$= 1 - \frac{1}{2!} + \frac{1}{3!} - \frac{1}{4!} + \cdots + (-1)^{n+1}\frac{1}{n!}. \qquad \text{since } \binom{n}{k}\frac{(n-k)!}{n!} = \frac{1}{k!}$$

We have that

$$e^x = 1 + x + \frac{x^2}{2!} + \frac{x^3}{3!} + \cdots,$$

and so

$$e^{-1} = 1 - 1 + \frac{1}{2!} - \frac{1}{3!} + \frac{1}{4!} - \frac{1}{5!} + \cdots.$$

Thus

$$1 - \frac{1}{2!} + \frac{1}{3!} - \frac{1}{4!} + \cdots = 1 - \frac{1}{e} \qquad \text{as } n \to \infty.$$

Therefore,

$$\mathbb{P}(A) = 1 - \frac{1}{e} \qquad \text{as } n \to \infty,$$

$$\mathbb{P}(A^c) = 1 - \mathbb{P}(A) = 1 - (1 - \frac{1}{e}) = \frac{1}{e} \qquad \text{as } n \to \infty.$$

PROBLEM (1.11.15). Two identical decks of cards, each containing N cards, are shuffled randomly. We say that a *k-matching* occurs if the two decks agree in exactly k places. Show that the probability that there is a k-matching is

$$\pi_k = \frac{1}{k!}\left(1 - \frac{1}{1!} + \frac{1}{2!} - \frac{1}{3!} + \cdots + \frac{(-1)^{N-k}}{(N-k)!}\right)$$

for $k = 0, 1, 2, \ldots, N$. We note that $\pi_k \simeq 1/(k!e)$ for large N and fixed k. Such matching probabilities are used in testing departures from randomness in circumstances such as psychological tests and wine-tasting competitions. (The convention is that $0! = 1$.)

SOLUTION. Let A be the event that a k-mathing occur and B be the event that 0-matching occur in $N - k$ remaining cards. Since A and B are independent, so

$$
\begin{aligned}
\pi_k &= \mathbb{P}(A \cap B) \\
&= \mathbb{P}(A)\mathbb{P}(B) \\
&= \binom{N}{k}\frac{(N-k)!}{N!}\mathbb{P}(B) \\
&= \binom{N}{k}\frac{(N-k)!}{N!}\left[1 - \frac{1}{1!} + \frac{1}{2!} - \cdots + (-1)^{N-k}\frac{1}{(N-k)!}\right] \\
&= \frac{1}{k!}\left(1 - \frac{1}{1!} + \frac{1}{2!} - \frac{1}{3!} + \cdots + \frac{(-1)^{N-k}}{(N-k)!}\right),
\end{aligned}
$$

as required. We note that $\pi_k \simeq 1/(k!e)$ for large N and fixed k.

PROBLEM (1.11.16). The buses which stop at the end of my road do not keep to the timetable. They should run every quarter hour, at $08.30, 08.45, 09.00, \ldots$, but in fact each bus is either five minutes early or five minutes late, the two possibilities being equally probable and different buses being independent. Other people arrive at the stop in such a way that, t minutes after the departure of one bus, the probability that no one is waiting for the next one is $e^{-t/5}$. What is the probability that no one is waiting at 09.00? One day, I come to the stop at 09.00 and find no one there; show that the chances are more than four to one that I have missed the nine o'clock bus.
You may use an approximation $e^3 \approx 20$. (Oxford 1977M)

SOLUTION. For the first part, let A be the event that no one is waiting is waiting at 09.00, B_1 be the event that the last bus depart at 08.55, B_2 be the event that the last bus depart at 08.50 and B_3 be the event that the last bus depart at 08.40. $\{B_1, B_2, B_3\}$ is a partition of the sample space (since exactly one of them must occur). It is easy to see that

$$\mathbb{P}(A_i) = \frac{1}{4}, \qquad\qquad \text{for } i = 1, 2, 3$$

$$\mathbb{P}(A \mid B_1) = e^{-1},$$

$$\mathbb{P}(A \mid B_2) = e^{-1} + e^{-2},$$

$$\mathbb{P}(A \mid B_3) = e^{-4}.$$

By Theorem 1.48,

$$
\begin{aligned}
\mathbb{P}(A) &= \mathbb{P}(B_1)\mathbb{P}(A \mid B_1) + \mathbb{P}(B_2)\mathbb{P}(A \mid B_2) + \mathbb{P}(B_3)\mathbb{P}(A \mid B_3) \\
&= \frac{1}{4}e^{-1} + \frac{1}{4}(e^{-1} + e^{-2}) + \frac{1}{4}e^{-4} \\
&= \frac{1}{4}(2e^{-1} + e^{-2} + e^{-4}).
\end{aligned}
$$

For the last part, by Bayes' theorem, Theorem 1.50,

$$
\begin{aligned}
\mathbb{P}(B_1 \mid A) &= \frac{\mathbb{P}(A \mid B_1)\mathbb{P}(B_1)}{\mathbb{P}(A)} \\
&= \frac{\frac{1}{2}e^{-1}}{\frac{1}{4}(2e^{-1} + e^{-2} + e^{-4})} \\
&= \frac{2e^3}{2e^3 + e^2 + 1} \ge 0.827.
\end{aligned}
$$

PROBLEM (1.11.17). A coin is tossed repeatedly; on each toss a head is shown with probability p, or a tail with probability $1 - p$. The outcomes of the tosses are independent. Let E denote the event that the first run of r successive heads occurs earlier that the first run of s successive tails. Let A denote the outcome of the first toss. Show that

$$\mathbb{P}(E \mid A = \text{head}) = p^{r-1} + (1 - p^{r-1})\mathbb{P}(E \mid A = \text{tail}).$$

Find a similar expression for $\mathbb{P}(E \mid A = \text{tail})$, and hence find $\mathbb{P}(E)$. (Oxford 1981M)

SOLUTION. For the first part, suppose $r = s = 1$. We have that $\mathbb{P}(E \mid A = \text{head}) = 1$ and

$$p^{r-1} + (1 - p^{r-1})\mathbb{P}(E \mid A = \text{tail}) = p^0 + 0 \cdot \mathbb{P}(E \mid A = \text{tail}) = 1.$$

Thus

$$\mathbb{P}(E \mid A = \text{head}) = p^{r-1} + (1 - p^{r-1})\mathbb{P}(E \mid A = \text{tail}).$$

Suppose $r = 2$, $s = 1$. We have that $\mathbb{P}(E \mid A = \text{head}) = p^2$ and

$$p^{r-1} + (1 - p^{r-1})\mathbb{P}(E \mid A = \text{tail}) = p^1 + (1 - p^1) \cdot 0 = p.$$

Thus

$$\mathbb{P}(E \mid A = \text{head}) \neq p^{r-1} + (1 - p^{r-1})\mathbb{P}(E \mid A = \text{tail}).$$

Suppose $r = s$. Let B be the event that the first run of r successive heads occurs in r first tosses ($\underset{r \text{ times}}{HH \ldots H} T \ldots$). Let C be the event that the first run of r successive heads occurs earlier that the first run of r successive tails and $A = \text{head}$. Thus $E \cap (A = \text{head}) = B \cup C$, $B \cap C = \emptyset$, and so

$$
\begin{aligned}
\mathbb{P}(E \cap (A = \text{head})) &= \mathbb{P}(B) + \mathbb{P}(C) \\
&= p^r + \mathbb{P}(A = \text{head})\mathbb{P}(B')\mathbb{P}(E \mid A = \text{tail}) \\
&= p^r + p(1 - p^{r-1})\mathbb{P}(E \mid A = \text{tail})
\end{aligned}
$$

where B' be the event that there are at least the tail occurs from second toss to rth toss. Thus

$$
\begin{aligned}
\mathbb{P}(E \mid A = \text{head}) &= \frac{\mathbb{P}(E \cap (A = \text{head}))}{\mathbb{P}(A = \text{head})} \\
&= \frac{p^r + p(1 - p^{r-1})\mathbb{P}(E \mid A = \text{tail})}{p} \\
&= p^{r-1} + (1 - p^{r-1})\mathbb{P}(E \mid A = \text{tail}).
\end{aligned}
$$

For the second part, let M be the event that r tails occur in r first tosses. Let N be the event that there are at least one head occur from the second toss to the rth toss. Then

$$E \mid (A = \text{tail}) = (A = \text{tail}) \cap N \cap (E \mid A = \text{head}).$$

Since $(A = \text{tail})$, N, $N \cap (E \mid A = \text{head})$ are independent events, so

$$\mathbb{P}(E \mid A = \text{tail}) = (1 - p)\left[1 - (1 - p)^{r-1}\right]\mathbb{P}(E \mid A = \text{head}).$$

Let $x = P(E \mid A = \text{head})$ and $y = P(E \mid A = \text{tail})$. From the above result, we hvae

$$x = p^{r-1} + (1 - p^{r-1})y$$

$$y = (1 - p)\left[1 - (1 - p)^{r-1}\right]x$$

$$x = p^{r-1} + (1 - p^{r-1})(1 - p)\left[1 - (1-p)^{r-1}\right]x$$

$$\implies \qquad p^{r-1} = \{1 - (1-p)[1 - (1-p)^{r-1}]\}x$$

$$\implies \qquad x = \frac{p^{r-1}}{1 - (1-p)[1 - (1-p)^{r-1}]} = \frac{p^{r-1}}{(1-p)^r + p}$$

$$y = (1-p)[1 - (1-p)^{r-1}]\frac{p^{r-1}}{(1-p)^r + p} = -\frac{p^{r-1}[(1-p)^r + p - 1]}{(1-p)^r + p}$$

We have

$$\mathbb{P}(E) = \mathbb{P}(A = \text{head})\mathbb{P}(E \mid A = \text{head}) + \mathbb{P}(A = \text{tail})\mathbb{P}(E \mid A = \text{tail})$$

$$= p\frac{p^{r-1}}{(1-p)^r + p} + (1-p)[-\frac{p^{r-1}[(1-p)^r + p - 1]}{(1-p)^r + p}]$$

$$= \frac{p^{r-1}\{p^2 - (1-p)^r + p[(1-p)^r - 1] + 1\}}{(1-p)^r + p}$$

PROBLEM (*1.11.18). Show that the axiom that $\mathbb{P}$ is countably additive is equivalent to the axiom that $\mathbb{P}$ is finitely additive and continuous. That is to say, let Ω be a set and $\mathcal{F}$ an event space of subsets of Ω. If $\mathbb{P}$ is a mapping from $\mathcal{F}$ into $[0, 1]$ satisfying
   (i) $P(\Omega) = 1$, $\mathbb{P}(\varnothing) = 0$;
   (ii)) if $A, B \in F$ and $A \cap B = \varnothing$ then $\mathbb{P}(A \cup B) = \mathbb{P}(A) + \mathbb{P}(B)$,
   (iii)) if $A_1, A_2, \ldots \in \mathcal{F}$ and $A_i \subseteq A_{i+1}$ for $i = 1, 2, \ldots$, then

$$\mathbb{P}(A) = \lim_{i \to \infty} \mathbb{P}(A_i), \qquad \text{where } A = \bigcup_{i=1}^{\infty} A_i,$$

then $\mathbb{P}$ satisfies $\mathbb{P}(\bigcup_i A_i) = \sum_i \mathbb{P}(A_i)$ for all sequences $A_1, A_2, \ldots$ of disjoint events.

SOLUTION. Firstly, we shall prove that P is finitely additive. Assume $A_1, A_2 \in \mathcal{F}$ and $A_1 \cap A_2 = \emptyset$, from the hypothesis (ii), we obtain that

$$\mathbb{P}(A_1 \cup A_2) = \mathbb{P}(A_1) + \mathbb{P}(A_2),$$

and so our statement holds for $n = 2$. Suppose that the statement holds for $n = k$, that is,

$$\mathbb{P}\left(\bigcup_{i=1}^{k} A_i\right) = \sum_{i=1}^{k} \mathbb{P}(A_i),$$

where $A_1, A_2, \ldots, A_k$ are disjoint events. If $n = k+1$, then

$$
\mathbb{P}\left(\bigcup_{i=1}^{k+1} A_i\right) = \mathbb{P}\left(\left(\bigcup_{i=1}^{k} A_i\right) \cup A_{k+1}\right)
$$

$$
= \mathbb{P}\left(\bigcup_{i=1}^{k} A_i\right) + \mathbb{P}\left(A_{k+1}\right)
$$

$$
= \sum_{i=1}^{k} \mathbb{P}\left(A_i\right) + \mathbb{P}\left(A_{k+1}\right)
$$

$$
= \sum_{i=1}^{k+1} \mathbb{P}\left(A_i\right).
$$

where $A_1, A_2, \ldots, A_k, A_{k+1}$ are disjoint events. Consider the sequence $A_1, A_2, \ldots$ of disjoint events. Let $B_k = \bigcup_{i=1}^{k} A_i$, $k \in \mathbb{N}$. The sequence $\{B_n\}$ of events is an increasing monotone sequence, that is $B_k \subseteq B_{k+1}$ for every $k \in \mathbb{N}$. We have that

$$
\mathbb{P}\left(\bigcup_{i=1}^{n} A_i\right) = \sum_{i=1}^{n} \mathbb{P}\left(A_i\right) = S_n
$$

where S_n is the nth partial sum of the series $\sum_{i=1}^{\infty} \mathbb{P}\left(A_i\right)$. The series $\sum_{i=1}^{\infty} \mathbb{P}\left(A_i\right)$ is a non negative and satisfying $0 \leq S_n = \mathbb{P}\left(\bigcup_{i=1}^{n} A_i\right) \leq \mathbb{P}(\Omega) = 1$ so it is a convergence series (Axiom (i)). Using Axiom (iii) to obtain that

$$
\mathbb{P}\left(\bigcup_{i=1}^{\infty} A_i\right) = \mathbb{P}\left(\lim_{n\to\infty} \bigcup_{i=1}^{n} A_i\right)
$$

$$
= \lim_{n\to\infty} \mathbb{P}\left(\bigcup_{i=1}^{n} A_i\right)
$$

$$
= \lim_{n\to\infty} \sum_{i=1}^{n} \mathbb{P}\left(A_i\right) \qquad \text{since } \mathbb{P} \text{ is finitely additive}
$$

$$
= \sum_{i=1}^{\infty} \mathbb{P}\left(A_i\right).
$$

PROBLEM (1.11.19). There are n socks in a drawer, three of which are red and the rest black. John chooses his socks by selecting two at random from the drawer, and puts them on. He is three times more likely to wear socks of different colours than to wear matching red socks. Find n.
For this value of n, what is the probability that John wears matching black socks? (Cambridge 2008)

SOLUTION. The number of ways to choose socks of different colour is

$$\binom{3}{1}\binom{n-3}{1} = 3(n-3).$$

The probability of choosing two socks of different colours is

$$\frac{3(n-3)}{\binom{n}{2}} = \frac{6(n-3)}{n(n-1)}.$$

The probability of choosing two red socks is

$$\frac{3}{\binom{n}{2}C_n^2} = \frac{6}{n(n-1)}.$$

Since the probability of wearing socks of different colours equals to three times the probability of wearing matching red socks, it follows that

$$\frac{6(n-3)}{n(n-1)} = 3 \cdot \frac{6}{n(n-1)},$$

giving $n = 6$. For $n = 6$, the probability of choosing two black socks is

$$\frac{\binom{3}{2}}{\binom{6}{2}} = \frac{2 \cdot 3}{6 \cdot 5} = \frac{1}{5}.$$

CHAPTER 2

Discrete random variables

2.1. Probability mass functions

EXERCISE (2.8). If X and Y are discrete random variables on the probability space $(\Omega, \mathcal{F}, \mathbb{P})$, show that U and V are discrete random variables on this space also, where

$$U(\omega) = X(\omega) + Y(\omega), \qquad V(\omega) = X(\omega)Y(\omega), \qquad \text{for } \omega \in \Omega.$$

SOLUTION. Because X and Y are discrete random variables, the image $X(\Omega)$ and $Y(\Omega)$ is a countable subset of $\mathbb{R}$, that is, $X(\Omega) = \{x_i \mid i \in\}$ and $Y(\Omega) = \{y_i \mid i \in \mathbb{N}\}$.

To show that U is discrete radom variable on $(\Omega, \mathcal{F}, \mathbb{P})$, we need to show that:
(1) the image $U(\Omega)$ is a countable subset of $\mathbb{R}$, and
(2) $\{\omega \in \Omega : U(\omega) = x\} \in \mathcal{F}$ for $x \in \mathbb{R}$.

Since $U(\omega) = X(\omega) + Y(\omega) = \bigcup_{i=1}^{\infty} \{x_i + Y(\Omega)\}$ and every set $\{x_i + Y(\Omega)\}$ is a countable set since $Y(\Omega)$ is a countable set.

The coutnable union of the countable sets is a countable set, so $U(\Omega) = \bigcup_{i=1}^{\infty} \{x_i + Y(\Omega)\}$ is a countable set.

For each $x \in \mathbb{R}$, we have

$$
\begin{aligned}
u^{-1}(x) &= \{\omega \in \Omega | U(\Omega) = x\} \\
&= \{\omega \in \Omega | X(\omega) + Y(\omega) = x\} \\
&= \{\omega \in \Omega | X(\omega) = x - Y(\omega)\} \\
&= \bigcup_{t \in Y(\Omega)} \left[\{\omega \in \Omega | X(\omega) = x - t\} \cap \{\omega \in \Omega | Y(\omega) = t\} \right].
\end{aligned}
$$

EXERCISE (2.9). Show that if $\mathcal{F}$ is the power set of Ω, then all functions which map into a countable subset of $\mathbb{R}$ are discrete random variables.

SOLUTION. Let X be a function which map Ω into a countable subset of $\mathbb{R}$. To show that X is discrete radom variable on $(\Omega, \mathcal{F}, \mathbb{P})$, we need to show that:

(1) the image $X(\Omega)$ is a countable subset of $\mathbb{R}$, and

(2) $\{\omega \in \Omega : X(\omega) = x\} \in \mathcal{F}$ for $x \in \mathbb{R}$. We have $\{\omega \in \Omega : X(\omega) = x\} \subset \Omega$ and since $\mathcal{F}$ is the power set of Ω so $\{\omega \in \Omega : X(\omega) = x\} \in \mathcal{F}$.

$X(\Omega)$ is a countable set by hypotheses.

Thus X is a discrete random variable.

EXERCISE (2.10). If E is an event of the probability space $(\Omega, \mathcal{F}, \mathbb{P})$ show that the *indicator function* of E, defined to be the function 1_E on Ω given by

$$1_E = \begin{cases} 1 & \text{if } \omega \in E, \\ 0 & \text{if } \omega \notin E, \end{cases}$$

is a discrete random variable.

SOLUTION. the image $1_F(\Omega) = \{1_E(\omega)|\omega \in |\Omega\} = \{0,1\}$ is a countable subset of $\mathbb{R}$, and

$$1_E^{-1}(x) = \{\omega \in \Omega : 1_E(\omega) = x\}$$
$$= \begin{cases} E & \text{if } x = 1, \\ E^c & \text{if } x = 0, \\ \emptyset & \text{if } x \neq 0 \text{ and } x \neq 1. \end{cases}$$

But $E \in \mathcal{F}, E^c = \Omega \backslash E \in \mathcal{F}$ and $\emptyset \in \mathcal{F}$ so $1_E^{-1}(x) \in \mathcal{F}$ for every $x \in \mathbb{R}$. Thus 1_E is a discrete random variable.

EXERCISE (2.11). Let $(\Omega, \mathcal{F}, \mathbb{P})$ be a probability space in which

$$\Omega = \{1, 2, 3, 4, 5, 6\}, \qquad \mathcal{F} = \{\varnothing, \{2, 4, 6\}, \{1, 3, 5\}, \Omega\}.$$

and let U, V, W be functions on defined by.

$$U(\omega) = \omega, \qquad V(\omega) = \begin{cases} 1 & \text{if } \omega \text{ is even,} \\ 0 & \text{if } \omega \text{ is odd,} \end{cases} \qquad W(\omega) = \omega^2,$$

for $\omega \in \Omega$. Determine which of U, V, W are discrete random variables on the probability space.

SOLUTION. Since $U^{-1}(1) = \{1\} \notin \mathcal{F}$, it follows that U is not a disrete random variable.

Note that the image $V(\Omega) = \{V(\omega) : \omega \in \Omega\} = \{0, 1\}$ is a countable subset of $\mathbb{R}$, and

$$V^{-1}(x) = \{\omega \in \Omega : V(\omega) = x\}$$

$$= \begin{cases} \{2,4,6\} & \text{if } x = 1, \\ \{1,3,5\} & \text{if } x = 0, \\ \varnothing & \text{if } x \neq 0 \text{ and } x \neq 1. \end{cases}$$

But $\{2,4,6\} \in \mathcal{F}, \{1,3,5\} \in \mathcal{F}$ and $\varnothing \in \mathcal{F}$ so $V^{-1}(x) \in \mathcal{F}$ for every $x \in \mathbb{R}$. Thus V is a discrete random variable.

Since $W^{-1}(1) = \{1\} \notin \mathcal{F}$, it follows that W is not a disrete random variable.

EXERCISE (2.12). For what value of c is the function p, defined by

$$p(k) = \begin{cases} \dfrac{c}{k(k+1)} & \text{if } k = 1,2,\ldots, \\ 0 & \text{otherwise}, \end{cases}$$

a mass function?

SOLUTION. The function p is a mass function if and only if

$$\sum_{k=1}^{\infty} p(k) = 1$$

This is equivalent to

$$c\sum_{k=1}^{\infty} \frac{1}{k(k+1)} = 1$$

We have that

$$c\sum_{k=1}^{n} \left(\frac{1}{k} - \frac{1}{k-1}\right) = 1 \iff c\left[\left(1 - \frac{1}{2}\right) + \left(\frac{1}{2} - \frac{1}{3}\right) + \cdots + \left(\frac{1}{n-1} - \frac{1}{n}\right)\right],$$

so

$$c\sum_{k=1}^{\infty} \frac{1}{k(k+1)} = 1$$

$$\iff \lim_{n\to\infty} c\left(1 - \frac{1}{n}\right) = 1$$

$$\iff c = 1.$$

2.2. Examples

EXERCISE (2.23). If X is a discrete random variable having the Poisson distribution with parameter λ, show that the probability that X is even is $e^{-\lambda} \cosh \lambda$.

SOLUTION. We have that

$$
\begin{aligned}
\mathbb{P}(X \text{ is even}) &= \sum_{k=0}^{\infty} p_X(X = 2k) \\
&= \sum_{k=0}^{\infty} \frac{1}{(2k)!} \lambda^k e^{-\lambda} \\
&= e^{-\lambda} \sum_{k=0}^{\infty} \frac{1}{(2k)!} \lambda^{2k} \\
&= e^{-\lambda} \cosh \lambda.
\end{aligned}
$$

EXERCISE (2.24). If X is a discrete random variable having the geometric distribution with parameter p, show that the probability that X is greater than k is $(1-p)^k$.

SOLUTION. We have that

$$
\begin{aligned}
\mathbb{P}(X > K) &= 1 - \mathbb{P}(1 \leq X \leq k) \\
&= 1 - (pq^0 + pq^1 + \cdots + pq^{k-1}) \\
&= 1 - p(1 + q + q^2 + \cdots + q^{k-1}) \\
&= 1 - p\frac{1 - q^k}{1 - q} \\
&= 1 - p\frac{1 - q^k}{p} \\
&= 1 - (1 - q^k) \\
&= q^k \\
&= (1 - p)^k,
\end{aligned}
$$

where $q = 1 - p$.

2.3. Functions of discrete random variables

EXERCISE (2.26). Let X be a discrete random variable having the Poisson distribution with parameter λ, and let $Y = \left| \sin(\frac{1}{2} \pi X) \right|$. Find the mass function of Y.

SOLUTION. Since X has the Poisson distribution with parameter λ, then

$$\operatorname{Im} X = \{0,1,2,\ldots\}.$$

.

If $k = 2m, = 0,1,2,\ldots$, then $y = \left|\sin\frac{1}{2}\pi k\right| = |\sin(m\pi)| = 0$

If $y = 2m+1$, $m = 0,1,2,\ldots$, then $y = \left|\sin\frac{1}{2}\pi k\right| = \left|\sin\frac{1}{2}\pi(2m+1)\right| = \left|\sin(\frac{\pi}{2} + m\pi)\right| = |(-1)^m| = 1$. Thus

$\operatorname{Im} Y = \{y \in Y : y = \left|\sin\frac{1}{2}\pi k\right|, k = 0,1,2,\ldots\} = \{\left|\sin\frac{1}{2}k\pi\right|, k = 0,1,2\ldots\} = \{0,1\}$

$$\begin{aligned}
p_Y(0) = \mathbb{P}(Y = 0) &= p_Y(0) = \mathbb{P}(Y = 0) \\
&= \mathbb{P}(X = 2m, m = 0,1,,2\ldots) \\
&= \sum_{m=0}^{\infty} p_X(2m) \\
&= e^{-\lambda} \sum_{k=0}^{\infty} \frac{\lambda^{2k}}{(2k)!} \\
&= e^{-\lambda} \cosh \lambda
\end{aligned}$$

$$\begin{aligned}
p_Y(1) &= 1 - p_Y(0) \\
&= 1 - e^{-\lambda} \cosh \lambda
\end{aligned}$$

The mass function of Y is

$$p_Y(x) = \begin{cases} e^{-\lambda} \cosh \lambda & \text{if } x = 0 \\ 1 - e^{-\lambda} \cosh \lambda & \text{if } x = 1 \\ 0 & \text{if } x \neq 0 \text{ and } x \neq 1 \end{cases}$$

2.4. Expectation

EXERCISE (2.37). If X has the binomial distribution with parameters n and $p = 1 - q$, show that

$$\mathbb{E}(X) = np, \qquad\qquad \mathbb{E}(X^2) = npq + n^2 p^2,$$

and deduce the variance of X.

SOLUTION (1). The mean of X is

$$\begin{aligned}
\mathbb{E}(X) &= \sum_{x \in \operatorname{Im} X} x \mathbb{P}(X = x) \\
&= \sum_{k=0}^{n} k \mathbb{P}(X = k) \\
&= \sum_{k=0}^{n} k \mathbb{P}(X = k) \\
&= \sum_{k=0}^{n} k \binom{n}{k} p^k q^{n-k} && \text{since } k \binom{n}{k} = n \binom{n-1}{k-1}) \text{ for } k \geq 1 \\
&= np \sum_{k=0}^{n} \binom{n-1}{k-1} p^{k-1} q^{n-k} \\
&= np \sum_{j=0}^{n-1} \binom{n-1}{j} p^j q^{n-1-j} && \text{reindex with } j = k - 1 \\
&= np(p+q)^{n-1} \\
&= np
\end{aligned}$$

and the mean of X^2 is

$$\begin{aligned}
\mathbb{E}(X^2) &= \sum_{k=0}^{n} k^2 \mathbb{P}(X = k) \\
&= \sum_{k=0}^{n} k^2 \binom{n}{k} p^k q^{n-k}
\end{aligned}$$

We have
$$\sum_{k=0}^{n} k \binom{n}{k} p^k q^{n-k} = np = \mathbb{E}(X).$$

Take derivative with respect to p in both sides, we obtain

$$\sum_{k=0}^{n} k^2 \binom{n}{k} p^{k-1} q^{n-k} - \sum_{k=0}^{n} k(n-k) \binom{n}{k} p^k q^{n-k-1} = n$$

since $\dfrac{dp}{dq} = -1$. Thus

$$\frac{1}{p} \sum_{k=0}^{n} k^2 \binom{n}{k} p^k q^{n-k} - \frac{n}{q} \sum_{k=0}^{n} k \binom{n}{k} p^k q^{n-k} + \frac{1}{q} \sum k^2 \binom{n}{k} p^k q^{n-k} = n.$$

X_i	0	1
$\mathbb{P}(X_i)$	q	p

This implies

$$\frac{1}{p}\mathbb{E}(X^2) - \frac{n}{q}\mathbb{E}(X) + \frac{1}{q}\mathbb{E}(X^2) = n$$

$$\Longleftrightarrow \qquad (\frac{1}{p} + \frac{1}{q})\mathbb{E}(X^2) - \frac{n}{q}np = n$$

since $(\mathbb{E}(X) = np)$. This implies

$$\frac{1}{pq}\mathbb{E}(X^2) = n + \frac{n^2 p}{q}$$

since $p + q = 1$. This implies

$$\mathbb{E}(X^2) = npq + n^2 p^2.$$

The variance of X

$$\text{var}\,(X) = \mathbb{E}(X^2) - \mathbb{E}(X)^2 = npq + n^2 p^2 - (np)^2 = npq$$

SOLUTION (2). Consider independence variables

$$X_i = \begin{cases} 1 & \text{if event } A \text{ occurs with probabaility } P \text{ for } i = 1, 2, \ldots, n, \\ 0 & \text{otherwise}, \end{cases}$$

Thus

$$X = \sum_{i=1}^{n} X_i$$

where
   Therefore

$$\mathbb{E}(X_i) = 0 \cdot q + 1 \cdot p = p$$

$$\mathbb{E}(X) = \mathbb{E}(\sum_{i=1}^{n} X_i) = \sum_{i=1}^{n} \mathbb{E}(X_i) = np.$$

EXERCISE (2.38). Show that $\text{var}(aX + b) = a^2 \text{var}(X)$ for $a, b \in R$.

SOLUTION. We have that

$$\begin{aligned}
\mathrm{var}(aX + b) &= \mathbb{E}\left((ax + b)^2\right) = \mathbb{E}\left(ax + b\right)^2 \\
&= \mathbb{E}\left(a^2 X^2 + 2abX + b^2\right) - (a\mathbb{E}(x) + b)^2 \\
&= a^2 E(X^2) + 2ab\mathbb{E}(X) + b^2 - a^2\left[\mathbb{E}(X)\right]^2 - 2ab\mathbb{E}(X) - b^2 \\
&= a^2 E(X^2) - a^2\left[\mathbb{E}(X)\right]^2 \\
&= a^2\left\{E(X^2) - \left[\mathbb{E}(X)\right]^2\right\} \\
&= a^2\mathrm{var}(X).
\end{aligned}$$

EXERCISE (2.39). Find $\mathbb{E}(X)$ and $\mathbb{E}(X^2)$ when X has the Poisson distribution with parameter λ, and hence show that the Poisson distribution has variance equal to its mean.

SOLUTION. The mean of X is

$$\begin{aligned}
\mathbb{E}(X) &= \sum_{x \in \mathrm{Im}X} x\mathbb{P}(X = x) \\
&= \sum_{k=0}^{\infty} k\mathbb{P}(X = k) \\
&= \sum_{k=0}^{\infty} k\frac{1}{k!}\lambda^k e^{-\lambda} \\
&= e^{-\lambda}\sum_{k=1}^{\infty} \frac{1}{(k-1)!}\lambda^k && \text{since the term involving } k = 0 \text{ vanishes} \\
&= e^{-\lambda}\lambda\sum_{k=1}^{\infty} \frac{1}{(k-1)!}\lambda^{k-1} \\
&= \lambda e^{-\lambda}\sum_{j=0}^{\infty} \frac{1}{j!}\lambda^j && \text{reindex with } j = k - 1 \\
&= \lambda e^{-\lambda}e^{\lambda} && \text{since } \sum_{k=0}^{\infty} \frac{1}{k!}x^k = e^k \\
&= \lambda,
\end{aligned}$$

and the mean of X^2 is

$$\mathbb{E}(X^2) = \sum_{x \in \text{Im} X} x^2 \mathbb{P}(X = x)$$

$$= \sum_{k=0}^{\infty} k^2 \mathbb{P}(X = k)$$

$$= \sum_{k=0}^{\infty} k^2 \frac{1}{k!} \lambda^k e^{-\lambda}$$

$$= e^{-\lambda} \sum_{k=1}^{\infty} \frac{k}{(k-1)!} \lambda^k \qquad \text{since the term involving } k = 0 \text{ vanishes.}$$

We have that

$$\mathbb{E}(X) = e^{-\lambda} \sum_{k=1}^{\infty} \frac{1}{(k-1)!} \lambda^k$$

$$= \lambda.$$

Differentiate this with respect to λ to obtain

$$-\sum_{k=1}^{\infty} \frac{1}{(k-1)!} e^{-\lambda} \lambda^k + \sum_{k=1}^{\infty} \frac{k}{(k-1)!} e^{-\lambda} \lambda^{k-1} = 1,$$

giving that

$$-\mathbb{E}(X) + \frac{1}{\lambda} \mathbb{E}(X^2) = 1.$$

Thus

$$\mathbb{E}(X^2) = \lambda + \lambda \mathbb{E}(\lambda) = \lambda + \lambda^2,$$

implying that

$$\text{var}(X) = \mathbb{E}(X^2) - [E(X)]^2$$

$$= \lambda + \lambda^2 - \lambda^2$$

$$= \lambda.$$

2.5. Conditional expectation and the partition theorem

2.6. Problems

PROBLEM (2.6.1). If X has the Poisson distribution with parameter λ, show that

$$\mathbb{E}\left(X(X-1)(X-2)\cdots(X-k)\right) = \lambda^{k+1}$$

for $k = 0, 1, 2, \ldots$.

SOLUTION. The mean of $X(X-1)(X-2)\cdots(X-k)$ is

$$
\begin{aligned}
\mathbb{E}\left(X(X-1)(X-2)\cdots(X-k)\right) &= \sum_{m=k+1}^{\infty} m(m-1)(m-2)\cdots \\
&\qquad (m-k)\frac{1}{m!}\lambda^m e^{-\lambda} \\
&= e^{-\lambda} \sum_{m=k+1}^{\infty} \frac{m!}{(m-k-1)!}\frac{1}{m!}\lambda^m \\
&= e^{-\lambda} \sum_{m=k+1}^{\infty} \frac{\lambda^m}{(m-k-1)!} \\
&= e^{-\lambda} \sum_{j=0}^{\infty} \frac{\lambda^{j+k+1}}{j!} \qquad \text{reindex with } j = m-k-1 \\
&= e^{-\lambda} \sum_{j=0}^{\infty} \frac{\lambda^j}{j!}\lambda^{k+1} \\
&= \lambda^{k+1} e^{-\lambda} \sum_{j=0}^{\infty} \frac{\lambda^j}{j!} \\
&= \lambda^{k+1} e^{-\lambda} e^{\lambda} \\
&= \lambda^{k+1}
\end{aligned}
$$

as required.

PROBLEM (2.6.2). Each toss of a coin results in heads with probability p (> 0). If $m(r)$ is the mean number of tosses up to and including the rth head, show that

$$m(r) = p[1 + m(r-1)] + (1-p)[1 + m(r)]$$

for $r = 1, 2, \ldots$, with the convention that $m(0) = 0$. Solve this difference equation by the method described in Appendix B.

SOLUTION. Let H be the event that the first toss gives head. The pair H, H^c is a partition of the sample space (since exactly one of them must occur). Let X be the event that rth head occur . It is easy to see that

$$\mathbb{E}(X = r \mid H) = 1 + m(r-1) \qquad\qquad \text{for } r = 1, 2, \ldots,$$

since if H occurs, then $X = r$ if and only if the first toss is followed by exactly $r - 1$ heads. Similarly,

$$\mathbb{E}(X = r \mid H^c) = 1 + m(r) \qquad \text{for } r = 1, 2, \ldots.$$

By the partition theorem, Theorem 2.42,

$$\mathbb{E}(X) = \mathbb{E}(X \mid B)\mathbb{P}(B) + \mathbb{E}(X \mid B^c)\mathbb{P}(B^c),$$

which is to say that

$$m(r) = p[1 + m(r - 1)] + (1 - p)[1 + m(r)]$$

for $r = 1, 2, \ldots$, with the convention that $m(0) = 0$, as required.

We proceed as follows in order to solve

$$m(r) = p[1 + m(r - 1)] + (1 - p)[1 + m(r)]$$

given that $m(0) = 0$ and $p + q = 1$. Transfer all the terms to the left-hand side

$$p[1 + m(r - 1)] + (1 - p)[1 + m(r)] - m(r) = 0;$$

this is equivalent to

$$-pm(r) + pm(r - 1) = -1. \tag{1}$$

If the right-hand side of (1) were zero, this would be identical to the homogeneous equation discussed in Example B.7. The new equation is solved in two steps. First, deem the right-hand side to be zero and solve as for the homogeneous case:

$$-pm(r) + pm(r - 1) = 0. \tag{2}$$

The auxiliary equation of (2) is

$$-p + p\theta^{-1} = 0$$

with roots $\theta = 1$. The general solution to (2) is therefore

$$m(r) = a1^r,$$

where a is an arbitrary constant. Then, augment this solution by some $m(r)$ which has to be given further thought:

$$m(r) = a + m(r).$$

This augmented $m(r)$ has to be such that when substituted into $-pm(r)+pm(r-1)$ the result is -1. In this book, it will always be possible to express $m(r)$ as the quadratic $A + Br + Cr^2$ with only one of the constants A, B and C non-zero. In the present case try $m(r) = Br$ and therefore require:

$$-pB(r) + pB(r - 1) = -1,$$

so

$$-pBr + pBr - pB = -1.$$

Hence

$$-pk = B = -1$$

so

$$B = \frac{1}{p}$$

giving

$$m(r) = \frac{r}{p} \qquad\qquad \text{for } r = 1, 2, \ldots$$

is a particular solution to (1). It follows that the general solution of (1) is

$$m(r) = a + \frac{r}{p} \qquad\qquad \text{for } r = 1, 2, \ldots$$

The constant a is found from the boundary conditions to be given by $a = 0$. Therefore the answer is $m(r) = r/p$.

PROBLEM (2.6.3). If X is a discrete random variable and $\mathbb{E}(X^2) = 0$, show that $\mathbb{P}(X = 0) = 1$. Deduce that, if $\operatorname{var}(X) = 0$, then $\mathbb{P}(X = \mu) = 1$, whenever $\mu = \mathbb{E}(X)$ is finite.

SOLUTION. Suppsose that X is a discrete random variable and $\mathbb{E}(X^2) = 0$. By (2.28),

$$\sum_{i=1}^{\infty} x_i^2 \mathbb{P}(X = x_i) = 0,$$

giving that

$$x_i^2 \mathbb{P}(X = x_i) = 0.$$

Thus $\mathbb{P}(X = x_i) = 0$ for $x_i \neq 0$. Hence

$$\mathbb{P}(X = 0) = 1 - \mathbb{P}(X_i)$$
$$= 1 - \mathbb{P}(\bigcup_{x_i \neq 0, x_i \in \mathrm{Im}(X)} \{\omega \colon X(\omega) \neq 0\})$$
$$= 1 - \sum_{x_i \neq 0, x_i \in \mathrm{Im}(X)} \mathbb{P}(X = x_i)$$
$$= 1$$

as required.

Let $Z = X - \mathbb{E}(X)$. By (2.33),

$$\mathrm{var}(X) = \mathbb{E}(Z^2).$$

If $\mathrm{var}(X) = 0$, this is equivalent to $\mathbb{E}(Z^2) = 0$, then $\mathbb{P}(Z = 0) = 1$ by the argument above. Thus $\mathbb{P}(X - \mathbb{E}(X) = 0) = 1$. Hence $\mathbb{P}(X = \mu) = 1$, where $\mu = \mathbb{E}(X)$ is finite.

PROBLEM (2.6.4). For what value of c and α is the function p, defined by

$$p(k) = \begin{cases} ck^\alpha & \text{for } k = 1, 2, \ldots, \\ 0 & \text{otherwie,} \end{cases}$$

a mass function?

SOLUTION. Mass functions sum up to 1, so that

$$1 = \sum_{k=1}^{\infty} p(k)$$
$$= c \sum_{k=1}^{\infty} k^\alpha,$$

giving that $\alpha < -1$ and $c = 1/\zeta(-a)$, where $\zeta(p) = \sum_{k} k^{-p}$ is the Riemann zeta function.

PROBLEM (2.6.4). *Lack-of-memory property.* If X has the geometric distribution with parameter p, show that

$$\mathbb{P}(X > m + n \mid X > m) = \mathbb{P}(X > n)$$

for $m, n = 0, 1, 2, \ldots$. We say that X has the 'lack-of-memory property' since, if we are given that $X - m > 0$, then the distribution of $X - m$ is the same as the original distribution of X. Show that the geometric distribution is the only distribution concentrated on the positive integers with the lack-of-memory property.

SOLUTION. For the first part, since X has the geometric distribution with parameter p $(= 1 - q)$, it follows that

$$\mathbb{P}(X = k) = pq^{k-1}$$

for $k = 1, 2, 3, \ldots$. We have that

$$
\begin{aligned}
\mathbb{P}(X > m + n \mid X > m) &= \frac{\mathbb{P}((X > m + n) \cap (X > m))}{P(X > m)} \\
&= \frac{\mathbb{P}(X > m + n)}{\mathbb{P}(X > m)} \qquad &&\text{since } m, n = 0, 1, 2, \ldots, \text{ so } m + n \geq n \\
&= \frac{\sum_{k=m++1}^{\infty} \mathbb{P}(X = k)}{\sum_{i=m+1}^{\infty} \mathbb{P}(X = i)} \\
&= \frac{\sum_{k=m+n+1}^{\infty} pq^{k-1}}{\sum_{i=m+1}^{\infty} pq^{i-1}} \\
&= \frac{p \sum_{j=m+n}^{\infty} q^j}{p \sum_{t=}^{\infty} q^t} \qquad &&\text{reindex with } j = k - 1 \text{ and } t = i - 1 \\
&= \frac{\frac{q^{m+n}}{1-q}}{\frac{q^m}{1-q}} \qquad &&\text{since } \sum_{k=l}^{\infty} r^k = \frac{r^k}{1 - r} \\
&= \frac{q^{n+m}}{q^m} \\
&= q^n,
\end{aligned}
$$

and

$$
\begin{aligned}
\mathbb{P}(X > n) &= \sum_{i=n+1}^{\infty} \mathbb{P}(X = i) \\
&= \sum_{i=m+1}^{\infty} pq^{i-1} \\
&= p \sum_{j=m}^{\infty} q^j \qquad &&\text{reindex with } j = i - 1 \\
&= p \frac{q^n}{1 - q} \\
&= q^n.
\end{aligned}
$$

Thus

$$\mathbb{P}(X > m + n \mid X > m) = \mathbb{P}(X > n)$$

as required.

For the last part, let X be the discrete random variable having lack-of-memory property and let $G(n)$ be the function on $\{0, 1, 2, \ldots\}$ given by $G(n) = \mathbb{P}(X > n)$. Then

$$
\begin{aligned}
G(m+n) &= \mathbb{P}(X > m+n) \\
&= \mathbb{P}(X > m+n \mid X > m)\mathbb{P}(X > m) \\
&\quad + \mathbb{P}(X > m+n \mid X \leq m)\mathbb{P}(X \leq m) \quad \text{by by the partition theorem, Theorem 1.48} \\
&= \mathbb{P}(X > m+n \mid X > m)\mathbb{P}(X > m) \quad\quad \text{since } \mathbb{P}(X > m+n \mid X \leq m) = 0 \\
&= \mathbb{P}(X > n)\mathbb{P}(X > m) \quad\quad\quad\quad\quad\; \text{since } X \text{ has the lack-of-memory property} \\
&= G(n)G(m) \\
&= G(m)G(n)
\end{aligned}
$$

for $m, n = 0, 1, 2, \ldots$. Thus

$$\mathbb{P}(X > k) = (\mathbb{P}(X > 1))^k$$

for $k = 2, 3, \ldots$. As a first step towards proving this show that

$$\mathbb{P}(X > 2) = (\mathbb{P}(X > 1))^2.$$

Define $p = \mathbb{P}(X = 1)$ and $q = \mathbb{P}(X > 1)$. We now have that

$$\mathbb{P}(X > k) = q^k,$$

for $k = 2, 3, \ldots$. Since the event $\{X > k - 1\}$ is the disjoint union of the events $\{X > k\}$ and $\{X = k\}$, it follows that

$$\mathbb{P}(X > k - 1) = \mathbb{P}(X > k) + \mathbb{P}(X = k),$$

which is to say that

$$
\begin{aligned}
\mathbb{P}(X = k) &= \mathbb{P}(X > k - 1) - \mathbb{P}(X > k), \\
&= q^{k-1} - q^k \\
&= q^{k-1}(1 - q) \\
&= pq^{m-1}
\end{aligned}
$$

for $k = 2, 3, \ldots$. But for $k = 1$,

$$
\begin{aligned}
\mathbb{P}(X = 1) &= p \\
&= pq^{k-1},
\end{aligned}
$$

trivially. Hence X takes values in $\{1, 2, 3, \ldots\}$ and

$$\mathbb{P}(X = k) = pq^{k-1} \qquad \text{for } k = 1, 2, 3, \ldots,$$

giving that X has the geometric distribution with parameter $p \in (0, 1)$.

PROBLEM (2.6.6). The random variable N takes non-negative integer values. Show that

$$\mathbb{E}(N) = \sum_{k=0}^{\infty} \mathbb{P}(N > k)$$

provided that the series on the right-hand side converges.
A fair die having two faces coloured blue, two red and two green, is thrown repeatedly. Find the probability that not all colours occur in the first k throws. Deduce that, if N is the random variable which takes the value n if all three colours occur in the first n throws but only two of the colours in the first $n - 1$ throws, then the expected value of N is $\dfrac{11}{2}$. (Oxford 1979M)

SOLUTION. For the first part, we have that

$$\sum_{k=0}^{m} \mathbb{P}(N > k) = \sum_{k=0}^{\infty} \sum_{i=k+1}^{\infty} \mathbb{P}(N = i) \qquad \text{since } \mathbb{P}(N > k) = \sum_{i=k+1}^{\infty} \mathbb{P}(N = i)$$

$$= \sum_{i=1}^{\infty} \sum_{k=0}^{n-1} \mathbb{P}(N = i) \qquad \text{change the order of summation}$$

$$= \sum_{i=0}^{\infty} n\mathbb{P}(N = i)$$

$$= \mathbb{E}(N),$$

as required.
For the second part, note that the probability that exactly one colour occurs in the first k throws is

$$3\left(\frac{1}{3}\right)^k$$

Furthermore, the probability that exactly two colours occurs in the first k throws is

$$3\left[\left(\frac{2}{3}\right)^k - \left(\frac{1}{3}\right)^k\right].$$

To see this, let H be the event that only two colours blue and green occur in the first k throws, E be the event that only two colours green and red occur in the first k throws and F be the event that only two colours blue and red occur in the first k throws. By the definition of the probability of the union of events (see Exercise 1.20),

$$\mathbb{P}(H \cup E \cup F) = \mathbb{P}(H) + \mathbb{P}(E) + \mathbb{P}(F) - \mathbb{P}(H \cap E) - \mathbb{P}(H \cap F) - \mathbb{P}(E \cap F) + \mathbb{P}(H \cap E \cap F)$$

$$= \frac{2^k}{3^k} + \frac{2^k}{3^k} + \frac{2^k}{3^k} - \frac{1}{3^k} - \frac{1}{3^k} - \frac{1}{3^k} + 0$$

$$= 3[(\frac{2}{3})^k - (\frac{1}{3})^k].$$

Hence the probability that not all colours occur in the first k throws is

$$3(\frac{1}{3})^k + 3[(\frac{2}{3})^k - (\frac{1}{3})^k] = \frac{3 \cdot 2^k - 3}{3^k}.$$

For the last part, we have that

$$\mathbb{E}(N) = \sum_{k=0}^{\infty} \mathbb{P}(N > k)$$

$$= \mathbb{P}(N > 0) + \mathbb{P}(N > 1) + \mathbb{P}(N > 2) + \sum_{k=3}^{\infty} \mathbb{P}(N > k)$$

$$= 1 + 1 + 1 + \sum_{k=3}^{\infty} \mathbb{P}(N > k)$$

$$= 3 + 3 \left[\left(\frac{2}{3}\right)^k - \left(\frac{1}{3}\right)^k \right]$$

$$= 3 + 3 \sum_{k=3}^{\infty} \left(\frac{2}{3}\right)^k - 3 \sum_{k=3}^{\infty} \left(\frac{1}{3}\right)^k$$

$$= 3 + 3 \frac{\left(\frac{2}{3}\right)^3}{1 - \frac{2}{3}} - 3 \frac{\left(\frac{1}{3}\right)^3}{1 - \frac{1}{3}}$$

$$= 3 + 9 \cdot \frac{8}{27} - \frac{9}{2} \cdot \frac{1}{27}$$

$$= 3 + \frac{8}{3} - \frac{1}{6}$$

$$= \frac{18 + 16 - 1}{6} = \frac{33}{6} = \frac{11}{2},$$

as required.

PROBLEM 2.6.1 (2.6.7). *Coupon-collecting problem.* There are c different types of coupon, and each coupon obtained is equally likely to be any one of the

c types. Find the probability that the first n coupons which you collect do not form a complete set, and deduce an expression for the mean number of coupons you will need to collect before you have a complete set.

SOLUTION. Let A_i be the event that we are having all types of coupon but c_i, $i = 1, 2, \ldots, c$. Then

$$\mathbb{P}(\bigcup_{i=1}^{c} A_i) = \sum_{i=1}^{c} \mathbb{P}(A_i) - \sum_{i<j} \mathbb{P}(A_i \cap A_j) + \sum_{i<j<k} \mathbb{P}(A_i \cap A_j) + \cdots + (-1)^{c+1} \mathbb{P}(\bigcap_{i=1}^{c} A_i)$$

and

$$\mathbb{P}(A_i) = \frac{(i-1)^{n-c+1}}{c^n}$$

for each $i \in \{1, 2, \ldots, c\}$. Furthermore,

$$\mathbb{P}(A_{i_1} \cap A_{i_2} \cap \cdots \cap A_{i_k}) = \frac{(c-k)^{n-c+k}}{c^n},$$

for $1 \le k \le c$. Note that

$$\sum_{i_1 < i_2 < \cdots < i_k} \mathbb{P}(A_{i_1} \cap A_{i_2} \cap \cdots \cap A_{i_k})$$

consists of $\binom{c}{k}$ terms for $1 \le k \le c$. Thus

$$\mathbb{P}(\bigcup_{i=1}^{c} A_i) = \binom{c}{1} \frac{(c-1)^{n-c+1}}{c^n} - \binom{c}{2} \frac{(c-1)^{n-c+1}}{c^n} + \cdots + (-1)^c \binom{c}{c-1} \frac{1}{c^n}$$

Let N be the random variable which takes the value k if the first $k-1$ coupons do not form a complete set, but the first k coupons are formed a complete set. Thus

$$\mathbb{P}(N > n) = \mathbb{P}(\bigcup_{i=1}^{c} A_i),$$

so

$$\mathbb{E}(N) = \sum_{n=0}^{\infty} \mathbb{P}(N > n)$$

$$= \sum_{n=0}^{c-1} \mathbb{P}(N > n) + \sum_{n=c}^{\infty} \mathbb{P}(N > n)$$

$$= c + \binom{c}{1} \sum_{n=c}^{\infty} \frac{(c-1)^{n-c+1}}{c^n} - \binom{c}{2} \sum_{n=c}^{\infty} \frac{(c-2)^{n-c+1}}{c^n} + \cdots + (-1)^c \binom{c}{1} \sum_{n=c}^{\infty} \frac{1}{c^n}$$

$$= c + \binom{c}{1} \frac{1}{(c-1)^{c-1}} \frac{\left(\frac{c-1}{c}\right)^c}{1 - \frac{c-1}{c}} - \binom{c}{2} \frac{1}{(c-1)^{c-2}} \frac{\left(\frac{c-2}{c}\right)^c}{1 - \frac{c-2}{c}} + \cdots + (-1)^c \binom{c}{c-1} \frac{\frac{1}{c^c}}{1 - \frac{1}{c}}$$

$$= c + \binom{c}{1} \frac{c-1}{c^{c-1}} - \frac{1}{2} \binom{c}{2} \frac{(c-2)^2}{c^{c-1}} + \cdots + (-1)^c \frac{1}{c-1} \binom{c}{c-1} \frac{1}{c^{c-1}}$$

$$= c + \frac{1}{c^{c-1}} \left[\frac{1}{2} \binom{c}{1}(c-1) - \frac{1}{2} \binom{c}{2}(c-2)^2 + \cdots + (-1)^c \frac{1}{c-1} \binom{c}{c-1} \right].$$

PROBLEM (*2.6.8). An ambidextrous student has a left and a right pocket, each initially containing n humbugs. Each time he feels hungry, he puts a hand into one of his pockets and, if it is not empty, he takes a humbug from it and eats it. On each occasion, he is equally likely to choose either the left or right pocket. When he first puts his hand into an empty pocket, the other pocket contains H humbugs. Show that if p_h is the probability that $H = h$, then

$$p_h = \binom{2n-h}{n} \frac{1}{2^{2n-h}} \qquad \text{for } h = 0, 1, \dots, n,$$

and find the expected value of H, by considering

$$\sum_{h=0}^{n} p_h, \qquad \qquad \sum_{h=0}^{n} h p_h, \qquad \qquad \sum_{h=0}^{n} (n-h) p_h,$$

or otherwise. (Oxford 1982M)

SOLUTION. This is the binomial distribution with parameters $2n - h$ and we may suppose without loss of generality that that the left pocket is empty and the right pocket contains $H = h$. The number of ways to take hambugs so that the left pocket is empty is that $\binom{2n-h}{n}$. Thus the probability p_H is that

$$p_h = \binom{2n-h}{n} \frac{1}{2^n} \frac{1}{2^{n-h}}$$

$$= \binom{2n-h}{n} \frac{1}{2^{2n-h}} \qquad \text{for } h = 0, 1, \dots, n.$$

For the last part, we first prove the formula

$$2(n-h)P_h = (2n-h)P_{h+1}.$$

Indeed,

$$2(n-h)P_h = 2(n-h)\binom{2n-h}{n}\frac{1}{2^{2n-h}}$$

$$= 2(n-h)\frac{(2n-h)!}{n!(n-h)!}\frac{1}{2^{2n-h}}$$

$$= \frac{(2n-h)!}{n!(n-h)!}\frac{1}{2^{2n-h-1}}$$

$$= (2n-h)\frac{(2n-h-1)!}{n!(n-h-1)!}\frac{1}{2^{2n-h-1}}$$

$$= (2n-h)\binom{2n-h-1}{n}\frac{1}{2^{2n-h-1}}$$

$$= (2n-h)P_{h+1}$$

Thus

$$\sum_{h=0}^{n-1} 2(n-h)P_h = \sum_{h=0}^{n-1}(2n-h)P_{h+1}$$

$$2n\sum_{h=0}^{n}P_h - 2np_n - 2\sum_{h=0}^{n}hP_h + 2np_n = 2n\sum_{h=0}^{n}P_h - 2np_0 - \sum_{h=0}^{n-1}(h+1)P_{h+1} + \sum_{h=0}^{n-1}p_{h+1}$$

$$2n - 2np_n - 2\mathbb{E}(H) + 2np_n = 2n - 2np_0 - \sum_{h=0}^{n}hp_h + 1 - p_0$$

$$-2\mathbb{E}(H) = -2np_0 - \mathbb{E}(H) + 1 - p_0$$

$$\mathbb{E}(H) = (2n+1)p_0 - 1.$$

PROBLEM (2.6.9). The probability of obtaining a head when a certain coin is tossed is p. The coin is tossed repeatedly until n heads occur in a row. Let X be the total number of tosses required for this to happen. Find the expected value of X.

SOLUTION. Let B_i, $i = 1, 2, \ldots, n$, be the event that the first $i-1$ tosses give heads and the ith toss gives tails and let B_{n+1} be the event that n tosses give heads. $\{B_1, B_2, \ldots B_{n+1}\}$ is a partition of the sample space. By the partition theorem, Theorem 2.42,

$$\mathbb{E}(X) = \sum_{i=1}^{n+1}\mathbb{P}(B_i)\mathbb{E}(X \mid B_i)$$

$$= (1-p)(1+\mathbb{E}(X)) + (1-p)p(2+\mathbb{E}(X)) + \cdots + (1-p)p^{n-1}(n+\mathbb{E}(X)) + p^n n$$

since $\mathbb{E}(X \mid B_i) = \mathbb{E}(x) + i$ for $i = 1, 2, \ldots, n$ and $\mathbb{E}(X \mid B_{n+1}) = n$, and $\mathbb{P}(B_i) = (1-p)p^{i-1}$ for $i = 1, 2, \ldots n$ and $\mathbb{P}(B_{n+1}) = p^n$. Thus

$$[1 - (1 - p)(1 + p + p^2 \cdots + p^{n-1})]\mathbb{E}(X) = (1 - p)[1 + 2p + \cdots + np^{n-1}] + p^n n.$$

Hence

$$[1 - (1 - p)\frac{1 - p^n}{1 - p}]\mathbb{E}(X) = (1 - p)[p + p^2 + \cdots + p^n]' + p$$

since $1 + p + p^2 + \cdots + p^{n-1} = \dfrac{1 - p^n}{1 - p}$. Therefore

$$p^n \mathbb{E}(X) = (1 - p)[p\frac{1 - p^n}{1 - p}] + p^n n \qquad\qquad \text{since } \sum_{i=1}^{n} p^i = p\frac{1 - p^n}{1 - p}$$

$$= (1 - p)\frac{[1 - (n+1)p^n](1 - p) + p - p^{n+1}}{(1 - p)^2} + p^n n$$

$$= \frac{1 - (n+1)p^n + np^{n+1}}{1 - p} + p^n n$$

$$= \frac{1 - p^n}{1 - p},$$

so

$$\mathbb{E}(X) = \frac{1 - p^n}{p^n(1 - p)}.$$

PROBLEM (2.6.10). A population of N animals has had a certain number a of its members captured, marked, and then released. Show that the probability P_n that it is necessary to capture n animals in order to obtain m which have been marked is

$$p_n = \frac{a}{N}\binom{a-1}{m-1}\binom{N-a}{n-m} / \binom{N-1}{n-1},$$

where $m \leq n \leq N - a + m$. Hence, show that

$$\frac{a}{N}\binom{a-1}{m-1}\frac{(N-a)!}{(N-1)!} \sum_{n=m}^{N-a+m} \frac{(n-1)!(N-n)!}{(n-m)!(N-a+m-n)!} = 1,$$

and that the expectation of n is $\dfrac{N+1}{a+1}m$. (Oxford 1972M)

SOLUTION. For the first part, let Y_m be the number of animals that it is necessary to capture (without re-release) to obtain m, which have been marked. For the event $\{Y_m = n\}$ to occur, it is necessary that:

(i) The nth animal is marked, which can occur in a ways.

(ii) The preceding $n - 1$ animals include exactly $m - 1$ marked and $n - m$ unmarked animals, which may occur in $\binom{a - 1}{m - 1}\binom{N - a}{n - m}$ ways.

The total number of ways of first selecting a distinct animal to fill the nth place, and then choosing $n - 1$ animals to fill the remaining $n - 1$ places is $N \cdot \binom{N - 1}{n - 1}$. Because these are assumed to be equally likely, the required probability is

$$
\begin{aligned}
p_n &= \mathbb{P}(Y_m = n) \\
&= \frac{a}{N}\binom{a - 1}{m - 1}\binom{N - a}{n - m} \bigg/ \binom{N - 1}{n - 1},
\end{aligned}
$$

where $m \leq n \leq N - a + m$, as required.

For the second part, we have that

$$
\sum_{n=m}^{N-1+m} p_n = 1.
$$

Thus

$$
\sum_{n=m}^{N-a+m} \frac{a}{N}\binom{a - 1}{m - 1} \frac{(N - a)!(n - 1)!(N - n)!}{(n - m)!(N - a - n + m)!(N - 1)!} = 1.
$$

Hence

$$
\frac{a}{N}\binom{a - 1}{N - 1}\frac{(N - a)!}{(N - 1)!} \sum_{n=m}^{N-a+m} \frac{(n - 1)!(N - n)!}{(n - m)!(N - a - n + m)!} = 1, \qquad (1)
$$

as required.

For the last part, we see from (1) that

$$
\begin{aligned}
\sum_{n=m}^{N-a+m} \frac{(n - 1)!(N - n)!}{(n - m)!(N - a - n + m)!} &= \frac{N}{a}\frac{(m - 1)(a - m)!}{(a - 1)!}\frac{(N - 1)!}{(N - a)!} \\
&= \frac{N!(m - 1)!(a - m)!}{a!(N - a)!} \\
&= \binom{N}{a}(m - 1)!(a - m)!.
\end{aligned}
$$

Thus

$$\sum_{n=m}^{N-a+m} \frac{(n-1)!(N-n)!}{(n-m)!(N-a-n+m)!(m-1)!(a-m)!} = \binom{N}{a}$$

so

$$\sum_{n=m}^{N-a+m} \binom{n-1}{m-1}\binom{N-n}{a-m} = \binom{N}{a}. \tag{2}$$

Applying (2) for $N+1$, $a+1$ and $m+1$ gives that

$$\sum_{n=m}^{N-a+m} \binom{n}{m}\binom{N-n}{a-m} = \binom{N+1}{a+1}.$$

The mean of n is

$$\begin{aligned}
\mathbb{E}(n) &= \sum_{n=m}^{N-a+m} np_n \\
&= \frac{a}{N}\binom{a-1}{m-1}\frac{(N-a)!}{(N-1)!}\sum_{n=m}^{N-a+m}\frac{n!(N-n)!}{(n-m)!(N-a-n+m)!} \\
&= m\binom{a}{m}\frac{(N-a)!}{N!}\sum_{n=m}^{N-a+m}\frac{n!(N-n)!}{(n-m)!(N-a-n+m)!} \\
&= m\binom{a}{m}\frac{(N-a)!}{N!}\sum_{n=m}^{N-a+m}\binom{n}{m}\binom{N-n}{a-m}m!(a-m)! \\
&= m\frac{a!}{m!(a-m)!}\frac{(N-a)!}{N!}\sum\binom{n}{m}\binom{N-n}{a-m}m!(a-m)! \\
&= m\frac{a!(N-a)!}{N!}\binom{N+1}{a+1} \\
&= m\frac{a!(N-a)!}{N!}\frac{(N+1)!}{(N-a)!(a+1)!} \\
&= m\frac{N+1}{a+1},
\end{aligned}$$

as required.

CHAPTER 3

Multivariate discrete distributions and independence

3.1. Bivariate discrete distributions

EXERCISE (3.8). Two cards are drawn at random from a deck of 52 cards. If X denotes the number of aces drawn and Y denotes the number of kings, display the joint mass function of X and Y in the tabular form of Table 3.1.

SOLUTION. We have that

$$p_{X,Y}(x=0,y=2) = \frac{\binom{4}{2}}{\binom{52}{2}} = \frac{4!}{2!2!} \cdot \frac{2!50!}{52!} = \frac{1}{13 \cdot 17},$$

$$p_{X,Y}(x=0,y=1) = \frac{\binom{44}{1}\binom{4}{1}}{\binom{52}{2}} = \frac{44!}{1!43!} \cdot \frac{4!}{1!3!} \cdot \frac{2!50!}{52!} = \frac{88}{13 \cdot 51},$$

$$p_{X,Y}(x=0,y=0) = \frac{\binom{44}{2}}{\binom{52}{2}} = \frac{44!}{2!42!} \cdot \frac{2!50!}{52!} = \frac{11 \cdot 43}{13.51},$$

$$p_{X,Y}(x=1,y=0) = \frac{\binom{4}{1} \cdot \binom{44}{1}}{\binom{52}{2}} = \frac{4!}{1!3!} \cdot \frac{44!}{1!43!} \cdot \frac{2!50!}{52!} = \frac{88}{13 \cdot 51},$$

$$p_{X,Y}(x=1,y=1) = \frac{\binom{4}{1}\binom{4}{1}}{\binom{52}{2}} = \frac{4!}{1!3!} \cdot \frac{4!}{1!3!} \cdot \frac{2!50!}{52!} = \frac{8}{13 \cdot 51},$$

$$p_{X,Y}(x=1,y=2) = 0,$$

$$p_{X,Y}(x=2,y=0) = \frac{\binom{4}{2}}{\binom{52}{2}} = \frac{4!}{2!2!} \cdot \frac{2!50!}{52!} = \frac{1}{13 \cdot 17}.$$

Thus

	$x = 0$	$x = 1$	$x = 2$
$y = 0$	$\dfrac{11 \cdot 43}{13 \cdot 51}$	$\dfrac{88}{13 \cdot 51}$	$\dfrac{1}{13 \cdot 17}$
$y = 1$	$\dfrac{88}{13 \cdot 51}$	$\dfrac{8}{13 \cdot 51}$	0
$y = 2$	$\dfrac{1}{13 \cdot 17}$	0	0

TABLE 1. The joint mass function of the pair X, Y.

EXERCISE (3.9). The pair of discrete random variables (X, Y) has joint mass function

$$\mathbb{P}(X = i, Y = j) = \begin{cases} \theta^{i+j+1} & \text{if } i, j = 0, 1, 2, \\ 0 & \text{otherwise,} \end{cases}$$

for some value of θ. Show that θ satisfies the equation

$$\theta + 2\theta^2 + 3\theta^3 + 2\theta^4 + \theta^5 = 1,$$

and find the marginal mass function of X in terms of θ.

SOLUTION. We have that

$$\sum_{i,j} \mathbb{P}(X = i, Y = j) = \theta + \theta^2 + \theta^3 + \theta^2 + \theta^3 + \theta^4 + \theta^3 + \theta^4 + \theta^5$$

$$= \theta + 2\theta^2 + 3\theta^3 + 2\theta^4 + \theta^5.$$

But

$$\sum_{x \in \mathrm{Im}\, X} \sum_{y \in \mathrm{Im}\, y} p_{X,Y}(x, y) = 1,$$

so

$$\theta + 2\theta^2 + 3\theta^3 + 2\theta^4 + \theta^5 = 1$$

The marginal mass function of X is

$$p_X(x) = \sum_y p_{X,Y}(x, y),$$

giving that

$$p_X(0) = p_{X,Y}(x = 0, y = 0) + p_{X,Y}(x = 0, y = 1) + p_{X,Y}(x = 0, y = 2)$$
$$= \theta + \theta^2 + \theta^3.$$

Thus

$$p_X(i) = \theta^{i+1} + \theta^{i+2} + \theta^{i+3}$$
$$= \theta^i(\theta + \theta^2 + \theta^3)$$

for $i = 0, 1, 2$.

3.2. Expectation in the multivariate case

EXERCISE (3.12). Suppose that (X, Y) has joint mass function

$$\mathbb{P}(X = i, Y = j) = \theta^{i+j+1} \qquad \text{for } i, j = 0, 1, 2.$$

Show that

$$\mathbb{E}(XY) = \theta^3 + 4\theta^4 + 4\theta^5$$

and

$$\mathbb{E}(X) = \theta^2 + 3\theta^3 + 3\theta^4 + 2\theta^5.$$

SOLUTION. We have that

$$\mathbb{E}(XY) = \sum_{x=0}^{2}\sum_{y=0}^{2}(xy)\mathbb{P}(X = x, Y = y)$$
$$= (1 \cdot 1)\mathbb{P}(X = 1, Y = 1) + (1 \cdot 2)\mathbb{P}(X = 1, Y = 2))$$
$$+ (2 \cdot 1)\mathbb{P}(X = 2, Y = 1) + (2 \cdot 2)\mathbb{P}(X = 2, Y = 2$$
$$= 1\theta^3 + 2\theta^4 + 2\theta^4 + 4\theta^5$$
$$= \theta^3 + 4\theta^4 + 4\theta^5$$

Note that $(ij)\mathbb{P}(X = i, Y = j) = 0$ for $i = 0$ or $j = 0$ and

$$\mathbb{E}(X) = \sum_{x=0}^{2}\sum_{y=0}^{2}x\mathbb{P}(X = x, Y = y)$$
$$= 1\mathbb{P}(X = 1, Y = 0) + 1\mathbb{P}(X = 1, Y = 1) + 1\mathbb{P}(X = 1, Y = 2)$$
$$+ 2\mathbb{P}(X = 2, Y = 0) + 2\mathbb{P}(X = 2, Y = 1) + 2\mathbb{P}(X = 2, Y = 2)$$
$$= 1\theta^2 + 1\theta^3 + 1\theta^4 + 2\theta^3 + 2\theta^4 + 2\theta^5$$
$$= \theta^2 + 3\theta^3 + 3\theta^4 + 2\theta^5$$

Note that $i\mathbb{P}(X = i, Y = j) = 0$ for $i = 0$.

3.3. Independence of discrete random variables

EXERCISE (3.21). Let X and Y be independent discrete random variables. Prove that

$$\mathbb{P}(X \geq x \text{ and } Y \geq y) = \mathbb{P}(X \geq x)P(Y \geq y)$$

for all $x, y \in \mathbb{R}$.

SOLUTION. Let $\{\operatorname{Im} X \geq x\} = \{x_1, x_2, \dots\}$ and $\{\operatorname{Im} Y \geq y\} = \{y_1, y_2, \dots\}$

$$
\begin{aligned}
\mathbb{P}(X \geq x \text{ and } Y \geq y) &= \sum_{i,j=1}^{\infty} \mathbb{P}(X = x_i \text{ and } Y = y_j) \\
&= \sum_{i,j=1}^{\infty} \mathbb{P}(X = x_i) \sum_{i,j=1}^{\infty} \mathbb{P}(Y = y_j) \quad \text{by independence} \\
&= \mathbb{P}(X \geq x)P(Y \geq y)
\end{aligned}
$$

EXERCISE (3.24). The *indicator function* of an event A is the function 1_A defined by

$$
1_A(\omega) = \begin{cases} 1 & \text{if } \omega \in A, \\ 0 & \text{if } \omega \notin A. \end{cases}
$$

Show that two events A and B are independent if and only if their indicator functions are independent random variables.

SOLUTION. Suppose that X and Y are independent, then $\mathbb{P}(A \cap B) = \mathbb{P}(A)\mathbb{P}(B)$.

$$
\begin{aligned}
p_{1_A,1_B}(0,0) &= \mathbb{P}(A^c \cap B^c) \\
&= \mathbb{P}(A^c)\mathbb{P}(B^c) \quad \text{(since } A \text{ and } B \text{ are independent so are } A^c \text{ and } B^c) \\
&= p_{1_A}(0)p_{1_B}(0)
\end{aligned}
$$

$$
\begin{aligned}
p_{1_A,1_B}(1,0) &= \mathbb{P}(A \cap B^c) \\
&= \mathbb{P}(A)\mathbb{P}(B^c) \quad \text{(since } A \text{ and } B \text{ are independent so are } A \text{ and } B^c) \\
&= p_{1_A}(1)p_{1_B}(0)
\end{aligned}
$$

$$
\begin{aligned}
p_{1_A,1_B}(0,1) &= \mathbb{P}(A^c \cap B) \\
&= \mathbb{P}(A^c)\mathbb{P}(B) \quad \text{(since } A \text{ and } B \text{ are independent so are } A^c \text{ and } B) \\
&= p_{1_A}(0)p_{1_B}(1)
\end{aligned}
$$

$$p_{1_A,1_B}(1,1) = \mathbb{P}(A \cap B)$$
$$= \mathbb{P}(A)\mathbb{P}(B)$$
$$= p_{1_A}(1)p_{1_B}(1).$$

Thus

$$p_{1_A,1_B}(i,j) = p_{1_A}(i)p_{1_B}(j)$$

for $i, j = 0, 1$. Hence 1_A and 1_B are independent random variables.

Conversely, suppose that 1_A and 1_B are independent random variables. We have

$$p_{1_A,1_B}(1,1) = \mathbb{P}(1_A = 1, 1_B = 1)$$
$$= \mathbb{P}(A \cap B).$$

But

$$p_{1_A,1_B}(1,1) = p_{1_A}(1)p_{1_B}(1) = \mathbb{P}(1_A = 1)\mathbb{P}(1_B = 1) = \mathbb{P}(A)\mathbb{P}(B).$$

Thus

$$\mathbb{P}(A \cap B) = \mathbb{P}(A)\mathbb{P}(B).$$

Therefore A and B are independent.

EXERCISE (3.25). If X and Y are independent discrete random variables, show that the two random variables $g(X)$ and $h(Y)$ are independent also, for any functions g and h which map $\mathbb{R}$ into $\mathbb{R}$.

SOLUTION. For $a, b \in \mathbb{R}$, we have

$$\mathbb{P}(g(X) = a, h(Y) = b) = \mathbb{P}(X = g^{-1}(a), Y = h^{-1}(b))$$
$$= \mathbb{P}(X = g^{-1}(a))\mathbb{P}(Y = h^{-1}(b)) \quad \text{since } X \text{ and } Y \text{ are independent}$$
$$= \mathbb{P}(g(X) = a)\mathbb{P}(h(Y) = b).$$

Thus $g(X)$ and $h(Y)$ are independent.

3.4. Sums of random variables

EXERCISE (3.29). If X and Y are independent discrete random variables, X having the Poisson distribution with parameter λ and Y having the Poisson distribution with parameter μ, show that $X + Y$ has the Poisson distribution with parameter $\lambda + \mu$. Give an example to show that the conclusion is not generally true if X and Y are dependent.

SOLUTION. By Theorem 3.27,

$\mathbb{P}(Z = z)$

$= \sum_{x \in \text{Im } X} \mathbb{P}(X = x)\mathbb{P}(Y = z - x)$

$= \sum_{x=0}^{\infty} \mathbb{P}(X = x)\mathbb{P}(Y = z - x)$

$= \mathbb{P}(X = 0)\mathbb{P}(Y = z) + \mathbb{P}(X = 1)\mathbb{P}(Y = z - 1)+$ since $z - x \geq 0$,

$\qquad \cdots + \mathbb{P}(Z = z)\mathbb{P}(Y = 0)$ so $x \leq z$ and $x \geq 0$

$= \dfrac{1}{0!}\lambda^0 e^{-\lambda} \cdot \dfrac{1}{z!}\mu^z e^{-\mu}$

$\quad + \dfrac{1}{1!}\lambda^1 e^{-\lambda} \cdot \dfrac{1}{(z-1)!}\mu^{z-1} e^{-\mu} + \cdots + \dfrac{1}{z!}\lambda^z e^{-\lambda} \cdot \dfrac{1}{0!}\mu^0 e^{-\mu}$

$= \sum_{x=0}^{z} \dfrac{1}{x!}\lambda^x e^{-\lambda} \dfrac{1}{(z-x)!}\mu^{z-x} e^{-\mu}$

$= \sum_{x=0}^{z} \dfrac{1}{x!(z-x)!}\lambda^x \mu^{z-x} e^{-\lambda-\mu}$

$= \dfrac{1}{z!}\sum_{x=0}^{z} \dfrac{z!}{x!(z-x)!}\lambda^x \mu^{z-x} e^{-(\lambda+\mu)}$ multiplying and dividing by $z!$

$= \dfrac{1}{z!}\sum_{x=0}^{z} \binom{z}{x}\lambda^x \mu^{z-x} e^{-(\lambda+\mu)}$ since $\binom{z}{x} = \dfrac{z!}{x!(z-x)!}$

$= \dfrac{1}{z!}(\lambda + \mu)^z e^{-(\lambda+\mu)}$ since $(\lambda + \mu)^z = \sum_{x=0}^{z} \binom{z}{x}\lambda^x \mu^{z-x}$.

Therefore $X + Y$ has the Poisson distribution with parameter $\lambda + \mu$. Take $Y = X$, so that $X + Y$ takes even values only—it cannot then have the Poisson distribution.

EXERCISE (3.30). If X has the binomial distribution with parameters m and p, Y has the binomial distribution with parameters n and p, and X and Y are independent, show that $X + Y$ has the binomial distribution with parameters $m + n$ and p.

SOLUTION. By Theorem 3.27,

$$\mathbb{P}(Z = z) = \sum_{x \in \mathrm{Im}\, X} \mathbb{P}(X = x)\mathbb{P}(Y = z - x)$$

$$= \sum_{x=0}^{\infty} \mathbb{P}(X = x)\mathbb{P}(Y = z - x)$$

$$= \mathbb{P}(X = 0)\mathbb{P}(Y = z) + \mathbb{P}(X = 1)\mathbb{P}(Y = z - 1)+$$

$$\cdots + \mathbb{P}(Z = z)\mathbb{P}(Y = 0)$$

$$= \binom{m}{0}p^0(1-p)^m\binom{n}{z}p^z(1-p)^0 + \binom{m}{1}p^1(1-p)^{n-1}\binom{n}{z-1}p^{z-1}(1-p)^1 +$$

$$\cdots + \binom{m}{z}p^z(1-p)^0\binom{n}{0}p^0(1-p)^z$$

$$= \sum_{x=0}^{z}\binom{m}{x}p^x(1-p)^m\binom{n}{z-x}p^{z-x}(1-p)^{n-(z-x)}$$

$$= \sum_{x=0}^{z}\binom{m}{x}\binom{n}{z-x}p^z(1-p)^{m+n-(z-x)}$$

$$=$$

We shall prove that $\sum_{x=0}^{z}\binom{m}{x}\binom{n}{z-x} = \binom{m+n}{z}$. Indeed, we have a group of people of m men and n women, the number way to choose z people out of group is that $\sum_{x=0}^{z}\binom{m}{x}\binom{n}{z-x}$ but this also equal to $\binom{m+n}{z}$. This complete tproof of the identity. Thus

$$\mathbb{P}(Z = z) = \binom{m+n}{z}p^z(1-p)^{m+n-(z-x)},$$

hence $Z = X + Y$ has the binomial distribution with parameters $m + n$ and p.

For $n = 2$, by Theorem 3.27, we have

$$P(X_1 + X_2 = 0) = \mathbb{P}(X_1 = 0)\mathbb{P}(X_2 = 0) = qq = q^2 = \binom{2}{0}p^0(1-p)^2 \qquad (q = 1 - p)$$

$$P(X_1 + X_2 = 1) = P(X_1 = 0)P(X_2 = 1) + \mathbb{P}(X_1 = 1)\mathbb{P}(X_2 = 0) = 2pq = \binom{2}{1}p^1(1-p)^1$$

$$P(X_1 + X_2 = 2) = P(X_1 = 1)P(X_2 = 1) = p^2 = \binom{2}{2}p^2(1-p)^0$$

Thus $X_1 + X_2$ has the binomial distribution with parameters 2 and p.

Suppose $S_n = X_1 + X_2 + \cdots + X_n$ has the binomial distribution with parameters n and p. That is,

$$P(S_n = k) = \binom{n}{k} p^k (1-p)^{n-k}$$

where $k = 0, 1, \ldots, n$. Consider $S_{n+1} = X_1 + X_2 + \cdots + X_n + X_{n+1} = S_n + X_{n+1}$

$$P(S_{n+1} = z) = \sum_{x=0}^{z} P(S_n = x) P(X_{n+1} = z - x).$$

We have $z - x = 0$ or $z - x = 1$, so $x = z$ or $x = z - 1$, so

$$\begin{aligned}
\mathbb{P}(S_{n+1} = z) &= \mathbb{P}(S_n = z) P(X_{n+1} = 0) + \mathbb{P}(S_n = z - 1)\mathbb{P}(X_{n+1} = 1) \\
&= \binom{n}{z} p^z (1-p)^{n-z}(1-p) + \binom{n}{z-1} p^{z-1}(1-p)^{n-(z-1)} p \\
&= \binom{n}{z} p^z (1-p)^{n-(z-1)} + \binom{n}{z-1} p^z (1-p)^{n-(z-1)} \\
&= \left[\binom{n}{z} + \binom{n}{z-1} \right] p^z (1-p)^{n-(z-1)} \\
&= \binom{n+1}{z} p^z (1-p)^{n-(z-1)} \qquad \text{(by Pascal's Identity)}
\end{aligned}$$

Thus S_{n+1} has the binomial distribution with parameters $n + 1$ and p.

By induction, S_n has the binomial distribution with parameters n and p for all $n \in \mathbb{N}$.

3.5. Indicator functions

EXERCISE (3.42). Let N be the number of the events $A_1, A_2, \ldots, A_n$ which occur. Show that[1]

$$\mathbb{E}(N) = \sum_{i=1}^{n} \mathbb{P}(A_i)$$

SOLUTION. Since

---

[1]A similar fact is valid for an infinite sequence $A_1, A_2, \ldots$, namely that the mean number of events that occur is $\sum_{i=1}^{\infty} \mathbb{P}(A_i)$. This is, however, harder to prove. See the footnote on p. 40.

$$1_{A_i}(\omega) = \begin{cases} 1 & \text{if } A_i \text{ occurs} \\ 0 & \text{otherwise} \end{cases}$$

it follows that

$$N = \sum_{i=1}^{n} 1_{A_i},$$

so that

$$\mathbb{E}(N) = \sum_{i=1}^{n} \mathbb{E}(1_{A_i}) = \sum_{i=1}^{n} \mathbb{P}(A_i)$$

3.6. Problems

PROBLEM (3.6.1). Let X and Y be independent discrete random variables, each having mass function given by

$$\mathbb{P}(X = k) = \mathbb{P}(Y = k) = pq^k \qquad \text{for } k = 0, 1, 2 \ldots,$$

where $0 < p = 1 - q < 1$. Show that

$$\mathbb{P}(X = k \mid X + Y = n) = \frac{1}{n+1} \qquad \text{for } k = 0, 1, 2 \ldots, n.$$

SOLUTION. We have that

$$\mathbb{P}(X = k \mid X + Y = n) = \frac{P(X = k, X + Y = n)}{P(X + Y = n)}$$

$$= \frac{P(X = k)P(Y = n - k)}{P(X + Y = n)}$$

$$P(X = k)P(Y = n - k) = pq^k pq^{n-k} = p^2 q^n$$

$$P(X + Y = n) = \sum_{k=0}^{n} P(X = k)P(Y = n - k) = \sum_{k=0}^{n} pq^k pq^{n-k} = \sum_{k=0}^{n} p^2 q^n =$$

$(n + 1)p^2 q^n$

Thus

$$\mathbb{P}(X = k \mid X + Y = n) = \frac{p^2 q^n}{(n+1)p^2 q^n} = \frac{1}{n+1} \text{ for } k = 0, 1, 2 \ldots, n.$$

PROBLEM (3.6.2). Independent random variables U and V each take the values -1 or 1 only, and

$$\mathbb{P}(U = 1) = a, \qquad \mathbb{P}(V = 1) = b,$$

where $0 < a, b < 1$. A third random variable W is defined by $W = UV$. Show that there are unique values of a and b such that U, V, and W are pairwise independent. For these values of a and b, are U, V, and W independent? Justify your answer. (Oxford 1971F)

SOLUTION. Since independent random variables U and V each take the values -1 or 1 only, so the third random variable $W = UV$ also takes the values -1 or 1 only.

$P(W = -1) = P(U = -1)P(V = 1) + P(U = 1)P(V = -1) = (1 - a)b + a(1 - b) = a + b - 2ab$

$P(W = 1) = P(U = 1)P(V = 1) + P(U = -1)P(V = -1) = ab + (1 - a)(1 - b) = -a - b + 2ab + 1$

$$
\begin{aligned}
\mathbb{P}(U = -1, W = -1) &= \mathbb{P}(U = -1, UV = -1) \\
&= \mathbb{P}(U = -1, V = 1) \\
&= \mathbb{P}(U = -1)\mathbb{P}(V = 1) \qquad \text{(since } U \text{ and } V \text{ are independent)} \\
&= (1 - a)b
\end{aligned}
$$

and

$$
\mathbb{P}(U = -1)\mathbb{P}(W = -1) \;=\; (1 - a)(a + b - 2ab) = 2a^2 b - a^2 - 3ab + a + b
$$

by Definititon 3.13

$$
\begin{aligned}
(1 - a)b &= (1 - a)(a + b - 2ab) \\
b &= a + b - 2ab \qquad \text{(since } 1 - a \neq 0)
\end{aligned}
$$

This implies $b = \dfrac{1}{2}$

$$
\begin{aligned}
\mathbb{P}(V = -1, W = -1) &= \mathbb{P}(V = -1, UV = 1) \\
&= \mathbb{P}(V = -1, U = 1) \\
&= \mathbb{P}(V = -1)\mathbb{P}(U = 1) \qquad \text{(since } U \text{ and } V \text{ are independent)} \\
&= (1 - b)a
\end{aligned}
$$

and

$$
\mathbb{P}(V = -1)\mathbb{P}(W = -1) \;=\; (1 - b)(a + b - 2ab)
$$

by Definition 3.13

$$(1 - b)a = (1 - b)(a + b - 2ab)$$
$$a = a + b - 2ab \quad (\text{since } 1 - b \neq 0)$$

This implies $a = \dfrac{1}{2}$. Plug $a = b = \dfrac{1}{2}$, we see that U, V, and W are pairwise independent. We have

$$\mathbb{P}(U = 1)\mathbb{P}(V = 1)\mathbb{P}(W = 1) = ab(-a - b + 2ab + 1) = \frac{1}{8}$$

and

$$\begin{aligned}
\mathbb{P}(U = 1, V = 1, W = 1) &= \mathbb{P}(U = 1, V = 1, UV = 1) \\
&= \mathbb{P}(U = 1, V = 1) \\
&= \mathbb{P}(U = 1)\mathbb{P}(V = 1) \\
&= ab = \frac{1}{4}.
\end{aligned}$$

Thus

$$\mathbb{P}(U = 1)\mathbb{P}(V = 1)\mathbb{P}(W = 1) \neq \mathbb{P}(U = 1, V = 1, W = 1)$$

for $a = b = \dfrac{1}{2}$. Therefore for these values of a and b, U, V, and W are not independent.

PROBLEM (3.6.3). If X and Y are discrete random variables, each taking only two distinct values, prove that X and Y are independent if and only if $\mathbb{E}(XY) = \mathbb{E}(X)\mathbb{E}(Y)$.

SOLUTION. The necessity of the condition is immediate from Theorem 3.19. To prove sufficiency, suppose X are discrete random variables taking only two distinct values x_1 and x_2, and Y be discrete random variables taking only two distinct values y_1 and y_2 ,and let $\mathbb{E}(XY) = \mathbb{E}(X)\mathbb{E}(Y)$. Then

$$\begin{aligned}
\mathbb{E}(XY) = {}& x_1 y_1 \mathbb{P}(X = x_1, Y = y_1) + x_1 y_2 \mathbb{P}(X = x_1, Y = y_2) \\
&+ x_2 y_1 \mathbb{P}(X = x_2, Y = y_1) + x_2 y_2 \mathbb{P}(X = x_2, Y = y_2)
\end{aligned}$$

and

$$\mathbb{E}(X)\mathbb{E}(Y) = [x_1\mathbb{P}(X = x_1) + x_2\mathbb{P}(X = x_2)]\,[y_1\mathbb{P}(Y = y_1) + y_2\mathbb{P}(Y = y_2)]$$
$$= \{x_1\,[\mathbb{P}(X = x_1, Y = y_1) + \mathbb{P}(X = x_1, Y = y_2)]$$
$$+ x_2\,[\mathbb{P}(X = x_2, Y = y_1) + \mathbb{P}(X = x_2, Y = y_2)]\}$$
$$\{y_1\,[\mathbb{P}(X = x_1, Y = y_1) + \mathbb{P}(X = x_2, Y = y_1)]$$
$$+ y_2\,[\mathbb{P}(X = x_1, Y = y_2) + \mathbb{P}(X = x_2, Y = y_2)]\}$$
$$= \{x_1\mathbb{P}(X = x_1, Y = y_1) + x_1\mathbb{P}(X = x_1, Y = y_2)$$
$$+ x_2\mathbb{P}(X = x_2, Y = y_1) + x_2\mathbb{P}(X = x_2, Y = y_2)\}$$
$$\{y_1\mathbb{P}(X = x_1, Y = y_1) + y_1\mathbb{P}(X = x_2, Y = y_1)$$
$$+ y_2\mathbb{P}(X = x_1, Y = y_2) + y_2\mathbb{P}(X = x_2, Y = y_2)\}$$

giving by $\mathbb{E}(XY) = \mathbb{E}(X)\mathbb{E}(Y)$ that

$$x_1 y_1 p_{X,Y}(x_1, y_1) + x_1 y_2 p_{X,Y}(x_1, y_2) + x_2 y_1 p_{X,Y}(x_2, y_1) + x_2 y_2 p_{X,Y}(x_2, y_2)$$
$$= [x_1 p_X(x_1) + x_2 p_X(x_2)]\,[y_1 p_Y(y_1) + y_2 p_Y(y_2)]$$

The joint mass function of the pair X, Y.

	x_1	x_2
y_1	a	b
y_2	c	d

where $a + b + c + d = 1$

$$x_1 y_1 a + x_1 y_2 c + x_2 y_1 b + x_2 y_2 d$$
$$= x_1 y_1 (a + c)(a + b) + x_1 y_2 (a + c)(c + d)$$
$$+ x_2 y_1 (b + a)(a + b) + x_2 y_2 (b + d)(c + d) \qquad (*)$$

We shall prove that if $E(XY) = E(X)E(Y)$, then $E((\alpha X + \beta)(\gamma Y + \delta)) = E(\alpha X + \beta)E((\gamma Y + \delta))$ where $\alpha, \beta, \gamma, \delta \in \mathbb{R}$. Indeed,

$$E((\alpha X + \beta)(\gamma Y + \delta)) = \alpha\gamma E(X, Y) + \alpha\delta E(X) + \beta\gamma E(Y) + \beta\gamma$$
$$= \alpha\gamma E(X)E(Y) + \alpha\delta E(X) + \beta\gamma(Y) + \beta\delta$$
$$= E(\alpha X + \beta)E(\gamma Y + \delta) \qquad (**)$$

Define X_1 and Y_1 by

$$X_1 = \frac{X - x_2}{x_1 - x_2} \qquad Y_1 = \frac{Y - y_2}{y_1 - y_2}.$$

Then the joint mass function of the pair X_1, Y_1 is

	$x_1' = 1$	$x_2' = 0$
$y_1' = 1$	a	b
$y_2' = 0$	c	d

Apply $(*)$ and $(**)$, we have

$$a = (a + c)(a + b)$$

Thus $P(X = x_1, Y = y_1) = P(X = x_1)P(Y = y_2)$. Then using

$$X_2 = \frac{X - x_2}{x_2 - x_1} \qquad Y_2 = \frac{Y - y_2}{y_2 - y_1},$$

we have $P(X = x_2, Y = y_2) = P(X = x_2)P(Y = y_2)$. Using

$$X_3 = \frac{X - x_2}{x_1 - x_2} \qquad Y_2 = \frac{Y - y_1}{y_2 - y_1},$$

and

$$X_4 = \frac{X - x_1}{x_2 - x_1} \qquad Y_4 = \frac{Y - y_1}{y_2 - y_1},$$

we have the remain formulas. So X and Y are independent random variables.

PROBLEM (3.6.4). Let $X_1, X_2, \ldots, X_n$ be independent discrete random variables, each having mass function

$$\mathbb{P}(X_i = k) = \frac{1}{N} \qquad \qquad \text{for } k = 1, 2, \ldots, N.$$

Find the mass functions of U_n and V_n, given by

$$U_n = \min\{X_1, X_2, \ldots, X_n\}, \qquad V_n = \max\{X_1, X_2, \ldots, X_n\}.$$

SOLUTION. For $k = 0, 1, 2, \ldots, N$, we have

$$\mathbb{P}(U_n \geq k) = \mathbb{P}(X_1 \geq k, X_2 \geq k, \ldots, X_n \geq k)$$

$$= \prod_{i=1}^{n} \mathbb{P}(X_i \geq k) \qquad \qquad \text{by Exercise 3.23}$$

$$= \prod_{i=1}^{n} [1 - \mathbb{P}(X_i < k)]$$

$$= [1 - \frac{k-1}{N}]^n \qquad \qquad \text{since } \mathbb{P}(X_i < k) = \sum_{j=1}^{k-1} \mathbb{P}(X_i = j) = \frac{k-1}{N}.$$

Moreover,

$$
\begin{aligned}
\mathbb{P}(U_n = k) &= \mathbb{P}(U_n \geq k) - \mathbb{P}(U_n \geq k+1) \\
&= [1 - \frac{k-1}{N}]^n - [1 - \frac{(k+1)-1}{N}]^n \\
&= [1 - \frac{k-1}{N}]^n - [1 - \frac{k+}{N}]^n
\end{aligned}
$$

for $k = 0, 1, 2, \ldots, N$. It is clear that if $k \geq N+1$, then $\mathbb{P}(U_k = k) = 0$.
  For $k = 0, 1, 2, \ldots, N$, we have

$$
\begin{aligned}
\mathbb{P}(V_n \leq k) &= \mathbb{P}(X_1 \leq k, X_2 \leq k, \ldots, X_n \leq k) \\
&= \prod_{i=1}^{n} \mathbb{P}(X_i \leq k) \qquad \text{(by Exercise 3.23)} \\
&= (\frac{k}{N})^n \qquad \text{(since } \mathbb{P}(X_i < k) = \sum_{j=1}^{k-1} \mathbb{P}(X_i = j) = \frac{k-1}{N})
\end{aligned}
$$

Moreover,

$$
\begin{aligned}
\mathbb{P}(V_n = k) &= \mathbb{P}(V_n \leq k) - \mathbb{P}(V_n \geq k-1) \\
&= [\frac{k}{N}]^n - [\frac{k-1}{N}]^n \\
&= \frac{k^n - (k-1)^n}{N^n}
\end{aligned}
$$

for $k = 0, 1, 2, \ldots, N$. It is clear that if $k \geq N+1$, then $\mathbb{P}(V_k = k) = 0$.

PROBLEM (3.6.5). Let X and Y be independent discrete random variables, X having the geometric distribution with parameter p and Y having the geometric distribution with parameter r. Show that $U = \min\{X, Y\}$ has the geometric distribution with parameter $p + r - pr$.

SOLUTION. Let $\{U = k\} = \{X = k, Y \geq k\} \cup \{Y = k, X \geq k\}$. Then

$$\mathbb{P}(U = k) = \mathbb{P}(X = k, Y \geq k) + \mathbb{P}(Y = k, X \geq k) - \mathbb{P}(\{X = k, Y \geq k\} \cap \{Y = k, X \geq k\}),$$

giving

$$\sum_{j=k}^{\infty} P(X=k)(Y=j)$$

$$+\sum_{j=k}^{\infty} P(Y=k, X=j) - P(X=k, Y=k) = pq^{k-1}\sum_{j=k}^{\infty} rs^{j-1} + rs^{k-1}\sum_{j=k}^{\infty} pq^{j-1} - pq^{k-1}rs^{k-1}$$

$$= p(1-p)^{k-1}\sum_{j=k}^{\infty} r(1-r)^{j-1} + r(1-r)^{k-1}\sum_{j=k}^{\infty} p(1-p)^{j-1}$$

$$- p(1-p)^{k-1}r(1-r)^{k-1}$$

$$= p('1-p)^{k-1}r\frac{(1-r)^{k-1}}{1-(1-r)} + rp(1-r)^{k-1}\frac{(1-p)^{k-1}}{1-(1-p)}$$

$$- pr[(1-r)(1-p)]$$

$$= p[(1-p)(1-r)]^{k-1} + r[(1-p)(1-r)]^{k-1}$$

$$- pr[(1-p)(1-r)]^{k-1}$$

$$= (p+r-pr)[(1-p)(1-r)]^{k-1}.$$

Let $s = p + r - pr$, then $1 - s = 1 - p - r + pr = (1-p)(1-r)$. So $\mathbb{P}(U = k) = s(1-s)^{k-1}$, therefore U has the geometric distribution with parameter $s = p + r - pr$.

PROBLEM (3.6.7). Let $X_1, X_2,...$ be discrete random variables, each having mean μ, and let N be a random variable which takes values in the non-negative integers and which is independent of the X_i. By conditioning on the value of N, show that

$$\mathbb{E}(X_1 + X_2 + \cdots + X_N) = \mu\mathbb{E}(N).$$

SOLUTION. Let B_i be the event that $B_i = \{\omega : N(\omega) = i-1\}$ for $i = 1, 2, \ldots$. Then B_i's form a partition of the sample space for $i = 1, 2, \ldots$. Define $S_N = X_1 + X_2 + \cdots + X_N$. Then

$$\mathbb{E}(S_N) = \sum_i \mathbb{E}(S_N \mid B_i)\mathbb{P}(B_i)$$

We have that

$$E(S_N \mid B_i) = E(S_{i-1})$$
$$= E(X_1 + X_2 + \cdots + X_{i-1})$$
$$= E(X_1) + E(X_2) + \cdots + E(X_{i-1})$$
$$= (i-1)E(X_1)$$
$$= (i-1)\mu.$$

Thus

$$\mathbb{E}(S_N) = \sum_i (i-1)\mu \mathbb{P}(N = i-1)$$

$$= \mu \sum_i (i-1)\mathbb{P}(N = i-1)$$

$$= \mu \mathbb{E}(N).$$

PROBLEM (3.6.8). Let $X_1, X_2, \ldots$ be independent, identically distributed random variables, and $S_n = X_1 + X_2 + \cdots + X_n$. Show that $\mathbb{E}(S_m/S_n) = m/n$ if $m \leq n$, and $\mathbb{E}(S_m/S_n) = 1 + (m-n)\mu E(1/S_n)$ if $m > n$, where $\mu = \mathbb{E}(X_1)$. You may assume that all the expectations are finite.

SOLUTION. For $m \leq n$, then

$$\mathbb{E}(\frac{S_m}{S_n}) = \mathbb{E}(\frac{X_1 + X_2 + \cdots + X_m}{S_n})$$

$$= \sum_{i=1}^m \mathbb{E}(\frac{X_i}{S_n})$$

$$= m\mathbb{E}(\frac{X_1}{S_n}) \qquad \text{since } \frac{X_i}{S_n} \text{ are identically distributed random variables.}$$

In particular, $m = n$, then $\mathbb{E}(1) = 1 = nE(\frac{X_1}{S_n})$. This implies $\mathbb{E}(\frac{X_1}{S_n}) = \frac{1}{n}$. Thus

$$\mathbb{E}(\frac{S_m}{S_n}) = \frac{m}{n}$$

For $m > n$,

$$\mathbb{E}(\frac{S_m}{S_n}) = \mathbb{E}(\frac{S_n}{S_n}) + \mathbb{E}(\sum_{i=n+1}^m \frac{X_i}{S_n})$$

$$= \mathbb{E}(1) + \sum_{i=n+1}^m \mathbb{E}(X_i)\mathbb{E}(\frac{1}{S_n}) \quad \text{since } X_i \text{ for } i \geq n+1 \text{ is independent with } 1/S_n$$

$$= 1 + (m-n)\mu\mathbb{E}(\frac{1}{S_n}).$$

PROBLEM (3.6.9). The random variables U and V each take the values ± 1. Their joint distribution is given by

$$\mathbb{P}(U = +1) = \mathbb{P}(U = -1) = \frac{1}{2},$$

$$\mathbb{P}(V = +1 \mid U = +1) = \frac{1}{3} = \mathbb{P}(V = -1 \mid U = -1),$$

$$\mathbb{P}(V = -1 \mid U = 1) = \frac{2}{3} = P(V = +1 \mid U = -1).$$

(a) Find the probability that $x^2 + Ux + V = 0$ has at least one real root.

(b) Find the expected value of the larger root, given that there is at least one real root.

(c) Find the probability that $x^2 + (U+V)x + U + V = 0$ has at least one real root.

(Oxford 1980M)

SOLUTION. (a) $x^2 + Ux + V = 0$ has at least one real root if and only if $U^2 - 4V \geq 0$. Since $V = \pm 1$, it follows that $U^2 - 4V \geq 0$ if and only if $V = -1$.

$$\mathbb{P}(V = -1) = \mathbb{P}(V = -1 \mid U = 1)\mathbb{P}(U = 1) + \mathbb{P}(V = -1 \mid U = -1)\mathbb{P}(U = -1) = \frac{1}{3}\frac{1}{2} + \frac{2}{3}\frac{1}{2} = \frac{1}{2}.$$

Thus the probability that $x^2 + Ux + V = 0$ has at least one real root is $1/2$.

(b) Let G be the random variable that taking the value is the larger root.

If $U = -1$ and $V = -1$, then $G = \dfrac{1 + \sqrt{5}}{2}$

$$
\begin{aligned}
P\left(G = \frac{1 + \sqrt{5}}{2}\right) &= P(U = -1, V = -1) \\
&= P(V = -1 \mid U = -1)P(U = -1) \\
&= \frac{1}{3} \cdot \frac{1}{2} = \frac{1}{6}
\end{aligned}
$$

If $U = 1$ and $V = -1$, then $G = \dfrac{-1 + \sqrt{5}}{2}$

$$
\begin{aligned}
P\left(G = \frac{-1 + \sqrt{5}}{2}\right) &= P(U = 1, V = -1) \\
&= P(V = -1 \mid U = 1)P(U = 1) \\
&= \frac{2}{3} \cdot \frac{1}{2} = \frac{1}{3}
\end{aligned}
$$

Thus

$$E(G) = \frac{1 + \sqrt{5}}{2}P\left(G = \frac{1 + \sqrt{5}}{2}\right) + \frac{-1 + \sqrt{5}}{2}P\left(G = \frac{-1 + \sqrt{5}}{2}\right) = \frac{1 + \sqrt{5}}{2} \cdot \frac{1}{6} +$$
$$\frac{-1 + \sqrt{5}}{2} \cdot \frac{1}{3} = \frac{\sqrt{5}}{2} - \frac{1}{6} = \frac{3\sqrt{5} - 1}{6}.$$

(c) Let $W = U + V$. Then $x^2 + (U+V)x + U + V = 0 \iff x^2 + Wx + W = 0$, and hence $x^2 + (U + V)x + U + V = 0$ has at least one real root if and only if $x^2 + Wx + W = 0$ has at least one real root. This means $W^2 - 4W \geq 0$. Since $W = U + V$, then W takes values $2, 0, -2$. Thus $W^2 - 4W \geq 0 \iff W = 0$ or $W = -2$.

$$P(W = 0) = P(U = -1, V = 1) + P(U = 1, V = -1) = P(V = 1 \mid U = -1)P(U = -1) + P(V = -1 \mid U = 1)P(U = 1)$$

$$= \frac{2}{3} \cdot \frac{1}{2} + \frac{2}{3} \cdot \frac{1}{2} = \frac{2}{3}$$

$$P(W = -2) = P(U = -1, V = -1) = P(V = -1 \mid U = -1)P(U = -1) =$$

$$\frac{1}{3} \cdot \frac{1}{2} = \frac{1}{6}$$

$$P(W = 0 \text{ or } W = -2) = P(W = 0) + P(W = -2) = \frac{2}{3} + \frac{1}{6} = \frac{5}{6}.$$

PROBLEM (3.6.10). A number N of balls are thrown at random into M boxes, with multiple occupancy permitted. Show that the expected number of empty boxes is $(M-1)^N/M^{N-1}$.

SOLUTION. Let Z_i be the indicator function that the ith box is empty. The total number of empty boxes is

$$S = Z_1 + Z_2 + \cdots + Z_M.$$

Also,

$$\mathbb{E}(Z_i) = \mathbb{P}(Z_i).$$

Since the probability that one particular ball does not land in the ith box is $(M-1)/M$, so the probability that all N balls do not fall in ith box is this

$$\mathbb{P}(Z_i) = \frac{(M-1)^N}{M^N},$$

so that

$$\mathbb{E}(S) = \sum_{i=1}^{M} \mathbb{E}(Z_i) = \sum_{i=1}^{M} \mathbb{P}(Z_i) = M\mathbb{P}(Z_1) = \frac{(M-1)^N}{M^{N-1}},$$

by symmetry.

PROBLEM (3.6.11). We are provided with a coin which comes up heads with probability p at each toss. Let $v_1, v_2, \ldots, v_n$ be n distinct points on a unit circle. We examine each unordered pair v_i, v_j in turn and toss the coin; if it comes up heads, we join v_i and v_j by a straight line segment (called an edge), otherwise we do nothing. The resulting network is called a *random graph*.

(a) the expected number of edges in the random graph is $\frac{1}{2}n(n-1)p$,

(b) the expected number of triangles (triples of points each pair of which is joined by an edge) is $\frac{1}{6}n(n-1)(n-2)p^3$.

SOLUTION. (a) Let N be the number of edges in the random graph, and A_{ij} be the event that there is an edge between v_i and v_j. Then

$$N = \sum_{1 \le i \ne j \le n} 1_{A_{i,j}},$$

so that

$$
\begin{aligned}
\mathbb{E}(N) &= \sum_{1 \le i \ne j \le n} \mathbb{E}(1_{A_{ij}}) \\
&= \sum_{1 \le i \ne j \le n} \mathbb{P}(A_{ij}) \\
&= \binom{n}{2} p \qquad\qquad \text{there are } \binom{n}{2} \text{ terms in the sum,} \\
&\qquad\qquad\qquad\qquad\qquad \mathbb{P}(A_{ij}) = p \\
&= \frac{1}{2} n(n{-}1)p.
\end{aligned}
$$

(b) Let M be the number of triangles in the random graph, and B_{ijk} be the event that there is a triangle $v_i v_j v_k$. Then

$$M = \sum_{1 \le i \ne j \ne k \le n} 1_{B_{i,jk}},$$

so that

$$
\begin{aligned}
\mathbb{E}(M) &= \sum_{1 \le i \ne j \ne k \le n} \mathbb{E}(1_{B_{ijk}}) \\
&= \sum_{1 \le i \ne j \ne k \le n} \mathbb{P}(B_{ijk}) \\
&= \binom{n}{3} p^3 \qquad\qquad \text{there are } \binom{n}{3} \text{ terms in the sum,} \\
&\qquad \mathbb{P}(B_{ijk}) = \mathbb{P}(A_{ij} \cap A_{ik} \cap A_{jk}) = \mathbb{P}(A_{ij})\mathbb{P}(A_{ik})\mathbb{P}(A_{jk}) = p^3 \\
&= \frac{1}{6} n(n-1)(n-2)p^3.
\end{aligned}
$$

PROBLEM (3.6.12). *Coupon-collecting problem.* There are c different types of coupon, and each coupon obtained is equally likely to be any one of the c types. Let Y_i be the additional number of coupons collected, after obtaining i distinct types, before a new type is collected. Show that Y_i has the geometric distribution with parameter $(c - i)/c$, and deduce the mean number of coupons you will need to collect before you have a complete set.

SOLUTION. Let N be the number of coupons you need to collect before you have a complete set. then

$$N = 1 + Y_1 + Y_2 + \cdots + Y_{c-1},$$

The probability of choosing a new coupon other than i obtained distinct types is $\dfrac{c-i}{c}$. The probability of getting $(k-1)$ consecutive coupons belonging to i obtained distinct types is $(\frac{i}{c})^{k-1}$. The probability of getting k additional coupons collected after obtaining i distinct types, before a new type is collected

$$\mathbb{P}(Y_i = k) \quad = \quad \frac{c-i}{c} \cdot (\frac{i}{c})^{k-1}$$

for $k = 1, 2, 3, \ldots.$ Thus Y_i has the geometric distribution with parameter $p = (c-i)/c$ and $i/c = 1 - (c-i)/c = 1 - p.$ We have

$$\mathbb{E}(Y_j) = \sum_{k \in \mathrm{Im}\, Y_j} k \mathbb{P}(Y_j = k)$$

$$= \sum_{k=1}^{\infty} k \mathbb{P}(Y_j = k) = \sum_{k=1}^{\infty} k \mathbb{P}(Y_j = k)$$

$$= \sum_{k=1}^{\infty} k \cdot \frac{c-j}{c} \cdot (\frac{j}{c})^{k-1} = \frac{c-j}{c} \sum_{k=1}^{\infty} k \cdot (\frac{j}{c})^{k-1}$$

$$= \frac{c-j}{c} \frac{d}{du} [\sum_{k=1}^{\infty} (\frac{j}{c})^k] \qquad \text{where } u = j/c$$

$$= \frac{c-j}{c} \frac{d}{du} [\frac{u}{1-u}] = \frac{c-j}{c} \frac{1}{(1-u)^2} = \frac{c-j}{c} \frac{1}{(1-\frac{j}{c})^2} = \frac{c}{c-j}$$

Thus

$$\mathbb{E}(N) = \mathbb{E}(1 + Y_1 + Y_2 + \cdots + Y_{c-1})$$
$$= \mathbb{E}(1) + \mathbb{E}(Y_1) + \mathbb{E}(Y_2) + \cdots + \mathbb{E}(Y_{c-1})$$
$$= 1 + \sum_{j=1}^{c-1} \mathbb{E}(Y_j)$$
$$= 1 + \sum_{j=1}^{c-1} \frac{c}{c-j}$$
$$= 1 + c \sum_{j=1}^{c-1} \frac{1}{c-j}$$
$$= \frac{c}{c} + c\left(\frac{1}{c-1} + \frac{1}{c-2} + \cdots + \frac{1}{1}\right)$$
$$= c\left(1 + \frac{1}{2} + \cdots + \frac{1}{c-1} + \frac{1}{c}\right)$$

PROBLEM (3.6.13). In Problem 3.6.12 above, find the expected number of different types of coupon in the first n coupons received.

SOLUTION. Let N be the number of different types of coupon in the first n coupons received. Let A_i be the event that at least one coupon of type ith is received, and let A_i^c be the event that there is no coupon of type ith in the first n coupons received. Then

$$N = \sum_{i=1}^{c} 1_{A_i},$$

so that

$$\mathbb{E}(N) = \sum_{i=1}^{c} \mathbb{E}(1_{A_i}) = \sum_{i=1}^{c} \mathbb{P}(A_i) = c\mathbb{P}(A_1) = c[1 - P(A_1^c)],$$

by symmetry. It is easily seen that $\mathbb{P}(A_1^c) = (1 - 1/c)^n$, and hence $\mathbb{E}(N) = c[1 - (1 - 1/c)^n]$ regardless of the value of n.

PROBLEM (3.6.14). Each time you flip a certain coin, heads appears with probability p. Suppose that you flip the coin a random number N of times, where N has the Poisson distribution with parameter λ and is independent of the outcomes of the flips. Find the distributions of the numbers X and Y of resulting heads and tails, respectively, and show that X and Y are independent.

SOLUTION. Let B_i be the event that $\{N = i\}$ for $i = 0, 1, 2, \ldots$. Then B_i's form a partition of the sample space. Let X be the numbers of of resulting heads. It is easy to see that for $m = 0, 1, 2, \ldots$,

$$\mathbb{P}(X = k \mid B_i) = \mathbb{P}(X = k \mid N = i) = \binom{n}{k} p^k (1-p)^{i-k} \qquad \text{for } k = 1, 2, \ldots,$$

since N is independent of the outcomes of the flips. Moreover, since N has the Poisson distribution with parameter λ,

$$\mathbb{P}(N = i) = \frac{1}{i!} \lambda^i e^{-\lambda} \qquad \text{for } i = 0, 1, 2, \ldots.$$

By the partition theorem, Theorem 1.48,

$$
\begin{aligned}
\mathbb{P}(X = k) &= \sum_i \mathbb{P}(X = k \mid B_i) \mathbb{P}(B_i) \\
&= \sum_{i=k}^{\infty} \binom{i}{k} p^k (1-p)^{i-k} \frac{1}{i!} \lambda^i e^{-\lambda} \\
&= \sum_{i=k}^{\infty} \frac{i!}{k!(i-k)!} p^k (1-p)^{i-k} \frac{1}{i!} \lambda^i e^{-\lambda} \\
&= \sum_{i=k}^{\infty} \frac{1}{k!(i-k)!} p^k (1-p)^{i-k} \lambda^i e^{-\lambda} \\
&= \frac{p^k}{k!(1-p)^k} e^{-\lambda} \sum_{i=k}^{\infty} \frac{1}{(i-k)!} (1-p)^i \lambda^i \\
&= \frac{p^k}{k!(1-p)^k} e^{-\lambda} \sum_{j=0}^{\infty} \frac{1}{j!} (1-p)^{j+k} \lambda^{j+k} \\
&= \frac{p^k}{k!(1-p)^k} e^{-\lambda} \sum_{j=0}^{\infty} \frac{(1-p)^j \lambda^j}{j!} \\
&= \frac{p^k}{k!(1-p)^k} e^{-\lambda} e^{(1-p)\lambda} \\
&= \frac{p^k}{k!(1-p)^k} e^{-\lambda p}
\end{aligned}
$$

We have

$$\mathbb{P}(X = k) = \sum_i \mathbb{P}(X = k \mid B_i)\mathbb{P}(B_i)$$

$$= \sum_{i=k}^{\infty} \binom{i}{k} p^k (1-p)^{i-k} \frac{1}{i!} \lambda^i e^{-\lambda}$$

$$= \sum_{i=k}^{\infty} \binom{i}{k} (p\lambda)^k (1-p)^{i-k} \frac{1}{i!} \lambda^i e^{-\lambda p} \lambda^{i-k} e^{-\lambda(1-p)}$$

$$= e^{-\lambda p}(p\lambda)^k e^{-\lambda(1-p)} \sum_{i=k}^{\infty} \binom{i}{k} \frac{(1-p)^{i-k}}{i!}$$

$$= e^{-\lambda p}(\lambda p)^k e^{-\lambda(1-p)} \sum_{i=k}^{\infty} \frac{i!}{k!(i-k)!} \cdot \frac{(1-p)^{i-k}}{i!}$$

$$= e^{-\lambda p}\frac{(\lambda p)^k}{k!} [e^{-\lambda(1-p)} \sum_{i=k}^{\infty} \frac{(1-p)^{i-k}}{(i-k)!}]$$

$$= e^{-\lambda p}\frac{(\lambda p)^k}{k!} e^{-\lambda(1-p)} \sum_{j=0}^{\infty} \frac{(1-p)^j}{j!} \qquad \text{reindex with } j = m - k$$

$$= e^{-\lambda p}\frac{(\lambda p)^k}{k!} e^{-\lambda(1-p)} e^{\lambda(1-p)} \qquad \text{use Maclaurin series } \sum_{j=0}^{\infty} \frac{\alpha^j}{j!} = e^{\alpha}$$

$$= e^{-\lambda p}\frac{(\lambda p)^k}{k!}.$$

Hence, X has the Poisson distribution with parameter λp.

Let Y be the numbers of of resulting tails. It is easy to see that

$$\mathbb{P}(Y = k) = e^{-\lambda(1-p)} \frac{[\lambda(1-p)]^k}{k!}$$

since tails appears with probability $1 - p$ and the roles of the appreance of a head and a tail are similar. Hence, Y has the Poisson distribution with parameter $\lambda(1 - p)$.

We have

$$\mathbb{P}(X = r, Y = s) = \mathbb{P}(X = r, Y = s \mid N = r + s) \qquad \text{since } N = X + Y$$
$$= \mathbb{P}(X = r \mid N = r + s)\mathbb{P}(Y = s \mid N = r + s)$$
$$= \binom{r + s}{s} p^x (1 - p)^s e^{-\lambda} \frac{\lambda^{r+s}}{(r + s)}$$
$$= \frac{(r + s)!}{r!s!} p^r (1 - p)^r e^{-\lambda} \frac{\lambda^{r-s}}{(r + s)!}$$
$$= [(\lambda p) \frac{e^{-\lambda p}}{r!}]\{[\lambda(1 - p)]^s \frac{e^{-\lambda(1-p)}}{s!}\}$$
$$= \mathbb{P}(X = r)\mathbb{P}(Y = s).$$

Hence, X and Y and Y are independent random variables.

PROBLEM (3.6.15). Let $(Z_n : 1 \leq n < \infty)$ be a sequence of independent, identically distributed random variables with

$$\mathbb{P}(Z_n = 0) = q, \qquad\qquad \mathbb{P}(Z_n = 1) = p,$$

where $p + q = 1$. Let A_i be the event that $Z_i = 0$ and $Z_{i-1} = 1$. If U_n is the number of times A_i occurs for $2 \leq i \leq n$, prove that $\mathbb{E}(U_n) = (n - 1)pq$, and find the variance of U_n. (Oxford 1977F)

SOLUTION. For $2 \leq i < j \leq n$, we have

$$P(A_i) = P(Z_i = 0, Z_{i-1} = 1)$$
$$= P(Z_i = 0)P(Z_{i-1} = 1) \qquad\qquad \text{by independence}$$
$$= qp$$
$$= P(Z_j = 0)P(Z_{j-1} = 1)$$
$$= P(Z_j = 0, Z_{j-1} = 1) \qquad\qquad \text{by independence}$$
$$= P(A_j)$$

Hence $P(A_i) = P(A_j) = pq$, for $2 \leq i < j \leq n$. Thus

$$\mathbb{E}(U_n) = \sum_{i=2}^{n} \mathbb{E}(1_{A_i})$$
$$= \sum_{i=2}^{n} \mathbb{P}(A_i)$$
$$= (n - 1)\mathbb{P}(A_2)$$
$$= (n - 1)pq$$

and the variance of U_n is

$$\mathrm{var}(U_n) = \mathbb{E}(U_n^2) - \mathbb{E}(U_n)^2$$

In

$$U_n^2 = \sum_{i=2}^{n} 1_{A_i}^2 + 2 \sum_{2 \le i < j} 1_{A_i} 1_{A_j}$$

$$= \sum_{i=2}^{n} 1_{A_i} + 2 \sum_{2 \le i < j} 1_{A_i \cap A_j} \qquad \text{since } 1_{A_i} 1_{A_j} = 1_{A_i \cap A_j}$$

Therefore,

$$\mathbb{E}(U_n^2) = \mathbb{E}\Big(\sum_{i=2}^{n} 1_{A_i} + 2 \sum_{2 \le i < j} 1_{A_i \cap A_j}\Big) = (n-1)pq + 2\frac{(n-3)(n-2)}{2}\mathbb{P}(A_i \cap A_j)$$

for $j \ge i+2$. Since $A_i \cap A_{i+1} = \varnothing$ and there are $(n-3)(n-2)/2$ terms $\mathbb{E}(1_{A_i \cap A_j})$ for $i \le j + 2$ in the second sum and $P(A_{i_1} \cap A_{j_1}) = P(A_{i_1} \cap A_{j_1}) = p^2 q^2$ for $j_1 \ge i_1 + 2$, $j_2 \ge i_2 + 2$. Thus

$$\begin{aligned}
\mathbb{E}(U_n^2) &= (n-1)pq + (n-3)(n-2)P(Z_i = 0, Z_{i-1} = 1, Z_j = 0, Z_{j-1} = 1)\\
&= (n-1)pq + (n-1)(n-2)P(Z_i = 0)P(Z_j = 0)P(Z_{i-1} = 0)P(Z_{j-1} = 0) \quad \text{for } j \ge i+1\\
&= (n-1)pq + (n-3)(n-2)p^2 q^2
\end{aligned}$$

Therefore

$$\begin{aligned}
\mathrm{var}(U_n) &= \mathbb{E}(U_n^2) - \mathbb{E}(U_n)^2\\
&= (n-1)pq + (n-3)(n-2)p^2 q^2 - [(n-1)pq]^2\\
&= (n-1)pq + (n-3)(n-2)p^2 q^2 - (n-1)^2 p^2 q^2\\
&= (n-1)pq + [n^2 - 5n + 6 - n^2 + 2n - 1]p^2 q^2\\
&= (n-1)pq - (3n-5)(pq)^2
\end{aligned}$$

PROBLEM (3.6.16). I throw two dice and record the scores S_1 and S_2. Let X be the sum $S_1 + S_2$ and Y the difference $S_1 - S_2$.

(a) Suppose the dice are fair, so that the values $1, 2, \ldots, 6$ are equally likely. Calculate the mean and variance of both X and Y. Find all the values of x and y at which the probabilities $\mathbb{P}(X = x)$, $\mathbb{P}(Y = y)$ are each either greatest or least. Determine whether the random variables X and Y are independent.

(b) Now suppose the dice give the values $1, 2, \ldots, 6$ with probabilities $p_1, p_2, \ldots, p_6$ and $q_1, q_2, \ldots, q_6$, respectively. Write down the values of $\mathbb{P}(X = 2)$, $\mathbb{P}(X = 7)$, and $\mathbb{P}(X = 12)$. By comparing $\mathbb{P}(X = 7)$ with $\sqrt{\mathbb{P}(X = 2)\mathbb{P}(X = 12)}$ and applying

the arithmetic/geometric mean inequality,[2] or otherwise, show that X cannot be uniformly distributed on the set $\{2, 3, \ldots, 12\}$.
(Cambridge 2009)

SOLUTION. We have that

	1	2	3	4	5	6
1	2	3	4	5	6	7
2	3	4	5	6	7	8
3	4	5	6	7	8	9
4	5	6	7	8	9	10
5	6	7	8	9	10	11
6	7	8	9	10	11	12

$$
\begin{aligned}
\mathbb{P}(X = 2) &= \mathbb{P}(X = 1, Y = 1) \\
&= \frac{1}{6} \cdot \frac{1}{6} = \frac{1}{36}
\end{aligned}
$$

$$
\begin{aligned}
\mathbb{P}(X = 3) &= \mathbb{P}(X = 1, Y = 2) + \mathbb{P}(X = 2, Y = 1) \\
&= \frac{1}{6} \cdot \frac{1}{6} + \frac{1}{6} \cdot \frac{1}{6} = \frac{2}{36}
\end{aligned}
$$

$$
\begin{aligned}
\mathbb{P}(X = 4) &= \mathbb{P}(X = 1, Y = 3) + \mathbb{P}(X = 2, Y = 2) + \mathbb{P}(X = 3, Y = 1) \\
&= \frac{1}{6} \cdot \frac{1}{6} + \frac{1}{6} \cdot \frac{1}{6} + \frac{1}{6} \cdot \frac{1}{6} = \frac{3}{36}
\end{aligned}
$$

$$
\begin{aligned}
\mathbb{P}(X = 5) &= \sum_{i+j=5} \mathbb{P}(S_1 = i)\mathbb{P}(S_2 = j) \\
&= \frac{4}{36}
\end{aligned}
$$

$$
\begin{aligned}
\mathbb{P}(X = 6) &= \sum_{i+j=6} \mathbb{P}(S_1 = i)\mathbb{P}(S_2 = j) \\
&= \frac{5}{36}
\end{aligned}
$$

---

[2]See the forthcoming Example 7.70 also.

$$\begin{aligned}
\mathbb{P}(X = 7) &= \sum_{i+j=7} \mathbb{P}(S_1 = i)\mathbb{P}(S_2 = j) \\
&= \frac{6}{36}
\end{aligned}$$

$$\begin{aligned}
\mathbb{P}(X = 8) &= \sum_{i+j=8} \mathbb{P}(S_1 = i)\mathbb{P}(S_2 = j) \\
&= \frac{5}{36}
\end{aligned}$$

$$\begin{aligned}
\mathbb{P}(X = 9) &= \sum_{i+j=9} \mathbb{P}(S_1 = i)\mathbb{P}(S_2 = j) \\
&= \frac{4}{36}
\end{aligned}$$

$$\begin{aligned}
\mathbb{P}(X = 10) &= \sum_{i+j=10} \mathbb{P}(S_1 = i)\mathbb{P}(S_2 = j) \\
&= \frac{3}{36}
\end{aligned}$$

$$\begin{aligned}
\mathbb{P}(X = 11) &= \sum_{i+j=11} \mathbb{P}(S_1 = i)\mathbb{P}(S_2 = j) \\
&= \frac{2}{36}
\end{aligned}$$

$$\begin{aligned}
\mathbb{P}(X = 12) &= \sum_{i+j=12} \mathbb{P}(S_1 = i)\mathbb{P}(S_2 = j) \\
&= \frac{1}{36}
\end{aligned}$$

Thus

$$\begin{aligned}
\mathbb{E}(X) &= \sum_{x=2}^{12} x\mathbb{P}(X = x) \\
&= 2 \cdot \frac{1}{36} + 3 \cdot \frac{2}{36} + 4 \cdot \frac{3}{36} + 5 \cdot \frac{4}{36} + 6 \cdot \frac{5}{36} + 7 \cdot \frac{6}{36} \\
&\quad + 8 \cdot \frac{5}{36} + 9 \cdot \frac{4}{36} + 10 \cdot \frac{3}{36} + 11 \cdot \frac{2}{36} + 12 \cdot \frac{1}{36} \\
&= 7
\end{aligned}$$

variance

$$
\begin{aligned}
\mathbb{E}(X^2) &= \sum_{x=2}^{12} x^2 \mathbb{P}(X = x) \\
&= 2^2 \cdot \frac{1}{36} + 3^2 \cdot \frac{2}{36} + 4^2 \cdot \frac{3}{36} + 5^2 \cdot \frac{4}{36} + 6^2 \cdot \frac{5}{36} + 7^2 \cdot \frac{6}{36} \\
&\quad + 8^2 \cdot \frac{5}{36} + 9^2 \cdot \frac{4}{36} + 10^2 \cdot \frac{3}{36} + 11^2 \cdot \frac{2}{36} + 12^2 \cdot \frac{1}{36} \\
&= \frac{329}{6}
\end{aligned}
$$

$$
\begin{aligned}
\mathrm{var}(X) &= \mathbb{E}(X^2) - \mathbb{E}(X)^2 \\
&= \frac{329}{6} - 7^2 \\
&= \frac{35}{6}
\end{aligned}
$$

	1	2	3	4	5	6
1	0	1	2	3	4	5
2	1	0	1	2	3	4
3	2	1	0	1	2	3
4	3	2	1	0	1	2
5	4	3	2	1	0	1
6	5	4	3	2	1	0

$$
\begin{aligned}
\mathbb{P}(X = 0) &= = \sum_{i<j,\,j-i=0} \mathbb{P}(S_1 = i)\mathbb{P}(S_2 = j) + \sum_{i>j,\,i-j=0} \mathbb{P}(S_1 = i)\mathbb{P}(S_2 = j) \\
&= \frac{6}{36}
\end{aligned}
$$

$$
\begin{aligned}
\mathbb{P}(X = 1) &= \sum_{i<j,\,j-i=1} \mathbb{P}(S_1 = i)\mathbb{P}(S_2 = j) + \sum_{i>j,\,i-j=1} \mathbb{P}(S_1 = i)\mathbb{P}(S_2 = j) \\
&= \frac{10}{36}
\end{aligned}
$$

$$\begin{aligned}
\mathbb{P}(X = 2) &= \sum_{i<j,\,j-i=2} \mathbb{P}(S_1 = i)\mathbb{P}(S_2 = j) + \sum_{i>j,\,i-j=2} \mathbb{P}(S_1 = i)\mathbb{P}(S_2 = j) \\
&= \frac{8}{36}
\end{aligned}$$

$$\begin{aligned}
\mathbb{P}(X = 3) &= \sum_{i<j,\,j-i=3} \mathbb{P}(S_1 = i)\mathbb{P}(S_2 = j) + \sum_{i>j,\,i-j=3} \mathbb{P}(S_1 = i)\mathbb{P}(S_2 = j) \\
&= \frac{6}{36}
\end{aligned}$$

$$\begin{aligned}
\mathbb{P}(X = 4) &= \sum_{i<j,\,j-i=4} \mathbb{P}(S_1 = i)\mathbb{P}(S_2 = j) + \sum_{i>j,\,i-j=4} \mathbb{P}(S_1 = i)\mathbb{P}(S_2 = j) \\
&= \frac{4}{36}
\end{aligned}$$

$$\begin{aligned}
\mathbb{P}(X = 5) &= \sum_{i<j,\,j-i=5} \mathbb{P}(S_1 = i)\mathbb{P}(S_2 = j) + \sum_{i>j,\,i-j=5} \mathbb{P}(S_1 = i)\mathbb{P}(S_2 = j) \\
&= \frac{2}{36}
\end{aligned}$$

$E(Y) = E(S_1) - E(S_2) = 0$ since $E(S_1) = E(S_2)$.
(b)

$$\begin{aligned}
\mathbb{P}(X = 2) &= \mathbb{P}(S_1 = 1, S_2 = 1) \\
&= p_1 q_1
\end{aligned}$$

$$\begin{aligned}
\mathbb{P}(X = 7) &= \mathbb{P}(S_1 = 1, S_2 = 6) + \mathbb{P}(S_1 = 2, S_2 = 5) + \mathbb{P}(S_1 = 3, S_2 = 4) \\
&\quad + \mathbb{P}(S_1 = 4, S_2 = 3) + \mathbb{P}(S_1 = 5, S_2 = 2) + \mathbb{P}(S_1 = 6, S_2 = 1) \\
&= p_1 q_6 + p_2 q_5 + p_3 q_4 + p_4 q_3 + p_5 q_2 + p_6 q_1
\end{aligned}$$

$$\begin{aligned}
\mathbb{P}(X = 12) &= \mathbb{P}(S_1 = 6, S_2 = 6) \\
&= p_6 q_6
\end{aligned}$$

$$
\begin{aligned}
\sqrt{\mathbb{P}(X=2)\mathbb{P}(X=12)} &= \sqrt{p_1 q_1 p_6 q_6} \\
&= \sqrt{(p_1 q_6)(p_6 q_1)} \\
&\leq \frac{(p_1 q_6)+(p_6 q_1)}{2} \qquad \text{apply the arithmetic/geometric} \\
&\phantom{\leq \frac{(p_1 q_6)+(p_6 q_1)}{2}} \quad\, \text{mean inequality} \\
&< p_1 q_6 + + p_6 q_1 \\
&< p_1 q_6 + p_2 q_5 + p_3 q_4 \\
&\quad + p_4 q_3 + p_5 q_2 + p_6 q_1 \\
&= \mathbb{P}(X=7)
\end{aligned}
$$

Thus X cannot be uniformly distributed on the set $\{2,3,\ldots,12\}$. Otherwise, the above inequality is an equality.

CHAPTER 4

Probability generating functions

4.1. Generating functions

EXERCISE (4.4). If $u_0, u_1, \ldots$ has generating function $U(s)$ and $v_0, v_1, \ldots$ has generating function $V(s)$, find $V(s)$ in terms of $U(s)$ when (a) $v_n = 2u_n$, (b) $v_n = u_n + 1$, (c) $v_n = nu_n$.

SOLUTION. (a) The sequence given by

$$v_n = 2u_n$$

has generating function

$$V(s) = \sum_{n=0}^{\infty}(2u_n)s^n = 2\sum_{n=0}^{\infty} u_n s^n = 2U(s) \quad \left(U(s) = \sum_{n=0}^{\infty} u_n s^n \text{ by the hypothesis}\right)$$

(b) The sequence given by

$$v_n = u_n + 1$$

has generating function

$$V(s) = \sum_{n=0}^{\infty}(u_n + 1)s^n$$

$$= \sum_{n=0}^{\infty}(u_n s^n + s^n)$$

$$= \sum_{n=0}^{\infty} u_n s^n + \sum_{n=0}^{\infty} s^n$$

$$= U(s) + \frac{1}{1-s} \qquad \left(U(s) = \sum_{n=0}^{\infty} u_n s^n \text{ by the hypothesis}\right)$$

(c) The sequence given by

$$v_n = nu_n$$

has generating function

$$V(s) = \sum_{n=0}^{\infty}(nu_n)s^n = \sum_{n=0}^{\infty} nu_n s^n = s(\sum_{n=0}^{\infty} u_n s^n)' = sU'(s)$$

EXERCISE (4.5). Let $0 < p = 1 - q < 1$. Of which sequence is $U(s) = 1/\sqrt{1 - 4pqs^2}$ the generating function?

SOLUTION. Prove that

$$(1 + x)^{\alpha} = \sum_{k=0}^{\infty} \binom{\alpha}{k} x^k \qquad\qquad \text{for } \alpha \in \mathbb{R}$$

where

$$\binom{\alpha}{k} = \frac{\alpha(\alpha - 1)\cdots(\alpha - k + 1)}{k!}$$

Define $f(x) = (1 + x)^{\alpha}$. Then

$$f^{(k)}(x) = \alpha(\alpha - 1)\cdots(\alpha - k + 1)(1 + x)^{\alpha - k}$$

for $k = 1, 2, \ldots$. This implies that

$$f^{(k)}(0) = \alpha(\alpha - 1)\cdots(\alpha - k + 1)$$

By the Maclautin expansion of $f(x)$, we have

$$f(x) = \sum_{k=0}^{\infty} \frac{f^{(k)}(0)}{k!} x^k = \sum_{k=0}^{\infty} \binom{\alpha}{k} x^k \qquad\qquad (1)$$

Apply (1) with $x = -4pqs^2$, $\alpha = -1/2$. Then

$$(1 - 4pqs^2)^{-1/2} = \sum_{k=0}^{\infty} \binom{-\frac{1}{2}}{k} (-4pqs^2)^k$$

$$= \sum_{k=0}^{\infty} \frac{(-\frac{1}{2})(-\frac{3}{2})(-\frac{5}{2}) \cdots (-\frac{2k-1}{2})}{k!} (-1)^k 4^k p^k q^k s^{2k}$$

$$= \sum_{k=0}^{\infty} (-1)^k \frac{1 \cdot 3 \cdot 5 \cdots (2k-1)}{2^k k!} (-1)^k 2^{2k} p^k q^k s^{2k}$$

$$= \sum_{k=0}^{\infty} \frac{1 \cdot 3 \cdot 5 \cdots (2k-1)}{k!} 2^k p^k q^k s^{2k}$$

$$= \sum_{k=0}^{\infty} \frac{1 \cdot 3 \cdot 5 \cdots (2k-1)}{k!k!} (2^k k!) p^k q^k s^{2k}$$

$$= \sum_{k=0}^{\infty} \frac{1 \cdot 3 \cdot 5 \cdots (2k-1)}{k!k!} [2 \cdot 4 \cdot 6 \cdots (2k)] p^k q^k s^{2k}$$

$$= \sum_{k=0}^{\infty} \frac{1 \cdot 2 \cdot 3 \cdot 4 \cdot 5 \cdot 6 \cdots (2k-1) \cdot (2k)}{k!k!} p^k q^k s^{2k}$$

$$= \sum_{k=0}^{\infty} \binom{2k}{k} p^k q^k s^{2k}$$

Thus

$$U(s) = 1/\sqrt{1 - 4pqs^2}$$

is the generating function of the sequence $u_{2k} = \binom{2k}{k} p^k q^k$, $u_{2k+1} = 0$.

Note. Since $U(s)$ is an even function, so its Taylor's expansion consits of the power of even degree only. Hence $u_{2k+1} = 0$.

Remark. If $U(s) = \sqrt{1 - 4pqs^2}$, then apply (1) with $x = -4pqs^2$, $\alpha = 1/2$. Then

$$
\begin{aligned}
(1 - 4pqs^2)^{1/2} &= \sum_{k=0}^{\infty} \binom{\frac{1}{2}}{k}(-4pqs^2)^k \\
&= \sum_{k=0}^{\infty} \frac{(\frac{1}{2})(-\frac{1}{2})(-\frac{3}{2})\cdots(-\frac{2k-3}{2})}{k!}(-1)^k 4^k p^k q^k s^{2k} \\
&= \sum_{k=0}^{\infty}(-1)^{k-1}\frac{1\cdot 3\cdot 5\cdots(2k-3)}{2^k k!}(-1)^k 2^{2k}p^k q^k s^{2k} \\
&= \sum_{k=0}^{\infty}-\frac{1\cdot 3\cdot 5\cdots(2k-3)}{k!}2^k p^k q^k s^{2k} \\
&= \sum_{k=0}^{\infty}-\frac{1\cdot 3\cdot 5\cdots(2k-3)}{k!k!}(2^k k!)p^k q^k s^{2k} \\
&= \sum_{k=0}^{\infty}-\frac{1}{(2k-1)}\cdot\frac{1\cdot 3\cdot 5\cdots(2k-3)(2k-1)}{k!k!}[2\cdot 4\cdot 6\cdots(2k)]p^k q^k s^{2k} \\
&= \sum_{k=0}^{\infty}-\frac{1}{(2k-1)}\cdot\frac{1\cdot 2\cdot 3\cdot 4\cdot 5\cdot 6\cdots(2k-3)\cdot(2k-1)\cdot(2k)}{k!k!}p^k q^k s^{2k} \\
&= \sum_{k=0}^{\infty}-\frac{1}{(2k-1)}\binom{2k}{k}p^k q^k s^{2k}
\end{aligned}
$$

Thus

$$
U(s) = \sqrt{1 - 4pqs^2}
$$

is the generating function of the sequence $u_{2k} = -\dfrac{1}{(2k-1)}\dbinom{2k}{k}p^k q^k$, $u_{2k+1}=0$

4.2. Integer-valued random variables

EXAMPLE (4.14). Let X be a random variable having the Bernoulli distribution with parameter p. Then

$$
\mathbb{P}(X = 0) = q, \qquad\qquad \mathbb{P}(X = 1) = p,
$$

where $p + q = 1$, and X has probability generating functio

$$
\begin{aligned}
G_X(s) &= p_X(0)s^0 + p_X(1)s^1 \\
&= q + ps.
\end{aligned}
$$

EXAMPLE (4.15). Let X be a random variable having the binomial distribution with parameters n and p. Then

$$
\mathbb{P}(X = k) = \binom{n}{k}p^k q^{n-k} \qquad\qquad \text{for } k = 0, 1, 2, \ldots, n,
$$

and X has probability generating function

$$\begin{aligned} G_X(s) &= \sum_{k=0}^{n} \binom{n}{k} p^k q^{n-k} s^k \\ &= \sum_{k=0}^{n} \binom{n}{k} q^{n-k} (ps)^k \\ &= (q+ps)^n. \end{aligned}$$

EXAMPLE (4.16). Let X be a random variable having the Poisson distribution with parameters λ. Then

$$\mathbb{P}(X=k) = \frac{1}{k!} \lambda^k e^{-\lambda} \qquad \text{for } k = 0, 1, 2, \ldots,$$

and X has probability generating function

$$\begin{aligned} G_X(s) &= \sum_{k=0}^{\infty} \frac{1}{k!} \lambda^k e^{-\lambda} s^k \\ &= e^{-\lambda} \sum_{k=0}^{n} \frac{1}{k!} (\lambda s)^k \\ &= e^{-\lambda} e^{\lambda s} \qquad \qquad \left(\text{use the Maclaurin series } \sum_{k=0}^{n} \frac{1}{k!} x^k = e^x\right) \\ &= e^{\lambda(s-1)}. \end{aligned}$$

EXAMPLE (4.17). Let X be a random variable having the negative binomial distribution with parameters n and p. Then

$$\mathbb{P}(X=k) = \binom{k-1}{n-1} p^n q^{k-n} \qquad \text{for } k = n, n+1, n+2, \ldots,$$

and X has probability generating function

$$G_X(s) = \sum_{k=n}^{\infty} \binom{k-1}{n-1} p^n q^{k-n} s^k$$

$$= \sum_{k=n}^{\infty} \frac{(n-1)!}{(n-1)!(k-n)!} p^n q^{k-n} s^k$$

$$= \sum_{k=n}^{\infty} \frac{n(n+1)\cdots(k-1)}{(k-n)!} p^n q^{k-n} s^k$$

$$= \sum_{j=0}^{\infty} (-1)^j \frac{(-n)(-n-1)\cdots(-k+1)}{j!} p^n q^j s^{n+j} \qquad \text{(put } k = n+j \text{ for } j = 0,1,2,\ldots)$$

$$= (ps)^n \sum_{j=0}^{\infty} (-1)^j \frac{(-n)(-n-1)\cdots(-n-j+1)}{j!} (qs)^j$$

$$= (ps)^n \sum_{j=0}^{\infty} (-1)^j \binom{-n}{j} (qs)^j$$

$$= (ps)^n \sum_{j=0}^{\infty} \binom{-n}{j} (-qs)^j$$

$$= (ps)^n (1-qs)^{-n}$$

$$= \left(\frac{ps}{1-qs}\right)^n$$

EXERCISE (4.18). If X is a random variable with probability generating function $G_X(s)$, and k is a positive integer, show that $Y = kX$ and $Z = X + k$ have probability generating functions

$$G_Y(s) = G_X(s^k), \qquad G_Z(s) = s^k G_X(s).$$

SOLUTION. $Y = kX$, for $i \in \operatorname{Im} Y$ then $i = kj$ for $j \in \{0,1,2,\ldots\}$.

$$
\begin{aligned}
G_Y(s) &= \sum_{j=0}^{\infty} \mathbb{P}(Y = kj) s^{kj} \\
&= \sum_{j=0}^{\infty} \mathbb{P}(kX = kj) s^{kj} \\
&= \sum_{j=0}^{\infty} \mathbb{P}(X = j) s^{kj} \\
&= \sum_{j=0}^{\infty} \mathbb{P}(X = j)(s^k)^j \\
&= G_X(s^k).
\end{aligned}
$$

$Z = X + k$, for $i \in \operatorname{Im} Z$ then $i = j + k$ for $j \in \{0,1,2,\ldots\}$

$$
\begin{aligned}
G_Z(s) &= \sum_{j=0}^{\infty} \mathbb{P}(Z = j + k)s^{j+k} \\
&= s^k \sum_{j=0}^{\infty} \mathbb{P}(X + k = j + k)s^j \\
&= s^k \sum_{j=0}^{\infty} \mathbb{P}(X = j)s^j \\
&= s^k G_X(s)
\end{aligned}
$$

EXERCISE (4.19). If X is uniformly distributed on $\{0, 1, 2, \ldots, a\}$, in that

(for $k = 0, 1, 2, \ldots, a,$) $$\mathbb{P}(X = k) = \frac{1}{a+1}$$

show that X has probability generating function

$$
G_X(s) = \frac{1 - s^{a+1}}{(a+1)(1-s)}.
$$

SOLUTION. We have that

$$
\begin{aligned}
G_X(s) &= \sum_{k=0}^{a} \mathbb{P}(X = k)s^k \\
&= \sum_{k=0}^{a} \frac{1}{a+1}s^k \\
&= \frac{1}{a+1} \sum_{k=0}^{a} s^k \\
&= \frac{1}{a+1} \cdot \frac{1 - s^{a+1}}{1 - s}.
\end{aligned}
$$

4.3. Moments

EXERCISE (4.30). Use the method of generating functions to show that a random variable having the Poisson distribution, parameter λ, has both mean and variance equal to λ.

SOLUTION. Let X have the Poisson distribution with parameter λ. It has probability generating function $G_X(s) = e^{\lambda(s-1)}$. Hence

$$
\begin{aligned}
\mathbb{E}(X) &= G_X'(1) = \lambda e^{\lambda(1-1)} = \lambda, \\
E(X^2) &= G_X''(1) + G_X'(1) = \lambda^2 e^{\lambda(1-1)} + \lambda = \lambda^2 + \lambda \\
\mathrm{var}(X) &= \mathbb{E}(X^2) - \mathbb{E}(X)^2 = (\lambda^2 + \lambda) - \lambda^2 = \lambda,
\end{aligned}
$$

EXERCISE (4.31). If X has the negative binomial distribution with parameters n and p, show that

$$\mathbb{E}(X) = n/p, \qquad \text{var}(X) = nq/p^2,$$

where $q = 1 - p$.

SOLUTION. Let X have the negative binomial distribution with parameters n and p. It has probability generating function $G_X(s) = [ps/(1-qs)]^n$ for $|s| < q^{-1}$ where $q = 1 - p$. Hence

$$
\begin{aligned}
G_X'(s) &= n\Big(\frac{ps}{1-qs}\Big)^{n-1}\frac{p(1-qs)+pqs}{(1-qs)^2} \\
&= n\Big(\frac{ps}{1-qs}\Big)^{n-1}\frac{p(1-qs)+qps}{(1-qs)^2} \\
&= np\frac{(ps)^{n-1}}{(1-qs)^{n+1}},
\end{aligned}
$$

$$
G_X''(s) = np\frac{(n-1)(ps)^{n-2}p(1-qs)^{n+1} + (ps)^{n-1}(n+1)(1-qs)^n q}{(1-qs)^{2n+2}}.
$$

This implies

$$
\begin{aligned}
G_X''(1) &= np\frac{(n-1)p^{2n} + (n+1)p^{2n-1}(1-p)}{p^{2n+2}} \\
&= \frac{n(n-1)p^{2n+1} + n(n+1)p^{2n}(1-p)}{p^{2n+2}} \\
&= \frac{p^{2n}(-2np + n^2 + n)}{p^{2n+2}} \\
&= \frac{n^2 + n - 2np}{p^2}.
\end{aligned}
$$

Hence

$$
\begin{aligned}
\mathbb{E}(X) = G_X'(1) &= np\frac{(p)^{n-1}}{(1-q)^{n+1}} = \frac{np^n}{p^{n+1}} = \frac{n}{p}, \\
\mathbb{E}(X^2) = G_X''(1) + G_X'(1) &= \frac{n^2 + n - 2np}{p^2} + \frac{n}{p}, \\
\text{var}(X) = \mathbb{E}(X^2) - \mathbb{E}(X)^2 &= \frac{n^2 + n - 2np}{p^2} + \frac{n}{p} - \frac{n^2}{p^2} \\
&= \frac{n - 2np + np}{p^2} = \frac{n - np}{p^2} = \frac{n(1-p)}{p^2} = \frac{nq}{p^2}.
\end{aligned}
$$

EXERCISE (4.32). Let X be a random variable taking values in the finite set $\{1, 2, \ldots, N\}$. The *Dirichlet* probability generating function of X is defined as the function $\Delta(s) = \mathbb{E}(X^{-s})$. Express the mean of X in terms of Δ. Similarly, express the mean of $\log X$ in terms of Δ. You may find it useful to recall that $(x^y - 1)/y \to \log x$ as $y \to 0$.

SOLUTION. The mean of X in terms of Δ, where Δ is defined as the function $\Delta(s) = \mathbb{E}(X^{-s})$, can be easily found by calculating Δ at the point $s = -1$. To see this when $s = -1$,

$$\Delta(-1) = \mathbb{E}(X^{-(-1)}) = \mathbb{E}(X).$$

If Δ is defined as the function $\Delta(s) = \mathbb{E}(s^{-X})$, we have that

$$\Delta(s) = \sum_{x=1}^{N} s^{-x} P(X = x)$$

so that

$$\Delta'(s) = \sum_{x=1}^{N} -xs^{-x-1}\mathbb{P}(X = x).$$

When $s = 1$,

$$\Delta'(1) = \sum_{x=1}^{N} -x\mathbb{P}(X = k) = -\mathbb{E}(X).$$

It follows that

$$\mathbb{E}(X) = -\Delta'(1) = -\left.\frac{d\Delta}{ds}\right|_{s=1}$$

If Δ is defined as the function $\Delta(s) = \mathbb{E}(X^{-s})$, the mean of $\log X$ in terms of Δ can be calculated by using the following argument:

$$\mathbb{E}(\log X) = \sum_{x=1}^{N} \log k\mathbb{P}(X = k)$$

$$= \sum_{x=1}^{N} (\lim_{y \to 0} \frac{x^y - 1}{y})\mathbb{P}(X = x)$$

$$= \sum_{x=1}^{N} \lim_{y \to 0} \frac{x^y \mathbb{P}(X = x) - \mathbb{P}(X = x)}{y}$$

$$= \sum_{x=1}^{N} \lim_{y \to 0} \frac{x^y \mathbb{P}(X = x) - \mathbb{P}(X = x)}{y}$$

$$= \lim_{y \to 0} \frac{\sum_{x=1}^{N} [x^y \mathbb{P}(X = x) - \mathbb{P}(X = x)]}{y}$$

$$= \lim_{y \to 0} \frac{\sum_{x=1}^{N} x^y \mathbb{P}(X = x) - \sum_{x=1}^{N} \mathbb{P}(X = x)}{y}$$

$$= \lim_{y \to 0} \frac{\Delta(-y) - 1}{y}$$

Alternateiely, we have that

$$\Delta(s) = \mathbb{E}(X^{-s}) = \sum_{x=1}^{N} x^{-s}\mathbb{P}(X = x).$$

It follows that

$$\Delta'(s) = \sum_{x=1}^{N} -x^{-s} \log x\mathbb{P}(X = x).$$

When $s = 0$,

$$\Delta'(0) = -\sum_{x=1}^{N} \log x\mathbb{P}(X = x) = -\mathbb{E}(\log X)$$

so that

$$\mathbb{E}(\log X) = -\Delta'(0)$$

$$= -\lim_{y \to 0} \frac{\Delta(y) - \Delta(0)}{y} \quad \text{by the definition of derivative of } \Delta \text{ at } s = 0$$

(since $\Delta(0) = \mathbb{E}(1) = 1$)

$$= \lim_{y \to 0} \frac{\Delta(-y) - 1}{y}.$$

Note that when $s = 1$,

$$\Delta'(1) = -\sum_{x=1}^{N} \frac{\log x}{x} \mathbb{P}(X = x) = -\mathbb{E}(\frac{\log X}{X})$$

so that

$$\mathbb{E}(\frac{\log X}{X}) = -\Delta'(1) = -\left.\frac{d\Delta}{ds}\right|_{s=1}.$$

4.4. Sums of independent random variables

EXERCISE (4.40). Use Theorem 4.33 to show that the sum of two independent random variables, having the Poisson distribution with parameters λ and μ respectively, has the Poisson distribution also, with parameter $\lambda + \mu$. Compare your solution to that of Exercise 3.29.

SOLUTION. Let X and Y be independent random variables with Poisson distributions having parameters λ and μ respectively. That is to say,

$$G_X(s) = e^{\lambda(s-1)}$$

and

$$G_Y(s) = e^{\mu(s-1)}.$$

Hence, if $Z = X + Y$, we have

$$G_Z(s) = G_{X+Y}(s)$$

(by Theorem 4.33)
$$= G_X(s)G_Y(s)$$
$$= e^{\lambda(s-1)}e^{\mu(s-1)}$$
$$= e^{(\lambda+\mu)(s-1)}.$$

By Uniqueness theorem for probability generating functions, Theorem 4.13, Z has the Poisson distribution with parameter $\lambda + \mu$.

EXERCISE (4.41). Use generating functions to find the distribution of $X + Y$, where X and Y are independent random variables, X having the binomial distribution with parameters m and p, and Y having the binomial distribution with parameters n and p. Deduce that the sum of n independent random variables, each having the Bernoulli distribution with parameter p, has the binomial distribution with parameters n and p.

SOLUTION. Let X and Y be independent random variables with binomial distributions having parameters m, p and n, p, respectively. That is to say,

$$G_X(s) = (q + ps)^m$$

and

$$G_Y(s) = (q + ps)^n.$$

Hence, if $Z = X + Y$, we have

$$\begin{aligned} G_Z(s) &= G_{X+Y}(s) \\ &= G_X(s)G_Y(s) \\ &= (q + ps)^m(q + ps)^n \\ &= (q + ps)^{m+n}. \end{aligned}$$

(by Theorem 4.33)

By Uniqueness theorem for probability generating functions, Theorem 4.13, Z has the binomial distribution with parameter $m + n$ and p.

Let X_i for $i \in \{1, 2, \ldots n\}$ be be independent random variables with Bernoulli distributions having parameter p. That is to say,

$$G_{X_i} = (q + ps)$$

Hence, if $S = X_1 + X_2 + \cdots + X_n$, we have

$$\begin{aligned} G_Z(s) &= G_{X_1+X_2+\cdots+X_n}(s) \\ &= \prod_{i=1}^{n} G_{X_i}(s) \\ &= (q + ps)^n. \end{aligned}$$

(by Theorem 4.33)

By Uniqueness theorem for probability generating functions, Theorem 4.13, S has the binomial distribution with parameters n and p.

EXERCISE (4.42). Each egg laid by a hen falls onto the concrete floor of the henhouse and cracks with probability p. If the number of eggs laid today by the hen has the Poisson distribution, parameter λ, use generating functions to show that the number of uncracked eggs has the Poisson distribution with parameter $\lambda(1-p)$.

SOLUTION. Let A_i be the event that the ith egg is laid today by the hen. For $i = 1, 2, \ldots, n$, we define the discrete random variable X_i by

$$X_i(A_i) = \begin{cases} 1 & \text{if the } i\text{th egg is uncracked,} \\ 0 & \text{if the } i\text{th egg is cracked.} \end{cases}$$

Each X_i takes values in $\{0, 1\}$ and has mass function given by

$$\mathbb{P}(X_i = 0) = p$$

and

$$\mathbb{P}(X_i = 1) = 1 - p.$$

Hence, each X_i has the Bernoulli distribution with parameter $1-p$. Let N be the number number of eggs laid today by the hen, and S be the number of uncracked eggs. Then

$$S = \sum_{i=1}^{N} X_i \qquad (N\text{is a discrete random variable})$$

Since N and X_i are independent random variables, we conclude from the random sum formula (4.37) that the tota; number S has probability generating function

$$G_S(s) = G_N(G_{X_1}(s)) = G_N(p + (1-p)s) \qquad \text{since } G_{X_1}(s) = p + (1-p)s$$

By our hypothesis then

$$G_N(s) = e^{\lambda(s-1)}$$

this implies that

$$G_S(s) = e^{\lambda[p+(1-p)s-1]} = e^{\lambda[(1-p)s-(1-p)]} = e^{\lambda(1-p)(s-1)}$$

By Uniqueness theorem for probability generating functions, Theorem 4.13, S has the Poisson distribution with parameter $\lambda(1-p)$.

4.5. Problems

PROBLEM (4.5.1). Let X have probability generating function $G_X(s)$ and let $u_n = \mathbb{P}(X > n)$. Show that the generating function $U(s)$ of the sequence $u_0, u_1, \ldots$ satisfies

$$(1 - s)U(s) = 1 - G_X(s),$$

whenever the series defining these generating functions converge.

SOLUTION. We have that

$$(1 - s)U(s) = U(s) - sU(s)$$

$$= \sum_{i=0}^{\infty} u_i s^i - \sum_{i=0}^{\infty} u_i s^{i+1}$$

$$= u_0 + \sum_{i=0}^{\infty} (u_i - u_{i-1})s^i$$

$$= u_0 + \sum_{i=0}^{\infty} [P(X \geq i + 1) - P(X \geq i)]s^i$$

(since $\mathbb{P}(X \geq i + 1) - \mathbb{P}(X \geq i) = -\mathbb{P}(X = i)$)

$$= u_0 - \sum_{i=1}^{\infty} \mathbb{P}(X = i)$$

(since $G_X(s) = \mathbb{P}(X = 0) + \sum_{i=1}^{\infty} \mathbb{P}(X = i)s^i$)

$$= \mathbb{P}(X \geq 1) - [G_X(s) - \mathbb{P}(X = 0)]$$

$$= \mathbb{P}(X = 0) + \mathbb{P}(X \geq 1)$$

$$= \sum_{i=0}^{\infty} \mathbb{P}(X = i) - G_X(s)$$

$$= 1 - G_X(s),$$

whenever the series defining these generating functions converge.

PROBLEM (4.5.2). A symmetrical die is thrown independently seven times. What is the probability that the total number of points obtained is 14? (Oxford 1974M)

PROBLEM. Consider

$$x_1 + x_2 + x_3 + x_4 + x_5 + x_6 = 14$$

such that $1 \leq x_i \leq 6$ for every $1 \leq i \leq 6$.

First, let $y_i = x_i - 1$ for $1 \leq i \leq 6$. We will count integer solutions of the equation

$y_1 + y_2 + y_3 + y_4 + y_5 + y_6 = 8$ with $0 \leq y_i \leq 5$, , as there is a straightforward bijection between such solutions and the solutions of the original equation. There are

$$\binom{8 + 6 - 1}{6 - 1} = \binom{13}{6}$$

non-negative solutions to this equation, when we ignore the upper bounds. Let A_i be the set of solutions with $y_i \geq 6$. Then we are interested in $\binom{13}{6}$ − $|A_1 \cup A_2 \cup A_3 \cup A_4 \cup A_5 \cup A_6|$. Applying inclusion-exclusion, we have

$$|A_1 \cup A_2 \cup A_3 \cup A_4 \cup A_5 \cup A_6| = \sum_{i=1}^{6} |A_i| - \sum_{1 \leq i < j \leq 6} |A_i \cap A_j|$$

Let x_i be the number of points obtained in ith throw for $i = 1, 2, \ldots, 7$. Then the problem reduces to finding the number of distinct positive integer-valued vectors $(x_1, x_2, \ldots, x_7)$ such that

$$x_1 + x_2 + x_3 + x_4 + x_5 + x_6 + x_7 = 14,$$

where $1 \leq x_i \leq 6$. Let $y_i = x_i - 1$ for $1 \leq i \leq 7$. We will count integer solutions of the equation

$$y_1 + y_2 + y_3 + y_4 + y_5 + y_6 + y_7 = 7$$

where $0 \leq y_i \leq 6$, as there is a straightforward bijection between such solutions and the solutions of the original equation. There are

$$\binom{7 + 7 - 1}{7 - 1} = \binom{13}{6}$$

non-negative solutions to this equation, when we ignore the upper bounds.

If $y_i = 7$ for some i, then $y_j = 0$ for $j \neq i$. In this case, there are 7 solutions.

If $y_i = 6$ for some i, then there exists some $j \neq i$ such that $y_j = 1$ and $y_k = 0$ for $k \neq i$ and $k \neq j$. In this case, there are $7 \cdot 6 = 42$ solutions. Thus the number of solutions satisfying $1 \leq x_i \leq 6$ for all i of the given equation is $\binom{13}{6} - 49$.

The probability that the total number of points obtained be 14 is that $\frac{1}{6^7}[\binom{13}{6} - 49]$.

PROBLEM (4.5.3). Three players, Alan, Bob, and Cindy, throw a perfect die in turn independently in the order $A, B, C, A, \ldots$ until one wins by throwing a 5 or a 6. Show that the probability generating function $F(s)$ for the random variable X which takes the value r if the game ends on the rth throw can be written as

$$F(s) = \frac{9s}{27 - 8s^3} + \frac{6s^2}{27 - 8s^3} + \frac{4s^3}{27 - 8s^3}.$$

Hence find the probabilities of winning for Alan, Bob, and Cindy. Find the mean duration of the game. (Oxford 1973M)

SOLUTION. Clearly, X has the geometric distribution with parameter $p = 2/6$ and

$$\mathbb{P}(X = r) = (\frac{2}{6})(\frac{4}{6})^{r-1} = (\frac{1}{3})(\frac{2}{3})^{r-1}$$

for $r = 1, 2, 3 \ldots$. Hence the pgf of X is then

$$\begin{aligned}
F(s) &= \sum_{k=0}^{\infty} s^k \mathbb{P}(X = k) \\
&= \sum_{k=1}^{\infty} s^k (\frac{1}{3})(\frac{2}{3})^{k-1} \quad\quad\quad (\text{since } \mathbb{P}(X = 0) = 0) \\
&= (\frac{1}{3})(\frac{3}{2}) \sum_{k=1}^{\infty} (\frac{2}{3})^k s^k \\
&= \frac{1}{2} \sum_{k=1}^{\infty} (\frac{2}{3} s)^k \\
&= \frac{1}{2} \cdot \frac{\frac{2}{3} s}{1 - \frac{2}{3} s} \\
&= \frac{s}{3 - 2s}
\end{aligned}$$

The probability of winning for Alan,

$$P_A = \sum_{k=0}^{\infty} \mathbb{P}(X = 3k + 1)$$

$$= \sum_{k=0}^{\infty} (\frac{2}{3})^{3k+1}$$

$$= \frac{1}{3} \sum_{k=0}^{\infty} (\frac{8}{27})^{k}$$

$$= \frac{1}{3} \cdot \frac{1}{1 - \frac{8}{27}}$$

$$= \frac{9}{19}.$$

The probability of winning for Bob,

$$P_B = \sum_{k=0}^{\infty} \mathbb{P}(X = 3k + 2)$$

$$= \sum_{k=0}^{\infty} (\frac{2}{3})^{3k+2}$$

$$= \frac{1}{3} \cdot \frac{2}{3} \sum_{k=0}^{\infty} (\frac{8}{27})^{k}$$

$$= \frac{2}{9} \cdot \frac{1}{1 - \frac{8}{27}}$$

$$= \frac{6}{19}.$$

Since X has probability generating function $F(s) = s/(3 - 2s)$, it follows that

$$\mathbb{E}(X) = F'(1)$$

$$= \frac{d}{ds}(\frac{s}{3 - 2s})\Big|_{s=1}$$

$$= \frac{3}{(3 - 2s)^2}\Big|_{s=1}$$

$$= \frac{3}{(3 - 2 \cdot 1)^2}$$

$$= 3$$

PROBLEM (4.5.4). A player undertakes trials, and the probability of success at each trial is p. A turn consists of a sequence of trials up to the first failure. Obtain the probability generating function for the total number of successes in N turns. Show that the mean of this distribution is $Np(1-p)^{-1}$ and find its variance. (Oxford 1974M)

SOLUTION. For $i = 1, 2, \ldots, N$, let X_i be the discrete random varaible that represent the number of successes in the ith turn.

It is easy to see that random variables X_i are independent and have identical distributions. Each X_i has mass function given by

(for $k = 0, 1, 2, \ldots,$) $\mathbb{P}(X_i = k) = p^k q$

and each X_i has probability generating function

$$
\begin{aligned}
G_{X_i}(s) &= \sum_{k=0}^{\infty} s^k \mathbb{P}(X_i = k) \\
&= \sum_{k=0}^{\infty} p^k q s^k \\
&= q \sum_{k=0}^{\infty} (ps)^k \\
&= \frac{q}{1 - ps}.
\end{aligned}
$$

It follows that the sum $S_N = X_1 + X_2 + \cdots + X_N$ of N independent random variables, each taking values in $\{0, 1, 2, \ldots\}$, has probability generating function given by

$$
G_{S_N}(s) = G_{X_1}(s) G_{X_2}(s) \cdots G_{X_N}(s) = [G_{X_1}(s)]^N = \left(\frac{q}{1 - ps}\right)^N.
$$

Hence

$$\mathbb{E}(S_N) = G'_{S_N}(1)$$

$$= \frac{d}{ds}\left(\frac{q}{1-ps}\right)^N\Big|_{s=1}$$

$$= N\left(\frac{q}{1-ps}\right)^{N-1}\frac{d}{ds}\left(\frac{q}{1-ps}\right)_{s=1}\Big|_{s=1}$$

$$= N\left(\frac{q}{1-ps}\right)^{N-1}\frac{pq}{(1-ps)^2}\Big|_{s=1}$$

$$= \frac{Npq^N}{(1-ps)^{N+1}}$$

$$= \frac{Np}{1-p},$$

$$\mathbb{E}(S_N^2) = G''_{S_N}(1) + G'_{S_N}(1)$$

$$= \frac{d}{ds}\frac{Npq^N}{(1-ps)^{N+1}}\Big|_{s=1} + \frac{Np}{1-p}$$

$$= \frac{Npq^N(-N-1)(-p)}{(1-ps)^{N+2}}\Big|_{s=1} + \frac{Np}{1-p}$$

$$= \frac{N(N+1)p^2q^N}{q^{N+2}} + \frac{Np}{1-p}$$

$$= \frac{N(N+1)p^2}{(1-p)^2} + \frac{Np}{1-p},$$

$$\text{var}(X) = E(S_N^2) - E(S_N)^2$$

$$= \frac{N(N+1)p^2}{(1-p)^2} + \frac{Np}{1-p} - \frac{N^2p^2}{(1-p)^2}$$

$$= \frac{N^2p^2 + Np^2 + Np(1-p) - N^2p^2}{(1-p)^2}$$

$$= \frac{Np(p+q)}{q^2}$$

$$= \frac{Np}{(1-p)^2}.$$

PROBLEM (4.5.5). Each year a tree of a particular type flowers once, and the probability that it has n flowers is $(1-p)p^n$, $n = 0, 1, 2, \ldots$, where $0 < p < 1$.

Each flower has probability $\frac{1}{2}$ of producing a ripe fruit, independently of all other flowers. Find the probability that in a given year
    (a) the tree produces r ripe fruits,
    (b) the tree had n flowers, given that it produces r ripe fruits.
(Oxford 1982M)

SOLUTION. (a) The number N of flowers has probability generating function

$$
\begin{aligned}
G_N(s) &= \sum_{k=0}^{\infty} s^k \mathbb{P}(X = k) \\
&= \sum_{k=0}^{\infty} (1-p) p^k s^k \\
&= (1-p) \sum_{n=0}^{\infty} (ps)^k \\
&= \frac{1-p}{1-ps}.
\end{aligned}
$$

Let X_i be the random variable that takes value 1 if the $i$the flower produce a ripe fruit, and takes value 0 otherwise. Each X_i has the Bernoulli distribution with parameter $\frac{1}{2}$, and consequently each X_i has probability generating function

$$
G_{X_i}(s) = \frac{1}{2} + \frac{1}{2}s.
$$

Since N and X_i are independent, we conclude from the random sum formula (4.37) that the total number $S = X_0 + X_1 + X_2 + \cdots + X_N$ of flowers producing ripe fruits has generating function

$$G_S(s) = G_N(G_{X_1}(s))$$

$$= \frac{1-p}{1 - p(\frac{1}{2} + \frac{1}{2}s)}$$

$$= \frac{2(1-p)}{(2-p) - ps}$$

$$= \frac{\frac{2(1-p)}{2-p}}{1 - \frac{p}{2-p}s}$$

$$= \frac{2(1-p)}{2-p} \cdot \frac{1}{1 - \frac{p}{2-p}s}$$

$$= \frac{2(1-p)}{2-p} \sum_{k=0}^{\infty} (\frac{p}{2-p}s)^k$$

$$= \sum_{k=0}^{\infty} \frac{2(1-p)p^k}{(2-p)^{k+1}} s^k,$$

giving

$$\mathbb{P}(S = r) = \frac{2(1-p)p^r}{(2-p)^{r+1}}$$

the coefficient in the sum above with respect to s^r.

(b) Let A be the event that the tree has n flowers, and let B be the event that the tree produces r ripe fruits,

$$P(A \mid B) = \frac{P(A \cap B)}{P(B)}$$

$$= P(B \mid A)\frac{P(A)}{P(B)}$$

The probability that the tree produces r ripe fruits, given that it has n flowers, is

$$P(B \mid A) = \binom{n}{r}(\frac{1}{2})^r(\frac{1}{2})^{n-r}$$

Thus

$$P(A \mid B) = \binom{n}{r}(\frac{1}{2})^r(\frac{1}{2})^{n-r}\frac{(1-p)p^n}{\frac{2(1-p)p^r}{(2-p)^{r+1}}} = \frac{\binom{n}{r}(\frac{1}{2})^n(1-p)p^n(2-p)^{r+1}}{2(1-p)p^r}$$

$$= \binom{n}{r}p^{n-r}(\frac{1}{2})^{n+1}(2-p)^{r+1}$$

PROBLEM (4.5.6). An unfair coin is tossed n times, each outcome is independent of all the others, and on each toss a head is shown with probability p. The total number of heads shown is X. Use the probability generating function of X to find

(a) the mean and variance of X,

(b) the probability that X is even,

(c) the probability that X is divisible by 3.

(Oxford 1980M)

SOLUTION. (a) The number X of heads after n tosses has the binomial distribution with parameters n and p, and consequently X has probability generating function

$$G_X(s) = \mathbb{E}(s^X)$$
$$= (q + ps)^n.$$

where $q = 1 - p$. Hence

$$\mathbb{E}(X) = G_X'(1) = np,$$
$$\mathbb{E}(X^2) = G_X''(1) + G_X'(1) = npq + n^2 p,$$
$$\mathrm{var}X = \mathbb{E}(X^2) - \mathbb{E}(X)^2 = npq,$$

in agreement with the calculations of Exercise 2.37.

(b) **Solution 1**. For $k = 0, 1, 2, \ldots, \left\lfloor \dfrac{n}{2} \right\rfloor$, we have that

$$\mathbb{P}(X = 2k) = \binom{n}{2k} p^{2k} q^{n-2k}$$

so that

$$\sum_{k=0}^{\lfloor \frac{n}{2} \rfloor} \binom{n}{2k} p^{2k} q^{n-2k}.$$

Solution 2. We have

$$G_X(s) = p_0 + p_1 s + p_2 s^2 + \cdots.$$

Observe that

$$G_X(1) = p_0 + p_1 + p_2 + \cdots$$
$$G_X(-1) = p_0 - p_1 + p_2 - \cdots$$

Thus

$$G_X(1) + G_X(-1) = 2p_0 + 2p_2 + 2p_4 + \cdots$$

so that

$$
\begin{aligned}
(p_0 + p_2 + p_4 + \cdots) &= \frac{1}{2}[G_X(1) + G_X(-1)] \\
&= \frac{1}{2}\{[(1-p) + p]^n + [(1-p) + p(-1)]^n\} \\
&= \frac{1}{2}[1 + (1-2p)^n]
\end{aligned}
$$

(c) **Solution 1.** For $k = 0, 1, 2, \ldots, \left\lfloor \frac{n}{3} \right\rfloor$, we have that

$$\mathbb{P}(X = 3k) = \binom{n}{2k} p^{3k} q^{n-3k}$$

so that

$$\sum_{k=0}^{\lfloor \frac{n}{3} \rfloor} \binom{n}{3k} p^{3k} q^{n-3k}.$$

Solution 2. We have

$$G_X(s) = p_0 + p_1 s + p_2 s^2 + \cdots.$$

Let ω and ω^2 be the primitive complex cube roots of unity. Thus There are 3 complex cube roots of unity: $1, \omega, \omega^2$.

$$
\begin{aligned}
G_X(1) &= p_0 + p_1 + p_2 + \cdots \\
G_X(\omega) &= p_0 + p_1\omega + p_2\omega^2 + \cdots \\
G_X(\omega^2) &= p_0 + p_1\omega^2 + p_2\omega^4 + \cdots
\end{aligned}
$$

Thus

$$
\begin{aligned}
G_X(1) + G_X(\omega) + G_X(\omega^2) &= (p_0 + p_1 + p_2 + \cdots) + (p_0 + p_1\omega + p_2\omega^2 + \cdots) + (p_0 + p_1\omega^2 + p_2\omega^4 + \cdots) \\
&= 3p_0 + p_1(1 + \omega + \omega^2) + p_2(1 + \omega^2 + \omega^4) + p_3(1 + \omega^3 + \omega^6) + \cdots \\
&= 3p_0 + p_1(1 + \omega + \omega^2) + p_2(1 + \omega + \omega^2) + p_3(1 + 1 + 1) + \cdots \\
&= 3p_0 + p_1 \cdot 0 + p_2 \cdot 0 + 3p_3 + \cdots
\end{aligned}
$$

so that

$$(p_0 + p_3 + p_6 + \cdots) = \frac{1}{3}[G_X(1) + G_X(\omega) + G_X(\omega^2)]$$
$$= \frac{1}{3}\{[(1-p)+p]^n + [(1-p)+p\omega]^n[(1-p)+p\omega^2]^n\}$$

PROBLEM (4.5.7). Let X and Y be independent random variables having Poisson distributions with parameters λ and μ, respectively. Prove that $X + Y$ has a Poisson distribution and that $\mathrm{var}(X + Y) = \mathrm{var}(X) + \mathrm{var}(Y)$. Find the conditional probability $\mathbb{P}(X = k \mid X + Y = n)$ for $0 \leq k \leq n$, and hence show that the conditional expectation of X given that $X + Y = n$, that is,

$$\mathbb{E}(X \mid X + Y = n) = \sum_{k=0}^{\infty} k\mathbb{P}(X = k \mid X + Y = n),$$

is $n\lambda/(\lambda + \mu)$. (Oxford 1983M)

SOLUTION. Let X and Y be independent random variables with Poisson distributions having parameters λ and μ, respectively. That is to say,

$$G_X(s) = e^{\lambda(s-1)}$$

and

$$G_Y(s) = e^{\mu(s-1)}.$$

Hence, if $Z = X + Y$, we have

(by Theorem 4.33)
$$\begin{aligned} G_Z(s) &= G_{X+Y}(s) \\ &= G_X(s)G_Y(s) \\ &= e^{\lambda(s-1)}e^{\mu(s-1)} \\ &= e^{(\lambda+\mu)(s-1)}. \end{aligned}$$

By Uniqueness theorem for probability generating functions, Theorem 4.13, $Z = X + Y$ has the Poisson distribution with parameter $\lambda + \mu$.

We have

$$\begin{aligned} \mathrm{var}(X+Y) &= \mathbb{E}[(X+Y)^2] - [\mathbb{E}(X+Y)]^2 \\ &= \mathbb{E}(X^2 + 2XY + Y^2) - [\mathbb{E}(X) + \mathbb{E}(Y)]^2 \\ &= E(X^2) + 2E(XY) + E(Y^2) - [E(X)]^2 - 2E(X)E(Y) - [E(Y)]^2 \end{aligned}$$

(since X and Y are independent, so $E(XY) = E(X)E(Y)$)
$$\begin{aligned} &= \{E(X^2) - [E(X)]^2\} + \{E(Y^2) - [E(Y)]^2\} \\ &= \mathrm{var}(X) + \mathrm{var}(Y) \end{aligned}$$

For $k = 0, 1, 2, \ldots, n$, we have that

$$\mathbb{P}(X = k \mid X + Y = n) = \frac{\mathbb{P}(X = k, Y = n - k)}{\mathbb{P}(X + Y = n)}$$

(since X and Y are independent)
$$= \frac{\mathbb{P}(X = k)\mathbb{P}(Y = n - k)}{\mathbb{P}(X + Y = n)}$$

(since $X + Y$ has Poisson distribution with parameter $\lambda + \mu$)
$$= \frac{[\frac{1}{k!}\lambda^k e^{-\lambda}][\frac{1}{(n-k)!}\mu^{n-k} e^{-\mu}]}{\frac{1}{n!}(\lambda + \mu)^n e^{-(\lambda+\mu)}}$$

$$= \frac{n! \lambda^k e^{-\lambda} \mu^{n-k} e^{-\mu}}{k!(n-k)!(\lambda + \mu)^n e^{-(\lambda+\mu)}}$$

$$= \binom{n}{k} \frac{\lambda^k \mu^{n-k}}{(\lambda + \mu)^n}$$

For $k = 0, 1, 2, \ldots, n$, we have that

$$\mathbb{E}(X = k \mid X + Y = n) = \sum_{k=0}^{\infty} k \mathbb{P}(X = k \mid X + Y = n)$$

$$= \sum_{k=0}^{n} k \binom{n}{k} \frac{\lambda^k \mu^{n-k}}{(\lambda + \mu)^n}$$

$$= \frac{1}{(\lambda + \mu)^n} \sum_{k=0}^{n} k \binom{n}{k} \lambda^k \mu^{n-k}$$

Use Binomial Theorem for $(\lambda + \mu)^n$

$$(\lambda + \mu)^n = \sum_{k=0}^{n} \binom{n}{k} \lambda^k \mu^{n-k}$$

Take the derivative in the variable λ, we have

$$n(\lambda + \mu)^{n-1} = \sum_{k=0}^{n} k \binom{n}{k} \lambda^{k-1} \mu^{n-k}$$

Multiply both sides by λ, we have

$$n\lambda(\lambda + \mu)^{n-1} = \sum_{k=0}^{n} k \binom{n}{k} \lambda^k \mu^{n-k}$$

Thus

$$\mathbb{E}(X = k \mid X + Y = n) = \frac{1}{(\lambda + \mu)^n} \sum_{k=0}^{n} k \binom{n}{k} \lambda^k \mu^{n-k}$$

$$= \frac{1}{(\lambda + \mu)^n} n\lambda(\lambda + \mu)^{n-1}$$

$$= \frac{n\lambda}{\lambda + \mu}.$$

PROBLEM 4.5.1 (*4.5.8). A fair coin is tossed a random number N of times, giving a total of X heads and Y tails. You showed in Problem 3.6.14 that X and Y are independent if N has the Poisson distribution. Use generating functions to show that the converse is valid too: if X and Y are independent and the generating function $G_N(s)$ of N is assumed to exist for values of s in a neighbourhood of $s = 1$, then N has the Poisson distribution.

SOLUTION. Since the coin is fair, so the probability of getting head is $p = 1/2$. For $= 1.2. \ldots , N$, we define the discrete random variable X_i by

$$X_i = \begin{cases} 1 & \text{if the } i\text{th toss is H,} \\ 0 & \text{if the } i\text{th toss is T.} \end{cases}$$

Each X_i has the Bernoulli distribution with parameter $p = 1/2$ and the probability generating function

$$G_{X_1}(s) = q + ps = \frac{1}{2} + \frac{1}{2}s.$$

By Random sum formula, Theorem 4.36,

$$G_X(s) = G_N(G_{X_1}(s))$$

$$= G_N(\frac{1}{2} + \frac{1}{2}s)$$

Similarly,

$$G_Y(s) = G_N(\frac{1}{2} + \frac{1}{2}s)$$

Since X and Y are independent, so X and $N - X$ are independent (since $Y = N - X$).

$$G_N(s) = G_{X+Y}(s)$$

(since X and Y are independent)
$$= G_X(s)G_Y(s)$$

(since $G_X(s) = G_Y(s)$)
$$= [G_X(s)]^2$$

$$= [G_N(\frac{1}{2} + \frac{1}{2}s)]^2$$

Let $G_N(s) = G(1 - s)$. Then $G_N(s) = G(1 - s)$. Thus

$$G_N(\frac{1}{2} + \frac{1}{2}s) = G(1 - \frac{1}{2} - \frac{1}{2}s)$$
$$= G(\frac{1}{2} - \frac{1}{2}s)$$
$$= G(\frac{1 - s}{2})$$

But since $G_N(s) = [G_N(\frac{1}{2} + \frac{1}{2}s)]^2$, so $G(1 - s) = [G(\frac{1 - s}{2})]^2$. Thus the function G has the property

$$G(t) = [G(\frac{t}{2})]^2 \qquad (1)$$

Use (1) n times, we obtain

$$G(t) = [G(\frac{t}{2})]^2 = [G(\frac{t}{2^2})]^{2^2} = \cdots = [G(\frac{t}{2^n})]^{2^n}$$

Use the Maclaurin expansion, we have

$$G_N(1 - s) = G_N(1) - G_N'(1) + o(s^2)$$

It implies that

$$G(s) = G_N(1) - G_N'(1)s + o(s^2)$$
$$= 1 - \mu s + o(s^2)$$

where $\mu = G_N'(1) = \mathbb{E}(N)$. Thus

$$G(s) = [G(\frac{s}{2^n})]^{2n} = [1 - \mu\frac{s}{2^n} + o(\frac{s^2}{4^n})] \qquad (2)$$

Sicne (2) holds for any s, so

$$G(s) = \lim_{n \to \infty} [1 - \frac{\mu s}{2^n} + o(\frac{s^2}{4^n})] = e^{-\mu s}$$

Thus

$$G_N(s) = G(1 - s) = e^{-\mu(1-s)} = e^{\mu(s-1)}$$

By Uniqueness theorem for probability generating functions, Theorem 4.13, N has the Poisson distribution with parameter μ.

PROBLEM 4.5.2 (4.5.9). *Coupon-collecting problem.* Each packet of a certain breakfast cereal contains one token, coloured either red, blue, or green. The coloured tokens are distributed randomly among the packets, each colour being equally likely. Let X be the random variable which takes the value j when I find my first red token in the jth packet which I open. Obtain the probability generating function of X, and hence find its expectation.
More generally, suppose that there are tokens of m different colours, all equally likely. Let Y be the random variable which takes the value j when I first obtain a full set, of at least one token of each colour, when I open my jth packet. Find the generating function of Y, and show that its expectation is $m(1 + \dfrac{1}{2} + \dfrac{1}{3} + \cdots + \dfrac{1}{m})$.
(Oxford 1985M)

SOLUTION. The the random variable X has the geometric distribution with parameter $p = \dfrac{1}{3}$, and consequently X has probability generating function

$$\begin{aligned}
G_X(s) &= \frac{ps}{1 - (1-p)s} \\
&= \frac{\frac{1}{3}s}{1 - (1 - \frac{1}{3})s} \\
&= \frac{s}{3 - 2s}.
\end{aligned}$$

Hence

$$\begin{aligned}
\mathbb{E}(X) &= G'_X(1) \\
&= \frac{3}{(3 - 2s)^2}\Big|_{s=1} \\
&= 3.
\end{aligned}$$

For $i = 0, 1, 2, \ldots, m - 1$, let Y_i be the additional number of tokens collected, after obtaining i distinct colours, before a new colour is collected. Thus each Y_i has the geometric distribution with parameter $(m - i)/m$ having probability generating function

$$G_{Y_i}(s) = \frac{\left(\frac{m-i}{m}\right)s}{1 - \left(1 - \frac{m-i}{m}\right)s}$$

$$= \frac{(m-i)s}{m - is}$$

for $i = 0, 1, 2, \ldots, m - 1$. Thus

$$Y = Y_0 + Y_1 + Y_2 + \cdots + Y_{m-1}$$

has probability generating function

$$G_Y(s) = G_{Y_0}(s)G_{Y_1}(s)G_{Y_2}(s)\cdots G_{Y_{m-1}}(s)$$

$$= \frac{(m-0)s}{m-0s} \cdot \frac{(m-1)s}{m-1s} \cdot \frac{(m-2)s}{m-2s} \cdots \frac{[m-(m-1)]s}{m-(m-1)s} \cdot$$

$$= s \cdot \frac{(m-1)s}{m-s} \cdot \frac{(m-2)s}{m-2s} \cdots \frac{s}{m-(m-1)s}$$

$$= \prod_{i=0}^{m-1} \frac{(m-i)s}{m-is}$$

We have that

$$G_Y'(s) = \frac{d}{ds} \prod_{i=0}^{m-1} \frac{(m-i)s}{m-is}$$

$$= \sum_{i=0}^{m-1} \left[\frac{d}{ds} \frac{(m-i)s}{m-is} \prod_{j\neq i} \frac{(m-j)s}{m-js}\right]$$

$$= \sum_{i=0}^{m-1} \left[\frac{m(m-i)}{(m-is)^2} \prod_{j\neq i} \frac{(m-j)s}{m-js}\right]$$

so that

$$G_Y'(1) = \sum_{i=0}^{m-1} \left[\frac{m(m-i)}{(m-is)^2} \prod_{j \neq i} \frac{(m-j)s}{m-js} \right] \Bigg|_{s=1}$$

$$= \sum_{i=0}^{m-1} \left[\frac{m(m-i)}{(m-i)^2} \prod_{j \neq i} \frac{m-j}{m-j} \right]$$

$$= \sum_{i=0}^{m-1} \left[\frac{m}{m-i} \prod_{j \neq i} \frac{m-j}{m-j} \right]$$

$$= \sum_{i=0}^{m-1} \frac{m}{m-i}$$

$$= m \sum_{i=0}^{m-1} \frac{1}{m-i}$$

$$= m \left(1 + \frac{1}{2} + \frac{1}{3} + \cdots + \frac{1}{m} \right)$$

Thus $\mathbb{E}(Y) = G_Y'(1) = m \left(1 + \dfrac{1}{2} + \dfrac{1}{3} + \cdots + \dfrac{1}{m} \right)$.

PROBLEM (4.5.10). Define the mean value of a discrete random variable and the probability generating function ϕ. Show that the mean value is $\phi'(1)$. If $\phi(s)$ has the form $p(s)/q(s)$ show that the mean value is $(p'(1) - q'(1))/q(1)$.

Two duellists, A and B, fire at each other in turn until one hits the other. Each duellist has the same probability of obtaining a hit with each shot fired, these probabilities being a for A and b for B. If A fires the first shot, calculate the probability that A wins the duel. Find also the probability distribution of the number of shots fired before the duel terminates. What is the expected number of shots fired? (Oxford 1976M)

SOLUTION. If X is a discrete random variable, the **expectation** of X is denoted by $\mathbb{E}(X)$ and defined by

$$\mathbb{E}(X) = \sum_{x \in \mathrm{Im}\, X} x \mathbb{P}(X = x)$$

whenever this sum converges absolutely, in that $\sum_x |x \mathbb{P}(X = x)| < \infty$.

The **probability generating function** (or **pgf**) of X is the function $\phi(s)$ defined by

$$\phi(s) = p_0 + p_1 s + p_2 s^2 + \cdots,$$

for all values of s for which the right-hand side converges absolutely.

Thus

$$\phi'(s) = \frac{d}{ds} \sum_{k=0}^{\infty} s^k \mathbb{P}(X = k)$$

$$= \sum_{k=0}^{\infty} \frac{d}{ds} s^k \mathbb{P}(X = k)$$

$$= \sum_{k=1}^{\infty} k s^{k-1} \mathbb{P}(X = k)$$

so that

$$\phi'(1) = \sum_{k=1}^{\infty} k 1^{k-1} \mathbb{P}(X = k)$$

$$= \sum_{x \in \text{Im } X} x \mathbb{P}(X = x)$$

where $\text{Im } X = \{0, 1, 2, \ldots\}$. Thus $\phi'(1) = \mathbb{E}(X)$ as required.

Let X has probability generating function $\phi(s)$ of the form $p(s)/q(s)$. Then

$$\phi(1) = \frac{p(1)}{q(1)}$$

$$= \sum_{x \in \text{Im } X} \mathbb{P}(X = x)$$

$$= 1$$

so that $p(1) = q(1)$. Hence

$$\phi'(1) = \frac{p'(1)q(1) - p(1)q'(1)}{q^2(1)}$$

(since $p(1) = q(1)$)

$$= \frac{[p'(1) - q'(1)]q(1)}{q^2(1)}$$

$$= \frac{p'(1) - q'(1)}{q(1)}$$

Thus $\mathbb{E}(X) = (p'(1) - q'(1))/q(1)$.

Let X be the random variable that takes value k at the kth shot and A wins the duel. It is easy to see that

$$\mathbb{P}(\text{A wins}) = \sum_{k=0}^{\infty} \mathbb{P}(X = 2k+1)$$

$$= \sum_{k=0}^{\infty} (1-a)^k (1-b)^k a$$

$$= \sum_{k=0}^{\infty} a[(1-a)^k(1-b)]^k$$

$$= \frac{a}{1-(1-a)(1-b)}$$

$$= \frac{a}{a+b-ab}.$$

Let Y be the random variable that takes value k when the duel terminate at kth shot. Thus

$$\mathbb{P}(Y = n) = \begin{cases} (1-a)^k(1-b)^{k-1}b & \text{if } n = 2k \\ (1-a)^k(1-b)^k a & \text{if } n = 2k+1 \end{cases}$$

for $k = 0, 1, 2, \ldots$. We have that

$$G_Y(s) = \sum_{k=1}^{\infty} (1-a)^k(1-b)^{k-1}bs^{2k} + \sum_{k=0}^{\infty}(1-a)^k(1-b)^k a s^{2k+1}$$

$$= \frac{b}{1-b} \sum_{k=1}^{\infty}(1-a)^k(1-b)^k s^{2k} + as \sum_{k=0}^{\infty}(1-a)^k(1-b)^k s^{2k}$$

$$= \frac{b}{1-b} \sum_{k=1}^{\infty}[(1-a)(1-b)s^2]^k + as \sum_{k=0}^{\infty}[(1-a)(1-b)s^2]^k$$

$$= \frac{b}{1-b} \cdot \frac{(1-a)(1-b)s^2}{1-(1-a)(1-b)s^2} + as \cdot \frac{1}{1-(1-a)(1-b)s^2}$$

$$= \frac{b(1-a)s^2 + as}{1-(1-a)(1-b)s^2}$$

so that

$$\mathbb{E}(Y) = G_Y'(1) = \frac{2b(1-a) + a + 2(1-a)(1-b)}{1-(1-a)(1-b)}$$

$$= \frac{2-a}{a+b-ab}$$

PROBLEM (4.5.11). There is a random number N of foreign objects in my soup, with mean μ and finite variance. Each object is a fly with probability p, and otherwise a spider; different objects have independent types. Let F be the number of flies and S the number of spiders.

(a) Show that $G_F(s) = G_N(ps + 1 - p)$. [You should present a clear statement of any general result used.]

(b) Suppose N has the Poisson distribution with parameter μ. Show that F has the Poisson distribution with parameter μp, and that F and S are independent.

(c) Let $p = \dfrac{1}{2}$ and suppose F and S are independent. [You are given nothing about the distribution of N.] Show that $G_N(s) = G_N(\frac{1}{2}[1 + s])^2$. By working with the function $H(s) = G_N(1 - s)$ or otherwise, deduce that N has a Poisson distribution.

You may assume that $[1 + (x/n) + o(n^{-1})]^n \to e^x$ as $n \to \infty$. (Cambridge 2002)

SOLUTION. (a) For $= 1.2. \ldots, N$, we define the discrete random variable F_i by

$$F_i = \begin{cases} 1 & \text{if the } i\text{th object is a fly,} \\ 0 & \text{if the } i\text{th object is a spider.} \end{cases}$$

Each F_i has the Bernoulli distribution with parameter p and the probability generating function

$$G_{F_1}(s) = ps + q = ps + 1 - p$$

Since N and the F_i are independent, we conclude from the random sum formula (4.37) that the total number $F = F_1 + F_2 + \cdots + F_N$ of flies has probability generating function

$$\begin{aligned} G_F(s) &= G_N(G_{F_1}(s)) \\ &= G_N(ps + 1 - p) \end{aligned}$$

(b) The number N of of foreign objects in my soup has the Poisson distribution with parameter μ, and consequently N has probability generating function

$$G_N(s) = e^{\mu(s-1)}.$$

Hence

$$G_F(s) = G_N(ps + 1 - p)$$
$$= e^{\mu(ps+1-p-1)}$$
$$= e^{\mu p(s-1)}.$$

By Uniqueness theorem for probability generating functions, Theorem 4.13, F has the Poisson distribution with parameter μp.

For $= 1.2. \ldots, N$, we define the discrete random variable S_i by

$$S_i = \begin{cases} 1 & \text{if the } i\text{th object is a spider,} \\ 0 & \text{if the } i\text{th object is a fly.} \end{cases}$$

Each S_i has the Bernoulli distribution with parameter $1 - p$ and the probability generating function

$$G_{S_1}(s) = (1 - p)s + p.$$

Since N and the S_i are independent, we conclude from the random sum formula (4.37) that the total number $S = S_1 + S_2 + \cdots + S_N$ of flies has probability generating function

$$G_F(s) = G_N(G_{S_1}(s))$$
$$= G_N((1 - p)s + p)$$
$$= e^{\mu[(1-p)s+p-1]}$$
$$= e^{\mu(1-p)(s-1)}.$$

By Uniqueness theorem for probability generating functions, Theorem 4.13, S has the Poisson distribution with parameter $\mu(1 - p)$.

We have

$$\begin{aligned}
\mathbb{P}(F = k, S = l) &= \mathbb{P}(F = k, N = k + l) \\
&= \mathbb{P}(F = k \mid N = k + l)\mathbb{P}(N = k + l) \\
&= [\binom{k + l}{k}p^k(1 - p)^l][\frac{1}{(k + l)!}\mu^{k+l}e^{-\mu}] \\
&= \frac{(k + l)!}{k!l!}p^k(1 - p)^l\frac{1}{(k + l)!}\mu^{k+l}e^{-\mu} \\
&= \frac{1}{k!l!}p^k(1 - p)^l\mu^k\mu^l e^{-\mu p}e^{-\mu(1-p)} \\
&= \frac{1}{k!}(\mu p)^k e^{-\mu p}\frac{1}{l!}[\mu(1 - p)]^l e^{-\mu(1-p)} \\
&= \mathbb{P}(F = k)\mathbb{P}(S = l).
\end{aligned}$$

Hence F and S are independent.

(c) Let $p = \frac{1}{2}$. Since $G_F(s) = G_N(ps + 1 - p)$ and $G_S(s) = G_N([1 - p]s + p)$, it follows that

$$G_F(s) = G_N(\frac{1}{2}[1 + s])$$

and

$$G_S(s) = G_N(\frac{1}{2}[1 + s]).$$

Since F and S are independent, so are F and $N - F$ are independent (since $S = N - F$).

$$\begin{aligned}
G_N(s) &= G_{F+S}(s) \\
&= G_F(s)G_S(s) \\
&= [G_F(s)]^2 \\
&= \{G_N(\frac{1}{2}[1 + s])\}^2
\end{aligned}$$

(since F and S are independent)

(since $G_F(s) = G_S(s)$)

Let $H(s) = G_N(1 - s)$. Thus

$$G_N(\frac{1}{2} + \frac{1}{2}s) = H(1 - \frac{1}{2} - \frac{1}{2}s)$$
$$= H(\frac{1}{2} - \frac{1}{2}s)$$
$$= H(\frac{1-s}{2})$$

But since $G_N(s) = [G_N(\frac{1}{2} + \frac{1}{2}s)]^2$, so $H(1-s) = [H(\frac{1-s}{2})]^2$. Thus the function H has the property

$$H(t) = [H(\frac{t}{2})]^2 \qquad (1)$$

use (1) n times, we obtain

$$H(t) = [H(\frac{t}{2})]^2 = [H(\frac{t}{2^2})]^{2^2} = \cdots = [H(\frac{t}{2^n})]^{2^n}$$

Use the Maclaurin expansion, we have

$$G_N(1-s) = G_N(1) - G_N'(1) + o(s^2)$$

This implies that

$$H(s) = G_N(1) - G_N'(1)s + o(s^2)$$
$$= 1 - \mu s + o(s^2)$$

where $\mu = G_N'(1) = \mathbb{E}(N)$. Thus

$$H(s) = [H(\frac{s}{2^n})]^{2n} = [1 - \mu\frac{s}{2^n} + o(\frac{s^2}{4^n})] \qquad (2)$$

Sicne (2) holds for any s, so

$$H(s) = \lim_{n \to \infty} [1 - \frac{\mu s}{2^n} + o(\frac{s^2}{4^n})] = e^{-\mu s}$$

Thus

$G_N(s) = H(1-s) = e^{-\mu(1-s)} = e^{\mu(s-1)}$. By Uniqueness theorem for probability generating functions, Theorem 4.13, N has the Poisson distribution with parameter μ.

CHAPTER 5

Distribution functions and density functions

5.1. Distribution functions

EXERCISE (5.11). Let X be a random variable taking integer values such that $\mathbb{P}(X = k) = p_k$ for $k = \ldots, -1, 0, 1, \ldots$. Show that the distribution function of X satisfies
$$F_X(b) - F_X(a) = p_{a+1} + p_{a+2} + \ldots + p_b$$
for all integers a, b with $a < b$.

SOLUTION. For $a < b$,

$$F_X(b) - F_X(a) = \mathbb{P}(a < X \leq b)$$
$$= \mathbb{P}\left(\bigcup_{k=a+1}^{b} (X = k) \right)$$
$$= \sum_{k=a+1}^{b} \mathbb{P}(X = k)$$
$$= \sum_{k=a+1}^{b} p_k$$
$$= p_{a+1} + p_{a+2} + \ldots + p_b.$$

EXERCISE (5.12). If X is a random variable and c is a real number such that $\mathbb{P}(X = c) > 0$, show that the distribution function $F_X(x)$ of X is discontinuous at the point $x = c$. Is the converse true?

SOLUTION. For $\epsilon > 0$,

$$\mathbb{P}(X = c) = \mathbb{P}(\{X \leq c\} \backslash \{X < c\})$$
$$= \mathbb{P}(X \leq c) - \mathbb{P}(X < c)$$
$$= \mathbb{P}(X \leq c) - \lim_{\epsilon \to 0} \mathbb{P}(X \leq c - \epsilon)$$
$$= \lim_{\epsilon \to 0} [\mathbb{P}(X \leq c) - \mathbb{P}(X \leq c - \epsilon)]$$

since the event $\{X \le c - \epsilon\}$ is a subset of the event $\{X \le c\}$. Hence

$$\mathbb{P}(X = c) = \lim_{\epsilon \to 0}[F_X(c) - F_X(c - \epsilon)].$$

Since $\mathbb{P}(X = c) > 0$, it follows that $\lim_{\epsilon \to 0}[F_X(c) - F_X(c - \epsilon)] > 0$ so that $F_X(c - \epsilon)$ does not approach to $F_X(c)$ as $\epsilon \uparrow 0$.

For $x < c$, the event $\{X \le x\}$ is a subset of the event $\{X < c\}$. Hence

$$
\begin{aligned}
\mathbb{P}(X \le x) &\le \mathbb{P}(X < c) \\
&= \mathbb{P}(\{X \le c\} \backslash \{X = c\}) \\
&= \mathbb{P}(X \le c) - \mathbb{P}(X = c) \\
&= F_X(c) - \mathbb{P}(X = c) \\
&< F_X(c)
\end{aligned}
$$

(since $\mathbb{P}(X = c) > 0$)

so that

$$F_X(x) < F_X(c)$$

for any $x < c$. This implies that

$$\lim_{\substack{x < c \\ x \to c}} F_X(x) < F_X(c).$$

Therefore the distribution function $F_X(x)$ of X is discontinuous at the point $x = c$

The converse is true since suppose that the distribution function $F_X(x)$ of X is discontinuous at the point $x = c$. Then

$$
\begin{aligned}
\mathbb{P}(X = c) &= \mathbb{P}(X \le c) - \mathbb{P}(X < c) \\
&= F_X(c) - \lim_{\substack{x < c \\ x \to c}} F_X(x)
\end{aligned}
$$

Note that $\lim_{\substack{x < c \\ x \to c}} F_X(x) < F_X(c)$ since $F_X(x)$ of X is discontinuous at the point $x = c$.

EXERCISE (5.13). Express the distribution function of $Y = \max\{0, X\}$ in terms of the distribution function F_X of X.

SOLUTION. For any $\omega \in \Omega$, we have

$$Y(\omega) = \max(0, X(\omega))$$
$$\geq 0.$$

Hence for $y < 0$,

$$\{Y \leq y\} = \varnothing$$

so that

$$\mathbb{P}(Y \leq y) = \mathbb{P}(\varnothing)$$
$$= 0.$$

Thus $F_y(y) = 0$ for any $y < 0$. If $y \geq 0$, then

$$\{Y \leq y\} = \max((0, X) \leq y)$$
$$= \{X \leq y\}$$

so $F_y(y) = F_X(y)$. Hence

$$F_Y(y) = \begin{cases} 0 & \text{if } x < 0, \\ F_X(y) & \text{if } y \leq 0. \end{cases}$$

EXERCISE (5.14). The real number m is called a *median* of the random variable X if

$$\mathbb{P}(X < m) \leq \frac{1}{2} \leq P(X \leq m).$$

Show that every random variable has at least one median.

5.2. Examples of distribution functions

EXERCISE (5.18). Show that if F_1 and F_2 are distribution functions, then so is the function $F(x) = \alpha F_1(x) + (1 - \alpha)F_2(x)$ for any α satisfying $0 \leq \alpha \leq 1$.

SOLUTION. We need to check that F satisfies (5.5) A non-negative combination of monotonic non-decreasing functions, is monotonic non-decreasing. Hence F is monotonic non-decreasing.

We need to check that F satisfies (5.6). We have that

$$\lim_{x \to -\infty} F(x) = \lim_{x \to -\infty} [\alpha F_1(x) + (1 - \alpha)F_2(x)]$$
$$= \alpha \lim_{x \to -\infty} F_1(x) + (1 - \alpha) \lim_{x \to -\infty} F_2(x)]$$

(since $\lim_{x \to -\infty} F_i(x) = 0$ for $i = 1, 2$) $= 0$.

We need to check that F satisfies (5.7). We have that

$$\lim_{x \to \infty} F(x) = \lim_{x \to \infty} [\alpha F_1(x) + (1 - \alpha) F_2(x)]$$

$$= \alpha \lim_{x \to \infty} F_1(x) + (1 - \alpha) \lim_{x \to \infty} F_2(x)]$$

(since $\lim_{x \to \infty} F_i(x) = 1$ for $i = 1, 2$) $\quad = \alpha + (1 - \alpha)$

$$= 1$$

We need to check that F satisfies (5.8). We have that

$$\lim_{\epsilon \downarrow 0} F(x + \epsilon) = \lim_{\epsilon \downarrow 0} [\alpha F_1(x + \epsilon) + (1 - \alpha) F_2(x + \epsilon)]$$

$$= \alpha \lim_{\epsilon \downarrow 0} F_1(x + \epsilon) + (1 - \alpha) \lim_{\epsilon \downarrow 0} F_2(x + \epsilon)]$$

(since F_i is continous from the right for $i = 1, 2$)

$$= \alpha F_1(x) + (1 - \alpha) F_2(x)$$

$$= F(x).$$

Hence F is a distribution function.

EXERCISE (5.19). Let

(for $x \in \mathbb{R}$.) $\qquad\qquad F(x) = c \int_{-\infty}^{x} e^{-|u|} \, du$

For what value of c is F a distribution function?

SOLUTION. We have that

$$\lim_{x \to \infty} F(x) = c \int_{-\infty}^{+\infty} e^{-|u|} \, du$$

$$= c[\int_{-\infty}^{0} e^{-|u|} \, du + \int_{0}^{+\infty} e^{-|u|} \, du]$$

$$= c[e^{u}\big|_{-\infty}^{0} + e^{-u}\big|_{0}^{\infty}]$$

(since $\lim_{u \to -\infty} e^{u} = \lim_{u \to \infty} e^{-u} = 0$) $\quad = c[1 - (-1)]$

$$= 2c$$

The function $F(x)$ satisfies (5.5), (5.6), and (5.8), so $F(x)$ is a distribution function if and only if $\lim_{x \to \infty} F(x) = 1 \iff 2c = 1 \iff c = \dfrac{1}{2}$.

5.3. Continuous random variables

EXERCISE (5.30). A random variable X has density function

$$f(x) = \begin{cases} 2x & \text{if } 0 < x < 1, \\ 0 & \text{otherwise.} \end{cases}$$

Find the distribution function of X.

SOLUTION. We have that

$$F(x) = \mathbb{P}(X \leq x)$$
$$= \int_{-\infty}^{x} f(u)\, du.$$

If $x < 0$, then

$$F(x) = \int_{-\infty}^{x} 0\, du$$
$$= 0.$$

If $0 \leq x < 1$, then

$$F(x) = \int_{-\infty}^{0} f(u)\, du + \int_{0}^{x} f(u)\, du$$
$$= \int_{-\infty}^{0} 0\, du + \int_{0}^{x} 2u\, du$$
$$= 0 + x^2$$
$$= x^2.$$

If $x \geq 1$, then

$$F(x) = \int_{-\infty}^{0} f(u)\, du + \int_{0}^{1} f(u)\, du + \int_{1}^{x} f(u)\, du$$
$$= \int_{-\infty}^{0} 0\, du + \int_{0}^{1} 2u\, du + \int_{1}^{x} 0\, du$$
$$= 0 + 1 + 0$$
$$= 1.$$

Thus the required distribution function is

$$F(x) = \begin{cases} 0 & \text{if } x < 0, \\ x^2 & \text{if } 0 \le x < 1, \\ 1 & \text{if } x \ge 1. \end{cases}$$

Note that $F(x)$ increases monotonically from 0 to 1 as is required for a distribution function. It should also be noted that $F(x)$ in this case is continuous.

EXERCISE (5.31). If X has density function

(for $x \in \mathbb{R}$,) $$f(x) = \frac{1}{2}e^{-|x|}$$

find the distribution function of X. This is called the *bilateral* (or *double*) *exponential* distribution.

SOLUTION. We have that

$$F(x) = \mathbb{P}(X \le x)$$
$$= \int_{-\infty}^{x} f(u)\,du.$$

If $x \le 0$, then

$$F(x) = \int_{-\infty}^{x} \frac{1}{2}e^{u}\,du$$
$$= \frac{1}{2}e^{x}$$

If $x > 0$, then

$$F(x) = \int_{-\infty}^{0} f(u)\,du + \int_{0}^{x} f(u)\,du$$
$$= \int_{-\infty}^{0} \frac{1}{2}e^{u}\,du + \int_{0}^{x} \frac{1}{2}e^{-u}\,du$$
$$= \frac{1}{2} - \frac{1}{2}e^{-u}\Big|_{0}^{x}$$
$$= \frac{1}{2} - \frac{1}{2}e^{-x} + \frac{1}{2}$$
$$= 1 - \frac{1}{2}e^{-x}$$

Thus the required distribution function is

$$F(x) = \begin{cases} \dfrac{1}{2}e^x & \text{if } x \le 0, \\ 1 - \dfrac{1}{2}e^{-x} & \text{if } x > 0. \end{cases}$$

Note that $F(x)$ increases monotonically from 0 to 1 as is required for a distribution function. It should also be noted that $F(x)$ in this case is continuous.

EXERCISE (5.32). If X has distribution function

$$F(x) = \begin{cases} \dfrac{1}{2(1+x^2)} & \text{for } -\infty < x \le 0, \\ \dfrac{1+2x^2}{2(1+x^2)} & \text{for } 0 < x < \infty, \end{cases}$$

show that X is continuous and find its density function.

SOLUTION. Let X have distribution function

$$F(x) = \begin{cases} \dfrac{1}{2(1+x^2)} & \text{for } -\infty < x \le 0, \\ \dfrac{1+2x^2}{2(1+x^2)} & \text{for } 0 < x < \infty. \end{cases}$$

Since

$$\lim_{x \downarrow 0} F(x) = \lim_{x \uparrow 0} F(x) = F(0),$$

it follows that F is is continuous at $x = 0$, and hence for all x and

$$F'(x) = \begin{cases} -\dfrac{x}{(1+x^2)^2} & \text{for } -\infty < x < 0, \\ \dfrac{x}{(1+x^2)^2} & \text{for } 0 < x < \infty. \end{cases}$$

Moroever,

$$\lim_{x \downarrow 0} \frac{F(x) - F(0)}{x} = \lim_{x \downarrow 0} \frac{-\frac{x}{(1+x^2)^2} - \frac{1}{2}}{x}$$

$$= \lim_{x \downarrow 0} \frac{1 + 2x^2 - (1 + x^2)}{2x(1 + x^2)}$$

$$= \lim_{x \downarrow 0} \frac{x}{2(1 + x^2)}$$

$$= 0$$

and

$$\lim_{x\uparrow 0} \frac{F(x) - F(0)}{x} = \lim_{x\uparrow 0} \frac{\frac{1}{(1+x^2)^2} - \frac{1}{2}}{x}$$

$$= \lim_{x\downarrow 0} \frac{1 - (1 + x^2)}{2x(1 + x^2)}$$

$$= \lim_{x\downarrow 0} \frac{-x}{2(1 + x^2)}$$

$$= 0$$

so that

$$\lim_{x\to 0} \frac{F(x) - F(0)}{x} = 0$$

and hence $F'(0) = 0$.

Let

$$f(x) = \begin{cases} -\dfrac{x}{(1 + x^2)^2} & \text{if } x < 0, \\ 0 & \text{if } x = 0, \\ \dfrac{x}{(1 + x^2)^2} & \text{if } x > 0. \end{cases}$$

Since f is a non-negative function and $F'(x) = f(x)$ for all x and we have

(by Newton-Leibniz formula) $\qquad \displaystyle\int_{-\infty}^{x} f(u)\,du = F(u)\big|_{-\infty}^{x}$

(since $F(-\infty) = \displaystyle\lim_{x\to-\infty} F(u) = \lim_{u\to-\infty} \frac{1}{2(1 + x^2)} = 0$) $\qquad = F(x)$

so that

$$F(x) = \int_{-\infty}^{x} f(u)\,du.$$

for $x \in \mathbb{R}$. This implies that X is a continuous random variable and its density function is $f(x)$ be defined by

$$f(x) = \begin{cases} -\dfrac{x}{(1 + x^2)^2} & \text{if } x < 0, \\ 0 & \text{if } x = 0, \\ \dfrac{x}{(1 + x^2)^2} & \text{if } x > 0. \end{cases}$$

EXERCISE (5.33). Find the distribution function of the so-called 'extreme value' density function

(for $x \in \mathbb{R}$.) $$f(x) = \exp(-x - e^{-x})$$

SOLUTION. We have that

$$
\begin{aligned}
F(x) &= \mathbb{P}(X \le x) \\
&= \int_{-\infty}^{x} f(u)\, du \\
&= \int_{-\infty}^{x} e^{-u - e^{-u}}\, du \\
&= \int_{-\infty}^{x} e^{-u} e^{-e^{-u}}\, du \\
\text{(since } d(-e^{-u}) = (-e^{-u})'\, du = e^{-u}\, du \text{)} \qquad &= \int_{-\infty}^{x} e^{-e^{-u}}\, d(-e^{-u}) \\
&= e^{-e^{-u}}\Big|_{-\infty}^{x} \\
&= e^{-e^{-x}} - \lim_{u \to -\infty} e^{-e^{-u}} \\
\text{(since } \lim_{u \to -\infty} e^{-e^{-u}} = 0 \text{)} \qquad &= e^{-e^{-x}} \\
\text{(for } x \in \mathbb{R} \text{.)} \qquad &= \exp(-e^{-x})
\end{aligned}
$$

5.4. Some common density functions

EXERCISE (5.45). For what values of its parameters is the gamma distribution also an exponential distribution?

SOLUTION. The gamma distribution also an exponential distribution if and only if

$$\frac{1}{\Gamma(w)} \lambda^w x^{w-1} e^{-\lambda x} = \lambda e^{-\lambda x}$$

Compare both sides, we have $w - 1$ so that $w = 1$. Then

$$
\begin{aligned}
\Gamma(1) &= \int_{0}^{\infty} e^{-x}\, dx \\
&= -e^{-x}\Big|_{0}^{\infty} \\
&= 1.
\end{aligned}
$$

So when $w = 1$,

$$\frac{1}{\Gamma(w)}\lambda^w x^{w-1}e^{-\lambda x} = \lambda e^{-\lambda x}$$

for $x > 0$. Thus the gamma distribution also an exponential distribution if and only if $w = 1$, arbitrary positive λ.

EXERCISE (5.46). Show that the gamma function $\Gamma(w)$ satisfies $\Gamma(w) = (w-1)\Gamma(w-1)$ for $w > 1$, and deduce that $\Gamma(n) = (n-1)!$ for $n = 1, 2, 3, \ldots$.

SOLUTION. We will use integration by parts with:

$$u = x^{w-1} \text{ and } dv = e^{-x}\,dx$$

to get

$$du = (w-1)x^{w-2}\,dx \text{ and } v = -e^{-x}.$$

Then, the integration by parts gives us:

$$\Gamma(w) = \lim_{b\to\infty}\left[-x^{w-1}e^{-x}\right]_{x=0}^{x=b} + (w-1)\int_0^\infty x^{w-2}e^{-x}\,dx.$$

Evaluating at $x = b$ and $x = 0$ for the first term, and using the definition of the gamma function (provided $w - 1 > 0$) for the second term, we have:

$$\Gamma(w) = -\lim_{b\to\infty}\left[\frac{b^{w-1}}{e^b}\right] + (w-1)\Gamma(w-1).$$

Since $b \to \infty$, we can consider $b > 1$. Take $m \in \mathbb{N}$ and $m > w - 1$, we have

$$0 < b^{w-1} < b^m.$$

Thus

$$0 < \frac{b^{w-1}}{e^b} < \frac{b^m}{e^b}.$$

Using L'Hospital's Rule m times, we obtain

$$\lim_{b\to\infty}\frac{b^m}{e^b} = \lim_{b\to\infty}\frac{m!}{e^b} = 0.$$

By squeeze theorem,

$$\lim_{b\to\infty}\frac{b^{w-1}}{e^b} = 0.$$

Thus

$$\Gamma(w) = (w-1)\Gamma(w-1).$$

By the fact that $\Gamma(w) = (w-1)\Gamma(w-1)$,

$$\begin{aligned}
\Gamma(n) &= (n-1)\Gamma(n-1) \\
&= (n-1)(n-2)\Gamma(n-2) \\
&= (n-1)(n-2)(n-3)\cdots(2)(1)\Gamma(1)
\end{aligned}$$

And, since by the definition of the gamma function,

$$\begin{aligned}
\Gamma(1) &= \int_0^\infty x^{1-1}e^{-x}\,dx \\
&= \int_0^\infty e^{-x}dx \\
&= 1,
\end{aligned}$$

we have

$$\Gamma(n) = (n-1)!$$

as was to be proved.

We can take the exponent and the natural log of the numerator without changing the limit. Doing so, we get:

$$-\lim_{b\to\infty}\left[\frac{b^{w-1}}{e^b}\right] = -\lim_{b\to\infty}\left\{\frac{\exp[(w-1)\ln b]}{\exp(b)}\right\}$$ Then, because both the numerator and denominator are exponents, we can write the limit as:

$$-\lim_{b\to\infty}\left[\frac{b^{w-1}}{e^b}\right] = -\lim_{b\to\infty}\left\{\exp[(w-1)\ln b - b]\right\}$$ Manipulating the limit a bit more, so that we can easily apply L'Hôpital's Rule, we get:

$$-\lim_{b\to\infty}\left[\frac{b^{w-1}}{e^b}\right] = -\lim_{b\to\infty}\left\{\exp\left[(w-1)b\left(\frac{\ln b}{b}-1\right)\right]\right\}$$

EXERCISE (5.47). Let

$$I = \int_{-\infty}^\infty e^{-x^2}\,dx.$$

By changing variables to polar coordinates, show that

$$I^2 = \int\int_{\mathbb{R}^2} e^{-x^2-y^2}\,dxdy = \int_{\theta=0}^{2\pi}\int_{r=0}^\infty e^{-r^2}r\,dr\,d\theta,$$

and deduce that $I = \sqrt{\pi}$.

SOLUTION. We have that

$$I = \int_{-\infty}^{\infty} e^{-x^2}\, dx.$$

It obviously does not matter what we call the variable, so we also have

$$I = \int_{-\infty}^{\infty} e^{-y^2}\, dy.$$

We can now multiply these two expressions together to get

$$I^2 = \int_{-\infty}^{\infty} e^{-x^2}\, dx \int_{-\infty}^{\infty} e^{-y^2}\, dy$$

(by Fubini's theorem)

$$= \int_{-\infty}^{\infty}\int_{-\infty}^{\infty} e^{-x^2-y^2}\, dxdy$$

$$= \int\int_{\mathbb{R}^2} e^{-x^2-y^2}\, dxdy.$$

We can rewrite this using polar coordinates, noting that $x^2 + y^2 = r^2$ and $dxdy = r\, dr\, d\theta$. We get

$$I^2 = \int_{\theta=0}^{2\pi}\int_{r=0}^{\infty} re^{-r^2}\, dr\, d\theta$$

$$= 2\pi \int_{r=0}^{\infty} re^{-r^2}\, dr.$$

We now substitute $u = r^2$, so u also runs from 0 to ∞ and $du = 2r\, dr$. The integral becomes

$$I^2 = 2\pi \int_{u=0}^{\infty} e^{-u} \cdot \frac{1}{2}\, du$$

$$= \pi[-e^{-u}]_{u=0}^{\infty}$$

$$= \pi((-0)-(-1))$$

$$= \pi$$

so $I = \sqrt{\pi}$.

$f(x) = \dfrac{1}{\sqrt{2\pi}} e^{-\frac{x^2}{2}}$ is the probability density functio of the random variable X having the standard normal distribution. So

$$\int_{-\infty}^{\infty} \frac{1}{\sqrt{2\pi}} e^{-\frac{x^2}{2}} = 1$$

The changing variable to $x = \sqrt{2}t$ then $x^2 = 2t^2$, $dx = \sqrt{2}\,dt$ and the intagral becomes

$$\int_{-\infty}^{\infty} \frac{1}{\sqrt{2\pi}} e^{-t^2} \sqrt{2}\,dt = 1$$

This implies that

$$\int_{-\infty}^{\infty} e^{-t^2}\,dt = \sqrt{\pi}$$

so

$$\int_{-\infty}^{\infty} e^{-x^2}\,dx = \sqrt{\pi}.$$

EXERCISE (5.48). Show that the density function

$$f(x) = \begin{cases} \dfrac{1}{\pi\sqrt{x(1-x)}} & \text{if } 0 < x < 1, \\ 0 & \text{otherwise,} \end{cases}$$

has distribution function with the form

(if $0 < x < 1$,) $$F(x) = c\sin^{-1}\sqrt{x}$$

and find the constant c.

We have

$$F(x) = \mathbb{P}(X \le x)$$
$$= \int_{-\infty}^{x} f(u)\,du.$$

If $x \le 0$, then

$$F(x) = \int_{-\infty}^{x} 0\,du$$
$$= 0.$$

If $0 < x < 1$, then

$$F(x) = \int_{-\infty}^{0} f(u)\,du + \int_{0}^{x} f(u)\,du$$

$$= \int_{-\infty}^{0} 0\,du + \int_{0}^{x} \frac{1}{\pi\sqrt{u(1-u)}}\,du$$

$$= 0 + \int_{0}^{x} \frac{1}{\pi\sqrt{u(1-u)}}\,du$$

$$= \frac{1}{\pi} \int_{0}^{\sin^{-1}\sqrt{x}} \frac{2\sin t \cos t}{\sqrt{\sin^2 t(1-\sin^2 t)}}\,dt$$

by the substitution $\sin^2 t = u \implies t = \sin^{-1}\sqrt{u}$. In general,

$$F(x) = \frac{2}{\pi} \int_{0}^{\sin^{-1}\sqrt{x}} \frac{\sin t \cos t}{\sqrt{\sin^2 t(1-\sin^2 t)}}\,dt$$

$$= \frac{2}{\pi} \int_{0}^{\sin^{-1}\sqrt{x}} dt$$

$$= \frac{2}{\pi}\, t\big|_{0}^{\sin^{-1}\sqrt{x}}$$

$$= \frac{2}{\pi} \sin^{-1}\sqrt{x}.$$

Compare this with $F(x) = c\sin^{-1}\sqrt{x}$, we conclude that $c = 2/\pi$.
    If $x \geq 1$, then

$$F(x) = \int_{-\infty}^{0} f(u)\,du + \int_{0}^{1} f(u)\,du + \int_{1}^{x} f(u)\,du$$

$$= \int_{-\infty}^{0} 0\,du + \int_{0}^{1} \frac{1}{\pi\sqrt{u(1-u)}}\,du + \int_{1}^{x} 0\,du$$

$$= 0 + \frac{2}{\pi} \sin^{-1}\sqrt{1} + 0$$

$$= 1.$$

Thus the required distribution function is

$$F(x) = \begin{cases} 0 & \text{if } x \leq 0, \\ \dfrac{2}{\pi} \sin^{-2}\sqrt{x} & \text{if } 0 < x < 1, \\ 1 & \text{if } x \geq 1. \end{cases}$$

Note that $F(x)$ increases monotonically from 0 to 1 as is required for a distribution function. It should also be noted that $F(x)$ in this case is continuous.

5.5. Functions of random variables

EXERCISE (5.54). Let X be a random variable with the exponential distribution, parameter λ. Find the density function of
  (a) $A = 2X + 5$,
  (b) $B = e^X$,
  (c) $C = (1 + X)^{-1}$,
  (d) $D = (1 + X)^{-2}$.

SOLUTION. (a) **Solution 1.** If X has the exponential distribution with parameter λ, that is to say,

$$f_X(x) = \begin{cases} 0 & \text{if } x \le 0 \\ \lambda e^{-\lambda x} & \text{if } x > 0, \end{cases}$$

then $A = 2X + 5$ has distribution function

$$\mathbb{P}(A \le y) = \mathbb{P}(2X + 5 < y)$$
$$= \mathbb{P}(X < \frac{y - 5}{2}).$$

If $(y - 5)/2 \le 0$, then $y \le 5$ and

$$\mathbb{P}(X < \frac{y - 5}{2}) = 0$$

If $0 < (y - 5)/2$, then $y > 5$, and we have

$$\mathbb{P}(X < \frac{y - 5}{2}) = \int_0^{\frac{y-5}{2}} \lambda e^{-\lambda x}$$
$$= -e^{-\lambda \mu}\Big|_0^{\frac{y-5}{2}}$$
$$= -e^{-\frac{\lambda}{2}(y-5)} + 1$$

Thus A has distribution function

$$F_A(y) = \begin{cases} 0 & \text{if } y \le 5, \\ 1 - e^{-\frac{\lambda}{2}(y-5)} & \text{if } y > 5. \end{cases}$$

Hence A has density function

$$f_A(y) = F_A'(y)$$

$$= \begin{cases} 0 & \text{if } y \leq 5, \\ \dfrac{\lambda}{2} e^{-\frac{\lambda}{2}(y-5)} & \text{if } y > 5. \end{cases}$$

Solution 2. We have $g(x) = 2x + 5$, then $g^{-1}(y) = \dfrac{y-5}{2}$. By Thereom 5.50,

$$f_A(y) = f_X[g^{-1}(y)] \frac{d}{dy}[g^{-1}(y)]$$

$$= \lambda e^{-\frac{\lambda}{2}(y-5)} \frac{d}{dy}\left(\frac{y-5}{2}\right)$$

$$= \frac{\lambda}{2} e^{-\frac{\lambda}{2}(y-5)}.$$

We have

$$x \leq 0 \iff x = \frac{y-5}{2} \leq 0 \iff y \leq 5$$

$$x > 0 \iff x = \frac{y-5}{2} > 0 \iff y > 5$$

Thus

$$f_A(y) = \begin{cases} 0 & \text{if } y \leq 5, \\ \dfrac{\lambda}{2} e^{-\frac{\lambda}{2}(y-5)} & \text{if } y > 5. \end{cases}$$

(b) $B = g(X) = e^X$ has distribution function

$$\mathbb{P}(B < y) = \mathbb{P}(e^X < y)$$

$$= \begin{cases} 0 & \text{if } y \leq 1, \\ \mathbb{P}(X < \ln y) & \text{if } y > 1. \end{cases}$$

Hence $f_B(y) = 0$ if $y \leq 1$, while for $y > 1$

$$f_B(y) = \frac{d}{dy}\mathbb{P}(B \le y)$$

$$= \frac{d}{dy}[F_X(\ln y)]$$

$$= \frac{d}{dy}[1 - e^{-\lambda \ln y}]$$

$$= \lambda y^{-\lambda-1}.$$

Thus

$$f_B(y) = \begin{cases} 0 & \text{if } y \le 1, \\ \lambda y^{-\lambda-1} & \text{IF } y > 1. \end{cases}$$

(c) Let $C = g(X) = (1+X)^{-1}$. Note that if $X \le 0$, then $P(X \le 0) = 0$ so that $P(\dfrac{1}{1+X} < y, X \le 0) = 0$. Hence we need only consider $X > 0$, so $y > 0$ C has distribution function

$$\mathbb{P}(B < y) = \mathbb{P}(\frac{1}{1+X} < y)$$

$$= \begin{cases} 0 & \text{if } y \ge 1 \\ \mathbb{P}(X > \dfrac{1}{y} - 1) & \text{if } y < 1 \end{cases}$$

$$= \begin{cases} 0 & \text{if } y \ge 1 \\ 1 - \mathbb{P}(X \le \dfrac{1}{y} - 1) & \text{if } y < 1 \end{cases}$$

Hence $f_B(y) = 0$ if $y \ge 1$, while for $y < 1$

$$f_B(y) = \frac{d}{dy}\mathbb{P}(B < y)$$

$$= \frac{d}{dy}[1 - \mathbb{P}(X \le \frac{1}{y} - 1)]$$

$$= \frac{d}{dy}[1 - (1 - e^{-\lambda(\frac{1}{y}-1)})]$$

$$= \frac{\lambda}{y^2}e^{-\lambda(\frac{1}{y}-1)}.$$

Thus

$$f_C(y) = \begin{cases} 0 & \text{if } y \geq 1, \\ \lambda y^{-2} \exp(-\lambda[x^{-1} - 1]) & \text{IF } y < 1. \end{cases}$$

(d) $C = g(X) = (1 + X)^{-2}$ has distribution function

$$\mathbb{P}(C < y) = \mathbb{P}(\frac{1}{(1+X)^2} < y)$$

$$= \begin{cases} 0 & \text{if } y \geq 1 \\ \mathbb{P}(X < -\sqrt{\dfrac{1}{y}} - 1 \text{ or } X > \sqrt{\dfrac{1}{y}} - 1) & \text{if } y < 1 \end{cases}$$

$$= \begin{cases} 0 & \text{if } y \geq 1 \\ 1 - \mathbb{P}(X \leq \dfrac{1}{y} - 1) & \text{if } y < 1 \end{cases}$$

$$\mathbb{P}(B < y) = \mathbb{P}(\frac{1}{(1+X)^2} < y)$$

$$= \mathbb{P}(X < -\sqrt{\frac{1}{y}} - 1 \text{ or } X > \sqrt{\frac{1}{y}} - 1)$$

$$= \mathbb{P}(X < -\sqrt{\frac{1}{y}} - 1) + \mathbb{P}(X > \sqrt{\frac{1}{y}} - 1)$$

$$= \mathbb{P}(X < -\sqrt{\frac{1}{y}} - 1) + 1 - \mathbb{P}(X \leq \sqrt{\frac{1}{y}} - 1)$$

$$= \{$$

Hence $f_B(y) = 0$ if $y \geq 1$, while for $y < 1$

$$f_B(y) = \frac{d}{dy}\mathbb{P}(B < y)$$

$$= \frac{d}{dy}[1 - \mathbb{P}(X \leq \frac{1}{y} - 1)]$$

$$= \frac{d}{dy}[1 - (1 - e^{-\lambda(\frac{1}{y} - 1)})]$$

$$= \frac{\lambda}{y^2}e^{-\lambda(\frac{1}{y} - 1)}).$$

Thus

$$f_B(y) = \begin{cases} 0 & \text{if } y \geq 1, \\ \lambda y^{-2} \exp(-\lambda[x^{-1} - 1]) & \text{if } y < 1. \end{cases}$$

EXERCISE (5.55). Show that if X has the normal distribution with parameters 0 and 1, then $Y = X^2$ has the χ^2 distribution with one degree of freedom.

SOLUTION. First, we seek the distribution of $Y = g(X) = X^2$:

$$\mathbb{P}(Y < y) = \mathbb{P}(X^2 < y)$$

$$= \begin{cases} 0 & \text{if } y < 0 \\ \mathbb{P}(-\sqrt{y} \leq X \leq \sqrt{y}) & \text{if } y \geq 0 \end{cases}$$

$$= \begin{cases} 0 & \text{if } y \geq 1 \end{cases}$$

Hence $f_Y(y) = 0$ if $y \leq 0$, while for $y > 0$

(if this derivative exists) $$f_Y(y) = \frac{d}{dy}\mathbb{P}(Y < y)$$

$$= \frac{d}{dy}[F_X(\sqrt{y}) - F_X(-\sqrt{y})]$$

$$= \frac{1}{2\sqrt{y}}[f_X(\sqrt{y}) + f_X(-\sqrt{y})]$$

$$= \frac{1}{2\sqrt{y}}[\frac{1}{\sqrt{2\pi}}e^{-\frac{1}{2}(\sqrt{y})^2} + \frac{1}{\sqrt{2\pi}}e^{-\frac{1}{2}(-\sqrt{y})^2}]$$

$$= \frac{1}{2\sqrt{y}} \cdot \frac{2}{\sqrt{2\pi}}e^{-\frac{1}{2}y}$$

$$= \frac{1}{\sqrt{2\pi}}y^{-\frac{1}{2}}e^{-\frac{1}{2}y}.$$

We have

$$\Gamma(\frac{1}{2}) = \int_0^\infty x^{\frac{1}{2}-1}e^{-x}\,dx$$

$$= \int_0^\infty x^{-\frac{1}{2}}e^{-x}\,dx$$

$$= \int_0^\infty \frac{e^{-x}}{\sqrt{x}}\,dx.$$

Let $t = \sqrt{x} \implies t^2 = x \implies dx = 2t\,dt$. This implies

$$\Gamma(\frac{1}{2}) = \int_0^\infty \frac{e^{-t^2}}{t} 2t\, dt$$

$$= \int_0^\infty 2e^{-t^2}\, dt$$

$$= 2\int_0^\infty e^{-t^2}\, dt$$

$$= \sqrt{\pi}$$

since $2\int_0^\infty e^{-t^2}\, dt = \int_{-\infty}^\infty e^{-t^2}\, dt = \sqrt{\pi}$ as $f(t) = e^{-t^2}$ is an even function. Hence

$$f_Y(y) = \frac{1}{\sqrt{2\pi}} y^{-\frac{1}{2}} e^{-\frac{1}{2}y}$$

$$= \frac{1}{2\Gamma(\frac{1}{2})} (\frac{1}{2}y)^{-\frac{1}{2}} e^{-\frac{1}{2}y}$$

Thus Y has density function

$$f_Y(y) = \begin{cases} \dfrac{1}{2\Gamma(\frac{1}{2})} (\frac{1}{2}y)^{-\frac{1}{2}} e^{-\frac{1}{2}y} & \text{if } y > 0, \\ 0 & \text{if } y \le 0. \end{cases}$$

so that has the χ^2 distribution with one degree of freedom.

5.6. Expectations of continuous random variables

EXERCISE (5.67). Show that a random variable with density function

$$f(x) = \begin{cases} \dfrac{1}{\pi\sqrt{x(1-x)}} & \text{if } 0 < x < 1, \\ 0 & \text{otherwise,} \end{cases}$$

has mean $\dfrac{1}{2}$.

SOLUTION. If X has density function

$$f(x) = \begin{cases} \dfrac{1}{\pi\sqrt{x(1-x)}} & \text{if } 0 < x < 1, \\ 0 & \text{otherwise,} \end{cases}$$

then

$$\mathbb{E}(X) = \int_{-\infty}^{\infty} x f_X(x)\, dx$$

(since $f_X(x) = 0$ for all $x \notin (0,1)$)
$$= \int_0^1 x \frac{1}{\pi \sqrt{x(1-x)}}\, dx$$

by the substitution $\sin^2 t = x \implies t = \sin^{-1}\sqrt{x}$ for $0 \le t \le \pi/2$. Thus $x = 0 \implies t = 0$ and $x = 1 \implies t = \pi/2$. Thus

$$\mathbb{E}(X) = \frac{2}{\pi} \int_0^{\pi/2} \sin^2 t \frac{\sin t \cos t}{\sqrt{\sin^2 t (1 - \sin^2 t)}}\, dt$$

$$= \frac{2}{\pi} \int_0^{\pi/2} \sin^2 t\, dt$$

$$= \frac{2}{\pi} \int_0^{\pi/2} \frac{1 - \cos(2t)}{2}\, dt$$

$$= \frac{2}{\pi} [\frac{1}{2}t - \frac{1}{4}\sin(2t)]_0^{\pi/2}$$

$$= \frac{2}{\pi} \cdot \frac{\pi}{4}$$

$$= \frac{1}{2}.$$

EXERCISE (5.68). The random variable X has density function
(for $0 \le x \le 1$) $\qquad\qquad f(x) = cx(1-x)$.
Determine c, and find the mean and variance of X.

SOLUTION. For $f(x)$ be the density function of X, X has to satisfy

$$\int_{-\infty}^{\infty} f_X(x)\, dx = 1$$

This becomes

(since $f(x) = 0$ for all $x \in (-\infty, 0) \cup (1, +\infty)$) $\qquad \int_0^1 cx(1-x)\, dx = 1$

$$c[\frac{x^2}{2} - \frac{x^3}{3}]_0^1 = 1$$

$$c[\frac{1}{2} - \frac{1}{3}] = 1$$

This implies $c = 6$.
    If X has density function

(for $0 \leq x \leq 1$) $f(x) = 6x(1 - x)$,

then

$$\mathbb{E}(X) = \int_{-\infty}^{\infty} x f_X(x) \, dx$$

$$= \int_0^1 x[6x(1 - x)] \, dx$$

$$= 6 \int_0^1 (x^2 - x^3) \, dx$$

$$= 6[\frac{x^3}{3} - \frac{x^4}{4}]_0^1$$

$$= 6[\frac{1}{3} - \frac{1}{4}]$$

$$= \frac{1}{2}.$$

$$\mathbb{E}(X^2) = \int_{-\infty}^{\infty} x^2 f_X(x) \, dx$$

$$= \int_0^1 x^2[6x(1 - x)] \, dx$$

$$= 6 \int_0^1 (x^3 - x^4) \, dx$$

$$= 6[\frac{x^4}{4} - \frac{x^5}{5}]_0^1$$

$$= 6[\frac{1}{4} - \frac{1}{5}]$$

$$= \frac{3}{10}.$$

Hence

$$\text{var}(X) = \mathbb{E}(X^2) - \mathbb{E}(X)^2 = \frac{3}{10} - \frac{1}{4} = \frac{1}{20}$$

EXERCISE (5.69). If X has the normal distribution with mean 0 and variance 1, find the mean value of $Y = e^{2X}$.

SOLUTION. If X has the normal distribution with mean 0 and variance 1, then X has parameters $\mu = 0$ and $\sigma^2 = 1$ and

$$\mathbb{E}(e^{2X}) = \int_{-\infty}^{\infty} e^{2x} \frac{1}{\sqrt{2\pi}} e^{-\frac{1}{2}x^2} \, dx$$

$$= \frac{1}{\sqrt{2\pi}} \int_{-\infty}^{\infty} e^{2x - \frac{1}{2}x^2} \, dx$$

$$= \frac{1}{\sqrt{2\pi}} \int_{-\infty}^{\infty} \left[e^{2 - \frac{1}{2}(x-2)^2} \right] dx$$

$$= \frac{1}{\sqrt{2\pi}} \int_{-\infty}^{\infty} e^{2} e^{-\frac{1}{2}(x-2)^2} \, dx$$

$$= \frac{e^2}{\sqrt{2\pi}} \int_{-\infty}^{\infty} e^{-\frac{1}{2}(x-2)^2} \, dx$$

$$= \frac{e^2}{\sqrt{2\pi}} \int_{-\infty}^{\infty} e^{-\frac{1}{2}u^2} \, du$$

By substitution $u = x - 2$. In general,

$$\mathbb{E}(e^{2X}) = \frac{e^2}{\sqrt{2\pi}} \int_{-\infty}^{\infty} e^{-\frac{1}{2}u^2} \, du$$

$$= e^2$$

since $\dfrac{1}{\sqrt{2\pi}} \displaystyle\int_{-\infty}^{\infty} e^{-\frac{1}{2}u^2} \, du = 1$ because this is the density function of standard normal distribution

5.7. Geometrical probability

5.8. Problems

PROBLEM (5.8.1). The *bilateral* (or *double*) exponential distribution has density function

(for $x \in \mathbb{R}$,)
$$f(x) = \frac{1}{2} c e^{-c|x|}$$

where $c \ (> 0)$ is a parameter of the distribution. Show that the mean and variance of this distribution are 0 and $2c^{-2}$, respectively.

SOLUTION. Snce X has the bilateral (or double) exponential distribution with parameter $c \ (> 0)$, it follows that

$$\mathbb{E}(X) = \int_{-\infty}^{\infty} x f(x)\, dx$$
$$= \int_{-\infty}^{\infty} x \frac{1}{2} c e^{-c|x|}\, dx$$
$$= 0 \qquad\qquad \text{since the function } f(x) = x\frac{1}{2}ce^{-c|x|} \text{ is odd,}$$

and

$$\mathbb{E}(X^2) = \int_{-\infty}^{\infty} x^2 f(x)\, dx$$
$$= \int_{-\infty}^{\infty} x^2 \frac{1}{2} c e^{-c|x|}\, dx$$
$$= c \int_{0}^{\infty} x^2 e^{-cx}\, dx.$$

Let $I = \int_{0}^{\infty} x^2 e^{-cx}\, dx$. We integrate by part. Let $u = x^2$ and $dv = e^{-cx}\, dx$. Then $du = 2x\, dx$ and $v = -\frac{1}{c}e^{-cx}$. By integration by parts, we have

$$I = -\frac{1}{c} x^2 e^{-cx} \Big|_{0}^{\infty} + \frac{2}{c} \int_{0}^{\infty} x e^{-cx}\, dx$$
$$= \frac{2}{c} \int_{0}^{\infty} x e^{-cx}\, dx$$

Let $I_2 = \int_{0}^{\infty} x e^{-cx}\, dx$. We integrate by part. Let $p = x$ and $dq = e^{-cx}\, dx$. Then $dp = dx$ and $q = -\frac{1}{c}e^{-cx}$. Using integration by parts, we have

$$I_2 = -\frac{1}{c} x e^{-cx} \Big|_{0}^{\infty} + \frac{1}{c} \int_{0}^{\infty} e^{-cx}\, dx = \frac{1}{c} \int_{0}^{\infty} e^{-cx}\, dx$$
$$= -\frac{1}{c^2} e^{-cx} \Big|_{0}^{\infty} = \frac{1}{c^2}$$

Thus

$$\mathbb{E}(X^2) = c \int_0^\infty x^2 e^{-cx}\, dx$$

$$= c \cdot \frac{2}{c} \int_0^\infty e^{-cx}\, dx$$

$$= c \cdot \frac{2}{c} \cdot \frac{1}{c^2}$$

$$= \frac{2}{c^2}$$

Hence

$$\mathrm{var}(X) = \mathbb{E}(X^2) - \mathbb{E}(X)^2$$

$$= \frac{2}{c^2}$$

PROBLEM (5.8.2). Let X be a random variable with the Poisson distribution, parameter λ. Show that, for $w = 1, 2, 3, \ldots$,

$$\mathbb{P}(X \geq w) = \mathbb{P}(Y \leq \lambda),$$

where Y is a random variable having the gamma distribution with parameters w and 1.

SOLUTION. For $w = 1, 2, 3, \ldots$,

$$\mathbb{P}(X \geq w) = 1 - \mathbb{P}(X \leq w - 1)$$

$$= 1 - e^{-\lambda} \sum_{k=0}^{w-1} \frac{1}{k!} \lambda^k.$$

Since Y has the gamma distribution with parameters w and 1, it follows that Y has density function

$$f_Y(y) = \begin{cases} \dfrac{1}{\Gamma(w)} y^{w-1} e^{-y} & \text{if } y > 0, \\ 0 & \text{if } y \leq 0, \end{cases}$$

where $\Gamma(w)$ is the gamma function, defined by

$$\Gamma(w) = \int_0^\infty x^{w-1} e^{-u}\, dx.$$

Thus

$$\mathbb{P}(Y \leq \lambda) = \int_0^\lambda f_Y(y)\,dy$$

$$= \int_0^\lambda \frac{1}{\Gamma(w)} y^{w-1} e^{-y}\,dy$$

$$= \frac{1}{\Gamma(w)} \int_0^\lambda y^{w-1} e^{-y}\,dy$$

$$= \frac{1}{\Gamma(w)} \left(\int_0^\infty y^{w-1} e^{-y}\,dy - \int_\lambda^\infty y^{w-1} e^{-y}\,dy \right)$$

$$= \frac{1}{\Gamma(w)} \left(\Gamma(w) - \int_\lambda^\infty y^{w-1} e^{-y}\,dy \right)$$

$$= 1 - \frac{1}{\Gamma(w)} \int_\lambda^\infty y^{w-1} e^{-y}\,dy$$

$$= 1 - \frac{1}{(w-1)!} (w-1)! e^{-\lambda} \sum_{k=0}^{w-1} \frac{1}{k!} \lambda^k$$

$$= 1 - e^{-\lambda} \sum_{k=0}^{w-1} \frac{1}{k!} \lambda^k.$$

Hence

$$\mathbb{P}(Y \leq \lambda) = \int_0^\lambda f_Y(y)\,dy$$

$$= \int_0^\lambda \frac{1}{\Gamma(w)} y^{w-1} e^{-y}\,dy$$

$$= \frac{1}{\Gamma(w)} \int_0^\lambda y^{w-1} e^{-y}\,dy$$

$$= \frac{1}{(w-1)!} \int_0^\lambda y^{w-1} e^{-y}\,dy$$

Let

$$I_n = \int_0^\lambda x^n e^{-x}\,dx.$$

Integrate by parts with $u = x^n$ and $dv = e^{-x}\,dx$. Then $du = nx^{n-1}\,dx$ and $v = -e^{-x}$. Thus

$$I_n = -x^n e^{-x}\big|_0^\lambda + n \int_0^\lambda x^{n-1} e^{-x}\, dx$$
$$= -\lambda^n e^{-\lambda} + n I_{n-1}$$

Divide both side by $n!$, we obtain

$$\frac{1}{n!} I_n = -\frac{\lambda^n e^{-\lambda}}{n!} + \frac{1}{(n-1)!} I_{n-1} \qquad (*)$$

Remember that

$$\mathbb{P}(Y \le \lambda) = \frac{1}{(w-1)!} \int_0^\lambda y^{w-1} e^{-y}\, dy$$
$$= \frac{1}{(w-1)!} I_{w-1}.$$

Apply (**) for this equation, we obtain

$$\frac{1}{(w-1)!} I_{w-1} = -\frac{\lambda^{w-1} e^{-\lambda}}{(w-1)!} + \frac{1}{(w-2)!} I_{w-2}$$
$$\frac{1}{(w-2)!} I_{w-2} = -\frac{\lambda^{w-2} e^{-\lambda}}{(w-2)!} + \frac{1}{(w-3)!} I_{w-3}$$
$$\vdots$$
$$\frac{1}{2!} I_2 = -\frac{\lambda^2 e^{-\lambda}}{2!} + I_1.$$

Add all above equations side by side and reduce, we obtain

$$\mathbb{P}(Y \le \lambda) = \frac{1}{(w-1)!} I_{w-1}$$
$$= -\frac{\lambda^{w-1} e^{-\lambda}}{(w-1)!} - \frac{\lambda^{w-2} e^{-\lambda}}{(w-2)!} - \cdots - \frac{\lambda^2 e^{-\lambda}}{2!} + I_1$$
$$= -\sum_{k=2}^{w-1} \frac{\lambda^k e^{-\lambda}}{k!} - \lambda e^{-\lambda} - e^{-\lambda} + 1 \qquad \text{since } I_1 = -\lambda e^{-\lambda} - e^{-\lambda} + 1$$
$$= 1 - \sum_{k=0}^{w-1} \frac{\lambda^k e^{-\lambda}}{k!}$$
$$= 1 - e^{-\lambda} \sum_{k=0}^{w-1} \frac{1}{k!} \lambda^k$$
$$= \mathbb{P}(X \ge w)$$

as required.

PROBLEM (5.8.3). The random variable X has density function proportional to $g(x)$, where g is a function satisfying

$$g(x) = \begin{cases} |x|^{-n} & \text{if } |x| \geq 1, \\ 0 & \text{otherwise,} \end{cases}$$

and n (≥ 2) is an integer. Find and sketch the density function of X, and determine the values of n for which both the mean and variance of X exist.

SOLUTION. The random variable X has density function

$$f_X(x) = \begin{cases} c|x|^{-n} & \text{if } |x| \geq 1, \\ 0 & \text{otherwise,} \end{cases}$$

for some constant c. For n (≥ 2) is an integer, density function integrates to 1, so that

$$\begin{aligned} 1 &= \int_{-\infty}^{\infty} f_X(x)\,dx \\ &= \int_{-\infty}^{-1} c(-x)^{-n}\,dx + \int_{1}^{\infty} cx^{-n}\,dx \\ &= -c\frac{(-x)^{-n+1}}{-n+1}\bigg|_{-\infty}^{-1} + c\frac{x^{-n+1}}{-n+1}\bigg|_{1}^{+\infty} \\ &= -\frac{c}{-n+1} - \frac{c}{-n+1} \\ &= \frac{2c}{n-1}, \end{aligned}$$

giving that $c = (n-1)/2$. Clearly,

(by (5.57))
$$\mathbb{E}(X) = \int_{-\infty}^{\infty} x f_X(x)\, dx$$

$$= \int_{-\infty}^{-1} xc(-x)^{-n}\, dx + \int_{1}^{\infty} xcx^{-n}\, dx$$

(since f_X)
$$= 0,$$

(by (5.59))
$$\mathbb{E}(X^2) = \int_{-\infty}^{\infty} x^2 f_X(x)\, dx$$

$$= \int_{-\infty}^{-1} x^2 c(-x)^{-n}\, dx + \int_{1}^{\infty} x^2 cx^{-n}\, dx$$

$$= -\frac{c}{3-n} - \frac{c}{3-n}$$

$$= \frac{2c}{n-3},$$

$$\mathrm{var}(X) = \mathbb{E}(X^2) - \mathbb{E}(X)^2$$

$$= \frac{2c}{n-3},$$

whenever the mean and variance of X exist, giving that $n \geq 4$.

PROBLEM (5.8.4). If X has the normal distribution with mean 0 and variance 1, find the density function of $Y = |X|$, and find the mean and variance of Y.

SOLUTION. Since X has the normal distribution with parameters $\mu = 0$ and $\sigma^2 = 1$, that is, X has density function

$$f_X(x) = \frac{1}{\sqrt{2\pi}} e^{-\frac{1}{2}x^2} \qquad \text{for } x \in \mathbb{R},$$

and $g(x) = |x|$, it follows that $Y = g(X) = |X|$ has distribution function

$$\mathbb{P}(Y \leq y) = \mathbb{P}(|X| \leq y)$$

$$= \begin{cases} 0 & \text{if } y < 0, \\ \mathbb{P}(-y \leq X \leq y) & \text{if } y \geq 0. \end{cases}$$

Hence $f_Y(y) = 0$ if $y < 0$, while for $y \geq 0$

$$\begin{aligned}
f_Y(y) &= \frac{d}{dy}\mathbb{P}(Y \le y) \\
&= \frac{d}{dy}[F_X(y) - F_X(-y)] \\
&= f_X(y) + f_X(-y) \\
&= 2f_X(y) \qquad\qquad\qquad\quad \text{since } f_X \text{ is even} \\
&= 2\frac{1}{\sqrt{2\pi}}e^{-\frac{1}{2}y^2} \\
&= \sqrt{\frac{2}{\pi}}e^{-\frac{1}{2}y^2}.
\end{aligned}$$

Thus

$$f_Y(y) = \begin{cases} 0 & \text{if } y < 0, \\ \sqrt{\dfrac{2}{\pi}}e^{-\frac{1}{2}y^2} & \text{if } y \ge 0. \end{cases}$$

Hence

(by (5.57))

$$\begin{aligned}
\mathbb{E}(Y) &= \int_{-\infty}^{\infty} y f_Y(y)\, dy \\
&= \int_0^{\infty} y\sqrt{\frac{2}{\pi}}e^{-\frac{1}{2}y^2}\, dy \\
&= \sqrt{\frac{2}{\pi}},
\end{aligned}$$

and

(by (5.59))

$$\begin{aligned}
\mathbb{E}(Y^2) &= \int_{-\infty}^{\infty} y^2 f_Y(y)\, dy \\
&= \int_0^{\infty} y^2\sqrt{\frac{2}{\pi}}e^{-\frac{1}{2}y^2}\, dy \\
&= 1,
\end{aligned}$$

giving by (5.62) that the variance of Y is

$$\begin{aligned}
\text{var}(X) &= \mathbb{E}(X^2) - \mathbb{E}(X)^2 \\
&= 1 - \frac{2}{\pi}.
\end{aligned}$$

PROBLEM (5.8.5). Let X be a random variable whose distribution function F is a continuous function. Show that the random variable Y, defined by $Y = F(X)$, is uniformly distributed on the interval $(0, 1)$.

SOLUTION. We have that

$$\operatorname{Im} Y = \{F(X(\omega)) : \omega \in \Omega\} = (0, 1)$$

since $F_X(x) \to 0$ as $x \to -\infty$ by (5.6) and $F_X(x) \to 1$ as $x \to \infty$ by (5.7). Hence $\mathbb{P}(Y \leq y) = 0$ if $y \leq 0$ and $\mathbb{P}(Y \leq y) = 1$ if $y \geq 1$. For $0 < y < 1$,

$$\mathbb{P}(Y < y) = \mathbb{P}(F(X) < y)$$

(since) $\qquad\qquad = \mathbb{P}(X < F^{-1}(y)) \qquad\qquad F \text{ is non-decreasing}$

$$= F(F^{-1}(y))$$

$$= y.$$

Thus

$$F_Y(y) = \begin{cases} 0 & \text{if } y \leq 0, \\ y & \text{if } 0 < y < 1, \\ 1 & \text{if } y \geq 1. \end{cases}$$

PROBLEM (*5.8.6). Let F be a distribution function, and let X be a random variable which is uniformly distributed on the interval $(0, 1)$. Let F^{-1} be the inverse function of F, defined by

$$F^{-1}(y) = \inf\{x : F(x) \geq y\}.$$

Show that the random variable $Y = F^{-1}(X)$ has distribution function F. This observation may be used in practice to generate pseudorandom numbers drawn from any given distribution.

SOLUTION. If X has distribution function F, and

$$g(y) = F^{-1}(y)$$

$$= \inf\{x : F(x) \geq y\},$$

then $Y = F^{-1}(X)$ has distribution function

$$F_Y(y) = \mathbb{P}(Y \le y)$$
$$= \mathbb{P}(F^{-1}(X) \le y)$$
$$= \mathbb{P}(X \le F(y)) \qquad \text{since } F \text{ is non-decreasing}$$
$$= F(y)$$

since $0 \le F(y) \le 1$ for all y and X is distributed on the interal $(0,1)$.

PROBLEM (5.8.7). If X is a continuous random variable taking non-negative values only, show that

$$\mathbb{E}(X) = \int_0^\infty [1 - F_X(x)]\, dx,$$

whenever this integral exists.

SOLUTION. We shall prove that

$$\mathbb{E}(X) = \int_0^\infty \mathbb{P}(X > x)\, dx.$$

We have that

$$\int_0^\infty \mathbb{P}(X > x)\, dx$$

$$= x\mathbb{P}(X > x)|_0^\infty - \int_0^\infty x \frac{d}{dx}[\mathbb{P}(X > x)]\, dx \qquad \begin{array}{l} \text{by integration by parts formula with} \\ u = \mathbb{P}(X > x), dv = dx \\ du = \dfrac{d}{dx}[\mathbb{P}(X > x)]\, dx, v = x \end{array}$$

$$= \lim_{x \to \infty} x[1 - F_X(x)] - \int_0^\infty x[1 - F_X(x)]'\, dx$$

$$= \lim_{x \to \infty} x[1 - F_X(x)] + \int_0^\infty x f_X(x)\, dx.$$

Since

$$\lim_{x \to \infty} x[1 - F_X(x)] = \lim_{x \to \infty} \frac{x}{\frac{1}{1 - F_X(x)}}$$

(by l'Hôpital's Rule)
$$= \lim_{x \to \infty} \frac{x}{\frac{f_X(x)}{[1 - F_X(x)]^2}}$$

$$= \lim_{x \to \infty} \frac{[1 - F_X(x)]^2}{f_X(x)}$$

$$= 0,$$

it follows that

$$\int_0^\infty \mathbb{P}(X > x)\, dx = \int_0^\infty x f_X(x)\, dx$$
$$= \mathbb{E}(X).$$

Hence

$$\mathbb{E}(x) = \int_0^\infty \mathbb{P}(X > x)\, dx$$
$$= \int_0^\infty [1 - \mathbb{P}(X \le x)]\, dx$$
$$= \int_0^\infty [1 - F_X(x)]\, dx$$

as required.

PROBLEM (*5.8.8). Use the result of Problem 5.8.7 to show that

$$\mathbb{E}(g(X)) = \int_{-\infty}^\infty g(x) f_X(x)\, dx$$

whenever X and $g(X)$ are continuous random variables and $g \colon \mathbb{R} \to [0, \infty)$.

SOLUTION. Applying the conclusion of Problem 5.8.7 to $Y = g(X)$, we obtain

$$\mathbb{E}(Y) = \int_0^\infty [1 - F_Y(x)]\,dx$$

$$= \int_0^\infty \mathbb{P}(Y \geq x)\,dx$$

$$= \int_0^\infty \mathbb{P}(g(X) \geq x)\,dx$$

$$= \int_0^\infty \mathbb{P}(X \in g^{-1}([0,\infty)))\,dx$$

$$= \int_0^\infty \int_{g^{-1}([0,\infty))} f_X(t)\,dtdx$$

$$= \int_{-\infty}^\infty \int_0^{g(t)} f_X(t)\,dtdx$$

$$= \int_{-\infty}^\infty dt \int_0^{g(t)} f_X(t)\,dx$$

$$= \int_{-\infty}^\infty g(t)f_X(t)\,dt$$

$$= \int_{-\infty}^\infty g(x)f_X(x)\,dx$$

as required.

PROBLEM (5.8.9). The random variable X' is said to be obtained from the random variable X by *truncation* at the point a if

$$X'(\omega) = \begin{cases} X(\omega) & \text{if } X(\omega) \leq a, \\ a & \text{if } X(\omega) > a. \end{cases}$$

Express the distribution function of X' in terms of the distribution function of X.

SOLUTION. Since X has distribution function F_X, and

$$g(x) = \begin{cases} x & \text{if } x \leq a, \\ a & \text{if } x > a, \end{cases}$$

it follows that $X' = g'(X)$ has distribution function

$$F_{X'}(y) = \mathbb{P}(X' \le y)$$
$$= \begin{cases} \mathbb{P}(X \le y) & \text{if } X(\omega) \le a, \\ \mathbb{P}(a \le y) & \text{if } X(\omega) > a. \end{cases}$$
$$= \begin{cases} F_X(y) & \text{if } X(\omega) \le a, \\ F_X(y) - F_X(a) & \text{if } X(\omega) > a. \end{cases}$$

If $y \le a$, then $F_{X'}(y) = \mathbb{P}(X' \le y) = \mathbb{P}(X \le y) = F_X(y)$ (since $y \le a$, then $X'(\omega) = y = X(\omega)$).

If $y > a$, then $F_{X'}(y) = \mathbb{P}(X' \le y) = \mathbb{P}(X' \le a) + \mathbb{P}(a < X' \le y) = F_X(a) = 1$ (since $\mathbb{P}(a < X' \le y) = 0$ by $X'(\omega) \le a$ for all ω and $(X' \le a) = \Omega$). Thus

$$F_{X'}(y) = \begin{cases} F_X(y) & \text{if } y \le a \\ 1 & \text{if } y > a \end{cases}$$

PROBLEM (5.8.10). Let X have the exponential distribution with parameter 1. Find the density function of $Y = (X - 2)/(X + 1)$.

SOLUTION. Since X has the exponential distribution with parameter λ, that is, X has density function

$$f_X(x) = \begin{cases} e^{-x} & \text{if } x > 0, \\ 0 & \text{if } x \le 0, \end{cases}$$

and $g(x) = (x - 2)/(x + 1)$, it follows that $Y = (X - 2)/(X + 1)$ has distribution function

$$F_Y(y) = \mathbb{P}(Y \le y)$$
$$= \mathbb{P}(\frac{X - 2}{X + 1} \le y)$$
$$= \mathbb{P}(X \le \frac{-y - 2}{y - 1})$$
$$= \begin{cases} 0 & \text{if } y \le -2 \text{ or } y \ge 1, \\ \mathbb{P}(-1 < X < \frac{-y - 2}{y - 1}) & \text{if } -2 < y < 1, \end{cases}$$

Hence $f_Y(y) = 0$ if $y \le -2$ or $y \ge 1$, while for $-2 < y < 1$

$$f_Y(y) = \frac{d}{dy}\mathbb{P}(Y \leq y)$$

$$= \frac{d}{dy}[F_X(\frac{-y-2}{y-1}) - F_X(-1)]$$

$$= \frac{3}{(y-1)^2}f_X(\frac{-y-2}{y-1})$$

$$= \frac{3}{(y-1)^2}e^{\frac{y+2}{y-1}}.$$

Thus

$$f_Y(y) = \begin{cases} \dfrac{3}{(y-1)^2}e^{\frac{y+2}{y-1}} & \text{if } -2 < y < 1, \\ 0 & \text{otherwise.} \end{cases}$$

PROBLEM (*5.8.13). A unit stick is broken at n random places, each uniform on $[0,1]$, and different breaks are chosen independently. Show that the resulting $n+1$ substicks can form a closed polygon with probability $1 - (n+1)/2^n$.

SOLUTION. Let X_k be the position of the kth break (in no special order). The pieces form a polygon if no piece is longer than the sum of the other lengths (since the straight segment connects two distinct points is the shortest among the curves), which is equivalent to each piece having length less than $\dfrac{1}{2}$ (since if we denote the length of ith piece by x_i, then $x_i < x_1 + x_2 + \cdots + x_{i-1} + x_{i+1} + \cdots + x_n$, and so $2x_i < \displaystyle\sum_{j=1}^{n} x_j = 1$, giving $x_i < \dfrac{1}{2}$ for $i = 1, 2, \ldots, n$). This fails to occur if and only if the disjoint union $A_0 \cup A_1 \cup \cdots \cup A_n$ occurs, where A_0 is the event there is no break in $(0, \frac{1}{2}]$, and A_k is the event of no break in $(X_k, X_k + \frac{1}{2}]$ for $k \geq 1$ (remember the permanent break at 1). Now,

$$\mathbb{P}(A_0) = \mathbb{P}(X_1 > \frac{1}{2}, X_2 > \frac{1}{2}, \ldots, X_n > \frac{1}{2})$$

$$= \mathbb{P}(X_1 > \frac{1}{2})\mathbb{P}(X_2 > \frac{1}{2}) \cdots \mathbb{P}(X_n > \frac{1}{2}) \qquad \text{by independence}$$

$$= (\frac{1}{2})^n,$$

and for $k \geq 1$,

$\mathbb{P}(A_k)$

$$= \int_0^1 \mathbb{P}(A_k \mid X_k = x)\, dx$$

$$= \int_0^{\frac{1}{2}} \mathbb{P}(X_i \in [0,1]\backslash(X_k, X_k + \tfrac{1}{2}) \text{ for } i \ne k)\, dx$$

$$= \int_0^{\frac{1}{2}} \prod_{i \ne k} \mathbb{P}(X_i \in [0,1]\backslash(X_k, X_k + \tfrac{1}{2}))\, dx$$

$$= \int_0^{\frac{1}{2}} (\tfrac{1}{2})^{n-1}\, dx \qquad\qquad \text{since } \mathbb{P}(X_i \in [0,1]\backslash(X_k, X_k + \tfrac{1}{2})) = \tfrac{1}{2} \text{ for } i \ne k$$

$$= (\tfrac{1}{2})^n.$$

Thus

$$\mathbb{P}(\bigcup_{i=0}^n A_i) = \sum_{i=0}^n \mathbb{P}(A_i) \qquad\qquad \text{by disjointness}$$

$$= (n+1)\frac{1}{2^n}.$$

Hence the probability that the resulting $n+1$ substicks can form a closed polygon is

$$\mathbb{P}((\bigcup_{i=0}^n A_i)^c) = 1 - \mathbb{P}(\bigcup_{i=0}^n A_i)$$

$$= 1 - \frac{n+1}{2^n},$$

as required.

PROBLEM (5.8.14). The random variable X is uniformly distributed on the interval $[0,1]$. Find the distribution and probability density function of Y, where

$$Y = \frac{3X}{1-X}.$$

(Cambridge 2003)

SOLUTION. Since X is uniformly distributed on the interval $[0,1]$ with distribution function

$$F_X(x) = \begin{cases} 0 & \text{if } x < 0, \\ x & \text{if } 0 \le x \le 1, \\ 1 & \text{if } x > 1, \end{cases}$$

and $g(x) = 3x/(1-x)$, it follows that $Y = 3X/(1-X)$ has distribution function

$$F_Y(y) = \mathbb{P}(Y \leq y)$$

$$= \mathbb{P}(\frac{3X}{1-X} \leq y)$$

$$= \begin{cases} 0 & \text{if } y < 0, \\ \mathbb{P}(X \leq \dfrac{y}{y+3}) & \text{if } y \geq 0. \end{cases}$$

$$= \begin{cases} 0 & \text{if } y < 0, \\ F_X(\dfrac{y}{y+3}) & \text{if } y \geq 0. \end{cases}$$

$$= \begin{cases} 0 & \text{if } y < 0, \\ \dfrac{y}{y+3} & \text{if } y \geq 0. \end{cases}$$

Hence $f_Y(y) = 0$ if $y < 0$, while for $y \geq 0$

$$f_Y(y) = \frac{d}{dy} F_Y(y)$$

$$= \frac{d}{dy} \mathbb{P}(Y \leq y)$$

$$= \frac{d}{dy}(\frac{y}{y+3})$$

$$= \frac{3}{(y+3)^2}.$$

Thus

$$f_Y(y) = \begin{cases} 0 & \text{if } y < 0, \\ \dfrac{3}{(y+3)^2} & \text{if } y \geq 0. \end{cases}$$

Part 2

Further Probability

CHAPTER 6

Multivariate distributions and independence

6.1. Random vectors and independence

EXERCISE (6.13). Show that two random variables X and Y are independent if and only if

$$\mathbb{P}(X > x, Y > y) = \mathbb{P}(X > x)\mathbb{P}(Y > y) \qquad \text{for } x, y \in \mathbb{R}.$$

SOLUTION. Suppose that A and B are two independent events. Then

$$\mathbb{P}(A \cap B) = \mathbb{P}(A)\mathbb{P}(B)$$

So

$$
\begin{aligned}
\mathbb{P}(A^c \cap B^c) &= \mathbb{P}((A \cup B)^c) && \text{by De Morgan's law} \\
&= 1 - \mathbb{P}(A \cup B) && \text{since } \mathbb{P}(A \cap B) = \mathbb{P}(A)\mathbb{P}(B) \\
&= 1 - [\mathbb{P}(A) + \mathbb{P}(B) - \mathbb{P}(A \cap B)] \\
&= 1 - \mathbb{P}(A) - \mathbb{P}(B) + \mathbb{P}(A)\mathbb{P}(B) \\
&= (1 - \mathbb{P}(A))(1 - \mathbb{P}(B)) = \mathbb{P}(A^c)\mathbb{P}(B^c)
\end{aligned}
$$

Therefore,

$$\mathbb{P}(A^c \cap B^c) = \mathbb{P}(A^c)\mathbb{P}(B^c).$$

Thus A^c and B^c are two independent events. It follows that A and B are independent if and only if A^c and B^c are independent event (since $(A^c)^c = A$, $(B^c) = B$)

For $A = (X > x)$, $B = (Y > y)$, X and Y are independent random variables iff $(X \leq x)$ and $(Y \leq y)$ are independent random variable, thus X and Y are independnent iff $(X > c)$ and $(Y > c)$ are independent events, that is, $\mathbb{P}(X > x, Y > y) = \mathbb{P}(X > x)\mathbb{P}(Y > y)$

EXERCISE (6.14). Let the pair (X, Y) of random variables have joint distribution function $F(x, y)$. Prove that

$$\mathbb{P}(a < X \leq b, c < Y \leq d) = F(b, d) + F(a, c) - F(a, d) - F(b, c)$$

for any $a, b, c, d \in \mathbb{R}$ such that $a < b$ and $c < d$.

EXERCISE (6.15). Prove that two random variables X and Y are independent if and only if

$$\mathbb{P}(a < X \leq b, c < Y \leq d) = \mathbb{P}(a < X \leq b)\mathbb{P}(c < Y \leq d)$$

for all $a, b, c, d \in \mathbb{R}$ satisfying $a < b$ and $c < d$.

SOLUTION. Suppose that X and Y are random variables with joint distribution function $F(x, y)$. Then

$$F(b, d) = \mathbb{P}(X \leq b, Y \leq d) = \mathbb{P}(X \leq b)\mathbb{P}(Y \leq d)$$

From Exercise 6.14, we have

$$\begin{aligned}
\mathbb{P}(a < X \leq b, c < Y \leq d) &= F(b, d) + F(a, c) - F(a, d) - F(b, c) \\
&= \mathbb{P}(X \leq b)\mathbb{P}(Y \leq d) + \mathbb{P}(X \leq a)\mathbb{P}(Y \leq c) - \mathbb{P}(X \leq a)\mathbb{P}(Y \leq d) \\
&\qquad - \mathbb{P}(X \leq b)\mathbb{P}(Y \leq c) \\
&= \mathbb{P}(X \leq a)[\mathbb{P}(Y \leq c) - \mathbb{P}(Y \leq d)] - \mathbb{P}(X \leq b)[\mathbb{P}(Y \leq c) - \mathbb{P}(Y \leq d)] \\
&= [\mathbb{P}(X \leq a) - \mathbb{P}(X \leq b)][\mathbb{P}(Y \leq c) - \mathbb{P}(Y \leq d)] \\
&= [\mathbb{P}(X \leq b) - \mathbb{P}(X \leq a)][\mathbb{P}(Y \leq d) - \mathbb{P}(Y \leq c)] \\
&= \mathbb{P}(a < X \leq b)\mathbb{P}(c < Y \leq d)
\end{aligned}$$

as required.

6.2. Joint density functions

EXERCISE (6.25). Random variables X and Y have joint density function

$$f(x, y) = \begin{cases} c(x^2 + \dfrac{1}{2}xy) & \text{if } 0 < x < 1, 0 < y < 2, \\ 0 & \text{otherwise.} \end{cases}$$

Find the value of the constant c and the joint distribution function of X and Y .

SOLUTION. Joint density functions integrate to 1, so that

$$1 = \int_{-\infty}^{\infty} \int_{-\infty}^{\infty} f(x,y) \, dx \, dy$$

$$= \int_{x=0}^{1} \int_{y=0}^{2} c(x^2 + \frac{1}{2}xy) \, dx \, dy$$

$$= \int_{0}^{1} (x^2 y + \frac{1}{4}xy^2)|_{y=0}^{2} \, dx$$

$$= c \int_{0}^{1} (2x^2 + x) \, dx$$

$$= c(\frac{2x^3}{3} + \frac{x^2}{2})|_{0}^{1}$$

$$= \frac{7}{6}c,$$

giving that $c = 6/7$. The joint distribution function of X and Y is

$$\mathbb{P}(X \le x, y \le y) = \int_{u=0}^{x} \int_{v=0}^{y} f(u,v) \, du \, dv$$

$$= \int_{u=0}^{x} \int_{v=0}^{y} \frac{6}{7}(u^2 + \frac{1}{2}uv) \, du \, dv$$

$$= \frac{6}{7} \int_{u=0}^{x} (u^2 v + \frac{1}{4}uv^2)|_{v=0}^{y} \, du$$

$$= \frac{6}{7} \int_{u=0}^{x} (y^2 y + \frac{1}{4}uy^2) \, du$$

$$= \frac{6}{7}(y\frac{u^3}{3} + \frac{1}{8}y^2 u^2)|_{u=0}^{x}$$

$$= \frac{6}{7}(\frac{x^3 y}{3} + \frac{1}{8}x^2 y^2).$$

Thus

$$F(x,y) = \begin{cases} \frac{6}{7}(\frac{1}{3}x^3 y + \frac{1}{8}x^2 y^2) & \text{if } 0 < x < 1, 0 < y < 2, \\ 0 & \text{otherwise.} \end{cases}$$

EXERCISE (6.26). Random variables X and Y have joint density function

$$f(x,y) = \begin{cases} e^{-x-y} & \text{if } x, y > 0, \\ 0 & \text{otherwise.} \end{cases}$$

Find $\mathbb{P}(X + Y \le 1)$ and $\mathbb{P}(X > Y)$.

SOLUTION. Suppose that X and Y have joint density function

$$f(x,y) = \begin{cases} e^{-x-y} & \text{if } x,y > 0, \\ 0 & \text{otherwise.} \end{cases}$$

Then

$$\mathbb{P}(X + Y \leq 1) = \iint_A f(x,y)\,dx\,dy$$

by Theorem 6.22, where $A = \{(x,y) \in \mathbb{R}^2 : x + y \leq 1\}$. Writing in the limits of integration, we find that

$$\begin{aligned}
\mathbb{P}(X + Y \leq 1) &= \int_{x=0}^{1} \int_{y=0}^{1-x} e^{-x-y}\,dx\,dy \\
&= \int_0^1 (-e^{-x-y})|_{y=0}^{1-x}\,dx \\
&= \int_0^1 (-e^{-1} + e^{-x})\,dx \\
&= (-e^{-1} - e^{-x})|_0^1 \\
&= e^{-1} - e^{-1} + 1 \\
&= 1 - 2e^{-1}.
\end{aligned}$$

Moreover,

$$\mathbb{P}(X + Y \leq 1) = \iint_B f(x,y)\,dx\,dy$$

by Theorem 6.22, where $B = \{(x,y) \in \mathbb{R}^2 : x > y\}$. Writing in the limits of integration, we find that

$$\mathbb{P}(X < Y) = \int_{x=0}^{\infty} \int_{y=0}^{x} e^{-x-y} \, dx \, dy$$

$$= \int_0^{\infty} -e^{-x-y}\big|_{y=0}^{x} \, dx$$

$$= \int_0^{\infty} (-e^{-2x} + e^{-x}) \, dx$$

$$= \frac{1}{2} e^{-2x} - e^{-x}\big|_0^{\infty}$$

$$= -\frac{1}{2} + 1$$

$$= \frac{1}{2}.$$

6.3. Marginal density functions and independence

EXERCISE (6.35). Let X and Y have joint density function

$$f(x, y) = \begin{cases} cx & \text{if } 0 < y < x < 1, \\ 0 & \text{otherwise.} \end{cases}$$

Find the value of the constant c and the marginal density functions of X and Y. Are X and Y independent?

SOLUTION. Joint density functions integrate to 1, so that

$$1 = \int_{-\infty}^{\infty} \int_{-\infty}^{\infty} f(x, y) \, dx \, dy$$

$$= \int_{x=0}^{1} \int_{y=0}^{x} cx \, dx \, dy$$

$$= c \int_0^1 xy\big|_{y=0}^{x} \, dx$$

$$= c \int_0^1 x^2 \, dx$$

$$= c \frac{x^3}{3}\bigg|_0^1$$

$$= \frac{1}{3} c,$$

giving that $c = 3$. The marginal density function of X is

$$f_X(x) = \int_{-\infty}^{\infty} f(x, y)\, dy$$

$$= \begin{cases} \int_0^x 3x\, dy & \text{if } 0 < x < 1, \\ 0 & \text{otherwise}, \end{cases}$$

$$= \begin{cases} 3\, xy\big|_{y=0}^{x} & \text{if } 0 < x < 1, \\ 0 & \text{otherwise}, \end{cases}$$

$$= \begin{cases} 3x^2 & \text{if } 0 < x < 1, \\ 0 & \text{otherwise}, \end{cases}$$

and the marginal density function of Y is

$$f_Y(y) = \int_{-\infty}^{\infty} f(x, y)\, dx$$

$$= \begin{cases} \int_y^1 3x\, dx & \text{if } 0 < y < 1, \\ 0 & \text{otherwise}, \end{cases}$$

$$= \begin{cases} \dfrac{3}{2}\, x^2\big|_{x=y}^{1} & \text{if } 0 < y < 1, \\ 0 & \text{otherwise}, \end{cases}$$

$$= \begin{cases} \dfrac{3}{2}(1 - y^2) & \text{if } 0 < y < 1, \\ 0 & \text{otherwise}, \end{cases}$$

Clearly, X and Y are dependent, since

$$f_X(x) f_Y(y) = \begin{cases} \dfrac{9}{2} x^2 (1 - y^2) & \text{if } 0 < y < x < 1, \\ 0 & \text{otherwise}, \end{cases}$$

$$\neq \begin{cases} cx & \text{if } 0 < y < x < 1, \\ 0 & \text{otherwise}, \end{cases}$$

$$= f(x, y).$$

EXERCISE (6.36). Random variables X, Y, and Z have joint density function

$$f(x, y, z) = \begin{cases} 8xyz & \text{if } 0 < x, y, z < 1, \\ 0 & \text{otherwise}. \end{cases}$$

Are X, Y, and Z independent? Find $\mathbb{P}(X > Y)$ and $\mathbb{P}(Y > Z)$.

SOLUTION. The marginal density function of X is

$$
\begin{aligned}
f_X(x) &= \int_{-\infty}^{\infty} \int_{-\infty}^{\infty} f(x, y, z)\, dy\, dz \\[2mm]
&= \begin{cases} \int_{y=0}^{1} \int_{z=0}^{1} 8xyz\, dy\, dz & \text{if } 0 < x < 1, \\ 0 & \text{otherwise,} \end{cases} \\[2mm]
&= \begin{cases} \int_{y=0}^{1} 4xyz^2 \big|_{z=0}^{1}\, dy & \text{if } 0 < x < 1, \\ 0 & \text{otherwise,} \end{cases} \\[2mm]
&= \begin{cases} \int_{0}^{1} 4xy\, dy & \text{if } 0 < x < 1, \\ 0 & \text{otherwise,} \end{cases} \\[2mm]
&= \begin{cases} 2xy^2 \big|_{0}^{1} & \text{if } 0 < x < 1, \\ 0 & \text{otherwise,} \end{cases} \\[2mm]
&= \begin{cases} 2x & \text{if } 0 < x < 1, \\ 0 & \text{otherwise.} \end{cases}
\end{aligned}
$$

The random variable Y and Z have this marginal density function also, and

$$
f(x, y, z) = f_X(x) f_Y(y) f_Z(z) \qquad \text{for } x, y \in \mathbb{R},
$$

so that X, Y and Z are independent. We have that

$$\mathbb{P}(X > Y) = \iiint_{ABDA'B'O} f(x, y, z)\, dx\, dy\, dz$$

$$= \int_{x=0}^{1} \int_{y=0}^{x} \int_{z=0}^{1} 8xyz\, dx\, dy\, dz$$

$$= \int_{x=0}^{1} \int_{y=0}^{x} 4xyz^2|_{z=0}^{1}\, dx\, dy$$

$$= \int_{x=0}^{1} \int_{y=0}^{x} 4xy\, dx\, dy$$

$$= \int_{x=0}^{1} 2xy^2|_{y=0}^{x}\, dx$$

$$= \int_{0}^{1} 2x^3\, dx$$

$$= \frac{x^4}{2}\Big|_{0}^{1}$$

$$= \frac{1}{2}.$$

Similarly, $\mathbb{P}(Y > Z) = 1/2$.

$$\mathbb{P}(Y > Z) = \iiint_{A'B'B.OC'C} f(x, y, z)\, dx\, dy\, dz$$

$$= \int_{x=0}^{1} \int_{y=0}^{1} \int_{z=0}^{y} 8xyz\, dx\, dy\, dz$$

6.4. Sums of continuous random variables

EXERCISE (6.45). If X and Y have joint density function

$$f(x, y) = \begin{cases} \dfrac{1}{2}(x + y)e^{-x-y} & \text{if } x, y > 0, \\ 0 & \text{otherwise,} \end{cases}$$

find the density function of $X + Y$.

SOLUTION. The sum $Z = X + Y$ of two jointly continuous random variables has density function (by (6.37)) $$f_Z(z) = \int_{-\infty}^{\infty} f(u, z - u)\, du$$

$$= \begin{cases} \int_0^z f(u, z - u)\, du & \text{if } z > 0, \\ 0 & \text{otherwise,} \end{cases}$$

since $f(u, z - u)\, du = 0$ unless $u > 0$ and $z - u > 0$. Thus, for $z > 0$,

$$f_Z(z) = \int_0^z \frac{1}{2} z e^{-z}\, du$$

$$= \frac{1}{2} z e^{-z} u \Big|_0^z$$

$$= \frac{1}{2} z^2 e^{-z}.$$

Hence

$$f_Z(z) = \begin{cases} \dfrac{1}{2} z^2 e^{-z} & \text{if } z > 0, \\ 0 & \text{otherwise.} \end{cases}$$

EXERCISE (6.46). If X and Y are independent random variables having the χ^2 distribution with m and n degrees of freedom, respectively, prove that $X + Y$ has the χ^2 distribution with $m + n$ degrees of freedom.

SOLUTION. $Z = X + Y$ has density function

(by (6.39)) $$f_Z(z) = \int_{-\infty}^{\infty} f_X(x) f_Y(z - x)\, dx$$

$$= \begin{cases} \int_0^z f_X(x) f_Y(z - x)\, dx & \text{if } z > 0, \\ 0 & \text{if } z \le 0, \end{cases}$$

since $f_X(x) f_Y(z - x) = 0$ unless $x > 0$ and $z - x > 0$. Thus, for $z > 0$,

$$f_Z(z) = \int_0^z \frac{1}{2\Gamma(\frac{1}{2}m)} \left(\frac{1}{2}x\right)^{\frac{1}{2}m - 1} e^{-\frac{1}{2}x} \frac{1}{2\Gamma(\frac{1}{2}n)} \left[\frac{1}{2}(z - x)\right]^{\frac{1}{2}n - 1} e^{-\frac{1}{2}(z - x)}\, dx$$

$$= A \int_0^z x^{\frac{1}{2}m - 1} e^{-\frac{1}{2}x} (z - x)^{\frac{1}{2}n - 1} e^{-\frac{1}{2}(z - x)}\, dx$$

where ???

EXERCISE (6.47). If X and Y are independent random variables, each having the normal distribution with mean 0 and variance 1, find the distribution of $X+Y$.

SOLUTION. Let X and Y be independent random variables, each having the normal distribution with mean 0 and variance 1. Then X and Y have dendity functions

$$f_X(x) = \frac{1}{\sqrt{2\pi}}\exp(-\frac{1}{2}x^2),$$

$$f_Y(y) = \frac{1}{\sqrt{2\pi}}\exp(-\frac{1}{2}y^2).$$

Then, for $z \in \mathbb{R}$, $Z = X + Y$ has density function

$$
\begin{aligned}
f_Z(z) &= \int_{-\infty}^{\infty} f_X(x)f_Y(z-x)\,dx \\
&= \int_{-\infty}^{\infty} \frac{1}{\sqrt{2\pi}}\exp(-\frac{1}{2}x^2)\frac{1}{\sqrt{2\pi}}\exp(-\frac{1}{2}(z-x)^2)\,dx \\
&= \frac{1}{2\pi}\int_{-\infty}^{\infty} \exp(-\frac{1}{2}x^2 - \frac{1}{2}(z-x)^2)\,dx \\
&= \frac{1}{2\pi}\int_{-\infty}^{\infty} \exp(-\frac{1}{2}x^2 - \frac{1}{2}z^2 + zx - \frac{1}{2}x^2)\,dx \\
&= \frac{1}{2\pi}\int_{-\infty}^{\infty} \exp(-x^2 + zx - \frac{1}{2}z^2)\,dx \\
&= \frac{1}{2\pi}\int_{-\infty}^{\infty} \exp(-(x - \frac{1}{2}z)^2 - \frac{1}{4}z^2)\,dx \\
&= A\int_{-\infty}^{\infty} \exp(-(x - \frac{1}{2}z)^2)\,dx
\end{aligned}
$$

where

$$A = \frac{1}{2\pi}\exp(-\frac{1}{4}z^2).$$

Substitute $u = x - \frac{1}{2}z$ in the last integral to obtain

$$f_Z(z) = A \int_{-\infty}^{\infty} \exp(-u^2)\,du$$

(since $\int_{-\infty}^{\infty} \exp(-u^2)\,du = \sqrt{\pi}$)
$$= \frac{1}{2\pi}\sqrt{\pi}\exp(-\frac{1}{4}z^2)$$

$$= \frac{1}{\sqrt{2}\sqrt{2\pi}}\exp(-\frac{1}{2}(\frac{z}{\sqrt{2}})^2)$$

The only distribution with density function of the form above is the normal distribution with with mean 0 and variance 2.

6.5. Changes of variables

EXERCISE (6.54). Let X and Y be independent random variables, each having the normal distribution with mean μ and variance σ^2. Find the joint density function of $U = X - Y$ and $V = X + Y$. Are U and V independent?

SOLUTION. The density function of X is

$$f_X(x) = \frac{1}{\sqrt{2\pi\sigma^2}}\exp(-\frac{1}{2\sigma^2}(x-\mu)^2),$$

and the density function of Y is

$$f_Y(x) = \frac{1}{\sqrt{2\pi\sigma^2}}\exp(-\frac{1}{2\sigma^2}(y-\mu)^2).$$

The random variables X and Y are independent, so that the joint density function of X and Y is

$$f_{X,Y}(x,y) = f_X(x)f_Y(y)$$
$$= \frac{1}{\sqrt{2\pi\sigma^2}}\exp(-\frac{1}{2\sigma^2}(x-\mu)^2)\frac{1}{\sqrt{2\pi\sigma^2}}\exp(-\frac{1}{2\sigma^2}(y-\mu)^2)$$
$$= \frac{1}{2\pi\sigma^2}\exp(-\frac{1}{2\sigma^2}(x-\mu)^2 - \frac{1}{\sigma^2}(y-\mu)^2).$$

The mapping T of this problem is given by $T(x,y) = (u,v)$, where

$$u = x - y, \qquad\qquad v = x + y,$$

and T is a bijection from $D = \{(x,y) : x, y \in \mathbb{R}\}$ to $S = \{(u,v) : u, v \in \mathbb{R}\}$ (or from $D = \mathbb{R}^2$ to $S = \mathbb{R}^2$). It has inverse $T^{-1}(u,v) = (x,y)$, where

$$x = \frac{1}{2}(u+v), \qquad\qquad y = \frac{1}{2}(-u+v).$$

The Jacobian of T^{-1} is

$$\begin{vmatrix} \dfrac{\partial x}{\partial u} & \dfrac{\partial x}{\partial v} \\[2mm] \dfrac{\partial y}{\partial u} & \dfrac{\partial y}{\partial v} \end{vmatrix} = \begin{vmatrix} \dfrac{1}{2} & \dfrac{1}{2} \\[2mm] -\dfrac{1}{2} & \dfrac{1}{2} \end{vmatrix} = \dfrac{1}{2},$$

giving by Jacobian's formula that U and V have joint density function

$$
\begin{aligned}
f_{U,V}(u,v) &= f_{X,Y}(x(u,v), y(u,v)) \, |J(u,v)| \\
&= \frac{1}{2} \cdot \frac{1}{2\pi\sigma^2} \exp(-\frac{1}{2\sigma^2}(x-\mu)^2 - \frac{1}{\sigma^2}(y-\mu)^2) \\
&= \frac{1}{4\pi\sigma^2} \exp(-\frac{1}{2\sigma^2}(\frac{1}{4}u^2 + \frac{1}{4}v^2 + uv + \mu^2 - u\mu - v\mu + \frac{1}{4}v^2 + \frac{1}{4}u^2 - uv + \mu^2)) \\
&= \frac{1}{4\pi\sigma^2} \exp(-\frac{1}{2\sigma^2}(\frac{1}{2}u^2 + \frac{1}{2}v^2 - 2v\mu + 2\mu^2)) \\
&= \frac{1}{4\pi\sigma^2} \exp(-\frac{1}{2\sigma^2}(\frac{u}{\sqrt{2}})^2) \exp(-\frac{1}{2\sigma^2}(\frac{v-2\mu}{\sqrt{2}})^2) \\
&= \frac{1}{\sqrt{2\pi(2\sigma^2)}} \exp(-\frac{1}{2\sigma^2}(\frac{1}{2}u^2)) \frac{1}{\sqrt{2\pi(2\sigma^2)}} \exp(-\frac{1}{2\sigma^2}(\frac{v-2\mu}{\sqrt{2}})^2)
\end{aligned}
$$

so that U and V are independent. The functions

$$g_U(u) = \frac{1}{\sqrt{2\pi(2\sigma^2)}} \exp(-\frac{1}{2\sigma^2}(\frac{1}{2}u^2))$$

and

$$g_V(v) = \frac{1}{\sqrt{2\pi(2\sigma^2)}} \exp(-\frac{1}{2\sigma^2}(\frac{v-2\mu}{\sqrt{2}})^2)$$

are density functions that respectively, having the normal distributions with mean 0 and variance $2\sigma^2$, and mean 2μ and $2\sigma^2$.

The marginal density function of U is

$$
\begin{aligned}
f_U(u) &= \int_{-\infty}^{\infty} f_{U,V}(u,v)\, dv \\
&= g_U(u) \int_{-\infty}^{\infty} g_V(v)\, dv
\end{aligned}
$$

(since $\displaystyle\int_{-\infty}^{\infty} g_V(v)\, dv = 1$.) $= g_U(u).$

Similarly, the marginal density function of V is

$$f_V(v) = \int_{-\infty}^{\infty} f_{U,V}(u,v)\,du$$

$$= g_V(v) \int_{-\infty}^{\infty} g_U(u)\,du$$

(since $\int_{-\infty}^{\infty} g_U(u)\,du = 1$.) $= g_V(v).$

EXERCISE (6.55). Let X and Y be random variables with joint density function

$$f(x,y) = \begin{cases} \dfrac{1}{4}e^{-\frac{1}{2}(x+y)} & \text{ì } x,y > 0, \\ 0 & \text{otherwise.} \end{cases}$$

Show that the joint density function of $U = \dfrac{1}{2}(X-Y)$ and $V = Y$ is

$$f_{U,V} = \begin{cases} \dfrac{1}{2}e^{-u-v} & \text{if } (u,v) \in A, \\ 0 & \text{otherwise,} \end{cases}$$

where A is a region of the (u,v) plane to be determined. Deduce that U has the bilateral exponential distribution with density function

$$f_U(u) = \frac{1}{2}e^{-|u|}$$

SOLUTION. The mapping T of this problem is given by $T(x,y) = (u,v)$, where

$$u = \frac{1}{2}(x-y), \qquad\qquad v = y,$$

and T is a bijection from $D = \{(x,y) : x,y > 0\}$ to $S = \{(u,v) : u > -\frac{1}{2}v, 0 < v < \infty, \}$. It has inverse $T^{-1}(u,v) = (x,y)$, where

$$x = 2u + v, \qquad\qquad y = v.$$

The Jacobian of T^{-1} is

$$\begin{vmatrix} \dfrac{\partial x}{\partial u} & \dfrac{\partial x}{\partial v} \\ \dfrac{\partial y}{\partial u} & \dfrac{\partial y}{\partial v} \end{vmatrix} = \begin{vmatrix} 2 & 1 \\ 0 & 1 \end{vmatrix} = 2,$$

giving by (6.51) that U and V have joint density function

$$f_{U,V}(u,v) = \begin{cases} f_{X,Y}(x(u,v), y(u,v)) \, |J(u,v)| & \text{if } u > -\frac{1}{2}v \text{ and } 0 < v < \infty, \\ 0 & \text{otherwise,} \end{cases}$$

$$= \begin{cases} \dfrac{1}{4} e^{-\frac{1}{2}[(2u+v)+v]} \, |2| & \text{if } u > -\frac{1}{2}v \text{ and } 0 < v < \infty, \\ 0 & \text{otherwise,} \end{cases}$$

$$= \begin{cases} \dfrac{1}{2} e^{-(u+v)} & \text{if } u > -\frac{1}{2}v \text{ and } 0 < v < \infty, \\ 0 & \text{otherwise.} \end{cases}$$

For $u > 0$,

$$\begin{aligned} f_U(u) &= \int_{-\infty}^{\infty} f_{U,V}(u,v) \, dv \\ &= \int_{-\infty}^{0} f_{U,V}(u,v) \, dv + \int_{0}^{\infty} f_{U,V}(u,v) \, dv \\ &= \int_{0}^{\infty} \frac{1}{2} e^{-(u+v)} \, dv \\ &= \frac{1}{2} e^{-u} \int_{0}^{\infty} e^{-v} \, dv \\ &= \frac{1}{2} e^{-u} [-e^{-v}]_{0}^{\infty} \\ &= \frac{1}{2} e^{-u} \cdot 1 \\ &= \frac{1}{2} e^{-u} \\ &= \frac{1}{2} e^{-|u|}. \end{aligned}$$

For $u \leq 0$,

$$f_U(u) = \int_{-\infty}^{\infty} f_{U,V}(u,v)\, dv$$

$$= \int_{-\infty}^{-2u} f_{U,V}(u,v)\, dv + \int_{-2u}^{\infty} f_{U,V}(u,v)\, dv$$

$$= \int_{-2u}^{\infty} \frac{1}{2} e^{-(u+v)}\, dv$$

$$= \frac{1}{2} e^{-u} \int_{-2u}^{\infty} e^{-v}\, dv$$

$$= \frac{1}{2} e^{-u} [-e^{-v}]_{-2u}^{\infty}$$

$$= \frac{1}{2} e^{-u} e^{2u}$$

$$= \frac{1}{2} e^{u}$$

$$= \frac{1}{2} e^{-|u|}.$$

The marginal density function of U is

(for $u \in \mathbb{R}$,) $$f_U(u) = \frac{1}{2} e^{-|u|}$$

so that U has the bilateral exponential distribution.

6.6. Conditional density functions

EXERCISE (6.60). Suppose that X and Y have joint density function

$$f(x,y) = \begin{cases} e^{-y} & 0 < x < y < \infty, \\ 0 & \text{otherwise.} \end{cases}$$

Find the conditional density functions of X given that $Y = y$, and of Y given that $X = x$.

SOLUTION. The marginal density function of X is

$$f_X(x) = \int_{-\infty}^{\infty} f(x,y)\, dy$$

$$= \int_{x}^{\infty} e^{-y}\, dy$$

$$= [-e^{-y}]_{x}^{\infty}$$

$$= e^{-x}$$

for $x > 0$, and the marginal density function of Y is

$$
\begin{aligned}
f_X(x) &= \int_{-\infty}^{\infty} f(x, y)\, dx \\
&= \int_0^y e^{-y}\, dx \\
&= e^{-y}[x]_0^y \\
&= e^{-y} y
\end{aligned}
$$

for $y > 0$, where it is understood that these functions take the value 0 off the specified domains. The conditional density function of Y given $X = x$ (> 0) is

$$
\begin{aligned}
f_{Y|X}(y \mid x) &= \frac{f_{X,Y}(x, y)}{f_X(x)} \\
&= \frac{e^{-y}}{e^{-x}} \\
&= e^{x-y}
\end{aligned}
$$

for $y > x$. The conditional density function of X given $Y = y$ is

$$
\begin{aligned}
f_{X|Y}(x \mid y) &= \frac{f_{X,Y}(x, y)}{f_Y(Y)} \\
&= \frac{e^{-y}}{e^{-y} y} \\
&= \frac{1}{y}
\end{aligned}
$$

for $0 < x < y$. It is clear that both these conditional density functions equal 0 if $x > y$.

EXERCISE (6.61). Let X and Y be independent random variables, each having the exponential distribution with parameter λ. Find the joint density function of X and $X + Y$, and deduce that the conditional density function of X, given that $X + Y = a$, is uniform on the interval $(0, a)$ for each $a > 0$. In other words, the knowledge that $X + Y = a$ provides no useful clue about the position of X in the interval $(0, a)$.

SOLUTION. The density function of X is

$$
f_X(x) = \begin{cases} \lambda e^{-\lambda x} & \text{if } x > 0, \\ 0 & \text{if } x \le 0, \end{cases}
$$

and the density function of Y is

$$f_Y(y) = \begin{cases} \lambda e^{-\lambda y} & \text{if } y > 0, \\ 0 & \text{if } y \leq 0. \end{cases}$$

The random variables X and Y are independent, so that the joint density function of X and Y is

$$f_{X,Y}(x,y) = f_X(x)f_Y(y)$$
$$= \begin{cases} \lambda^2 e^{-\lambda(x+y)} & \text{if } x > 0 \text{ and } y > 0, \\ 0 & \text{otherwise.} \end{cases}$$

Let $U = X$ and $V = X + Y$. The mapping T of this problem is given by $T(x,y) = (u,v)$, where

$$u = x, \qquad\qquad v = x + y,$$

and T is a bijection from $D = \{(x,y) : x, y > 0\}$ to $S = \{(u,v) : 0 < u < \infty, v > u\}$. It has inverse $T^{-1}(u,v) = (x,y)$, where

$$x = u, \qquad\qquad y = -u + v.$$

The Jacobian of T^{-1} is

$$\begin{vmatrix} \dfrac{\partial x}{\partial u} & \dfrac{\partial x}{\partial v} \\ \dfrac{\partial y}{\partial u} & \dfrac{\partial y}{\partial v} \end{vmatrix} = \begin{vmatrix} 1 & 0 \\ -1 & 1 \end{vmatrix} = 1,$$

giving by Jacobian formula, (6.51) that U and V have joint density function

$$f_{U,V}(u,v) = \begin{cases} f_{X,Y}(x(u,v), y(u,v))\,|J(u,v)| & \text{if } u > 0 \text{ and } v > u, \\ 0 & \text{otherwise,} \end{cases}$$
$$= \begin{cases} \lambda^2 e^{-\lambda[u+(-u+v)]} & \text{if } u > 0 \text{ and } v > u, \\ 0 & \text{otherwise,} \end{cases}$$
$$= \begin{cases} \lambda^2 e^{-\lambda v} & \text{if } u > 0 \text{ and } v > u, \\ 0 & . \end{cases}$$

The marginal density function of V is

$$f_V(v) = \int_{-\infty}^{\infty} f_{U,V}(u,v)\, du$$

$$= \int_0^v \lambda^2 e^{-\lambda v}\, du$$

$$= \lambda^2 e^{-\lambda v} v$$

for $v > 0$. The conditional density function of U given $V = a$ (> 0) is

$$f_{U|V}(u \mid a) = \frac{f_{U,V}(u,a)}{f_V(a)}$$

$$= \frac{\lambda^2 e^{-\lambda a}}{\lambda^2 e^{-\lambda a} a}$$

$$= \frac{1}{a}$$

for $0 < u < a$. Thus the conditional density function of X given $X + Y = a$ (> 0) is

$$f_{X|X+Y}(x,a) = \frac{1}{a}$$

for $0 < x < a$, so that X given that $X + Y = a$ is uniform on the interval $(0, a)$ for each $a > 0$.

6.7. Expectations of continuous random variables

EXERCISE (6.72). Let the pair (X, Y) be uniformly distributed on the unit disc, so that

$$f_{X,Y}(x,y) = \begin{cases} \pi^{-1} & \text{if } x^2 + y^2 \le 1, \\ 0 & \text{otherwise.} \end{cases}$$

Find $\mathbb{E}(\sqrt{X^2 + Y^2})$ and $\mathbb{E}(X^2 + Y^2)$.

SOLUTION. We have that

$$\mathbb{E}(\sqrt{X^2 + Y^2}) = \iint_D \sqrt{x^2 + y^2} f_{X,Y}(x,y)\, dx\, dy$$

by Theorem 6.62, where $D = \{(x,y) : x^2 + y^2 \le 1\}$. Changing variables to polar coordinates, we find that

$$\mathbb{E}(\sqrt{X^2 + Y^2}) = \int_{\theta=0}^{2\pi} \int_{r=0}^{1} r\pi^{-1} r \, dr \, d\theta$$

$$= \pi^{-1} \int_{\theta=0}^{2\pi} [\frac{1}{3}r^3]_{r=0}^{1} \, d\theta$$

$$= \frac{1}{3}\pi^{-1} \int_{\theta=0}^{2\pi} d\theta$$

$$= \frac{1}{3}\pi^{-1} [\theta]_{\theta=0}^{2\pi}$$

$$= \frac{2}{3}.$$

Similarly,

$$\mathbb{E}(X^2 + Y^2) = \iint_D (x^2 + y^2) f_{X,Y}(x, y) \, dx \, dy$$

(by)

$$= \int_{\theta=0}^{2\pi} \int_{r=0}^{1} r^2 \pi^{-1} r \, dr \, d\theta$$

$$= \pi^{-1} \int_{\theta=0}^{2\pi} [\frac{1}{4}r^4]_{r=0}^{1} \, d\theta$$

$$= \frac{1}{4}\pi^{-1} \int_{\theta=0}^{2\pi} d\theta$$

$$= \frac{1}{4}\pi^{-1} [\theta]_{\theta=0}^{2\pi}$$

$$= \frac{1}{2}.$$

EXERCISE (6.71). Give an example of a pair of dependent and jointly continuous random variables X, Y for which $\mathbb{E}(XY) = \mathbb{E}(X)\mathbb{E}(Y)$.

SOLUTION. Let X and Z be independent, X having the normal distribution with mean 0, and variance 1, and Z taking the values ± 1 each with probability $\frac{1}{2}$. The density function of X is

$$f_X(x) = \frac{1}{\sqrt{2\pi}} \exp(-\frac{1}{2}x^2) \qquad \text{for } x \in \mathbb{R},$$

and the mass function of Z is given by

$$p_Z(-1) = \frac{1}{2} \qquad p_Z(1) = \frac{1}{2} \qquad p_Z(z) = 0 \text{ if } z \neq \pm 1.$$

Define $Y = XZ$. The joint density function of Y is

$$f_Y(y) = f_{X,Z}(tz)$$

$$= \begin{cases} \dfrac{1}{2\sqrt{2\pi}} \exp(-\dfrac{1}{2}t^2) & \text{if } z = -1, \\ \dfrac{1}{2\sqrt{2\pi}} \exp(-\dfrac{1}{2}t^2) & \text{if } z = 1, \\ 0 & \text{otherwise.} \end{cases}$$

We have that

(by Theorem 2.42)

$$\mathbb{E}(XY) = E(XY \mid Z = -1)\mathbb{P}(Z = -1) + \mathbb{E}(XY \mid Z = 1)\mathbb{P}(Z = 1)$$
$$= \frac{1}{2}\mathbb{E}(X^2) + \frac{1}{2}\mathbb{E}(-X^2)$$
$$= 0.$$

On the other hand, $\mathbb{E}(X) = 0$, giving that $\mathbb{E}(XY) = \mathbb{E}(X)\mathbb{E}(Y)$.

We have that

$$\mathbb{P}(X \leq 0, Y \leq 0) = \mathbb{P}(X \leq 0, -X \leq 0)$$
$$= \mathbb{P}(X = 0)$$
$$= 0$$

On the other hand,

$$\mathbb{P}(X \leq 0) = \frac{1}{2}$$

and

$$\mathbb{P}(Y \leq 0) = \frac{1}{2}$$

giving that

$$\mathbb{P}(X \leq 0, Y \leq 0) \neq \mathbb{P}(X \leq 0)\mathbb{P}(Y \leq 0)$$

which is to says that X and Y are dependent. (similar to Example 3.22)

EXERCISE (6.72). If X and Y have joint density function

$$f(x, y) = \begin{cases} e^{-y} & \text{if } 0 < x < y < \infty, \\ 0 & \text{otherwise,} \end{cases}$$

find $\mathbb{E}(X \mid Y = y)$ and $\mathbb{E}(Y \mid X = x)$.

SOLUTION. The marginal density function of X is

$$
\begin{aligned}
f_X(x) &= \int_{-\infty}^{\infty} f(x,y)\,dy \\
&= \int_{x}^{\infty} e^{-y}\,dy \\
&= [-e^{-y}]_{x}^{\infty} \\
&= e^{-x}
\end{aligned}
$$

for $x > 0$, and the marginal density function of Y is

$$
\begin{aligned}
f_X(x) &= \int_{-\infty}^{\infty} f(x,y)\,dx \\
&= \int_{0}^{y} e^{-y}\,dx \\
&= e^{-y}[x]_{0}^{y} \\
&= e^{-y}y
\end{aligned}
$$

for $y > 0$, where it is understood that these functions take the value 0 off the specified domains. The conditional density function of Y given $X = x$ (> 0) is

$$
\begin{aligned}
f_{Y|X}(y \mid x) &= \frac{f_{X,Y}(x,y)}{f_X(x)} \\
&= \frac{e^{-y}}{e^{-x}} \\
&= e^{x-y}
\end{aligned}
$$

for $y > x$. The conditional density function of X given $Y = y$ is

$$
\begin{aligned}
f_{X|Y}(x \mid y) &= \frac{f_{X,Y}(x,y)}{f_Y(Y)} \\
&= \frac{e^{-y}}{e^{-y}y} \\
&= \frac{1}{y}
\end{aligned}
$$

for $0 < x < y$. It is clear that both these conditional density functions equal 0 if $x > y$.

We have that

$$E(X \mid Y = y) = \int_{-\infty}^{\infty} x f_{X\mid Y}(x \mid y)\, dx$$

$$= \int_{0}^{y} x \frac{1}{y}\, dx$$

$$= \frac{1}{y} [\frac{x^2}{2}]_{x=0}^{y}$$

$$= \frac{1}{2} y$$

and

$$E(Y \mid X = x) = \int_{-\infty}^{\infty} y f_{Y\mid X}(y \mid x)\, dy$$

$$= \int_{x}^{\infty} y e^{x-y}\, dy$$

$$= e^{x} \int_{x}^{\infty} y e^{-y}\, dy$$

$$= e^{x} \{ [-y e^{-y}]_{y=x}^{\infty} + \int_{x}^{\infty} e^{-y} dy \}$$

$$= e^{x} (x e^{-x} + e^{-x})$$

$$= e^{x} e^{-x} (x + 1)$$

$$= x + 1.$$

6.8. Bivariate normal distribution

EXERCISE (6.79). Let the pair (X, Y) have the bivariate normal density function of (6.76), and let U and V be given by (6.78). Show that U and V have the standard bivariate normal distribution. Hence or otherwise show tha

$$\mathbb{E}(XY) - \mathbb{E}(X)E(Y) = \rho \sigma_1 \sigma_2$$

and that

$$\mathbb{E}(Y \mid X) = \mu_2 + \rho \sigma_2 (x - \mu_1)/\sigma_1.$$

SOLUTION. The pair (X, Y) has the bivariate normal density function

(for $x, y \in \mathbb{R}$,) $$f_{X,Y}(x, y) = \frac{1}{2\pi \sigma_1 \sigma_2 \sqrt{1 - \rho^2}} e^{-\frac{1}{2} Q(x,y)}$$

where Q is the quadratic form

$$Q(x,y) = \frac{1}{1-\rho^2}[(\frac{x-\mu_1}{\sigma_1})^2 - 2\rho(\frac{x-\mu_1}{\sigma_1})(\frac{y-\mu_2}{\sigma_2}) + (\frac{y-\mu_2}{\sigma_2})^2]$$

and $\mu_1, \mu_2 \in \mathbb{R}$, $\sigma_1, \sigma_2 > 0$, $-1 < \rho < 1$. Let

$$U = \frac{X - \mu_1}{\sigma_1}, \qquad\qquad V = \frac{Y - \mu_2}{\sigma_2}.$$

The mapping T of this problem is given by $T(x,y) = (u,v)$, where

$$u = \frac{x - \mu_1}{\sigma_1}, \qquad\qquad v = \frac{y - \mu_2}{\sigma_2},$$

and T is a bijection from $D = \{(x,y) : x,y \in \mathbb{R}\}$ to $S = \{(u,v) : u,v \in \mathbb{R}\}$. It has inverse $T^{-1}(u,v) = (x,y)$, where

$$x = \sigma_1 u + \mu_1, \qquad\qquad y = \sigma_2 v + \mu_2.$$

The Jacobian of T^{-1} is

$$\begin{vmatrix} \dfrac{\partial x}{\partial u} & \dfrac{\partial x}{\partial v} \\[2mm] \dfrac{\partial y}{\partial u} & \dfrac{\partial y}{\partial v} \end{vmatrix} = \begin{vmatrix} \sigma_1 & 0 \\ 0 & \sigma_2 \end{vmatrix} = \sigma_1 \sigma_2,$$

giving by Jacobian formula, (6.51) that U and V have joint density function

$$\begin{aligned}
f_{U,V}(u,v) &= f_{X,Y}(x(u,v), y(u,v)) \, |J(u,v)| \\
&= \frac{1}{2\pi\sigma_1\sigma_2\sqrt{1-\rho^2}} e^{-\frac{1}{2(1-\rho^2)}(u^2 - 2\rho uv + v^2)} \sigma_1 \sigma_2 \\
&= \frac{1}{2\pi\sqrt{1-\rho^2}} e^{-\frac{1}{2(1-\rho^2)}(u^2 - 2\rho uv + v^2)}
\end{aligned}$$

so that U and V have the standard bivariate normal distribution.

We have that

$$\begin{aligned}
\mathbb{E}(XY) - \mathbb{E}(X)\mathbb{E}(Y) &= \mathbb{E}((\sigma_1 U + \mu_2)(\sigma_2 V + \mu_2)) - \mathbb{E}(\sigma_1 U + \mu_2)\mathbb{E}(\sigma_2 V + \mu_2) \\
&= \mathbb{E}(\sigma_1\sigma_2 U + \sigma_1\mu_2 U + \sigma_2\mu_1 V + \mu_1\mu_2) - [\sigma_1\mathbb{E}(U) + \mu_1][\sigma_2\mathbb{E}(V) + \mu_2] \\
&= \rho\sigma_1\sigma_2 + \mu_1\mu_2 - \mu_1\mu_2 \\
&= \rho\sigma_1\sigma_2,
\end{aligned}$$

as required, since $\mathbb{E}(UV) = \rho$ and $\mathbb{E}(U) = \mathbb{E}(V) = 0$.

The conditional expectation of Y given $X = x$ is

$$\mathbb{E}(Y \mid X = x) = \mathbb{E}(\sigma_2 V + \mu_2 \mid \sigma_1 U + \mu_1 = x)$$
$$= \mathbb{E}(\sigma_2 V + \mu_2 \mid U = \frac{x - \mu_1}{\sigma_1})$$
$$= \sigma_2 \mathbb{E}(V \mid U = \frac{x - \mu_1}{\sigma_1}) + \mu_2$$
$$= \sigma_2 \rho \frac{x - \mu_1}{\sigma_1} + \mu_2,$$

as required, since $\mathbb{E}(\mu_2 \mid U = x) = \mu_2$ and $E(\sigma_2 V \mid U = x) = \sigma_2 \mathbb{E}(V \mid U = x) = \sigma_2 \rho x$.

EXERCISE (6.80). Let the pair (X, Y) have the bivariate normal distribution of (6.76), and let $a, b \in \mathbb{R}$. Show that $aX + bY$ has a univariate normal distribution, possibly with zero variance.

SOLUTION (1). The pair (X, Y) has the bivariate normal density function (6.76), that is,

(for $x, y \in \mathbb{R}$,) $$f_{X,Y}(x, y) = \frac{1}{2\pi\sigma_1\sigma_2\sqrt{1 - \rho^2}} e^{-\frac{1}{2}Q(x,y)}$$

where Q is the quadratic form

$$Q(x, y) = \frac{1}{1 - \rho^2}[(\frac{x - \mu_1}{\sigma_1})^2 - 2\rho(\frac{x - \mu_1}{\sigma_1})(\frac{y - \mu_2}{\sigma_2}) + (\frac{y - \mu_2}{\sigma_2})^2]$$

and $\mu_1, \mu_2 \in \mathbb{R}$, $\sigma_1, \sigma_2 > 0$, $-1 < \rho < 1$.

Firstly, we shall show that if T has the normal distribution with mean μ and variance σ^2, then kT, where k is a real constant, has the normal distribution. If $k > 0$, then the distributuion of kT is

$$F_{kT}(x) = \mathbb{P}(kT < x)$$
$$= \mathbb{P}(T < \frac{x}{k})$$
$$= \frac{1}{\sqrt{2\pi\sigma^2}} \int_{-\infty}^{x/k} \exp(-\frac{1}{2\sigma^2}(t - \mu)^2)) \, dt.$$

In this case, the density function of kT is

$$f_{kT}(x) = \frac{d}{dx} F_{kT}(x)$$

$$= \frac{1}{k\sqrt{2\pi\sigma^2}} \exp(-\frac{1}{2\sigma^2}(\frac{x}{k} - \mu)^2)$$

$$= \frac{1}{\sqrt{2\pi(k\sigma)^2}} \exp(-\frac{1}{2(k\sigma)^2}(x - k\mu)^2)$$

so that kT has the normal distribution with mean $k\mu$ and variance $(k\sigma)^2$. If $k < 0$, then the distributuion of kT is

$$F_{kT}(x) = \mathbb{P}(kT < x)$$

$$= \mathbb{P}(T > \frac{x}{k})$$

$$= 1 - \mathbb{P}(T \leq \frac{x}{k})$$

$$= 1 - \frac{1}{\sqrt{2\pi\sigma^2}} \int_{-\infty}^{x/k} \exp(-\frac{1}{2\sigma^2}(t - \mu)^2)) \, dt.$$

In this case, the density function of kT is

$$f_{kT}(x) = \frac{d}{dx} F_{kT}(x)$$

$$= -\frac{1}{k\sqrt{2\pi\sigma^2}} \exp(-\frac{1}{2\sigma^2}(\frac{x}{k} - \mu)^2)$$

$$= \frac{1}{\sqrt{2\pi(-k\sigma)^2}} \exp(-\frac{1}{2(-k\sigma)^2}(x - k\mu)^2)$$

so that kT has the normal distribution with mean $k\mu$ and variance $(-k\sigma)^2$. If $k = 0$, then kT has the normal distribution, so long as one allows degenerate normal distributions with zero variances. The converse is true, so long as one allows $k \neq 0$: $T = (1/k)(kT)$.

Secondly, we shall show that if T has the normal distribution with mean μ and variance σ^2, then $T + a$, where a is a real constant, has the normal distribution. In fact, the distribution function of $T + a$ is

$$F_{T+a}(x) = \mathbb{P}(T + a < x)$$

$$= \mathbb{P}(T < x - a)$$

$$= \frac{1}{\sqrt{2\pi\sigma^2}} \int_{-\infty}^{x-a} \exp(-\frac{1}{2\sigma^2}(t - \mu)^2)) \, dt.$$

The density function of $T + a$ is

$$f_{kT}(x) = \frac{d}{dx} F_{T+a}(x)$$

$$= \frac{1}{\sqrt{2\pi\sigma^2}} \exp(-\frac{1}{2\sigma^2}(x - a - \mu)^2)$$

$$= \frac{1}{\sqrt{2\pi\sigma^2}} \exp(-\frac{1}{2\sigma^2}[x - (a + \mu)]^2)$$

so that $T + a$ has the normal distribution with mean $a + \mu$ and variance $(k\sigma)^2$. The converse is true: $T = (T + a) + (-a)$.

Let U and V be given by (6.78), that is,

$$U = \frac{X - \mu_1}{\sigma_1}, \qquad\qquad V = \frac{Y - \mu_2}{\sigma_2}.$$

Then $aX + bY = a\sigma_1 U + b\sigma_2 V + (a\mu_1 + b\mu_2)$. We can assume that $a \neq 0$ and $b \neq 0$. Using the above two facts, we deduce that $aX + bY$ has the normal distribution if and only if $a\sigma_1 U + b\sigma_2 V$ has the normal distribution. But $a\sigma_1 U + b\sigma_2 V$ has the normal distribution if and only if $U + \alpha V$, where $\alpha \neq 0$, has the normal distribution. The distribution function of $U + \alpha V$ is

$$F_{U+\alpha V}(z) = \mathbb{P}(U + \alpha V < z)$$

$$= \int_{v=-\infty}^{(z-u)/|\alpha|} \int_{u=-\infty}^{\infty} F_{U,V}(u, v)\, du\, dv,$$

where

$$F_{U,V}(u, v) = \frac{1}{2\pi\sqrt{1-\rho^2}} \exp(-\frac{1}{2(1-\rho^2)}(u^2 - 2\rho uv + v^2)).$$

The density function of $U + \alpha V$ is

$$f_{U+\alpha V}(z) = \frac{d}{dz} F_{U+\alpha V}(z)$$

$$= \int_{-\infty}^{\infty} \frac{1}{2\pi|\alpha|\sqrt{1-\rho^2}} \exp(-\frac{1}{2(1-\rho^2)}[u^2 - 2\rho u(\frac{z-u}{\alpha}) + (\frac{z-u}{\alpha})^2])\, du$$

$$= \frac{1}{2\pi|\alpha|\sqrt{1-\rho^2}} \int_{-\infty}^{\infty} \exp(-\frac{1}{2(1-\rho^2)}[(1 + \frac{2\rho}{\alpha} + \frac{1}{\alpha^2})u^2 - (\frac{2\rho z}{\alpha} + \frac{2z}{\alpha^2})u + \frac{z^2}{\alpha^2}])\, du.$$

$$= A \int_{-\infty}^{\infty} \exp(-\frac{1}{2}(au^2 + bu + u))\, du$$

where

$$A = \frac{1}{2\pi |\alpha| \sqrt{1-\rho^2}}, \quad a = \frac{\alpha^2 + 2\rho\alpha + 1}{\alpha^2(1-\rho^2)}, \quad b = -\frac{2(\rho\alpha + 1)z}{\alpha^2(1-\rho^2)}, \quad c = \frac{z^2}{\alpha^2(1-\rho^2)}.$$

We have that

$$f_{U+\alpha V}(z) = \frac{1}{2\pi |\alpha| \sqrt{1-\rho^2}} \int_{-\infty}^{\infty} \exp(-\frac{1}{2}(au^2 + bu + c))\, du$$

$$= \frac{1}{2\pi |\alpha| \sqrt{1-\rho^2}} \int_{-\infty}^{\infty} \exp(-\frac{1}{2}[(\sqrt{a}x + \frac{b}{2\sqrt{a}})^2 + c - \frac{b^2}{4a}])\, dx$$

Substitute $t = \sqrt{a}u + \frac{b}{2\sqrt{a}}$ in the last integral to obtain

$$f_{U+\alpha V}(z) = \frac{1}{2\pi |\alpha| \sqrt{1-\rho^2}} \int_{-\infty}^{\infty} \frac{1}{\sqrt{a}} \exp(-\frac{1}{2}(t^2 + c - \frac{b^2}{4a}))\, dt$$

$$= \frac{1}{2\pi |\alpha| \sqrt{1-\rho^2}} [\frac{1}{\sqrt{a}} \exp(-\frac{1}{2}(c - \frac{b^2}{4a})) \int_{-\infty}^{\infty} e^{-\frac{1}{2}t^2}\, dt]$$

$$= \frac{1}{2\pi |\alpha| \sqrt{1-\rho^2}} [\frac{\sqrt{2\pi}}{\sqrt{a}} \exp(-\frac{1}{2}(c - \frac{b^2}{4a}))].$$

$$= \frac{1}{2\pi |\alpha| \sqrt{1-\rho^2}} \frac{\sqrt{2\pi}}{\sqrt{\frac{\alpha^2+2\rho\alpha+1}{\alpha^2(1-\rho^2)}}} \exp(-\frac{1}{2}[\frac{z^2}{\alpha^2(1-\rho^2)} - \frac{4(1+\rho\alpha)^2 z^2}{\alpha^4(1-\rho^2)^2} \cdot \frac{\alpha^2(1-\rho^2)}{4(\alpha^2+2\rho\alpha+1)}])$$

$$= \frac{1}{\sqrt{2\pi(\alpha^2 + 2\rho\alpha + 1)}} \exp(-\frac{1}{2}[\frac{\alpha^2(1-\rho^2)z^2}{\alpha^2(1-\rho^2)(\alpha^2+2\rho\alpha+1)}])$$

$$= \frac{1}{\sqrt{2\pi(\alpha^2 + 2\rho\alpha + 1)}} \exp(-\frac{1}{2(\alpha^2+2\rho\alpha+1)}z^2)$$

so that $U+\alpha V$ has the normal distribution with mean 0 and variance $(\alpha^2+2\rho\alpha+1)$.

SOLUTION (2). By changing of variables as in (6.78), the pair (X, Y) has the standard bivariate normal distribution. We shall first find the joint density function of $U = X$ and $V = aX + bY$ by the method of change of variables, and then find the marginal density function of V.

We consider first the case $b \neq 0$. The mapping T of this case is given by $T(x, y) = (u, v)$, where

$$u = x, \qquad\qquad v = ax + by,$$

and T is a bijection from $D = \{(x, y) : x, y \in \mathbb{R}\}$ to $S = \{(u, v) : u, v \in \mathbb{R}\}$. It has inverse $T^{-1}(u, v) = (x, y)$, where

$$x = u, \qquad\qquad y = -\frac{a}{b}u + \frac{1}{b}v.$$

The Jacobian of T^{-1} is

$$\begin{vmatrix} \dfrac{\partial x}{\partial u} & \dfrac{\partial x}{\partial v} \\[2mm] \dfrac{\partial y}{\partial u} & \dfrac{\partial y}{\partial v} \end{vmatrix} = \begin{vmatrix} 1 & 0 \\[1mm] -\dfrac{a}{b} & \dfrac{1}{b} \end{vmatrix} = \frac{1}{b},$$

giving by Jacobian formula, (6.51) that U and V have joint density function

$$\begin{aligned}
f_{U,V}(u,v) &= f_{X,Y}(x(u,v), y(u,v)) \, |J(u,v)| \\
&= \frac{1}{2\pi |b| \sqrt{1-\rho^2}} e^{-\frac{1}{2(1-\rho^2)}[u^2 - 2\rho u(-\frac{a}{b}u + \frac{1}{b}v) + (-\frac{a}{b}u + \frac{1}{b}v)^2]} \\
&= \frac{1}{2\pi |b| \sqrt{1-\rho^2}} e^{-\frac{1}{2(1-\rho^2)}[(1 + 2\rho\frac{a}{b} + \frac{a^2}{b^2})u^2 - \frac{2}{b^2}(\rho b + a)uv + \frac{1}{b^2}v^2]}.
\end{aligned}$$

For $m > 0$, then

$$\begin{aligned}
\int_{-\infty}^{\infty} e^{-\frac{1}{2}(mu^2 + fu + g)} \, du &= \int_{-\infty}^{\infty} e^{-\frac{1}{2}[(\sqrt{m} + \frac{f}{2\sqrt{m}})^2 + g - \frac{f^2}{4m}]} \, du \\
&= e^{-\frac{1}{2}(g - \frac{f^2}{4m})} \int_{-\infty}^{\infty} \frac{1}{\sqrt{m}} e^{-\frac{1}{2}t^2} \, dt \\
&= \frac{\sqrt{2\pi}}{\sqrt{m}} e^{-\frac{1}{2}(g - \frac{f^2}{4m})}.
\end{aligned}$$

The marginal density function fo V is

$$\begin{aligned}
f_V(v) &= \int_{-\infty}^{\infty} f_{U,V}(u,v) \, du \\
&= \frac{1}{2\pi |b| \sqrt{1-\rho^2}} \cdot \frac{\sqrt{2\pi}}{\frac{\sqrt{a^2 + 2\rho ab + b^2}}{|b|\sqrt{1-\rho^2}}} e^{-\frac{1}{2(1-\rho^2)}[\frac{v^2}{b^2} - \frac{4(\rho b + a)^2}{4b^4(1+2\rho\frac{a}{b}+\frac{a^2}{b^2})}v^2]} \\
&= \frac{1}{\sqrt{2\pi}\sqrt{a^2 + 2\rho ab + b^2}} e^{-\frac{1}{2(1-\rho^2)b^2}(1 - \frac{\rho^2 b^2 + 2\rho ab + a^2}{b^2 + 2\rho ab + a^2})v^2} \\
&= \frac{1}{\sqrt{2\pi}\sqrt{a^2 + 2\rho ab + b^2}} e^{-\frac{1}{2(1-\rho^2)b^2} \cdot \frac{(1-\rho^2)b^2}{b^2 + 2\rho ab + a^2}v^2} \\
&= \frac{1}{\sqrt{2\pi(a^2 + 2\rho ab + b^2)}} e^{-\frac{1}{2(a^2 + 2\rho ab + b^2)}v^2},
\end{aligned}$$

so that $V = aX + bY$, where $b \neq 0$, has the normal distribution with mean 0 and variance $a^2 + 2\rho ab + b^2$.

We consider next the case $b = 0$. In this case, we could do the same as in the first case; however we can use the moment generating function the shorten the problem. The moment generating function of V is

$$M_V(t) = \mathbb{E}(e^{aXt})$$
$$= \mathbb{E}(e^{(at)X})$$
$$= M_X(at),$$

where

$$M_X(t) = e^{-\frac{1}{2}t^2},$$

giving that

$$M_V(t) = e^{\frac{1}{2}a^2 t^2},$$

which we recognize by (7.58) as the moment generating function of the normal distribution with mean 0 and variance a^2.

6.9. Problems

PROBLEM (6.9.1). If X and Y are independent random variables with density functions f_X and f_Y, respectively, show that $U = XY$ and $V = X/Y$ have density functions

$$f_U(u) = \int_{-\infty}^{\infty} f_X(x) f_Y(u/x) \frac{1}{|x|} \, dx, \qquad f_V(v) = \int_{-\infty}^{\infty} f_X(vy) f_Y(y) \, |y| \, dy.$$

SOLUTION. If X and Y are independent, then $f_{X,Y}(x,y) = f_X(x) f_Y(y)$. For the first part, we shall find the joint density function of $W = X$ and $U = XY$, and then find the marginal density function of U. The mapping T of this part is given by $T(x,y) = (w,u)$, where

$$w = x, \qquad\qquad u = xy,$$

and T is a bijection from $D = \{(x,y) : x \in \mathbb{R}, y \in \mathbb{R}\}$ to $S = \{(w,u) : w \neq 0, u \in \mathbb{R}\}$. It has inverse $T^{-1}(w,u) = (x,y)$, where

$$x = w, \qquad\qquad y = \frac{u}{w}.$$

The Jacobian of T^{-1} is

$$\begin{vmatrix} \dfrac{\partial x}{\partial w} & \dfrac{\partial x}{\partial u} \\[2ex] \dfrac{\partial y}{\partial w} & \dfrac{\partial y}{\partial u} \end{vmatrix} = \begin{vmatrix} 1 & 0 \\[1ex] -\dfrac{u}{w^2} & \dfrac{1}{w} \end{vmatrix} = \frac{1}{w},$$

giving by Jacobian formula, (6.51) that W and U have joint density function

$$f_{W,U}(w,u) = \begin{cases} f_{X,Y}(x(w,u),y(w,u))\,|J(w,u)| & \text{if } w \neq 0, \\ 0 & \text{otherwise,} \end{cases}$$

$$= \begin{cases} f_X(w)f_Y(u/w)\left|\dfrac{1}{w}\right| & \text{if } w \neq 0, \\ 0 & \text{otherwise.} \end{cases}$$

The marginal density function of U is

$$f_U(u) = \int_{-\infty}^{\infty} f_{W,U}(w,u)\,dw$$

$$= \int_{-\infty}^{\infty} f_X(w)f_Y(u/w)\left|\frac{1}{w}\right|\,dw$$

$$= \int_{-\infty}^{\infty} f_X(x)f_Y(u/x)\frac{1}{|x|}\,dx$$

as required. For the second part, we shall find the joint density function of $W = Y$ and $V = X/Y$, and then find the marginal density function of V. The mapping T of this part is given by $T(x,y) = (w,v)$, where

$$w = y, \qquad\qquad v = \frac{x}{y},$$

and S is a bijection from $D = \{(x,y) : x \in \mathbb{R}, y \in \mathbb{R}\}$ to $S = \{(w,v) : w \neq 0, v \in \mathbb{R}\}$. It has inverse $T^{-1}(w,v) = (x,y)$, where

$$x = wv, \qquad\qquad y = w.$$

The Jacobian of S^{-1} is

$$\begin{vmatrix} \dfrac{\partial x}{\partial w} & \dfrac{\partial x}{\partial v} \\ \dfrac{\partial y}{\partial w} & \dfrac{\partial y}{\partial v} \end{vmatrix} = \begin{vmatrix} v & w \\ 1 & 0 \end{vmatrix} = -w,$$

giving by Jacobian formula, (6.51) that W and V have joint density function

$$f_{W,V}(w,v) = \begin{cases} f_{X,Y}(x(w,v),y(w,v))\,|J(w,v)| & \text{if } v \neq 0, \\ 0 & \text{otherwise,} \end{cases}$$

$$= \begin{cases} f_X(wv)f_Y(w)\,|-w| & \text{if } w \neq 0, \\ 0 & \text{otherwise.} \end{cases}$$

The marginal density function of V is

$$f_V(v) = \int_{-\infty}^{\infty} f_{W,V}(w, v)\, dw$$

$$= \int_{-\infty}^{\infty} f_X(wv) f_Y(v)\, |-w|\, dw$$

$$= \int_{-\infty}^{\infty}\int_{-\infty}^{\infty} f_X(vy) f_Y(y)\, |y|\, dy\, dx$$

as required.

PROBLEM (6.9.2). Is the function G, defined by

$$G(x, y) = \begin{cases} 1 & \text{if } x + y \geq 0, \\ 0 & \text{otherwise}, \end{cases}$$

the joint distribution function of some pair of random variables? Justify your answer.

SOLUTION. No. Clearly,

$$\frac{\partial^2}{\partial x\, \partial y} G(x, y) = 0$$

for all x and y, and it is the case that

$$\int_{-\infty}^{\infty}\int_{-\infty}^{\infty} \frac{\partial^2}{\partial x\, \partial y} G(x, y)\, dx\, dy = \int_{-\infty}^{\infty}\int_{-\infty}^{\infty} 0\, dx\, dy$$

$$= 0$$

$$\neq 1,$$

giving that $\dfrac{\partial^2}{\partial x\, \partial y} G(x, y)$ is not a joint density function, so that $G(x, y)$ is not a joint distribution function.

PROBLEM (6.9.3). Let (X, Y, Z) be a point chosen uniformly at random in the unit cube $(0, 1)^3$. Find the probability that the quadratic equation $Xt^2 + Yt + Z = 0$ has two distinct real roots.

SOLUTION. By the quadratic formula, the quadratic equation $Xt^2 + Yt + Z = 0$ has two distinct real roots if and only if $Y^2 - 4XZ > 0$. That is to say, $Y > \sqrt{4XZ}$. Let $A = \{(x, y, z)\colon \sqrt{4xz} < y \leq 1, 0 \leq x, z \leq 1\}$. Then

$$\mathbb{P}(Y > 2\sqrt{XZ}) = \mathbb{P}((X, Y, Z) \in A)$$

$$= \frac{\text{volume}\,(A)}{\text{volume}\,((0,1)^3)}$$

since (X, Y, Z) is uniformly distributed on the unit cube $(0, 1)^3$. The volume of A is

$$
\begin{aligned}
\text{volume}\,(A) &= \iiint_A dx\,dy\,dz \\
&= \int_{z=1/4}^{1} \int_{x=0}^{1/(4z)} \int_{y=2\sqrt{xz}}^{1} dx\,dy\,dz + \int_{z=0}^{1/4} \int_{x=0}^{1} \int_{y=2\sqrt{xz}}^{1} dx\,dy\,dz \\
&= \int_{z=1/4}^{1} \int_{x=0}^{1/(4z)} (1 - 2\sqrt{xz})\,dx\,dz + \int_{z=0}^{1/4} \int_{x=0}^{1} (1 - 2\sqrt{xz})\,dx\,dz \\
&= \int_{1/4}^{1} [x - \tfrac{4}{3}\sqrt{z}x^{3/2}]_{x=0}^{1/(4z)}\,dz + \int_{z=0}^{1/4} [1 - 2\sqrt{xz}]_{x=0}^{1}\,dz \\
&= \int_{1/4}^{1} \frac{1}{12z}\,dz + \int_{0}^{1/4} (1 - \tfrac{4}{3}\sqrt{z})\,dz \\
&= [\tfrac{1}{12}\log z]_{1/4}^{1} + [z - \tfrac{8}{9}z^{3/2}]_{0}^{1/4} \\
&= \frac{1}{12}\log 4 + \frac{5}{36} \\
&= \frac{5}{36} + \frac{1}{6}\log 2,
\end{aligned}
$$

so that

$$
\begin{aligned}
\mathbb{P}(Y > 2\sqrt{XZ}) &= \frac{\text{volume}\,(A)}{\text{volume}\,((0,1)^3)} \\
&= \frac{5}{36} + \frac{1}{6}\log 2,
\end{aligned}
$$

since the volume of the unit cube $(0, 1)^3$ is 1.

PROBLEM (6.9.4). Show that if X and Y are independent random variables having the exponential distribution with parameters λ and μ, respectively, then $\min\{X, Y\}$ has the exponential distribution with parameter $\lambda + \mu$.

SOLUTION. The distribution function of $Z = \min\{X, Y\}$ is

$$\mathbb{P}(Z \leq z) = \mathbb{P}(\min\{X, Y\} \leq z)$$
$$= 1 - \mathbb{P}(\min\{X, Y\} > z)$$
$$= 1 - \mathbb{P}(X > z, Y > z) \qquad \text{since } \min\{X, Y\} > u$$
$$\phantom{= 1 - \mathbb{P}(X > z, Y > z)} \qquad \text{if and only if } X > u \text{ and } Y > u$$
$$= 1 - \mathbb{P}(X > z)\mathbb{P}(Y > z) \qquad \text{by independence}$$
$$= 1 - [1 - \mathbb{P}(X \leq z)][1 - \mathbb{P}(Y \leq z)]$$
$$= \begin{cases} 1 - (1-0)(1-0) & \text{if } z \leq 0, \\ 1 - [1 - (1 - e^{-\lambda z})][1 - (1 - e^{-\mu z})] & \text{if } z \geq 0, \end{cases}$$
$$= \begin{cases} 0 & \text{if } z \leq 0, \\ 1 - e^{-(\lambda + \mu)z} & \text{if } z \geq 0, \end{cases}$$

so that $\min\{X, Y\}$ has the exponential distribution with parameter $\lambda + \mu$.

PROBLEM (6.9.5). *Lack-of-memory property.* If X has the exponential distribution, show that

$$\mathbb{P}(X > u + v \mid X > u) = \mathbb{P}(X > v) \qquad \text{for } u, v > 0.$$

This is called the 'lack of memory' property, since it says that, if we are given that $X > u$, then the distribution of $X - u$ is the same as the original distribution of X. Show that if Y is a positive, continuous random variable with the lack-of-memory property above, then Y has the exponential distribution.

SOLUTION. The solution to this problem is adapted from the proof of Theorem 11.26.

If X is exponentially distributed with parameter λ then, for $u, v \geq 0$,

$$\mathbb{P}(X > u + v \mid X > u) = \frac{\mathbb{P}(X > u + v \text{ and } X > u)}{\mathbb{P}(X > u)}$$

$$\text{(since)} \qquad = \frac{\mathbb{P}(X > u + v)}{\mathbb{P}(X > u)} \qquad u \leq u + v$$

$$= \frac{e^{-\lambda(u+v)}}{e^{-\lambda u}} \qquad \text{from Example 5.22}$$

$$= e^{-\lambda v}$$

$$= \mathbb{P}(X > v), \qquad\qquad (6.9.5.1)$$

so that X has the lack-of-memory property.

Conversely, suppose that X is positive and continuous, and has the lack-of-memory property. Let $G(u) = \mathbb{P}(X > u)$ for $u \geq 0$. The left-hand side of (6.9.5.1) is

$$\mathbb{P}(X > u + v \mid X > u) = \frac{\mathbb{P}(X > u + v)}{\mathbb{P}(X > u)} = \frac{G(u+v)}{G(u)},$$

and so G satisfies the 'functional equation'

$$G(u + v) = G(u)G(v) \qquad\qquad \text{for } u, v > 0. \qquad\qquad (6.9.5.2)$$

The function $G(u)$ is non-increasing in the real variable u, and all non-zero non-increasing solutions of (6.9.5.2) are of the form

$$G(u) = e^{-\lambda u} \qquad\qquad \text{for } u \geq 0, \qquad\qquad (6.9.5.3)$$

where λ is some constant. It is an interesting exercise in analysis to derive (6.9.5.2) from (6.9.5.2), and we shall check this as follows. First, we note that $G(0) = 1$ by setting $v = 0$. Next, we differentiate throughout (6.9.5.2) with respect to v, noting that G must be differentiable by the continuity of X and the Fundamental Theorem of Calculus, to obtain

$$G'(u + v) = G(u)G'(y).$$

In particular, setting $y = 0$ gives

$$G'(u) = G(u)G'(0).$$

Therefore, letting $\lambda = -G'(0)$, we have

$$G'(u) = -\lambda G(u) \qquad\qquad\qquad G(0) = 1,$$

which has solution $G(u) = e^{-\lambda u}$ as required. Since G is a decreasing function, we must have $\lambda > 0$.

PROBLEM (6.9.6). Let $X_1, X_2, \ldots, X_n$ be independent random variables, each having distribution function F and density function f. Find the distribution function of U and the density functions of U and V, where $U = \min\{X_1, X_2, \ldots, X_n\}$ and $V = \max\{X_1, X_2, \ldots, X_n\}$. Show that the joint density function of U and V is

$$f_{U,V}(u, v) = n(n - 1)f(u)f(v)[F(v) - F(u)]^{n-2} \qquad\qquad \text{if } u < v.$$

SOLUTION. The distribution function of $U = \min\{X_1, X_2, \ldots, X_n\}$ is

$$F_U(u) = \mathbb{P}(U \le u)$$
$$= \mathbb{P}(\min\{X_1, X_2, \ldots, X_n\} \le u)$$
$$= 1 - \mathbb{P}(\min\{X_1, X_2, \ldots, X_n\} > u)$$
$$= 1 - \mathbb{P}(X_1 > u, X_2 > u, \ldots X_n > u) \qquad \text{since } \min\{X_1, X_2, \ldots, X_n\} > u$$
$$\Leftrightarrow X_1 > u, X_2 > u, \ldots X_n > u$$
$$= 1 - \mathbb{P}(X_1 > u)\mathbb{P}(X_2 > u) \cdots \mathbb{P}(X_n > u) \qquad \text{by independence}$$
$$= 1 - [1 - \mathbb{P}(X_1 \le u)][1 - \mathbb{P}(X_2 \le u)] \cdots [1 - \mathbb{P}(X_n \le u)]$$
$$= 1 - [1 - F(u)][1 - F(u)] \cdots [1 - F(u)]$$
$$= 1 - [1 - F(u)]^n.$$

Differentiate this equation with respect to u, where possible, to obtain

$$f_U(u) = \frac{d}{du} F_U(u)$$
$$= \frac{d}{du} \{1 - [1 - F(u)]^n\}$$
$$= n f(u)[1 - F(u)]^{n-1}.$$

The distribution function of $V = \max\{X_1, X_2, \ldots, X_n\}$ is

$$F_V(v) = \mathbb{P}(V \le v)$$
$$= \mathbb{P}(\max\{X_1, X_2, \ldots, X_n\} \le v)$$
$$= \mathbb{P}(X_1 \le v, X_2 \le v, \ldots X_n \le v) \qquad \text{since } \max\{X_1, X_2, \ldots, X_n\} \le v$$
$$\Leftrightarrow X_1 \le v, X_2 \le v, \ldots, \text{ and } X_n \le v$$
$$= \mathbb{P}(X_1 \le v)\mathbb{P}(X_2 \le v) \cdots \mathbb{P}(X_n \le v) \qquad \text{by independence}$$
$$= F(v)F(v) \cdots F(v)$$
$$= [F(v)]^n.$$

Differentiate this equation with respect to v, where possible, to obtain

$$f_V(v) = \frac{d}{dv} F_V(v)$$
$$= \frac{d}{dv} [F(v)]^n$$
$$= n f(v)[F(v)]^{n-1}.$$

For $u < v$, the joint distribution function of U and V is

$F_{U,V}(u,v)$

$= \mathbb{P}(U \le u, V \le v)$

$= \mathbb{P}(\min\{X_1, X_2, \dots, X_n\} \le u, \max\{X_1, X_2, \dots, X_n\} \le v)$

$= \mathbb{P}(\max\{X_1, X_2, \dots, X_n\} \le v)$

$\quad - \mathbb{P}(\min\{X_1, X_2, \dots, X_n\} > u, \max\{X_1, X_2, \dots, X_n\} \le v)$

$= \mathbb{P}(V \le v) - \mathbb{P}(u < X_1 \le v, u < X_2 \le v, \dots, u < X_n \le v)$

$\qquad\qquad\qquad\qquad\qquad \min\{X_1, X_2, \dots, X_n\} > u$
$\qquad\qquad\qquad\qquad\qquad\quad \text{and}$
$\qquad\qquad\qquad\qquad\qquad \max\{X_1, X_2, \dots, X_n\} \le v$
$\qquad\qquad\qquad\qquad \Leftrightarrow u < X_1 \le v, u < X_2 \le v,$
$\qquad\qquad\qquad\qquad\qquad \dots, u < X_n \le v$

$= \mathbb{P}(V \le v) - \mathbb{P}(u < X_1 \le v)\mathbb{P}(u < X_2 \le v) \cdots \mathbb{P}(u < X_n \le v)$

$= [F(v)]^n - [F(v) - F(u)][F(v) - F(u)] \cdots [F(v) - F(u)]$ $\qquad$ by independence

$= [F(v)]^n - [F(v) - F(u)]^n.$

Differentiate this equation with respect to u, where possible, to obtain

$$\frac{\partial}{\partial u} F_{U,V}(u,v) = \frac{\partial}{\partial u} \{[F(v)]^n - [F(v) - F(u)]^n\}$$
$$= nf(u)[F(v) - F(u)]^{n-1},$$

and differentiate this equation with respect to v, where possible, to obtain

$$\frac{\partial^2}{\partial u\, \partial v} F_{U,V}(u,v) = n(n-1)f(u)f(v)[F(v) - F(u)]^{n-2},$$

giving that the joint density function of U and V is

$$f_{U,V}(u,v) = n(n-1)f(u)f(v)[F(v) - F(u)]^{n-2} \qquad\qquad \text{if } u < v,$$

as required.

PROBLEM (6.9.7). Let $X_1, X_2, \dots$ be independent, identically distributed, continuous random variables. Define N as the index such that

$$X_1 \ge X_2 \ge \cdots \ge X_{N-1} \text{ and } X_{N-1} < X_N.$$

Prove that $\mathbb{P}(N = k) = (k-1)/k!$ and that $\mathbb{E}(N) = e$.

SOLUTION. We note that if X and Y are ontinuous random variables, then $\mathbb{P}(X = Y) = 0$. Henceforth, it is reasonable to assume that

$$X_1 > X_2 > \cdots > X_{k-1} \text{ and } X_{k-1} < X_k.$$

The number of permutations of $\{X_1, X_2, \dots, X_k\}$ is $k!$. There are $k - 1$ cases occur for this event, such as, $X_k > X_1 > X_2 > \cdots > X_{k-1}$, $X_1 > X_k > X_2 >$

$\cdots > X_{k-1}, \ldots, X_1 > X_2 > \cdots > X_{k-2} > X_k > X_{k-1}$. There are $k - 1$ cases occur for this event. Thus

$$\mathbb{P}(N = k) = \frac{k-1}{k!},$$

as required.

The mean of N is

$$
\begin{aligned}
\mathbb{E}(N) &= \sum_{k \in \operatorname{Im} N} k\mathbb{P}(N = k) \\
&= \sum_{k=2}^{\infty} k\frac{k-1}{k!} \\
&= \sum_{k=2}^{\infty} \frac{1}{(k-2)!} \\
&= \sum_{n=0}^{\infty} \frac{1}{n!} \qquad\qquad \text{reindex with } n = k - 2 \\
&= e,
\end{aligned}
$$

as required.

PROBLEM (6.9.8). Show that there exists a constant c such that the function

$$f(x, y) = \frac{c}{(1 + x^2 + y^2)^{3/2}} \qquad\qquad \text{for } x, y \in \mathbb{R}$$

is a joint density function. Show that both marginal density functions of f are the density function of the Cauchy distribution.

SOLUTION. Joint density functions integrate to 1, so that

$$
\begin{aligned}
1 &= \int_{-\infty}^{\infty} \int_{-\infty}^{\infty} f(x, y)\, dx\, dy \\
&= \int_{-\infty}^{\infty} \int_{-\infty}^{\infty} \frac{c}{(1 + x^2 + y^2)^{3/2}}\, dx\, dy.
\end{aligned}
$$

Change variables to polar coordinates in the last integral to obtain

$$
\begin{aligned}
1 &= \int_{\theta=0}^{2\pi} \int_{r=0}^{\infty} \frac{c}{(1 + r^2)^{3/2}} r\, dr\, d\theta \\
&= 2\pi \int_{0}^{\infty} \frac{c}{(1 + r^2)^{3/2}} r\, dr.
\end{aligned}
$$

Substitute $t = 1 + r^2$ in the last integral to obtain

$$1 = 2\pi \int_1^\infty \frac{c}{2t^{3/2}} \, dt$$

$$= -2\pi [\frac{c}{\sqrt{t}}]_1^\infty$$

$$= 2\pi c,$$

giving that $c = 1/(2\pi)$.

We now evaluate $I = \int_{-\infty}^\infty \frac{1}{(a + y^2)^{3/2}} \, dy$ where $a > 0$. We have that

$$I = \int_{-\infty}^\infty \frac{\frac{1}{a^{3/2}} \, dy}{[1 + (\frac{y}{\sqrt{a}})^2]^{3/2}}$$

$$= \int_{-\infty}^\infty \frac{\frac{1}{a} \, d(\frac{y}{\sqrt{a}})}{[1 + (\frac{y}{\sqrt{a}})^2]^{3/2}}$$

Substitute $t = y/\sqrt{a}$ in the last integral to obtain

$$I = \frac{1}{a} \int_{-\infty}^\infty \frac{dt}{(1 + t^2)^{3/2}}$$

Let $t = \tan\phi$ where $-\pi/2 < \phi < \pi/2$, then $1 + t^2 = 1 + \tan^2\phi = \frac{1}{\cos^2\phi}$ and $dt = \frac{1}{\cos^2\phi} \, d\phi$

$$I = \frac{1}{a} \int_{-\pi/2}^{\pi/2} \frac{\frac{1}{\cos^2\phi} \, d\phi}{(\frac{1}{\cos^2\phi})^{3/2}} = \frac{1}{a} \int_{-\pi/2}^{\pi/2} \cos\phi \, d\phi$$

$$= \frac{1}{a} [\sin\phi]_{-\pi/2}^{\pi/2} = \frac{1}{a}(1 + 1) = \frac{2}{a}$$

Apply the integral above for $a = 1 + x^2$, we have that

$$f_X(x) = \int_{-\infty}^\infty \frac{1}{2\pi} \cdot \frac{1}{(1 + x^2 + y^2)^{3/2}} \, dy$$

$$= \frac{1}{2\pi} \cdot \frac{2}{1 + x^2}$$

$$= \frac{1}{\pi(1 + x^2)} \qquad\qquad \text{for } x \in \mathbb{R},$$

so that X has the Cauchy distribution. A similar calculation shows that Y has this distribution also.

PROBLEM (6.9.9). Let X and Y have joint density function

$$f(x,y) = \begin{cases} \dfrac{1}{4}(x+3y)e^{-(x+y)} & \text{if } x, y \geq 0, \\ 0 & \text{otherwise.} \end{cases}$$

Find the marginal density function of Y. Show that $\mathbb{P}(Y > X) = \dfrac{5}{8}$.

SOLUTION. The marginal density function of Y is

$$f_Y(y) = \int_{-\infty}^{\infty} f(x,y)\,dx$$

$$= \int_0^{\infty} \frac{1}{4}(x+3y)e^{-(x+y)}\,dx$$

$$= \frac{1}{4}\{[-(x+3y)e^{-(x+y)}]_{x=0}^{\infty} + \int_{x=0}^{\infty} e^{-(x+y)}\,dx\} \quad \begin{array}{l} \text{by integration by parts formula with} \\ u = x+3y, dv = e^{-(x+y)}\,dx \\ du = dx, v = -e^{-(x+y)} \end{array}$$

$$= \frac{1}{4}\{3ye^{-y} - [e^{-(x+y)}]_{x=0}^{\infty}\}$$

$$= \frac{1}{4}(3ye^{-y} + e^{-y})$$

$$= \frac{1}{4}(3y+1)e^{-y}$$

for $0 < y < \infty$.

We have that

$$\mathbb{P}(Y > X) = \iint_A f(x,y)\,dx\,dy$$

by Theorem 6.22, where $A = \{(x,y) \in R^2 : y > x\}$. Writing in the limits of integration, we find that

$$\mathbb{P}(Y > X) = \int_{y=0}^{\infty} [\int_{x=0}^{y} \frac{1}{4}(x+3y)e^{-(x+y)}\,dx]\,dy$$

$$= \int_{y=0}^{\infty} I\,dy$$

where I is the integral given by

$$I = \int_{x=0}^{y} \frac{1}{4}(x+3y)e^{-(x+y)}\,dx$$

by integration by parts formula with

$$\left(\quad \begin{matrix} u = x+3y, dv = e^{-(x+y)}\,dx \\ du = dx, v = -e^{-(x+y)} \end{matrix} \quad\right)$$

$$= \frac{1}{4}\{[-(x+3y)e^{-(x+y)}]_{x=0}^{y} + \int_{x=0}^{y} e^{-(x+y)}\,dx\}$$

$$= \frac{1}{4}(-4ye^{-2y} + 3ye^{-y} - e^{-2y} + e^{-y}).$$

$$= \frac{1}{4}[e^{-y}(3y+1) + e^{-2y}(-4y-1)]$$

Thus

$$\mathbb{P}(Y > X) = \int_{0}^{\infty} \frac{1}{4}[e^{-y}(3y+1) + e^{-2y}(-4y-1)]\,dy$$

$$= \frac{1}{4}[\int_{0}^{\infty} e^{-y}(3y+1)\,dy + \int_{0}^{\infty} e^{-2y}(-4y-1)\,dy]$$

$$= \frac{1}{4}(J+K)$$

where J and K are the integrals given by

$$J = \int_{0}^{\infty} e^{-y}(3y+1)\,dy$$

$$= [-e^{-y}(3y+1)]_{0}^{\infty} + \int_{0}^{\infty} 3e^{-y}\,dy$$

by integration by parts formula with
$$u = 3y+1, dv = e^{-y}\,dy$$
$$du = 3dy, v = -e^{-y}$$

$$= [-e^{-y}(3y+1)]_{0}^{\infty} + [-3e^{-y}]_{0}^{\infty}$$

$$= [-3e^{-y}y - e^{-y} - 3e^{-y}]_{0}^{\infty}$$

$$= [-3e^{-y}y - 4e^{-y}]_{0}^{\infty}$$

$$= 4$$

and

$$K = \int_0^\infty e^{-2y}(-4y - 1)\,dy$$

by integration by parts formula with
$$u = -4y - 1, dv = e^{-2y}\,dy$$
$$du = -4dy, v = -\frac{1}{2}e^{-2y}$$

$$= [-\frac{1}{2}e^{-2y}(-4y - 1)]_0^\infty + \int_0^\infty 2e^{-2y}\,dy$$

$$= [-\frac{1}{2}e^{-2y}(-4y - 1)]_0^\infty + [-e^{-2y}]_0^\infty$$

$$= [2e^{-2y}y + \frac{1}{2}e^{-2y} - e^{-2y}]_0^\infty$$

$$= [2e^{-2y}y + \frac{3}{2}e^{-2y}]_0^\infty$$

$$= -\frac{3}{2}$$

Therefore

$$\mathbb{P}(Y > X) = \frac{1}{4}(4 - \frac{3}{2})$$
$$= \frac{5}{8},$$

as required.

PROBLEM (6.9.10). Let S_n be the sum of n independent, identically distributed random variables having the exponential distribution with parameter λ. Show that S_n has the gamma distribution with parameters n and λ. For given $t > 0$, show that $N_t = \max\{n \colon S_n \le t\}$ has a Poisson distribution.

SOLUTION. For the first part, we shall prove by induction on n. Consider first the case $n = 2$. Then $S_2 = X_1 + X_2$, where X_1 and X_2 are independent, identically distributed random variables having the exponential distribution with parameter λ, has density function

$$f_{S_2}(z) = \int_{-\infty}^\infty f_{X_1}(x)f_{X_2}(s - x)\,dx$$
$$= \begin{cases} \int_0^z f_{X_1}(x)f_{X_2}(s - x)\,dx & \text{if } z > 0, \\ 0 & \text{otherwise,} \end{cases}$$

since $f_{X_1}(x)f_{X_2}(z - x) = 0$ unless $x > 0$ and $z - x > 0$. Thus, for $z > 0$,

$$f_{S_2}(z) = \int_0^z \lambda e^{-\lambda x} \lambda e^{-\lambda(z-x)}\, dx$$

$$= \int_0^z \lambda^2 e^{-\lambda z} dx$$

$$= [\lambda^2 e^{-\lambda z} x]_{x=0}^z$$

$$= \lambda^2 z e^{-\lambda z}.$$

$$= \frac{1}{\Gamma(2)} \lambda^2 z^{2-1} e^{-\lambda z}.$$

The only distribution with density function of the form above is the gamma distribution with parameters 2 and λ. Hence the result is true for $n = 2$. Let $m \geq 2$ and suppose that the result is true for $n \leq m$. Then it is true that $S_m = X_1 + X_2 + \cdots + X_m$, where $X_1, X_2, \ldots, X_m$ independent, identically distributed random variables having the exponential distribution with parameter λ, has the gamma distribution with parameters m and λ. That is to say,

$$f_{S_m}(z) = \begin{cases} \dfrac{1}{\Gamma(m)} \lambda^m z^{m-1} e^{-\lambda z} & \text{if } z > 0, \\ 0 & \text{if } z \leq 0, \end{cases}$$

so that $S_{m+1} = X_1 + X_2 + \cdots + X_{m+1}$, where $X_1, X_2, \ldots, X_{m+1}$ independent, identically distributed random variables having the exponential distribution with parameter λ, has density function

$$f_{S_{m+1}}(z) = \int_{-\infty}^{\infty} f_{S_m}(x) f_{X_{m+1}}(z-x)\, dx$$

$$= \begin{cases} \displaystyle\int_0^z f_{S_m}(x) f_{X_{m+1}}(z-x)\, dx & \text{if } z > 0, \\ 0 & \text{otherwise.} \end{cases}$$

since $f_{S_m}(x) f_{X_{m+1}}(z-x) = 0$ unless $x > 0$ and $z - x > 0$. Thus, for $z > 0$,

$$f_{S_{m+1}}(z) = \int_0^z \frac{1}{\Gamma(m)} \lambda^m x^{m-1} \lambda e^{-\lambda(z-x)}\, dx$$

$$= \frac{1}{\Gamma(m)} \lambda^{m+1} e^{-\lambda z} [\frac{x^m}{m}]_0^z$$

$$= \frac{1}{m\Gamma(m)} \lambda^{m+1} z^m e^{-\lambda z}$$

$$= \frac{1}{\Gamma(m+1)} \lambda^{m+1} z^m e^{-\lambda z}.$$

The only distribution with density function of the form above is the gamma distribution with parameters $m+1$ and λ. Therefore S_n has the gamma distribution with parameters n and λ.

For the second part, we note that

$$\mathbb{P}(N_t = n) = \mathbb{P}(S_n \le t < S_{n+1})$$
$$= \iint_A f_{S_n, S_{n+1}}(x, y)\, dx\, dy$$

by Theorem 6.22, where $A = \{(x, y) \in \mathbb{R}^2 : x \le t < y\}$. Writing in the limits of integration, we find that

$$\mathbb{P}(N_t = n) = \int_{x=0}^{t} \int_{y=t}^{\infty} f_{S_n, S_{n+1}}(x, y)\, dx\, dy$$
$$= \int_{x=0}^{t} \int_{y=t}^{\infty} f_{S_{n+1}|S_n}(y \mid x) f_{S_n}(x)\, dx\, dy.$$

The conditional distribution function of S_{n+1} given $S_n = u$ is

$$\mathbb{P}(S_{n+1} \le y \mid S_n = x) = \mathbb{P}(S_n + X_{n+1} \le y \mid S_n = x)$$
$$= \mathbb{P}(x + X_{n+1} \le y)$$
$$= \mathbb{P}(X_{n+1} \le y - x).$$

We differentiate this with respect to v, to obtain

$$f_{S_{n+1}|S_n}(y \mid x) = f_{X_{n+1}}(y - x).$$

Hence

$$\mathbb{P}(N_t = n) = \int_{x=0}^{t} \int_{y=t}^{\infty} f_{X_{n+1}}(y - x) f_{S_n}(x)\, dx\, dy$$
$$= \int_{x=0}^{t} \int_{y=t}^{\infty} f_{X_{n+1}}(y - x) f_{S_n}(x)\, dx\, dy$$
$$= \int_{x=0}^{t} \int_{y=t}^{\infty} \lambda e^{-\lambda(y-x)} \frac{1}{\Gamma(n)} \lambda^n x^{n-1} e^{-\lambda x}\, dx\, dy$$
$$= \lambda^{n+1} \frac{1}{\Gamma(n)} \int_{x=0}^{t} \int_{y=t}^{\infty} e^{-\lambda(y-x)} x^{n-1} e^{-\lambda x}\, dx\, dy$$
$$= \frac{1}{n!} (\lambda t)^n e^{-\lambda t},$$

giving that N_t has the Poisson distribution with parameter λt.

PROBLEM (6.9.11). An aeroplane drops medical supplies to two duellists. With respect to Cartesian coordinates whose origin is at the target point, both the x and y coordinates of the landing point of the supplies have normal distributions which are independent. These two distributions have the same mean 0 and variance σ^2. Show that the expectation of the distance between the landing point and the target is $\sigma\sqrt{\pi/2}$. What is the variance of this distance? (Oxford 1976M)

SOLUTION. Let X and Y be coordinates of the landing point of the supplies. The joint density function of X and Y is

$$f_{X,Y}(x,y) = \frac{1}{2\pi\sigma^2} \exp(-\frac{1}{2\sigma^2}(x^2 + y^2)).$$

The distance $\sqrt{X^2 + Y^2}$ between the landing point and the target has expectation

$$\mathbb{E}(\sqrt{X^2 + Y^2}) = \int_{-\infty}^{\infty}\int_{-\infty}^{\infty} \sqrt{x^2 + y^2} f_{X,Y}(x,y)\, dx\, dy$$
$$= \int_{-\infty}^{\infty}\int_{-\infty}^{\infty} \sqrt{x^2 + y^2}\, \frac{1}{2\pi\sigma^2} \exp(-\frac{1}{2\sigma^2}(x^2 + y^2))\, dx\, dy$$

by Theorem 6.62. Changing variables to polar coordinates, we find that

$$\mathbb{E}(\sqrt{X^2 + Y^2}) = \int_{\theta=0}^{2\pi}\int_{r=0}^{\infty} r\, \frac{1}{2\pi\sigma^2} \exp(-\frac{1}{2\sigma^2}r^2)r\, dr\, d\theta$$
$$= \frac{1}{2\pi\sigma^2} \int_{\theta=0}^{2\pi} d\theta \int_{r=0}^{\infty} r^2 \exp(-\frac{1}{2\sigma^2}r^2)\, dr$$
$$= \frac{1}{\sigma^2} I,$$

where I is an integral given by

$$I = \int_0^\infty r^2 e^{-\frac{1}{2\sigma^2}r^2}\, dr$$

$$= [-r^2\sigma^2 e^{-\frac{1}{2\sigma^2}r^2}]_0^\infty + \sigma^2 \int_0^\infty e^{-\frac{1}{2\sigma^2}r^2}\, dr \qquad$$

by integration by parts formula with
$$u = r, dv = re^{-\frac{1}{2\sigma^2}r^2}\, dr$$
$$du = dr, v = -\sigma^2 e^{-\frac{1}{2\sigma^2}r^2}$$

$$= \sigma^2 \int_0^\infty \sqrt{2}\sigma e^{-t^2}\, dt \qquad\qquad \text{by the substitution } t = \frac{1}{\sqrt{2\sigma^2}}r$$

$$= \frac{\sigma^2}{2} \int_{-\infty}^\infty \sqrt{2}\sigma e^{-t^2}\, dt$$

$$= \frac{\sigma^2}{2}\sqrt{2}\sigma \int_{-\infty}^\infty e^{-t^2}\, dt$$

$$(\text{since } \int_{-\infty}^\infty e^{-x^2}\, dx = 1)$$

$$= \frac{\sqrt{2}}{2}\sigma^3 \sqrt{\pi},$$

giving that

$$\mathbb{E}(\sqrt{X^2 + Y^2}) = \frac{1}{\sigma^2}\frac{\sqrt{2}}{2}\sigma^3 \sqrt{\pi}$$

$$= \sigma\sqrt{\frac{\pi}{2}},$$

as required. Alternatively, we note that

$$\mathbb{E}(\sqrt{X^2 + Y^2}) = \int_{\theta=0}^{2\pi}\int_{r=0}^\infty r \frac{1}{2\pi\sigma^2} \exp(-\frac{1}{2\sigma^2}r^2)r\, dr\, d\theta$$

$$= \frac{1}{\sqrt{2\pi\sigma^2}} \int_{\theta=0}^{2\pi} d\theta \int_{r=0}^\infty r^2 \frac{1}{\sqrt{2\pi\sigma^2}} \exp(-\frac{1}{2\sigma^2}r^2)\, dr$$

$$= \frac{\sqrt{2\pi}}{\sqrt{\sigma^2}}\cdot\frac{1}{2} \int_{r=-\infty}^\infty r^2 \frac{1}{\sqrt{2\pi\sigma^2}} \exp(-\frac{1}{2\sigma^2}r^2)\, dr \qquad \text{since the integrand is even}$$

$$= \sqrt{\frac{\pi}{2\sigma^2}}\sigma^2 = \sigma\sqrt{\frac{\pi}{2}},$$

as required, since

$$\text{var}(X) = \int_{-\infty}^\infty x^2 \frac{1}{\sqrt{2\pi\sigma^2}} \exp(-\frac{1}{2\sigma^2}x^2)\, dx = \sigma^2,$$

where X has the normal distribution with parameters $\mu = 0$ and σ^2 (see Example 5.65). The mean of $X^2 + Y^2$ is

$$\mathbb{E}(X^2 + Y^2) = \int_{-\infty}^{\infty} \int_{-\infty}^{\infty} (x^2 + y^2) f_{X,Y}(x, y) \, dx \, dy$$

$$= \int_{-\infty}^{\infty} \int_{-\infty}^{\infty} (x^2 + y^2) \frac{1}{2\pi\sigma^2} \exp(-\frac{1}{2\sigma^2}(x^2 + y^2)) \, dx \, dy$$

by Theorem 6.62. Changing variables to polar coordinates, we find that

$$\mathbb{E}(X^2 + Y^2) = \int_{\theta=0}^{2\pi} \int_{r=0}^{\infty} r^2 \frac{1}{2\pi\sigma^2} \exp(-\frac{1}{2\sigma^2} r^2) r \, dr \, d\theta$$

$$= \frac{1}{2\pi\sigma^2} \int_{\theta=0}^{2\pi} d\theta \int_{r=0}^{\infty} r^3 \exp(-\frac{1}{2\sigma^2} r^2) \, dr$$

$$= \frac{1}{\sigma^2} J,$$

where J is an integral given by

$$J = \int_0^{\infty} r^3 e^{-\frac{1}{2\sigma^2} r^2} \, dr$$

$$= \int_{-\infty}^{0} 2\sigma^4 t e^t \, dt \qquad\qquad \text{by the substitution } t = -\frac{1}{2\sigma^2} r^2$$

$$= 2\sigma^4 \int_{-\infty}^{0} t e^t \, dt$$

$$= 2\sigma^4 \{[e^t t]_{-\infty}^{0} - \int_{-\infty}^{0} e^t \, dt\} \qquad \begin{array}{c} \text{by integration by parts formula with} \\ u = t, dv = e^t \, dt \\ du = dt, v = e^t \end{array}$$

$$= 2\sigma^4 \{0 - (-1)\}$$

$$= 2\sigma^4.$$

Hence

$$\mathbb{E}(X^2 + Y^2) = \frac{1}{\sigma^2} 2\sigma^4$$

$$= 2\sigma^2.$$

The variance of $\sqrt{X^2 + Y^2}$ is

$$\text{var}(\sqrt{X^2 + Y^2}) = \mathbb{E}(X^2 + Y^2) - [\mathbb{E}(\sqrt{X^2 + Y^2})]^2$$

$$= 2\sigma^4 - \sigma^2 \frac{\pi}{2}$$

$$= \sigma^2 (2 - \frac{1}{2}\pi).$$

PROBLEM (6.9.12). X and Y are independent random variables normally distributed with mean zero and variance σ^2. Find the expectation of $\sqrt{X^2 + Y^2}$. Find the probabilities of the following events, where a, b, c, and α are positive constants such that $b < c$ and $\alpha < \frac{1}{2}\pi$:

(a) $\sqrt{X^2 + Y^2} < a$,
(b) $0 < \tan^{-2}(Y/X) < \alpha$ and $Y > 0$.

SOLUTION. The expectation equals $\sigma\sqrt{\pi/2}$ (see Problem 6.9.11).
(a) The joint density function of X and Y is

$$f_{X,Y}(x, y) = \frac{1}{2\pi\sigma^2} \exp(-\frac{1}{2\sigma^2}(x^2 + y^2)).$$

The distribution function of $\sqrt{X^2 + Y^2}$ is

$$\mathbb{P}(\sqrt{X^2 + Y^2} < a) = \mathbb{P}(X^2 + Y^2 < a)$$
$$= \iint_A f_{X,Y}(x, y)\, dx\, dy$$
$$= \iint_A \frac{1}{2\pi\sigma^2} \exp(-\frac{1}{2\sigma^2}(x^2 + y^2))\, dx\, dy$$

by Theorem 6.22, where $A = \{(x, y) \in \mathbb{R}^2 : x^2 + y^2 < a\}$. Changing variables to polar coordinates, show that, we find that

$$\mathbb{P}(\sqrt{X^2 + Y^2} < a) = \int_{\theta=0}^{2\pi} \int_{r=0}^{\infty} \frac{1}{2\pi\sigma^2} e^{-\frac{1}{2\sigma^2}r^2} r\, dr\, d\theta$$
$$= 2\pi \frac{1}{2\pi\sigma^2}[(-\sigma^2)e^{-\frac{1}{2\sigma^2}r^2}]_0^a$$
$$= 1 - \exp(-\frac{1}{2\sigma^2}a^2).$$

(b) Let $R^2 = X^2 + Y^2$ and $\Theta = \tan^{-1}(Y/X)$.
We have that

$$\mathbb{P}(R^2 < a, 0 < \Theta < \alpha) = \iint_B f_{X,Y}(x, y)\, dx\, dy$$

by Theorem 6.22, where $B = \{(x, y) \in \mathbb{R}^2 : x^2 + y^2 < a \text{ and } 0 < \tan^{-1}(y/x) < \alpha\}$. Changing variables to polar coordinates, show that, we find that

$$F_{R^2,\Theta}(a,\alpha) = \mathbb{P}(R^2 < a, 0 < \Theta < \alpha)$$

$$= \int_{\theta=0}^{\alpha} \int_{r=0}^{\sqrt{a}} \frac{1}{2\pi\sigma^2} e^{-\frac{1}{2\sigma^2}r^2} r\, dr\, d\theta$$

$$= \alpha \frac{1}{2\pi\sigma^2} [(-\sigma^2)e^{-\frac{1}{2\sigma^2}r^2}]_0^{\sqrt{a}}$$

$$= \frac{\alpha}{2\pi}[1 - \exp(-\frac{1}{2\sigma^2}a)] \qquad \text{for } a > 0.$$

For $a > 0$ and $0 \le \alpha \le 2\pi$, the joint density function of R^2 and Θ is

$$f_{R^2,\Theta}(a,\alpha) = \frac{\partial^2}{\partial a\, \partial\alpha} F_{R^2,\Theta}(a,\alpha)$$

$$= \frac{1}{2\pi}\left(\frac{1}{2\sigma^2} e^{-\frac{1}{2\sigma^2}a}\right).$$

The marginal density function of R^2 is

$$f_{R^2}(a) = \int_{\alpha=0}^{2\pi} f_{R^2,\Theta}(a,\alpha)\, d\alpha$$

$$= \int_{\alpha=0}^{2\pi} \frac{1}{2\pi}\left(\frac{1}{2\sigma^2} e^{-\frac{1}{2\sigma^2}a}\right) d\alpha$$

$$= \frac{1}{2\sigma^2} e^{-\frac{1}{2\sigma^2}a}.$$

The marginal density function of Θ is

$$f_\Theta(\alpha) = \int_{a=0}^{\infty} f_{R^2,\Theta}(a,\alpha)\, da$$

$$= \int_{a=0}^{\infty} \frac{1}{2\pi}\left(\frac{1}{2\sigma^2} e^{-\frac{1}{2\sigma^2}a}\right) d\alpha$$

$$= \frac{1}{2\pi}.$$

Thus

$$f_{R^2,\Theta}(a,\alpha) = f_{R^2}(a) f_\Theta(\alpha)$$

giving that R^2 and Θ are independent. Moreover, R^2 has an expenential distribution with parameter $\dfrac{1}{2\sigma^2}$ and Θ has uniform distribution on $(0, 2\pi)$. Therefore,

$$\mathbb{P}(0 < \tan^{-1}(Y/X) < \alpha, Y > 0) = \int_0^\alpha \frac{1}{2\pi} \, d\alpha = \frac{\alpha}{2\pi}$$

PROBLEM (6.9.13). The independent random variables X and Y are both exponentially distributed with parameter λ, that is, each has density function

$$f(t) = \begin{cases} \lambda e^{-\lambda t} & \text{if } t > 0, \\ 0 & \text{otherwise.} \end{cases}$$

(a) Find the (cumulative) distribution and density functions of the random variables $1 - e^{-\lambda X}$, $\min\{X, Y\}$, and $X - Y$.

(b) Find the probability that $\max\{X, Y\} \le aX$, where a is a real constant. (Oxford 1982M)

SOLUTION. (a) The distribution function of $Z = 1 - e^{-\lambda X}$ is

$$
\begin{aligned}
F_Z(z) &= \mathbb{P}(Z \le z) \\
&= \mathbb{P}(1 - e^{-\lambda X} < z) \\
&= \mathbb{P}(e^{-\lambda X} > 1 - z) \\
&= \mathbb{P}(-\lambda X > \log(1 - z)) \qquad\qquad \text{for } 0 < z < 1 \\
&= \mathbb{P}(X < -\frac{1}{\lambda} \log(1 - z)) \\
&= F_X(-\frac{1}{\lambda} \log(1 - z)) \\
&= 1 - e^{-\lambda(-\frac{1}{\lambda} \log(1-z))} \\
&= z.
\end{aligned}
$$

Thus $Z = 1 - e^{-\lambda x}$ has a uniform distribution on $(0, 1)$.

The distribution function of $Z = \min\{X, Y\}$ is

$$
\begin{aligned}
\mathbb{P}(Z \le z) &= \mathbb{P}(\min\{X, Y\} \le z) \\
&= 1 - \mathbb{P}(\min\{X, Y\} > z) \\
&= 1 - \mathbb{P}(X > z, Y > z) &&\text{since } \min\{X, Y\} > u \\
&&&\text{if and only if } X > u \text{ and } Y > u \\
&= 1 - \mathbb{P}(X > z)\mathbb{P}(Y > z) &&\text{by independence} \\
&= 1 - [1 - \mathbb{P}(X \le z)][1 - \mathbb{P}(Y \le z)] \\
&= \begin{cases} 1 - (1 - 0)(1 - 0) & \text{if } z \le 0, \\ 1 - [1 - (1 - e^{-\lambda z})][1 - (1 - e^{-\lambda z})] & \text{if } z \ge 0, \end{cases} \\
&= \begin{cases} 0 & \text{if } z \le 0, \\ 1 - e^{-2\lambda z} & \text{if } z \ge 0, \end{cases}
\end{aligned}
$$

so that $\min\{X, Y\}$ has the exponential distribution with parameter 2λ.

Let $U = X$ and $V = X - Y$. The mapping T of this problem is given by $T(x, y) = (u, v)$, where

$$u = x, \qquad\qquad v = x - y,$$

and T is a bijection from $D = \{(x, y) : x, y \in \mathbb{R}\}$ to $S = \{(u, v) : u, v \in \mathbb{R}\}$ (or from $D = \mathbb{R}^2$ to $S = \mathbb{R}^2$). It has inverse $T^{-1}(u, v) = (x, y)$, where

$$x = u, \qquad\qquad y = u - v.$$

The Jacobian of T^{-1} is

$$\begin{vmatrix} \dfrac{\partial x}{\partial u} & \dfrac{\partial x}{\partial v} \\[2mm] \dfrac{\partial y}{\partial u} & \dfrac{\partial y}{\partial v} \end{vmatrix} = \begin{vmatrix} 1 & 0 \\ 1 & -1 \end{vmatrix} = -1,$$

giving by (6.51) that U and V have joint density function

$$\begin{aligned} f_{U,V}(u, v) &= \begin{cases} f_{X,Y}(x(u, v), y(u, v)) \, |J(u, v)| & \text{if } 0 < u < v, \\ 0 & \text{otherwise,} \end{cases} \\[2mm] &= \begin{cases} \lambda e^{-\lambda u} \lambda e^{-\lambda(u-v)} \, |-1| & \text{if } 0 < u < v, \\ 0 & \text{otherwise,} \end{cases} \\[2mm] &= \begin{cases} \lambda^2 e^{-\lambda(2u-v)} & \text{if } 0 < u < v, \\ 0 & \text{otherwise.} \end{cases} \end{aligned}$$

For $v > 0$,

$$\begin{aligned} f_V(v) &= \int_{-\infty}^{\infty} f_{U,V}(u, v) \, du \\ &= \int_{u=v}^{\infty} \lambda^2 e^{-\lambda(2u-v)} \, du \\ &= \lambda^2 \left(-\frac{1}{2\lambda}\right) e^{-\lambda(2u-v)} \Big|_{u=v}^{\infty} \\ &= \frac{\lambda}{2} e^{-\lambda v} \\ &= \frac{\lambda}{2} e^{-\lambda |v|}, \end{aligned}$$

since $|v| = v$ if $v > 0$. For $v \leq 0$,

$$f_V(v) = \int_{-\infty}^{\infty} f_{U,V}(u,v)\, du$$

$$= \int_{u=0}^{\infty} \lambda^2 e^{-\lambda(2u-v)}\, du$$

$$= \lambda^2 \left(-\frac{1}{2\lambda}\right) e^{-\lambda(2u-v)}\big|_{u=0}^{\infty}$$

$$= \frac{\lambda}{2} e^{\lambda v}$$

$$= \frac{\lambda}{2} e^{-\lambda|v|},$$

since $|v| = -v$ if $v \leq 0$. The marginal density function of V is

(for $v \in \mathbb{R}$,)
$$f_V(v) = \frac{\lambda}{2} e^{-\lambda|v|}$$

giving that $X - Y$ has the bilateral exponential distribution.

(b) If $a \leq 0$, then $\max\{X,Y\} > 0 \geq aX$ since $aX \leq 0$, so that $\mathbb{P}(\max(X,Y)) = 0$. If $0 < a \leq 1$, then $\max\{X,Y\} \geq X > aX$ since $X > 0$, so that $\mathbb{P}(\max(X,Y) \leq aX) = 0$. If $a \geq 1$, we have that

$$\mathbb{P}(\max\{X,Y\} \leq aX) = \mathbb{P}(X \leq aX, Y \leq aX)$$
$$= \mathbb{P}(Y \leq aX)$$
$$= \iint_A f_{X,Y}(x,y)\, dx\, dy$$

by Theorem 6.22, where $A = \{(x,y) \in \mathbb{R}^2 : 0 < x, y < \infty, y \leq ax\}$. Writing in the limits of integration, we find that

$$\mathbb{P}(\max\{X,Y\} \le aX) = \int_{x=0}^{\infty} \int_{y=0}^{ax} e^{-\lambda(x+y)} \, dx \, dy$$

$$= \lambda^2 \int_{x=0}^{\infty} -\frac{1}{\lambda} e^{-\lambda(x+y)} |_{y=0}^{ax} \, dx$$

$$= \lambda^2 \int_{0}^{\infty} [-\frac{1}{\lambda} + \frac{1}{\lambda} e^{-\lambda x}] \, dx$$

$$= \frac{1}{a+1} e^{-\lambda(a+1)} - e^{-\lambda x} |_{0}^{\infty}$$

$$= -\frac{1}{a+1} + 1$$

$$= \frac{a}{a+1}.$$

PROBLEM (6.9.14). The independent random variables X and Y are normally distributed with mean 0 and variance 1.

(a) Show that $W = 2X - Y$ is normally distributed, and find its mean and variance.

(b) Find the mean of $Z = X^2/(X^2 + Y^2)$.

(c) Find the mean of V/U, where $U = \max\{|X|, |Y|\}$ and $V = \min\{|X|, |Y|\}$. (Oxford 1985M)

SOLUTION. (a) We shall find the joint density function of $S = X$ and $W = 2X - Y$, and then find the marginal density function of W. The mapping T of this part is given by $T(x, y) = (s, w)$, where

$$s = x, \qquad\qquad w = 2x - y,$$

and S is a bijection from $D = \{(x, y) : x \in \mathbb{R}, y \in \mathbb{R}\}$ to $S = \{(s, w) : s \in \mathbb{R}, w \in \mathbb{R}\}$. It has inverse $T^{-1}(s, w) = (x, y)$, where

$$x = s, \qquad\qquad y = 2s - w.$$

The Jacobian of S^{-1} is

$$\begin{vmatrix} \dfrac{\partial x}{\partial s} & \dfrac{\partial x}{\partial w} \\ \dfrac{\partial y}{\partial s} & \dfrac{\partial y}{\partial w} \end{vmatrix} = \begin{vmatrix} 1 & 0 \\ 2 & -1 \end{vmatrix} = -1,$$

giving by Jacobian formula, (6.51) that S and W have joint density function

$$f_{S,W}(s, w) = f_{X,Y}(x(s, w), y(s, w)) \, |J(s, w)|$$

$$= \frac{1}{2\pi} \exp(-\frac{1}{2}[s^2 + (2s - w)^2]) \, |-1| \, .$$

$$= \frac{1}{2\pi} \exp(-\frac{1}{2}(5s^2 - 4sw + w^2))$$

The marginal density function of W is

$$f_W(w) = \int_{-\infty}^{\infty} f_{S,W}(s, w)\, ds$$

$$= \int_{-\infty}^{\infty} \frac{1}{2\pi} e^{-\frac{1}{2}(5s^2 - 4sw + w^2)}\, ds$$

$$= \frac{1}{2\pi} \int_{-\infty}^{\infty} e^{-\frac{1}{2}[(\sqrt{5}s - \frac{2}{\sqrt{5}}w)^2 + \frac{1}{5}w^2]}\, ds$$

$$= \frac{1}{2\pi} e^{-\frac{1}{2}(\frac{1}{5}w^2)} \int_{-\infty}^{\infty} e^{-\frac{1}{2}(\sqrt{5}s - \frac{2}{\sqrt{5}}w)^2}\, ds$$

$$= \frac{1}{2\pi} e^{-\frac{1}{2\pi(5)}(w^2)} \int_{-\infty}^{\infty} \frac{1}{\sqrt{5}} e^{-\frac{1}{2}t^2}\, dt \qquad \text{by substitution } t = \sqrt{5}s - \frac{2}{\sqrt{5}}w$$

$$= \frac{1}{2\pi\sqrt{5}} e^{-\frac{1}{2\pi(\sqrt{5})^2}(w^2)} \int_{-\infty}^{\infty} e^{-\frac{1}{2}t^2}\, dt$$

$$\left(\text{since } \frac{1}{\sqrt{2\pi}} \int_{-\infty}^{\infty} e^{-\frac{1}{2}x^2}\, dx = 1\right)$$

$$= \frac{1}{2\pi\sqrt{5}} e^{-\frac{1}{2\pi(\sqrt{5})^2}(w^2)} \sqrt{2\pi}$$

$$= \frac{1}{\sqrt{2\pi(\sqrt{5})^2}} e^{-\frac{1}{2\pi(\sqrt{5})^2}(w^2)},$$

giving that W has the normal distribution with mean 0 and variance $(\sqrt{5})^2$.

(b) The mean of $Z = X^2/(X^2 + Y^2)$ is

$$
\begin{aligned}
\mathbb{E}(X^2/(X^2+Y^2)) &= \int_{-\infty}^{\infty}\int_{-\infty}^{\infty} \frac{x^2}{x^2+y^2} f_{X,Y}(x,y)\,dx\,dy \\
&= \int_{-\infty}^{\infty}\int_{-\infty}^{\infty} \frac{x^2}{x^2+y^2}\frac{1}{2\pi} e^{-\frac{1}{2}(x^2+y^2)}\,dx\,dy \\
&= \frac{1}{2\pi}\int_{\theta=0}^{2\pi}\int_{r=0}^{\infty} \frac{r^2\cos^2\theta}{r^2} e^{-\frac{1}{2}r^2} r\,dr\,d\theta \\
&= \frac{1}{2\pi}\int_{0}^{2\pi}\cos^2\theta d\theta \int_{0}^{\infty} e^{-\frac{1}{2}r^2} r\,dr \qquad \text{by Fubini's theorem} \\
&= \frac{1}{2\pi}\int_{0}^{2\pi}\frac{1+\cos(2\theta)}{2}\,d\theta \\
&= \frac{1}{2\pi}(\frac{1}{2}\theta + \frac{\sin 2\theta}{4})\big|_{0}^{2\pi} \\
&= \frac{\pi}{2\pi} \\
&= \frac{1}{2}.
\end{aligned}
$$

(c) Let $T = V/U$. Then

$$
\begin{aligned}
T &= \frac{\max\{|X|,|Y|\}}{\min\{|X|,|Y|\}} \\
&= \begin{cases} \dfrac{|X|}{|Y|} & \text{if } |X|\le|Y|, \\[2mm] \dfrac{|Y|}{|X|} & \text{if } |X|>|Y|. \end{cases}
\end{aligned}
$$

The mean of T is

$$
\mathbb{E}(T) = \iint_A \frac{|x|}{|y|} f_{X,Y}\,dx\,dy + \iint_B \frac{|y|}{|x|} f_{X,Y}\,dx\,dy
$$

by Theorem 6.62, where $A = \{(x,y)\in\mathbb{R}^2 \colon |x|\le|y|\}$ and $B = \{(x,y)\in\mathbb{R}^2 \colon |x| > |y|\}$. Interchanging the roles of x and y, we find that

$$
\mathbb{E}(T) = 2\iint_A \frac{|x|}{|y|} f_{X,Y}\,dx\,dy.
$$

Writing in the limits of integration, we find that

$$E(T) = 8 \int_{x=0}^{\infty} \int_{y=x}^{\infty} \frac{x}{y} \cdot \frac{1}{2\pi} e^{-\frac{1}{2}(x^2+y^2)} \, dx \, dy$$

$$= 8 \frac{1}{2\pi} \int_{\theta=\pi/4}^{\pi/2} \int_{r=0}^{\infty} \frac{r \cos\theta}{r \sin\theta} e^{-\frac{1}{2}r^2} r \, dr \, d\theta \quad \text{by changing variables to polar coordinates}$$

$$= \frac{4}{\pi} \int_{\pi/4}^{\pi/2} \frac{\cos\theta}{\sin\theta} \, d\theta \int_{0}^{\infty} e^{-\frac{1}{2}r^2} r \, dr \quad \text{by Fubini's theorem}$$

$$= \frac{4}{\pi} \int_{\sqrt{2}/2}^{1} \frac{1}{t} \, dt \int_{0}^{\infty} e^{-\frac{1}{2}r^2} r \, dr \quad \text{by the substitution } t = \sin\theta$$

$$= (\frac{4}{\pi} \log|t| \, |_{\sqrt{2}/2}^{1})(-e^{-\frac{1}{2}r^2} |_0^\infty)$$

$$= -\frac{4}{\pi} \log(\frac{\sqrt{2}}{2})$$

$$= \frac{2}{\pi} \log 2.$$

PROBLEM (6.9.15). Let X and Y be independent random variables, X having the normal distribution with mean 0 and variance 1, and Y having the χ^2 distribution with n degrees of freedom. Show that

$$T = \frac{X}{\sqrt{Y/n}}$$

has density function

$$f(t) = \frac{1}{\sqrt{\pi n}} \frac{\Gamma(\frac{1}{2}(n+1))}{\Gamma(\frac{1}{2}n)} (1 + \frac{t^2}{n})^{-\frac{1}{2}(n+1)} \qquad \text{for } t \in \mathbb{R}.$$

T is said to have the *t-distribution* with n degrees of freedom.

SOLUTION. We shall find the joint density function of $T = X/\sqrt{Y/n}$ and $W = Y$, and then find the marginal density function of T. The joint dentiy function of X and Y is

$$f_{X,Y}(x,y) = \begin{cases} \dfrac{1}{\sqrt{2\pi}} e^{-\frac{1}{2}x^2} \dfrac{1}{2\Gamma(\frac{1}{2}n)} (\frac{1}{2}y)^{\frac{1}{2}n-1} e^{-\frac{1}{2}y} & \text{if } x \in \mathbb{R}, 0 < y < \infty, \\ 0 & \text{otherwise.} \end{cases}$$

The mapping M of this problem is given by $M(x,y) = (t,w)$, where

$$t = \frac{x}{\sqrt{y/n}}, \qquad\qquad w = y,$$

and M is a bijection from $D = \{(x, y) : x \in \mathbb{R}, 0 < y < \infty\}$ to $S = \{(t, w) : t \in \mathbb{R}, 0 < w < \infty\}$. It has inverse $M^{-1}(t, w) = (x, y)$, where

$$x = t\sqrt{\frac{w}{n}}, \qquad\qquad y = w.$$

The Jacobian of T^{-1} is

$$\begin{vmatrix} \dfrac{\partial x}{\partial t} & \dfrac{\partial x}{\partial w} \\[2mm] \dfrac{\partial y}{\partial t} & \dfrac{\partial y}{\partial w} \end{vmatrix} = \begin{vmatrix} \sqrt{\dfrac{w}{n}} & \dfrac{t}{2\sqrt{n}\sqrt{w}} \\[2mm] 0 & 1 \end{vmatrix} = \sqrt{\frac{w}{n}},$$

giving by Jacobian formula, (6.51) that T and W have joint density function

$$f_{T,W}(t, w) = \begin{cases} f_{X,Y}(x(t, w), y(t, w))\,|J(t, w)| & \text{if } t \in \mathbb{R}, w > 0, \\ 0 & \text{otherwise,} \end{cases}$$

$$= \begin{cases} \dfrac{1}{\sqrt{2\pi}} e^{-\frac{1}{2}\frac{w}{n}t^2} \dfrac{1}{2\Gamma(\frac{1}{2}n)}\left(\dfrac{1}{2}w\right)^{\frac{1}{2}n-1} e^{-\frac{1}{2}w}\sqrt{\dfrac{w}{n}} & \text{if } t \in \mathbb{R}, w > 0, \\ 0 & \text{otherwise.} \end{cases}$$

The marginal density function of T is

$$f_T(t) = \int_{-\infty}^{\infty} f_{T,W}(t, w)\, dw$$

$$= \int_0^{\infty} \frac{1}{\sqrt{2\pi}} e^{-\frac{1}{2}\frac{w}{n}t^2} \frac{1}{2\Gamma(\frac{1}{2}n)}\left(\frac{1}{2}w\right)^{\frac{1}{2}n-1} e^{-\frac{1}{2}w}\sqrt{\frac{w}{n}}\, dw$$

$$= \frac{1}{\sqrt{2\pi}}\frac{1}{2\Gamma(\frac{1}{2}n)}\left(\frac{1}{2}\right)^{\frac{1}{2}n-1}\frac{1}{\sqrt{n}}\int_0^{\infty} w^{\frac{1}{2}(n+1)-1} e^{-\frac{1}{2}(1+\frac{1}{n}t^2)w}\, dw$$

Substitute $v = \dfrac{1}{2}(1 + \dfrac{1}{n}t^2)w \implies dv = \dfrac{1}{2}(1 + \dfrac{1}{n}t^2)\, dw$ and $w = \dfrac{2v}{1 + \frac{1}{n}t^2}$

$$f_T(t) = \frac{1}{\sqrt{2\pi}}\frac{1}{2\Gamma(\frac{1}{2}n)}\left(\frac{1}{2}\right)^{\frac{1}{2}n-1}\frac{1}{\sqrt{n}}\int_0^{\infty} w^{\frac{1}{2}(n+1)-1} e^{-\frac{1}{2}(1+\frac{1}{n}t^2)w}\, dw$$

$$= \frac{1}{\sqrt{2\pi}}\frac{1}{2\Gamma(\frac{1}{2}n)}\left(\frac{1}{2}\right)^{\frac{1}{2}n-1}\frac{1}{\sqrt{n}}\int_0^{\infty} \frac{2^{\frac{1}{2}(n+1)-1} v^{\frac{1}{2}(n+1)-1}}{(1+\frac{1}{n}t^2)^{\frac{1}{2}(n+1)-1}} e^{-v}\frac{2}{1+\frac{1}{n}t^2}\, dv$$

$$= \frac{1}{\sqrt{\pi}}\frac{1}{\Gamma(\frac{1}{2}n)}\frac{1}{\sqrt{n}}\frac{1}{(1+\frac{1}{n}t^2)^{\frac{1}{2}(n+1)}}\int_0^{\infty} v^{\frac{1}{2}(n+1)-1} e^{-v}\, dv$$

(for $t \in \mathbb{R}$,)

$$= \frac{1}{\sqrt{\pi n}}\frac{\Gamma(\frac{1}{2}(n+1))}{\Gamma(\frac{1}{2}n)}\left(1 + \frac{t^2}{n}\right)^{-\frac{1}{2}(n+1)}$$

since

$$\int_0^\infty v^{\frac{1}{2}(n+1)-1}e^{-v}\,dv = \Gamma(\frac{1}{2}(n+1)),$$

by the definition of the gamma function.

PROBLEM (6.9.16). Let X and Y be independent random variables with the χ^2 distribution, X having m degrees of freedom and Y having n degrees of freedom. Show that

$$U = \frac{X/m}{Y/n}$$

has density function

$$f(u) = \frac{m\Gamma(\frac{1}{2}(m+n))}{n\Gamma(\frac{1}{2}m)\Gamma(\frac{1}{2}n)} \cdot \frac{(mu/n)^{\frac{1}{2}m-1}}{[1+(mu/n)]^{\frac{1}{2}(m+n)}} \qquad \text{for } u > 0.$$

U is said to have the F-distribution with m and n degrees of freedom.

SOLUTION. We shall find the joint density function of $W = X/m$ and $U = \frac{X/m}{Y/n}$, and then find the marginal density function of U. The joint dentiy function of X and Y is

$$f_{X,Y}(x,y) = \frac{1}{4\Gamma(\frac{1}{2}m)\Gamma(\frac{1}{2}n)}(\frac{1}{2}x)^{\frac{1}{2}m-1}(\frac{1}{2}y)^{\frac{1}{2}n-1}e^{-\frac{1}{2}(x+y)} \qquad \text{for } x,y > 0.$$

The mapping T of this problem is given by $T(x,y) = (w,u)$, where

$$w = \frac{x}{m}, \qquad\qquad u = \frac{x/m}{y/n},$$

and T is a bijection from $D = \{(x,y) : x,y > 0\}$ to $S = \{(w,u) : w,u > 0\}$. It has inverse $T^{-1}(w,u) = (x,y)$, where

$$x = mw, \qquad\qquad y = n\frac{w}{u}.$$

The Jacobian of T^{-1} is

$$\begin{vmatrix} \dfrac{\partial x}{\partial w} & \dfrac{\partial x}{\partial u} \\ \dfrac{\partial y}{\partial w} & \dfrac{\partial y}{\partial u} \end{vmatrix} = \begin{vmatrix} m & 0 \\ \dfrac{n}{u} & -\dfrac{nw}{u^2} \end{vmatrix} = -\frac{mnw}{u^2},$$

giving by Jacobian formula, (6.51) that T and W have joint density function

$$f_{W,U}(w,u) = f_{X,Y}(x(w,u),y(w,u))\,|J(w,u)|$$

$$= \frac{1}{4\Gamma(\frac{1}{2}m)\Gamma(\frac{1}{2}n)}(\frac{1}{2}mw)^{\frac{1}{2}m-1}(\frac{1}{2}n\frac{w}{u})^{\frac{1}{2}n-1}e^{-\frac{1}{2}(mw+n\frac{w}{u})}\frac{mnw}{u^2} \qquad \text{for } w,u > 0$$

The marginal density function of T is

$$f_U(u) = \int_{-\infty}^{\infty} f_{W,U}(w, u) \, dw$$

$$= \int_0^{\infty} \frac{1}{4\Gamma(\frac{1}{2}m)\Gamma(\frac{1}{2}n)} (\frac{1}{2}mw)^{\frac{1}{2}m-1} (\frac{1}{2}n\frac{w}{u})^{\frac{1}{2}n-1} e^{-\frac{1}{2}(mw+n\frac{w}{u})} \frac{mnw}{u^2} \, dw$$

$$= \frac{1}{4\Gamma(\frac{1}{2}m)\Gamma(\frac{1}{2}n)} (\frac{1}{2})^{\frac{1}{2}(m+n)-2} m^{\frac{1}{2}m} n^{\frac{1}{2}n} (\frac{1}{u})^{\frac{1}{2}n+1} \int_0^{\infty} w^{\frac{1}{2}(m+n)-1} e^{-\frac{1}{2}(\frac{mu+n}{u})w} \, dw$$

Substitute $v = \frac{1}{2}(\frac{mu+n}{u})w \implies dv = \frac{1}{2}(m + \frac{n}{u}) \, dw$ and $w = \frac{2uv}{mu+n}$

$$f_U(u) = \frac{1}{\Gamma(\frac{1}{2}m)\Gamma(\frac{1}{2}n)} (\frac{1}{2})^{\frac{1}{2}(m+n)} m^{\frac{1}{2}m} n^{\frac{1}{2}n} (\frac{1}{u})^{\frac{1}{2}n+1}$$

$$\int_0^{\infty} (\frac{2uv}{mu+n})^{\frac{1}{2}(m+n)-1} e^{-v} \frac{2u}{mu+n} \, dv$$

$$= \frac{1}{\Gamma(\frac{1}{2}m)\Gamma(\frac{1}{2}n)} m^{\frac{1}{2}m} n^{\frac{1}{2}n} u^{\frac{1}{2}m-1} \frac{1}{(mu+n)^{\frac{1}{2}(m+n)}}$$

$$\int_0^{\infty} v^{\frac{1}{2}(m+n)-1} e^{-v} \, dv$$

$$= \frac{\Gamma(\frac{1}{2}(m+n))}{\Gamma(\frac{1}{2}m)\Gamma(\frac{1}{2}n)} \cdot \frac{(mu)^{\frac{1}{2}m-1} n^{\frac{1}{2}n} n^{-\frac{1}{2}(m+n)} m}{(1 + \frac{mu}{n})^{\frac{1}{2}(m+n)}} \qquad \text{since } \int_0^{\infty} v^{\frac{1}{2}(m+n)-1} e^{-v} \, dv = \Gamma(\frac{1}{2}(m+n))$$

$$= \frac{\Gamma(\frac{1}{2}(m+n))}{\Gamma(\frac{1}{2}m)\Gamma(\frac{1}{2}n)} \cdot \frac{(\frac{mu}{n})^{\frac{1}{2}m-1} m}{(1 + \frac{mu}{n})^{\frac{1}{2}(m+n)} n}$$

$$= \frac{m\Gamma(\frac{1}{2}(m+n))}{n\Gamma(\frac{1}{2}m)\Gamma(\frac{1}{2}n)} \cdot \frac{(mu/n)^{\frac{1}{2}m-1}}{[1 + (mu/n)]^{\frac{1}{2}(m+n)}} \qquad \text{for } u > 0,$$

as required.

PROBLEM (6.9.17). In a sequence of dependent Bernoulli trials, the conditional probability of success at the ith trial, given that all preceding trials have resulted in failure, is p_i ($i = 1, 2, \ldots$). Give an expression in terms of the p_i for the probability that the first success occurs at the nth trial.

Suppose that $p_i = 1/(i+1)$ and that the time intervals between successive trials are independent random variables, the interval between the $(n-1)$th and the nth trials being exponentially distributed with density $n^\alpha \exp(-n^\alpha x)$, where α is a given constant. Show that the expected time to achieve the first success is finite if and only if $\alpha > 0$. (Oxford 1975F)

SOLUTION. First, for $i = 1, 2, \ldots$, we define the discrete random variable X_i by

$$X_i = \begin{cases} 1 & \text{if the } i\text{th trial is a success,} \\ 0 & \text{if the } i\text{th trial is a fail,} \end{cases}$$

giving by the chain rule of probability (also called the general product rule) that the probability that the first success occurs at the nth trial is

$\mathbb{P}(X_n = 1, X_1 = 0, X_2 = 0,$

$\qquad \ldots, X_{n-1} = 0) = \mathbb{P}(X_n = 1 \mid X_{n-1} = X_{n-2} = \cdots = X_1 = 0)$

$\qquad\qquad \mathbb{P}(X_{n-1} = X_{n-2} = \cdots = X_1 = 0)$

$\qquad\qquad = \mathbb{P}(X_n = 1 \mid X_{n-1} = X_{n-2} = \cdots = X_1 = 0)\mathbb{P}(X_{n-1} = 0 \mid X_{n-2} = \cdots = X_1 = 0)$

$\qquad\qquad \mathbb{P}(X_{n-2} = \cdots = X_1 = 0)$

$$\vdots$$

$\qquad\qquad = \mathbb{P}(X_n = 1 \mid X_{n-1} = \cdots = X_1 = 0)\mathbb{P}(X_{n-1} = 0 \mid X_{n-2} = \cdots = X_1 = 0)$

$\qquad\qquad \mathbb{P}(X_{n-2} = 0 \mid X_{n-3} = \cdots = X_1 = 0) \cdots \mathbb{P}(X_2 = 0 \mid X_1 = 0)\mathbb{P}(X_1 = 0)$

$\qquad\qquad = p_n(1 - p_{n-1})(1 - p_{n-2}) \cdots (1 - p_2)(1 - p_1),$

since

$$\mathbb{P}(X_i = 0 \mid X_{i-1} = \cdots = X_1 = 0) = 1 - \mathbb{P}(X_i = 1 \mid X_{i-1} = \cdots = X_1 = 0)$$
$$= 1 - p_i.$$

For the second part, since $p_i = 1/(i+1)$, it follows that

$$\mathbb{P}(X_i = 1, X_{i-1} = X_{i-2} = \cdots X_1 = 0) = \frac{1}{i+1}(1 - \frac{1}{i}) \cdots (1 - \frac{1}{2})$$
$$= \frac{1}{i+1} \cdot \frac{i-1}{i} \cdot \frac{i-2}{i-1} \cdots \frac{2}{3} \cdot \frac{1}{2}$$
$$= \frac{1}{(i+1)i}.$$

Let X be the time to achieve the first success. The mean of X is

$$\mathbb{E}(X) = \sum_{i=1}^{\infty} \mathbb{E}(X \mid X_i = 1, X_{i-1} = \cdots = X_1 = 0)\mathbb{P}(X_i = 1, X_{i-1} = \cdots = X_1 = 0)$$

$$= \sum_{i=1}^{\infty}[\sum_{j=1}^{i}(\int_0^{\infty} t j^{\alpha} e^{-j^{\alpha} t} \, dt)]\frac{1}{(i+1)i}$$

$$= \sum_{i=1}^{\infty}(\sum_{j=1}^{i} \frac{1}{j^{\alpha}})\frac{1}{(i+1)i}.$$

If $\alpha > 0$, then the series $\sum_{j=1}^{\infty} \frac{1}{j^{\alpha}}$ converges to some finite number A. Hence

$$\mathbb{E}(X) \leq \sum_{i=1}^{\infty} A \frac{1}{(i+1)i}$$

$$= A[(\frac{1}{1} - \frac{1}{2}) + (\frac{1}{2} - \frac{1}{3}) + \cdots]$$

$$= A.$$

Conversely, if the expected time to achieve the first success is finite, that is to say $\mathbb{E}(X)$ is finite, then the series $\sum_{i=1}^{\infty} (\sum_{j=1}^{i} \frac{1}{j^{\alpha}}) \frac{1}{(i+1)i}$ converges. Thus the general term $\sum_{j=1}^{i} \frac{1}{j^{\alpha}} \cdot \frac{1}{(i+1)i}$ is bounded, giving that the series $\sum_{j=1}^{\infty} \frac{1}{j^{\alpha}}$ converges, implying that $\alpha > 0$ since the series $\sum_{j=1}^{\infty} \frac{1}{j^{\alpha}}$ converges if and only if $\alpha > 0$.

Therefore, the expected time to achieve the first success is finite if and only if $\alpha > 0$.

PROBLEM (6.9.18). Let $a, b > 0$. Independent positive random variables X and Y have probability densities

$$\frac{1}{\Gamma(a)} x^{a-1} e^{-x}, \qquad\qquad \frac{1}{\Gamma(b)} y^{b-1} e^{-y}, \qquad\qquad \text{for } x, y \geq 0,$$

respectively, and U and V are defined by

$$U = X + Y, \qquad\qquad\qquad V = \frac{X}{X+Y}.$$

Prove that U and V are independent, and find their distributions. Deduce that

$$\mathbb{E}(\frac{X}{X+Y}) = \frac{\mathbb{E}(X)}{\mathbb{E}(X) + \mathbb{E}(Y)}.$$

(Oxford 1971F)

SOLUTION. The joint density function of X and Y is

$$f_{X,Y}(x, y) = \frac{1}{\Gamma(a)} x^{a-1} e^{-x} \frac{1}{\Gamma(b)} y^{b-1} e^{-y}$$

(for $x, y \geq 0$.)
$$= \frac{1}{\Gamma(a)\Gamma(b)} x^{a-1} y^{b-1} e^{-(x+y)}$$

The mapping T of this part is given by $T(x, y) = (u, v)$, where

$$u = x + y, \qquad\qquad v = \frac{x}{x + y},$$

and S is a bijection from $D = \{(x, y) : x, y > 0\}$ to $S = \{(u, v) : 0 < u < \infty, 0 < v < 1\}$. It has inverse $T^{-1}(u, v) = (x, y)$, where

$$x = uv, \qquad\qquad y = u(1 - v).$$

The Jacobian of S^{-1} is

$$\begin{vmatrix} \dfrac{\partial x}{\partial u} & \dfrac{\partial x}{\partial v} \\[2mm] \dfrac{\partial y}{\partial u} & \dfrac{\partial y}{\partial v} \end{vmatrix} = \begin{vmatrix} v & u \\ (1 - v) & -u \end{vmatrix} = -u,$$

giving by Jacobian formula, (6.51) that U and V have joint density function

$$
f_{U,V}(u, v) = \begin{cases} f_{X,Y}(x(u, v), y(u, v)) \, |J(u, v)| & \text{if } u > 0 \text{ and } 0 < v < 1, \\ 0 & \text{otherwise,} \end{cases}
$$

$$
= \begin{cases} \dfrac{1}{\Gamma(a)\Gamma(b)} (uv)^{a-1} [u(1 - v)]^{b-1} e^{-[uv + u(1 - v)]} u & \text{if } u > 0 \text{ and } 0 < v < 1, \\ 0 & \text{otherwise,} \end{cases}
$$

$$
= \begin{cases} \dfrac{1}{\Gamma(a)\Gamma(b)} u^{a+b-1} v^{a-1} (1 - v)^{b-1} e^{-u} & \text{if } u > 0 \text{ and } 0 < v < 1, \\ 0 & \text{otherwise.} \end{cases}
$$

Since $f_{U,V}(u, v)$ is in the form of $g(u)h(v)$, it follows that U and V are independent. The marginal density function of U is

$$
f_U(u) = \int_{-\infty}^{\infty} f_{U,V}(u, v) \, dv
$$

$$
= \begin{cases} \displaystyle\int_0^1 f_{U,V}(u, v) \, dv & \text{if } u > 0 \\ 0 & \text{otherwise,} \end{cases}
$$

since $f_{U,V}(u, v) = 0$ unless $u > 0$ and $0 < v < 1$. Thus, for $u > 0$,

$$f_U(u) = \int_0^1 \frac{1}{\Gamma(a)\Gamma(b)} u^{a+b-1} v^{a-1} (1-v)^{b-1} e^{-u} \, dv$$

$$= \frac{1}{\Gamma(a)\Gamma(b)} u^{a+b-1} e^{-u} \int_0^1 v^{a-1} (1-v)^{b-1} \, dv$$

(by (6.44)) $$= \frac{1}{\Gamma(a)\Gamma(b)} u^{a+b-1} e^{-u} \frac{\Gamma(a)\Gamma(b)}{\Gamma(a+b)}$$

$$= \frac{1}{\Gamma(a+b)} u^{a+b-1} e^{-u}.$$

The marginal density function of V is

(by Theorem 6.31)

$$f_V(v) = \frac{f_{U,V}(u,v)}{f_U(u)}$$

$$= \begin{cases} \dfrac{1}{\Gamma(a)\Gamma(b)} u^{a+b-1} v^{a-1} (1-v)^{b-1} e^{-u} \Gamma(a+b) \dfrac{1}{u^{a+b-1} e^{-u}} & \text{if } 0 < v < 1, \\ 0 & \text{otherwise,} \end{cases}$$

$$= \begin{cases} v^{a-1} (1-v)^{b-1} & \text{if } 0 < v < 1, \\ 0 & \text{otherwise.} \end{cases}$$

Since U and V are independent, it follows that

$$\mathbb{E}(UV) = \mathbb{E}(U)\mathbb{E}(V).$$

Hence,

$$\mathbb{E}\left(\frac{X}{X+Y}(X+Y)\right) = \mathbb{E}\left(\frac{X}{X+Y}\right)\mathbb{E}(X+Y),$$

giving that

$$\mathbb{E}(X) = \mathbb{E}\left(\frac{X}{X+Y}\right)\mathbb{E}(X+Y).$$

Thus

$$\mathbb{E}\left(\frac{X}{X+Y}\right) = \frac{\mathbb{E}(X)}{\mathbb{E}(X+Y)} = \frac{\mathbb{E}(X)}{\mathbb{E}(X)+\mathbb{E}(Y)},$$

as required.

PROBLEM (6.9.19). Let X_1, X_2, X_3 be independent χ^2 random variables with r_1, r_2, r_3 degrees of freedom.

(a) Show that $Y_1 = X_1/X_2$ and $Y_2 = X_1 + X_2$ are independent and that Y_2 is a χ^2 random variable with $r_1 + r_2$ degrees of freedom.

(b) Deduce that the following random variables are independent:

$$\frac{X_1/r_1}{X_2/r_2} \qquad \text{and} \qquad \frac{X_3/r_3}{(X_1 + X_2)/(r_1 + r_2)}.$$

(Oxford 1982F)

SOLUTION. (a) The joint density function of X_1 and X_2 is

$$f_{X_1,X_2}(x,y) = \begin{cases} \dfrac{1}{2\Gamma(\frac{1}{2}r_1)}(\frac{1}{2}x)^{\frac{1}{2}r_1-1}e^{-\frac{1}{2}x}\dfrac{1}{2\Gamma(\frac{1}{2}r_2)}(\frac{1}{2}y)^{\frac{1}{2}r_2-1}e^{-\frac{1}{2}y} & \text{if } x,y > 0, \\ 0 & \text{otherwise,} \end{cases}$$

$$= \begin{cases} \dfrac{1}{4\Gamma(\frac{1}{2}r_1)\Gamma(\frac{1}{2}r_2)}(\frac{1}{2})^{\frac{1}{2}(r_1+r_2)-2}x^{\frac{1}{2}r_1-1}y^{\frac{1}{2}r_2-1}e^{-\frac{1}{2}(x+y)} & \text{if } x,y > 0, \\ 0 & \text{otherwise.} \end{cases}$$

The mapping T of this part is given by $T(x,y) = (u,v)$, where

$$u = \frac{x}{y}, \qquad\qquad v = x + y,$$

and S is a bijection from $D = \{(x,y) : x,y > 0\}$ to $S = \{(u,v) : u,v > 0\}$. It has inverse $T^{-1}(u,v) = (x,y)$, where

$$x = \frac{uv}{u+1}, \qquad\qquad y = \frac{v}{u+1}.$$

The Jacobian of S^{-1} is

$$\begin{vmatrix} \dfrac{\partial x}{\partial u} & \dfrac{\partial x}{\partial v} \\ \dfrac{\partial y}{\partial u} & \dfrac{\partial y}{\partial v} \end{vmatrix} = \begin{vmatrix} \dfrac{v}{(u+1)^2} & \dfrac{u}{u+1} \\ -\dfrac{v}{(u+1)^2} & \dfrac{1}{u+1} \end{vmatrix} = \frac{v}{(u+1)^2}\cdot\frac{1}{u+1} + \frac{v}{(u+1)^2}\cdot\frac{u}{u+1} = \frac{v}{(u+1)^2},$$

giving by Jacobian formula, (6.51) that Y_1 and Y_2 have joint density function

$$f_{Y_1,Y_2}(u,v) = \begin{cases} f_{X_1,X_2}(x(u,v),y(u,v))\,|J(u,v)| & \text{if } u,v > 0, \\ 0 & \text{otherwise,} \end{cases}$$

$$= \begin{cases} \dfrac{1}{4\Gamma(\frac{1}{2}r_1)\Gamma(\frac{1}{2}r_2)}(\frac{1}{2})^{\frac{1}{2}(r_1+r_2)-2}(\frac{uv}{u+1})^{\frac{1}{2}r_1-1}(\frac{v}{u+1})^{\frac{1}{2}r_2-1}e^{-\frac{1}{2}(\frac{uv}{u+1}+\frac{v}{u+1})}\dfrac{v}{(u+1)^2} & \text{if } u,v > 0, \\ 0 & \text{otherwise,} \end{cases}$$

$$= \begin{cases} \dfrac{1}{4\Gamma(\frac{1}{2}r_1)\Gamma(\frac{1}{2}r_2)}(\frac{1}{2})^{\frac{1}{2}(r_1+r_2)-2}u^{\frac{1}{2}r_1-1}(\frac{1}{u+1})^{\frac{1}{2}(r_1+r_2)}v^{\frac{1}{2}(r_1+r_2)-1}e^{-\frac{1}{2}v} & \text{if } u,v > 0, \\ 0 & \text{otherwise,} \end{cases}$$

Since $f_{Y_1,Y_2}(u,v)$ is in the form of $g(u)h(v)$, it follows that Y_1 and Y_2 are independent. The marginal density function of Y_1 is

$$
\begin{aligned}
f_{Y_1}(u) &= \int_{-\infty}^{\infty} f_{U,V}(u,v)\,dv \\
&= \begin{cases} \displaystyle\int_0^{\infty} f_{U,V}(u,v)\,dv & \text{if } u > 0 \\ 0 & \text{otherwise,} \end{cases}
\end{aligned}
$$

since $f_{Y_1,Y_2}(u,v) = 0$ unless $u, v > 0$. Thus, for $v > 0$,

$$
\begin{aligned}
f_{Y_1}(u) \\
&= \int_0^{\infty} \frac{1}{4\Gamma(\frac{1}{2}r_1)\Gamma(\frac{1}{2}r_2)} (\frac{1}{2})^{\frac{1}{2}(r_1+r_2)-2} \\
&\qquad u^{\frac{1}{2}r_1-1}(\frac{1}{u+1})^{\frac{1}{2}(r_1+r_2)} v^{\frac{1}{2}(r_1+r_2)-1} e^{-\frac{1}{2}v}\,dv \\
&= \frac{1}{4\Gamma(\frac{1}{2}r_1)\Gamma(\frac{1}{2}r_2)} (\frac{1}{2})^{\frac{1}{2}(r_1+r_2)-2} u^{\frac{1}{2}r_1-1}(\frac{1}{u+1})^{\frac{1}{2}(r_1+r_2)} \\
&\qquad \int_0^{\infty} v^{\frac{1}{2}(r_1+r_2)-1} e^{-\frac{1}{2}v}\,dv \\
&= \frac{1}{4\Gamma(\frac{1}{2}r_1)\Gamma(\frac{1}{2}r_2)} (\frac{1}{2})^{\frac{1}{2}(r_1+r_2)-2} u^{\frac{1}{2}r_1-1}(\frac{1}{u+1})^{\frac{1}{2}(r_1+r_2)} \\
&\qquad \int_0^{\infty} (2t)^{\frac{1}{2}(r_1+r_2)-1} e^{-t}\,dt && \text{by the substitution } t = \frac{1}{2}v \\
&= \frac{1}{4\Gamma(\frac{1}{2}r_1)\Gamma(\frac{1}{2}r_2)} (\frac{1}{2})^{\frac{1}{2}(r_1+r_2)-2} u^{\frac{1}{2}r_1-1}(\frac{1}{u+1})^{\frac{1}{2}(r_1+r_2)} 2^{\frac{1}{2}(r_1+r_2)-1} \\
&\qquad \int_0^{\infty} t^{\frac{1}{2}(r_1+r_2)-1} e^{-t}\,dt \\
&= \frac{1}{4\Gamma(\frac{1}{2}r_1)\Gamma(\frac{1}{2}r_2)} (\frac{1}{2})^{\frac{1}{2}(r_1+r_2)-2} u^{\frac{1}{2}r_1-1}(\frac{1}{u+1})^{\frac{1}{2}(r_1+r_2)} 2^{\frac{1}{2}(r_1+r_2)-1} \\
&\qquad \Gamma(\frac{r_1+r_2}{2}) && \text{by (5.41)} \\
&= \frac{1}{2}\frac{\Gamma(\frac{r_1+r_2}{2})}{\Gamma(\frac{1}{2}r_1)\Gamma(\frac{1}{2}r_2)} u^{\frac{1}{2}r_1-1}(\frac{1}{u+1})^{\frac{1}{2}(r_1+r_2)}.
\end{aligned}
$$

The marginal density function of Y_2 is

(by Theorem 6.31)

$$f_{Y_2}(v) = \frac{f_{Y_1,Y_2}(u,v)}{f_{Y_1}(u)}$$

$$= \begin{cases} \dfrac{1}{4\Gamma(\frac{1}{2}r_1)\Gamma(\frac{1}{2}r_2)}(\dfrac{1}{2})^{\frac{1}{2}(r_1+r_2)-2}u^{\frac{1}{2}r_1-1}(\dfrac{1}{u+1})^{\frac{1}{2}(r_1+r_2)}v^{\frac{1}{2}(r_1+r_2)-1}e^{-\frac{1}{2}v}2 \\[3mm] \qquad \dfrac{\Gamma(\frac{1}{2}r_1)\Gamma(\frac{1}{2}r_2)}{\Gamma(\frac{r_1+r_2}{2})}u^{-(\frac{1}{2}r_1-1)}(\dfrac{1}{u+1})^{-\frac{1}{2}(r_1+r_2)} & \text{if } v > 0, \\[3mm] 0 & \text{otherwise}, \end{cases}$$

$$= \begin{cases} \dfrac{1}{2\Gamma(\frac{1}{2}r_1)\Gamma(\frac{1}{2}r_2)}(\dfrac{1}{2}v)^{\frac{1}{2}(r_1+r_2)-1}e^{-\frac{1}{2}v} & \text{if } v > 0, \\[3mm] 0 & \text{otherwise}, \end{cases}$$

so that Y_2 is a χ^2 random variable with $r_1 + r_2$ degrees of freedom.

(b) We note that if X and Y are are independent, then $g(X)$ and $h(Y)$ are independent for all functions $g, h\colon \mathbb{R} \to \mathbb{R}$. Let

$$g(\frac{X_1}{X_2}) = \frac{r_2}{r_1}\frac{X_1}{X_2} = \frac{X_1/r_1}{X_2/r_2} \qquad \text{and} \qquad h(X_1 + X_2) = \frac{X_3/r_3}{(X_1+X_2)/(r_1+r_2)}.$$

Since X_1/X_2 and $X_1 + X_2$ are independent, then

$$\frac{X_1/r_1}{X_2/r_2} \qquad \text{and} \qquad \frac{X_3/r_3}{(X_1+X_2)/(r_1+r_2)}$$

are independent.

PROBLEM (6.9.20). Let X and Y be random variables with the vector (X,Y) uniformly distributed on the region $R = \{(x,y)\colon 0 < y < x < 1\}$. Write down the joint probability density function of (X,Y). Find $\mathbb{P}(X + Y + 1)$. Find the probability density function $f_X(x)$ of X, and also find $\mathbb{E}(X)$. Find the conditional probability density function $f_{Y|X}(y \mid x)$ of Y given that $X = x$, and also find $\mathbb{E}(Y \mid X = x)$. (Oxford 2005)

SOLUTION. The joint density function of X and Y is

$$f_{X,Y}(x,y) = \begin{cases} \dfrac{1}{\text{area}\,(R)} & \text{if } (x,y) \in R \\[3mm] 0 & \text{otherwise}. \end{cases}$$

Let $A = R \cap \{(x, y) \in \mathbb{R}^2 : x + y < 1\}$. Then

$$
\begin{aligned}
P(X + Y < 1) &= \iint_A 2 \, dx \, dy \\
&= \int_{y=0}^{\frac{1}{2}} \int_{x=y}^{1-y} 2 \, dx \, dy \\
&= 2 \int_0^{\frac{1}{2}} (1 - 2y) \, dy \\
&= 2(y - y^2)|_0^{\frac{1}{2}} \\
&= \frac{1}{2}.
\end{aligned}
$$

The probability density function of X is

$$
\begin{aligned}
f_X(x) &= \int_{-\infty}^{\infty} f_{X,Y}(x, y) \, dy \\
&= \begin{cases} \int_0^x 2 \, dy & \text{if } 0 \leq x \leq 1 \\ 0 & \text{otherwise.} \end{cases} \\
&= \begin{cases} 2x & \text{if } 0 < x < 1 \\ 0 & \text{otherwise.} \end{cases}
\end{aligned}
$$

The mean of X is

$$
\begin{aligned}
\mathbb{E}(X) &= \int_{-\infty}^{\infty} x f_X(x) \, dx \\
&= \int_0^1 x(2x) \, dx \\
&= \frac{2}{3} x^3 \Big|_0^1 \\
&= \frac{2}{3}.
\end{aligned}
$$

The conditional probability density function of Y given that $X = x$ is

$$f_{Y|X}(y \mid x) = \frac{f_{X,Y}(x,y)}{f_X(x)}$$

$$= \begin{cases} \dfrac{2}{2x} & \text{if } 0 < y < x < 1, \\ 0 & \text{otherwise,} \end{cases}$$

$$= \begin{cases} \dfrac{1}{x} & \text{if } 0 < y < x < 1, \\ 0 & \text{otherwise.} \end{cases}$$

The mean of Y given that $X = x$ is

$$\mathbb{E}(Y \mid X) = \int_0^x y \frac{1}{x} \, dy$$

$$= \frac{1}{2x} y^2 \big|_{y=0}^{x}$$

$$= \frac{1}{2}x \qquad \text{for } 0 < x < 1.$$

PROBLEM (6.9.21). Let X and Y be independent random variables, each uniformly distributed on $[0, 1]$. Let $U = \min\{X, Y\}$ and $V = \max\{X, Y\}$. Show that $\mathbb{E}(U) = \dfrac{1}{3}$, and hence find the covariance of U and V. (Cambridge 2007)

SOLUTION. The joint distribution function of U and V is

$$\begin{aligned}
F_{U,V}(u, v) = \mathbb{P}(U < u, V < v) &= \mathbb{P}(\min\{X, Y\} < u, \max\{X, Y\} < v) \\
&= \mathbb{P}(\max\{X, Y\} < v) \\
&\quad - \mathbb{P}(\min\{X, Y\} \geq u, \max\{X, Y\} < v) \\
&= \mathbb{P}(X < v, Y < v) \\
&\quad - \mathbb{P}(u \leq X < v, u \leq Y < v) \qquad \begin{array}{l} \text{since } \min\{X, Y\} \geq u \\ \text{and } \max\{X, Y\} < v \\ \Leftrightarrow u \leq X < v, u \leq Y < v \end{array} \\
&= F_{X,Y}(v, v) - \mathbb{P}(u \leq X < v)\mathbb{P}(u \leq Y < v) \quad \text{by independence} \\
&= v^2 - (v - u)^2,
\end{aligned}$$

for $0 \leq u \leq v \leq 1$, since

$$f_X(x) = \begin{cases} 1 & \text{if } 0 < x < 1 \\ 0 & \text{otherwise,} \end{cases}$$

and

$$f_Y(y) = \begin{cases} 1 & \text{if } 0 < y < 1 \\ 0 & \text{otherwise.} \end{cases}$$

The joint density function of U and V is

$$\begin{aligned}
f_{U,V}(u,v) &= \frac{\partial^2 F_{U,V}(u,v)}{\partial u\,\partial v} \\
&= 2 \text{ if } 0 \leq u \leq v \leq 1.
\end{aligned}$$

The marginal density function of U is

$$\begin{aligned}
f_U(u) &= \int_u^1 2\,dv \\
&= 2v\Big|_u^1 \\
&= 2(1-u) \text{ if } 0 \leq u \leq 1.
\end{aligned}$$

The mean of U is

$$\begin{aligned}
\mathbb{E}(U) &= \int_0^1 2u(1-u)\,du \\
&= 2\int_0^1 (u-u^2)\,du \\
&= u^2 - \frac{2}{3}u^2\Big|_0^1 \\
&= \frac{1}{3}.
\end{aligned}$$

The covariane of U and V is

$$\begin{aligned}
\operatorname{cov}(U,V) &= \mathbb{E}([U-\mathbb{E}(U)])\mathbb{E}([V-\mathbb{E}(V)]) \\
&= \mathbb{E}(UV - U\mathbb{E}(V) - V\mathbb{E}(U) + \mathbb{E}(U)\mathbb{E}(V)) \\
&= \mathbb{E}(UV) - \mathbb{E}(U)\mathbb{E}(V) - \mathbb{E}(V)\mathbb{E}(U) + \mathbb{E}(U)\mathbb{E}(V) \\
&= \mathbb{E}(UV) - \mathbb{E}(U)\mathbb{E}(V)
\end{aligned}$$

The mean of UV is

$$
\begin{aligned}
E(UV) &= \int_{u=0}^{1} \int_{v=u}^{1} 2uv \, du \, dv \\
&= \int_{0}^{1} 2u \frac{1}{2} v^2 |_{v=u}^{1} \, du \\
&= \int_{0}^{1} uv^2 |_{v=u}^{1} \, du \\
&= \int_{0}^{1} (u - u^3) \, du \\
&= (\frac{u^2}{2} - \frac{u^2}{4}) |_{0}^{1} \\
&= \frac{1}{2} - \frac{1}{4} \\
&= \frac{1}{4}.
\end{aligned}
$$

The marginal density function of V is

$$
\begin{aligned}
f_V(v) &= \int_{u=0}^{v} 2 \, du \\
&= 2u |_{u=0}^{v} \\
&= 2v.
\end{aligned}
$$

The mean of V is

$$
\begin{aligned}
E(V) &= \int_{0}^{1} 2v^2 \, dv \\
&= \frac{2}{3} v^3 |_{0}^{1} \\
&= \frac{2}{3}.
\end{aligned}
$$

The covariance of U and V is

$$
\begin{aligned}
\operatorname{cov}(U, V) &= \frac{1}{4} - \frac{1}{3} \cdot \frac{2}{3} \\
&= \frac{1}{36}.
\end{aligned}
$$

PROBLEM (*6.9.22). Three crew members of Dr Who's spacecraft Tardis are teleported to the surface of the spherical planet Zog. Their positions X, Y, Z are independent and uniformly distributed on the surface. Find the probability density function of the angle$\angle XCY$, where C is the centre of Zog. Two people positioned on the surface at A and B are in direct radio communication if and only if $\angle ACB < \frac{1}{2}\pi$.

(a) Find the probability that Z is in direct radio communication with either X or Y, conditional on the event that $\phi := \angle XCY$ satisfies $\phi < \frac{1}{2}\pi$.

b) Find the probability that Z is in direct radio communication with both X and Y, conditional on the event that $\phi > \frac{1}{2}\pi$.

Deduce that the probability that all three crew members can keep in touch is $(\pi + 2)/(4\pi)$.

PROBLEM (6.9.24). Let X and Y be independent non-negative random variables with densities f and g, respectively. Find the joint density function of $U = X$ and $V = X + aY$, where a is a positive constant.
Let X and Y be independent and exponentially distributed random variables, each with density

(for $x \geq 0$.) $$f(x) = \lambda e^{-\lambda x}$$

Find the density of $X + \frac{1}{2}Y$. Is it the same as the density of $\max\{X,Y\}$? (Cambridge 2007)

SOLUTION. The joint density function of X and Y is

(for $x, y \geq 0$) $$f_{X,Y}(x, y) = f(x)g(y).$$

The mapping T of this problem is given by $T(x, y) = (u, v)$, where

$$u = x, \qquad\qquad v = x + ay,$$

and T is a bijection from $D = \{(x, y) : x, y \geq 0\}$ to $S = \{(u, v) : u, v \geq 0\}$. It has inverse $T^{-1}(u, v) = (x, y)$, where

$$x = u, \qquad\qquad y = \frac{v - u}{a}.$$

The Jacobian of S^{-1} is

$$\begin{vmatrix} \dfrac{\partial x}{\partial u} & \dfrac{\partial x}{\partial v} \\ \dfrac{\partial y}{\partial u} & \dfrac{\partial y}{\partial v} \end{vmatrix} = \begin{vmatrix} 1 & 0 \\ -\dfrac{1}{a} & \dfrac{1}{a} \end{vmatrix} = \frac{1}{a},$$

giving by Jacobian formula, (6.51) that U and V have joint density function

$$f_{U,V}(u, v) = \begin{cases} f_{X,Y}(x(u,v), y(u,v))\,|J(u,v)| & \text{if } u, v \geq 0, \\ 0 & \text{otherwise,} \end{cases}$$

$$= \begin{cases} \dfrac{1}{a}f(u)g(\dfrac{v - u}{a}) & \text{if } u, v \geq 0, \\ 0 & \text{otherwise,} \end{cases}$$

Apply the above result for the sepcial case where $f(x) = g(x) = \lambda e^{-\lambda x}$ for $x \geq 0$ and $a = \dfrac{1}{2}$ to obtain,

$$f_{U,V}(u,v) = \begin{cases} 2\lambda e^{-\lambda u} \lambda e^{-\lambda 2(v-u)} & \text{if } 0 \leq u \leq v, \\ 0 & \text{otherwise,} \end{cases}$$

$$= \begin{cases} 2\lambda^2 e^{-\lambda(2v-u)} & \text{if } 0 \leq u \leq v, \\ 0 & \text{otherwise.} \end{cases}$$

The marginal density function of $V = X + \dfrac{1}{2}Y$ is

$$f_V(v) = \int_0^v 2\lambda^2 e^{-\lambda(2v-u)} \, du$$

$$= 2\lambda^2 e^{-2\lambda v} \frac{e^{\lambda u}}{\lambda}\Big|_{u=0}^v$$

(for $v \geq 0$,)
$$= 2\lambda e^{-2\lambda v}(e^{\lambda v} - 1).$$

Let $Z = \max\{X, Y\}$. The distribution function of Z is

$$\begin{aligned} F_Z(z) &= \mathbb{P}(Z \leq z) \\ &= \mathbb{P}(\max\{X, Y\} \leq z) \\ &= \mathbb{P}(X \leq z, Y \leq z) \end{aligned}$$

(by independence)
$$\begin{aligned} &= \mathbb{P}(X \leq z)\mathbb{P}(Y \leq z) \\ &= \begin{cases} 0 & \text{if } z \leq 0, \\ (1 - e^{-\lambda z})^2 & \text{if } z > 0. \end{cases} \end{aligned}$$

The density function of Z is

$$f_Z(z) = \begin{cases} 0 & \text{if } z \leq 0, \\ 2\lambda e^{-\lambda z}(1 - e^{-\lambda z}) & \text{if } z > 0, \end{cases}$$

giving that the density of $X + \dfrac{1}{2}Y$ is not the same as the density of $\max\{X, Y\}$.

SOLUTION (6.9.25). Let X and Y have the bivariate normal density function

$$f(x,y) = \frac{1}{2\pi\sqrt{1-\rho^2}} \exp\{-\frac{1}{2(1-\rho^2)}(x^2 - 2\rho xy + y^2)\} \qquad \text{for } x, y \in \mathbb{R}.$$

for fixed $\rho \in (-1, 1)$. Let $Z = (Y - \rho X)/\sqrt{1 - \rho^2}$. Show that X and Z are independent $N(0, 1)$ variables. Hence or otherwise determine $\mathbb{P}(X > 0, Y > 0)$. (Cambridge 2008)

SOLUTION. For the first part, we shall use the Jacobian method to find the joint pdf of $W = X$ and Z. The mapping T of this part is given by $T(x, y) = (w, z)$, where

$$w = x, \qquad\qquad z = \frac{y - \rho x}{\sqrt{1 - \rho^2}},$$

and T is a bijection from $D = \{(x, y) : x, y \in \mathbb{R}\}$ to $S = \{(w, z) : w, z \in \mathbb{R}\}$. It has inverse $T^{-1}(w, z) = (x, y)$, where

$$x = w, \qquad\qquad y = \rho w + \sqrt{1 - \rho^2} z.$$

The Jacobian of S^{-1} is

$$\begin{vmatrix} \dfrac{\partial x}{\partial w} & \dfrac{\partial x}{\partial z} \\ \dfrac{\partial y}{\partial w} & \dfrac{\partial y}{\partial z} \end{vmatrix} = \begin{vmatrix} 1 & 0 \\ \rho & \sqrt{1 - \rho^2} \end{vmatrix} = \sqrt{1 - \rho^2},$$

giving by Jacobian formula, (6.51) that W and Z have joint density function

$$f_{W,Z}(w, z) = \frac{1}{2\pi\sqrt{1 - \rho^2}} \exp\{-\frac{1}{2(1 - \rho^2)}[w^2 - 2\rho w(\rho w + \sqrt{1 - \rho^2} z) + (\rho w + \sqrt{1 - \rho^2} z)^2]\}\sqrt{1 - \rho^2}$$

$$= \frac{1}{2\pi} \exp\{-\frac{1}{2(1 - \rho^2)}(1 - \rho^2)(w^2 + z^2)\}$$

(for $w, z \in \mathbb{R}$.)

$$= \frac{1}{2\pi} \exp\{-\frac{1}{2}(w^2 + z^2)\}$$

The marginal density function of W is

$$f_W(w) = \int_{-\infty}^{\infty} f_{W,Z}(w, z)\, dz$$

$$= \int_{-\infty}^{\infty} \frac{1}{2\pi} e^{-\frac{1}{2}(w^2 + z^2)}\, dz$$

$$= \frac{1}{2\pi} e^{-\frac{1}{2}w^2} \int_{-\infty}^{\infty} e^{-\frac{1}{2}z^2}\, dz$$

$$= \frac{1}{2\pi} e^{-\frac{1}{2}w^2} \sqrt{2\pi}$$

(for $w \in \mathbb{R}$,) $\qquad\qquad = \frac{1}{\sqrt{2\pi}} e^{-\frac{1}{2}w^2}$

so that W has the normal distribution with mean 0 and variance 1. By symmetry, the random variable Z has this distribution also, and

(for $u, v \in \mathbb{R}$,)
$$f_{W,Z}(w, z) = f_W(w) f_Z(z)$$

so that U and V are independent.

For the second part, we have that

$$\mathbb{P}(X > 0, Y > 0) = \iint_A f_{X,Y}(x, y) \, dx \, dy$$

by Theorem 6.22, where $A = \{(x, y) \in \mathbb{R}^2 : x, y > 0\}$. Writing in the limits of integration, we find that

$$\mathbb{P}(X > 0, Y > 0) = \int_{x=0}^{\infty} \int_{y=0}^{\infty} \frac{1}{2\pi \sqrt{1 - \rho^2}} e^{-\frac{1}{2(1-\rho^2)}(x^2 - 2\rho xy + y^2)} \, dx \, dy$$

(by changing variables to polar coordinates)

$$= \frac{1}{2\pi \sqrt{1 - \rho^2}} \int_{\theta=0}^{\frac{\pi}{2}} \int_{r=0}^{\infty} e^{-\frac{1}{2(1-\rho^2)}(r^2 - r^2 \rho \sin 2\theta)} r \, dr \, d\theta$$

$$= \frac{1}{2\pi \sqrt{1 - \rho^2}} \int_{\theta=0}^{\frac{\pi}{2}} -e^{-\frac{1}{2(1-\rho^2)}(1 - \rho \sin 2\theta) r^2} \frac{1 - \rho^2}{1 - \rho \sin 2\phi} \Big|_{r=0}^{\infty} \, d\theta$$

$$= \frac{\sqrt{1 - \rho^2}}{2\pi} \int_0^{\frac{\pi}{2}} \frac{1}{1 - \rho \sin 2\theta} \, d\theta$$

(by the substitution)

$$= \frac{\sqrt{1 - \rho^2}}{2\pi} \int_0^{\infty} \frac{1}{(1 + t^2)(1 - \rho \frac{2t}{1+t^2})} \, dt \qquad\qquad t = \tan \theta$$

$$= \frac{\sqrt{1 - \rho^2}}{2\pi} \int_0^{\infty} \frac{1}{1 - 2\rho t + t^2} \, dt$$

$$= \frac{\sqrt{1 - \rho^2}}{2\pi} \int_0^{\infty} \frac{1}{(t - \rho)^2 + (1 - \rho^2)} \, dt$$

$$= \frac{\sqrt{1 - \rho^2}}{2\pi} \cdot \frac{1}{1 - \rho^2} \int_0^{\infty} \frac{1}{1 + (\frac{t-\rho}{\sqrt{1-\rho^2}})^2} \, dt$$

$$= \frac{\sqrt{1 - \rho^2}}{2\pi} \cdot \frac{1}{1 - \rho^2} \sqrt{1 - \rho^2} \tan^{-1} \frac{t - \rho}{\sqrt{1 - \rho^2}} \Big|_{t=0}^{\infty}$$

$$= \frac{1}{2\pi} \left(\frac{\pi}{2} - \tan^{-1} \frac{-\rho}{\sqrt{1 - \rho^2}} \right).$$

Alternatively, we have that

$$\mathbb{P}(X > 0, Y > 0) = \mathbb{P}(W > 0, \rho W + \sqrt{1 - \rho^2} Z > 0)$$

$$= \iint_A f_{W,Z}(w, z) \, dw \, dz$$

by Theorem 6.22, where $A = \{(w, z) \in \mathbb{R}^2 : w > 0, z > -\rho w/\sqrt{1 - \rho^2}\}$. Writing in the limits of integration, we find that

$$\mathbb{P}(X > 0, Y > 0) = \int_{w=0}^{\infty} \int_{z=-\frac{\rho u}{\sqrt{1-\rho^2}}}^{\infty} \frac{1}{2\pi} e^{-\frac{1}{2}(w^2+z^2)} \, dw \, dz$$

(by changing variables to polar coordinates)

$$= \frac{1}{2\pi} \int_{\theta=\tan^{-1} \frac{-\rho}{\sqrt{1-\rho^2}}}^{\frac{\pi}{2}} \int_{r=0}^{\infty} e^{-\frac{1}{2}r^2} r \, dr \, d\theta$$

$$= \frac{1}{2\pi} \left(\frac{\pi}{2} - \tan^{-1} \frac{-\rho}{\sqrt{1-\rho^2}} \right)(-e^{-\frac{1}{2}r^2})|_0^{\infty}$$

$$= \frac{1}{2\pi} \left(\frac{\pi}{2} - \tan^{-1} \frac{-\rho}{\sqrt{1-\rho^2}} \right).$$

PROBLEM (6.9.26). Let X and Y be random variables with the joint probability density function

(for $x, y > 0$.) $$f_{X,Y}(x, y) = \frac{1}{4} e^{-\frac{1}{2}(x+y)}$$

Show that the joint probability density function of $U = \frac{1}{2}(X - Y)$ and $V = Y$ is

$$f_{U,V}(u, v) = \begin{cases} \dfrac{1}{2} e^{-u-v} & \text{if } (u, v) \in A \\ 0 & \text{otherwise,} \end{cases}$$

where A is a region of the (u, v) plane to be determined. Deduce that U has probability density function

() $$f_U(u) = \frac{1}{2} e^{-|u|}, \qquad\qquad -\infty < u < \infty.$$

(Oxford 2008)

SOLUTION. The mapping T of this problem is given by $T(x, y) = (u, v)$, where

$$u = \frac{1}{2}(x - y), \qquad\qquad v = y,$$

and T is a bijection from $D = \{(x, y) : x, y > 0\}$ to $A = \{(u, v) : 2u+v > 0, v > 0\}$. It has inverse $T^{-1}(u, v) = (x, y)$, where

$$x = 2u + v, \qquad\qquad y = v.$$

The Jacobian of S^{-1} is

$$\begin{vmatrix} \dfrac{\partial x}{\partial u} & \dfrac{\partial x}{\partial v} \\[2ex] \dfrac{\partial y}{\partial u} & \dfrac{\partial y}{\partial v} \end{vmatrix} = \begin{vmatrix} 2 & 1 \\ 0 & 1 \end{vmatrix} = 2,$$

giving by Jacobian formula, (6.51) that U and V have joint density function

$$f_{U,V}(u,v) = \begin{cases} \dfrac{1}{4} e^{-\frac{1}{2}[(2u+v)+v]} 2 & \text{if } (u,v) \in A \\ 0 & \text{otherwise,} \end{cases}$$

$$= \begin{cases} \dfrac{1}{2} e^{-u-v} & \text{if } (u,v) \in A \\ 0 & \text{otherwise.} \end{cases}$$

The marginal density function of U is

$$f_U(u) = \int_{-\infty}^{\infty} f_{U,V}(u,v)\, dv$$

$$= \begin{cases} \displaystyle\int_{0}^{\infty} \dfrac{1}{2\pi} e^{-u-v}\, dv & \text{if } u \geq 0 \\ \displaystyle\int_{-2u}^{\infty} \dfrac{1}{2\pi} e^{-u-v}\, dv & \text{if } u < 0 \end{cases}$$

$$= \begin{cases} \dfrac{1}{2} e^{-u} & \text{if } u \geq 0 \\ \dfrac{1}{2} e^{u} & \text{if } u < 0 \end{cases}$$

$(-\infty < u < \infty,)$
$$= \dfrac{1}{2} e^{-|u|},$$

as required.

PROBLEM (6.9.27). (a) Suppose that the continuous random variables X and Y are independent with probability density functions f and g, both of which are symmetric about zero.

(i) Find the joint probability density function of (U, V), where $U = X$ and $V = Y/X$.

(ii) Show that the marginal density function of V is

$$f_V(v) = 2 \int_0^{\infty} x f(x) g(xv)\, dx.$$

(iii) Let X and Y be independent normal random variables, each with mean 0, and with non-zero variances a^2 and b^2, respectively. Show that $V = Y/X$ has probability density function

$$f_V(v) = \frac{c}{\pi(c^2 + v^2)} \qquad \text{for } -\infty < v < \infty,$$

where $c = b/a$. Hence find $\mathbb{P}(|Y| < |X|)$.

(b) Now let X and Y be independent random variables, each uniformly distributed on the interval $(0, 1)$. By considering the random variables $U = Y$ and $V = XY^2$, or otherwise, find the probability density function of V.
(Oxford 2010)

SOLUTION. (a) For part (i), the mapping T of this part is given by $T(x, y) = (u, v)$, where

$$u = x, \qquad\qquad v = \frac{y}{x},$$

and T is a bijection from $D = \{(x, y) \in \mathbb{R}^2\}$ to $S = \{(u, v) \in \mathbb{R}^2 : u \neq 0\}$. It has inverse $T^{-1}(u, v) = (x, y)$, where

$$x = u, \qquad\qquad y = uv.$$

The Jacobian of S^{-1} is

$$\begin{vmatrix} \dfrac{\partial x}{\partial u} & \dfrac{\partial x}{\partial v} \\ \dfrac{\partial y}{\partial u} & \dfrac{\partial y}{\partial v} \end{vmatrix} = \begin{vmatrix} 1 & 0 \\ v & u \end{vmatrix} = u,$$

giving by Jacobian formula, (6.51) that U and V have joint density function

$$f_{U,V}(u, v) = \begin{cases} f(u)g(uv)\,|u| & \text{if } (u, v) \in S \\ 0 & \text{otherwise.} \end{cases}$$

For part (ii), the marginal density function of V is

$$\begin{aligned} f_V(v) &= \int_{-\infty}^{\infty} f_{U,V}(u, v)\,du \\ &= \int_{-\infty}^{\infty} f(u)g(uv)\,|u|\,du \\ &= 2\int_{0}^{\infty} u f(x)g(uv)\,du \\ &= 2\int_{0}^{\infty} x f(x)g(xv)\,dx, \end{aligned}$$

(since the integrand is even)

as required. For the first part of part (iii), we shall use the Jacobian method with $U = X$ and $V = Y/X$. The density functions of X and Y are

$$f_X(x) = \frac{1}{\sqrt{2\pi a^2}} \exp(-\frac{1}{2a^2}x^2)$$

and

$$f_Y(y) = \frac{1}{\sqrt{2\pi b^2}} \exp(-\frac{1}{2b^2}y^2),$$

both of which are symmetric about zero. It follows that we may calculate the marginal density function of V by applying the results of part (i) and (ii) to the random variable V to obtain

$$f_V(v) = 2 \int_0^\infty x f_X(x) f_Y(xv)\, dx$$

$$= 2 \int_0^\infty x \frac{1}{\sqrt{2\pi a^2}} e^{-\frac{1}{2a^2}x^2} \frac{1}{\sqrt{2\pi b^2}} e^{-\frac{1}{2b^2}x^2 v^2}\, dx$$

$$= \frac{1}{\pi ab} \int_0^\infty e^{-\frac{1}{2}(\frac{b^2}{a^2} + \frac{v^2}{b^2})x^2} x\, dx$$

(by the substitution)

$$= \frac{1}{\pi ab} \int_0^\infty \frac{a^2 b^2}{b^2 + a^2 v^2} e^{-t}\, dt \qquad\qquad t = \frac{1}{2}(\frac{1}{a^2} + \frac{v^2}{b^2})x^2$$

$$= \frac{1}{\pi ab} \cdot \frac{a^2 b^2}{b^2 + a^2 v^2}(-e^{-t})|_{t=0}^\infty$$

$$= \frac{ab}{\pi(b^2 + a^2 v^2)}$$

$$= \frac{\frac{ab}{a^2}}{\pi(\frac{b^2 + a^2 v^2}{a^2})}$$

$$= \frac{\frac{b}{a}}{\pi[(\frac{b}{a})^2 + v^2]}$$

$$= \frac{c}{\pi(c^2 + v^2)} \qquad\qquad \text{for } -\infty < v < \infty,$$

where $c = b/a$, as required. For the second part of part (iii), we have that

$$\mathbb{P}(|Y| < |X|) = \iint_A f_{X,Y}(x, y)\, dx\, dy$$

by Theorem 6.22, where $A = \{(x, y) \in \mathbb{R}^2 : |y| < |x|\}$. Writing in the limits of integration, we find that

$$\mathbb{P}(|Y| < |X|) = 4 \int_{x=0}^{\infty} \int_{y=0}^{x} \frac{1}{\sqrt{2\pi a^2}} e^{-\frac{1}{2a^2}x^2} \frac{1}{\sqrt{2\pi b^2}} e^{-\frac{1}{2a^2}y^2} \, dx \, dy$$

Alternatively, we have that

$$
\begin{aligned}
\mathbb{P}(|Y| < |X|) &= \mathbb{P}\left(\left|\frac{Y}{X}\right| < 1\right) \\
&= \mathbb{P}(|V| < 1) \\
&= \mathbb{P}(-1 < V < 1) \\
&= \int_{-1}^{1} f_V(v) \, dv \\
&= \int_{-1}^{1} \frac{c}{\pi(c^2 + v^2)} \, dv \\
&= \frac{c}{\pi} \int_{-1}^{1} \frac{1}{c^2 + v^2} \, dv \\
&= \frac{1}{\pi c} \int_{-1}^{1} \frac{1}{1 + (\frac{v}{c})^2} \, dv \\
&= \frac{1}{\pi c} \int_{-1}^{1} \frac{c}{1 + (\frac{v}{c})^2} \, d\left(\frac{v}{c}\right) \\
&= \frac{1}{\pi} \tan^{-1} \frac{v}{c} \Big|_{v=-1}^{1} \\
&= \frac{1}{\pi} \left(\tan^{-1} \frac{1}{c} - \tan^{-1} \frac{-1}{c}\right) \\
&= \frac{2}{\pi} \tan^{-1} \frac{1}{c}
\end{aligned}
$$

(by Theorem 5.27) — aligned to the fourth line.

(since $\tan^{-1}(-\alpha) = -\tan^{-1}\alpha$) — aligned to the last line.

(b) Since X and Y are independent, the joint density function of X and Y is

$$
\begin{aligned}
f_{X,Y}(x,y) &= f_X(x) f_Y(y) \\
&= \begin{cases} 1 & \text{if } 0 < x, y < 1 \\ 0 & \text{otherwise.} \end{cases}
\end{aligned}
$$

The mapping T of this part is given by $T(x,y) = (u,v)$, where

$$u = y, \qquad\qquad v = xy^2,$$

and T is a bijection from $D = \{(x,y) \in \mathbb{R}^2 : 0 < x, y < 1\}$ to $S = \{(u,v) \in \mathbb{R}^2 : 0 < u < 1, 0 < v < u^2\}$. It has inverse $T^{-1}(u,v) = (x,y)$, where

$$x = \frac{v}{u^2}, \qquad\qquad y = u.$$

The Jacobian of T^{-1} is

$$\begin{vmatrix} \dfrac{\partial x}{\partial u} & \dfrac{\partial x}{\partial v} \\[2mm] \dfrac{\partial y}{\partial u} & \dfrac{\partial y}{\partial v} \end{vmatrix} = \begin{vmatrix} -\dfrac{2v}{u^3} & \dfrac{1}{u^2} \\[2mm] 1 & 0 \end{vmatrix} = -\frac{1}{u^2},$$

giving by Jacobian formula, (6.51) that U and V have joint density function

$$f_{U,V}(u,v) = \begin{cases} \dfrac{1}{u^2} & \text{if } (u,v) \in S \\ 0 & \text{otherwise.} \end{cases}$$

The marginal density of V is

$$\begin{aligned}
f_V(v) &= \int_{-\infty}^{\infty} f_{U,V}(u,v)\, du \\
&= \begin{cases} \displaystyle\int_{\sqrt{v}}^{1} \frac{1}{u^2}\, du & \text{if } 0 < v < 1, \\ 0 & \text{otherwise,} \end{cases} \\
&= \begin{cases} -\dfrac{1}{u}\Big|_{u=\sqrt{v}}^{1} & \text{if } 0 < v < 1, \\ 0 & \text{otherwise,} \end{cases} \\
&= \begin{cases} \dfrac{1}{\sqrt{v}} - 1 & \text{if } 0 < v < 1, \\ 0 & \text{otherwise.} \end{cases}
\end{aligned}$$

PROBLEM (6.9.28). (a) Define the distribution function F of a random variable, and also its density function f, assuming F is differentiable. Show that

$$f(x) = -\frac{d}{dx}\mathbb{P}(X > x).$$

(b) Let U, V be independent random variables, each with the uniform distribution on $[0,1]$. Show that

$$\mathbb{P}(V^2 > U > x) = \frac{1}{3} - x + \frac{2}{3}x^{3/2} \qquad\qquad \text{for } x \in (0,1).$$

(c) What is the probability that the random quadratic equation $x^2 + 2Vx + U = 0$ has real roots?

(d) Given that the two roots R_1, R_2 of the above quadratic are real, what is the probability that both $|R_1| \leq 1$ and $|R_2| \leq 1$?

SOLUTION. (a) The function $F_X : \mathbb{R} \to [0,1]$ is called the distribution function of a random variable X if and only if

$$F(x) = \mathbb{P}(X \leq x).$$

The non-negative function f_X is called the density function of a random X if and only if the distribution function $F_X(x)$ of X may be written in the form

$$F(x) = \mathbb{P}(X \leq x) = \int_{-\infty}^{x} f(x)\, du \qquad \text{for } x \in \mathbb{R}.$$

for some , we say that X has (probability) density function (or pdf) f.

We have that

(since F is differentiable)
$$\begin{aligned}
f(x) &= \frac{d}{dx}F(x) \\
&= \frac{d}{dx}\mathbb{P}(X \leq x) \\
&= \frac{d}{dx}(1 - \mathbb{P}(X > x)) \\
&= -\frac{d}{dx}\mathbb{P}(X > x),
\end{aligned}$$

as required.

(b) Since U and V are independent random variables, each with the uniform distribution on $[0,1]$, it follows that the joint density function of U and V is

$$\begin{aligned}
f_{U,V}(u,v) &= f_U(u)f_V(v) \\
&= \begin{cases} 1 & \text{if } 0 < u, v < 1 \\ 0 & \text{otherwise.} \end{cases}
\end{aligned}$$

We have that

$$\mathbb{P}(V^2 > U > x) = \iint_A f_{X,Y}(x,y)\, dx\, dy$$

by Theorem 6.22, where $A = \{(u,v) \in \mathbb{R}^2 : x < u < 1, \sqrt{u} < v < 1\}$. Writing in the limits of integration, we find that

$$\mathbb{P}(V^2 > U > x) = \int_{u=x}^{1}\int_{v=\sqrt{u}}^{1} du\, dv$$

$$= \int_{x}^{1}(1 - \sqrt{u})\, du$$

$$= u - \frac{2}{3}u^{3/2}\big|_{x}^{1}$$

$$= \frac{1}{3} - x + \frac{2}{3}x^{3/2} \qquad\qquad \text{for } x \in (0,1).$$

(c) By the quadratic formula, the random quadratic equation $x^2 + 2Vx + U = 0$ has real roots if and only if $V^2 - U \geq 0$. That is to say, $V^2 \geq U$. We have that

$$\mathbb{P}(V^2 \geq U) = \mathbb{P}(V^2 > U > 0)$$

$$= \frac{1}{3},$$

by applying the result of part (b) with $x = 0$.

(d) **Wrong Solution:** Given that the two roots R_1, R_2 of the above quadratic are real, both $|R_1| \leq 1$ and $|R_2| \leq 1$ if and only if the derivative of the quadratic to be negative at -1 and positive at 1. That is to say, $V^2 > U > 0$.

$$\mathbb{P}(|R_1| \leq 1, |R_2| \leq 1 \mid V^2 > U > 0) = \frac{\mathbb{P}(|R_1| \leq 1, |R_2| \leq 1, V^2 > U > 0)}{\mathbb{P}(V^2 > U > 0)}$$

$$= \frac{\mathbb{P}(-2 + 2V < 0, 2 + 2V > 0, V^2 > U > 0)}{\mathbb{P}(V^2 > U > 0)}$$

$$= \frac{\mathbb{P}(V < 1, V > -1, V^2 > U > 0)}{\mathbb{P}(V^2 > U > 0)}$$

$$= \frac{\mathbb{P}(V^2 < 1, V^2 > U > 0)}{\mathbb{P}(V^2 > U > 0)}$$

$$= \frac{\mathbb{P}(V^2 > U > 0)}{\mathbb{P}(V^2 > U > 0)}$$

$$= 1.$$

Right Solution: Note that the quadratic equation $x^2 + 2Vx + U = 0$ has two real roots R_1, R_2 such that both $|R_1| \leq 1$ and $|R_2| \leq 1$ if and only if

$$\begin{cases} V^2 - U \geq 0, \\ f(-1) \geq 0, \\ f(1) \geq 0, \\ -1 \leq -\dfrac{2V}{2} \leq 1, \end{cases}$$

which is to say that

$$\begin{cases} V^2 \geq U \\ U - 2V + 1 \geq 0 \\ U + 2V + 1 \geq 0 \\ -1 \leq V \leq 1 \end{cases}$$

where $f(x) = x^2 + 2Vx + U$. We have that

$$\mathbb{P}(V^2 \geq U, U - 2V + 1 \geq 0, U + 2V + 1 \geq 0, -1 \leq V \leq 1) = \iint_A f_{U,V}(u,v) \, du \, dv$$

by Theorem 6.22, where $A = \{(u,v) \in \mathbb{R}^2 : 0 \leq u \leq 1, \sqrt{u} \leq v \leq \dfrac{u+1}{2}\}$. Writing in the limits of integration, we find that

$$\begin{aligned} \mathbb{P}(V^2 \geq U, U - 2V + 1 \geq 0, U + 2V + 1 \geq 0, -1 \leq V \leq 1) &= \int_{u=0}^{1} \int_{\sqrt{u}}^{\frac{u+1}{2}} du \, dv \\ &= \int_0^1 \left(\frac{u+1}{2} - \sqrt{u} \right) du \\ &= \frac{u^2}{4} + \frac{1}{2}u - \frac{2}{3}u^{\frac{3}{2}} \Big|_0^1 \\ &= \frac{1}{12}. \end{aligned}$$

The probability that both $|R_1| \leq 1$ and $|R_2| \leq 1$ given that the two roots R_1, R_2 of the quadratic are real is

$$\begin{aligned} \mathbb{P}(|R_1| \leq 1, |R_2| \leq 1 \mid V^2 \geq U) &= \frac{\mathbb{P}(|R_1| \leq 1, |R_2| \leq 1, V^2 \geq U)}{\mathbb{P}(V^2 \geq U)} \\ &= \frac{\mathbb{P}(V^2 \geq U, U - 2V + 1 \geq 0, U + 2V + 1 \geq 0, -1 \leq V \leq 1)}{\mathbb{P}(V^2 \geq U)} \\ &= \frac{1}{12} \cdot 3 \\ &= \frac{1}{4}. \end{aligned}$$

CHAPTER 7

Moments, and moment generating functions

7.1. A general note

7.2. Moments

EXERCISE (7.10). If X is uniformly distributed on (a, b), show that

(for $k = 1, 2, \ldots$.)
$$\mathbb{E}(X^k) = \frac{b^{k+1} - a^{k+1}}{(b-a)(k+1)}$$

SOLUTION. Since X is uniformly distributed on (a, b), it follows that

(by Theorem 5.58)
$$\mathbb{E}(X^k) = \int_a^b x^k \frac{1}{b-a}\, dx$$

$$= \frac{1}{(b-a)(k+1)} x^{k+1} \big|_a^b$$

(for $k = 1, 2, \ldots,$)
$$= \frac{b^{k+1} - a^{k+1}}{(b-a)(k+1)}$$

as required.

EXERCISE (7.11). If X has the gamma distribution with parameters w and λ, show that

(for $k = 1, 2, \ldots$.)
$$\mathbb{E}(X^k) = \frac{\Gamma(w+k)}{\lambda^k \Gamma(w)}$$

SOLUTION. Since X has the gamma distribution with parameters w and λ, it follows that

(by Theorem 5.58)

$$\mathbb{E}(X^k) = \int_0^\infty x^k \frac{1}{\Gamma(w)} \lambda^w x^{w-1} e^{-\lambda x} \, dx$$

$$= \frac{1}{\Gamma(w)} \int_0^\infty \lambda^w x^{k+w-1} e^{-\lambda x} \, dx$$

$$= \frac{1}{\lambda^k \Gamma(w)} \int_0^\infty \lambda^{w+k} x^{w+k-1} e^{-\lambda x} \, dx$$

(for $k = 1, 2, \ldots,$)

$$= \frac{\Gamma(w+k)}{\lambda^k \Gamma(w)}$$

as required.

EXERCISE (7.12). If X has the χ^2 distribution with n degrees of freedom, show that

(for $k = 1, 2, \ldots.$)

$$\mathbb{E}(X^k) = 2^k \frac{\Gamma(k + \frac{1}{2}n)}{\Gamma(\frac{1}{2}n)}$$

SOLUTION. Since X has the χ^2 distribution with n degrees of freedom, it follows that

(by Theorem 5.58)

$$\mathbb{E}(X^k) = \int_0^\infty x^k \frac{1}{2\Gamma(\frac{1}{2}n)} (\frac{1}{2}x)^{\frac{1}{2}n-1} e^{-\frac{1}{2}x} \, dx$$

$$= \frac{1}{\Gamma(\frac{1}{2}n)} \int_0^\infty (\frac{1}{2})^{\frac{1}{2}n} x^{k+\frac{1}{2}n-1} e^{-\frac{1}{2}x} \, dx$$

$$= 2^k \frac{1}{\Gamma(\frac{1}{2}n)} \int_0^\infty (\frac{1}{2})^{k+\frac{1}{2}n} x^{k+\frac{1}{2}n-1} e^{-\frac{1}{2}x} \, dx$$

(for $k = 1, 2, \ldots,$)

$$= 2^k \frac{\Gamma(k + \frac{1}{2}n)}{\Gamma(\frac{1}{2}n)}$$

as required.

7.3. Variance and covariance

EXERCISE (7.35). If X and Y have the bivariate normal distribution with parameters μ_1, μ_2, σ_1, σ_2, ρ (see (6.76)), show that

$$\text{cov}(X, Y) = \rho \sigma_1 \sigma_2 \qquad \text{and} \qquad \rho(X, Y) = \rho.$$

SOLUTION. Since X and Y have the bivariate normal distribution with parameters μ_1, μ_2, σ_1, σ_2, ρ, it follows that (by (7.21)) $\text{cov}(X,Y) = \mathbb{E}(XY) - \mathbb{E}(X)\mathbb{E}(Y)$

EXERCISE (7.36). Let $X_1, X_2, \ldots$ be a sequence of uncorrelated random variables, each having variance σ^2. If $S_n = X_1 + X_2 + \cdots + X_n$, show that

$$\text{cov}(S_m, S_n) = \text{var}(S_m) = m\sigma^2 \qquad \text{if } m < n.$$

SOLUTION. By (7.21),

$$\text{cov}(S_m, S_n) = \mathbb{E}(S_m S_n) - \mathbb{E}(S_m)\mathbb{E}(S_n)$$

$$= \mathbb{E}(\sum_{i=1}^{m} X_i^2 + \sum_{\substack{i \neq j \\ i = 1,2,\ldots,m \\ j = 1,2,\ldots,n}} \mathbb{E}(X_i X_j) - \mathbb{E}(\sum_{i=1}^{m} X_i)\mathbb{E}(\sum_{i=1}^{n} X_j)$$

$$= \sum_{i=1}^{m} \mathbb{E}(X_i^2) + \sum_{\substack{i \neq j \\ i = 1,2,\ldots,m \\ j = 1,2,\ldots,n}} \mathbb{E}(X_i X_j) - \sum_{i=1}^{m} \mathbb{E}(X_i) \sum_{j=1}^{n} \mathbb{E}(X_j)$$

$$= \sum_{i=1}^{m} \{\mathbb{E}(X_i^2) - [\mathbb{E}(X_j)]^2\} + \sum_{\substack{i \neq j \\ i = 1,2,\ldots,m \\ j = 1,2,\ldots,n}} [\mathbb{E}(X_i X_j) - \mathbb{E}(X_i)\mathbb{E}(X_j)]$$

$$= m\text{var}(X_1),$$

since $X_1, X_2, \ldots$ are a sequence are uncorrelated random variables, each having variance σ^2.

EXERCISE (7.37). Show that $\text{cov}(X,Y) = 1$ in the case when X and Y have joint density function

$$f(x,y) = \begin{cases} \dfrac{1}{y} e^{-y-x/y} & \text{if } x, y > 0, \\ 0 & \text{otherwise.} \end{cases}$$

SOLUTION. By (7.21),

$$\operatorname{cov}(X, Y) = \mathbb{E}(XY) - \mathbb{E}(X)\mathbb{E}(Y).$$

The mean of X may be calculated directly from (5.59) in the usual way. This calculation is a little complicated since the marginal density function X is not easy to calculate, and it is simpler to use the following trick. Solving $\mathbb{E}(Y)$ first. The marginal density function of Y is

$$
\begin{aligned}
f_X(x) &= \int_{-\infty}^{\infty} f(x, y)\, dx \\
&= \begin{cases} \int_0^{\infty} \dfrac{1}{y} e^{-y-\frac{x}{y}}\, dx & \text{if } y > 0, \\ 0 & \text{otherwise,} \end{cases} \\
&= \begin{cases} [-e^{-y-\frac{x}{y}}]_{x=0}^{\infty} & \text{if } y > 0, \\ 0 & \text{otherwise,} \end{cases} \\
&= \begin{cases} e^{-y} & \text{if } y > 0, \\ 0 & \text{otherwise.} \end{cases}
\end{aligned}
$$

The mean of Y is

$$
\begin{aligned}
\mathbb{E}(Y) &= \int_0^{\infty} y e^{-y}\, dy \\
&= \int_0^{\infty} y\, d(-e^{-y}) \\
&= [-y e^{-y}]_0^{\infty} + \int_0^{\infty} e^{-y}\, dy \\
&= [-e^{-y}]_0^{\infty} \\
&= 1.
\end{aligned}
$$

The conditional expectation of X given $Y = y$ is

$$\mathbb{E}(X \mid Y = y) = \int_0^\infty x \frac{\frac{1}{y} e^{-y - \frac{x}{y}}}{e^{-y}} \, dx$$

$$= \int_0^\infty \frac{x}{y} e^{-\frac{x}{y}} \, dx$$

$$= \frac{1}{y} \{ [-xy e^{-\frac{x}{y}}]_{x=0}^\infty + \int_0^\infty y e^{-\frac{x}{y}} \, dx \} \qquad \begin{array}{l} \text{by integration by parts formula with} \\ u = x, dv = e^{-\frac{x}{y}} \, dx \\ du = dx, v = -y e^{-\frac{x}{y}} \end{array}$$

$$= \int_{x=0}^\infty e^{-\frac{x}{y}} \, dx$$

$$= [-y e^{-\frac{x}{y}}]_{x=0}^\infty$$

$$= y.$$

The mean of X is

$$\mathbb{E}(X) = \int_0^\infty \mathbb{E}(X \mid Y = y) f_Y(y) \, dy \qquad \text{by Theorem 6.69}$$

$$= \int_0^\infty y e^{-y} \, dy$$

$$= \mathbb{E}(Y)$$

$$= 1.$$

The mean of XY is

$$\mathbb{E}(XY) = \int_{x=0}^{\infty} \int_{y=0}^{\infty} xy\frac{1}{y}e^{-y-\frac{x}{y}} \, dx \, dy$$

$$= \int_{x=0}^{\infty} \int_{y=0}^{\infty} xe^{-y-\frac{x}{y}} \, dx \, dy$$

$$= \int_{y=0}^{\infty} (\int_{x=0}^{\infty} xe^{-y-\frac{x}{y}} \, dx) \, dy$$

$$= \int_{y=0}^{\infty} (\int_{x=0}^{\infty} x \, d(-ye^{-y-\frac{x}{y}})) \, dy$$

$$= \int_{y=0}^{\infty} \{[-xye^{-y-\frac{x}{y}}]_{x=0}^{\infty} + \int_{x=0}^{\infty} ye^{-y-\frac{x}{y}} \, dx\} \, dy$$

$$= \int_{y=0}^{\infty} \{[-y^2 e^{-y-\frac{x}{y}}]_{x=0}^{\infty}\} \, dy$$

$$= \int_{y=0}^{\infty} y^2 e^{-y} \, dy$$

$$= \int_{0}^{y} y^2 d(-e^{-y})$$

$$= [-y^2 e^{-y}]_0^{\infty} + 2\int_0^{\infty} ye^{-y} \, dy$$

$$= 2\int_0^{\infty} y d(-e^{-y})$$

$$= [-2ye^{-y}]_{y=0}^{\infty} + 2\int_0^{\infty} e^{-y} \, dy$$

$$= [-2e^{-y}]_0^{\infty}$$

$$= 2.$$

Hence

$$\mathrm{cov}(X,Y) = \mathbb{E}(XY) - \mathbb{E}(X)\mathbb{E}(Y).$$
$$= 2 - 1 \cdot 1$$
$$= 1,$$

as required.

7.4. Moment generating functions

EXERCISE (7.59). Find the moment generating function of a random variable having
(a) the gamma distribution with parameters w and λ,

(b) the Poisson distribution with parameter λ.

SOLUTION. (a) If X has the gamma distribution with parameters w and λ, the moment generating function of X is

$$
\begin{aligned}
M_X(t) &= \int_0^\infty e^{tx} \frac{1}{\Gamma(w)} \lambda^w x^{w-1} e^{-\lambda x} \, dx \\
&= \frac{\lambda^w}{\Gamma(w)} \int_0^\infty x^{w-1} e^{-(\lambda-t)x} \, dx \\
&= \frac{\lambda^w}{\Gamma(w)} \int_0^\infty \left(\frac{u}{\lambda-t}\right)^{w-1} e^{-u} \frac{1}{\lambda-t} \, du \quad \text{by the substitution } u = (\lambda-t)x \\
&= \frac{\lambda^w}{\Gamma(w)(\lambda-t)^w} \int_0^\infty u^{w-1} e^{-u} \, du \\
&= \frac{\lambda^w}{\Gamma(w)(\lambda-t)^w} \Gamma(w) \qquad\qquad \text{since } \int_0^\infty x^{w-1} e^{-x} \, dx = \Gamma(w) \\
&= \left(\frac{\lambda}{\lambda-t}\right)^w \qquad\qquad\qquad\quad \text{if } t < \lambda.
\end{aligned}
$$

(b) If X has the Poisson distribution with parameter λ, the moment generating function of X is

$$
\begin{aligned}
M_X(t) &= \sum_{k=0}^\infty e^{tk} \frac{1}{k!} \lambda^k e^{-\lambda} \\
&= e^{-\lambda} \sum_{k=0}^\infty \frac{(\lambda e^t)^k}{k!} \\
&= e^{-\lambda} e^{\lambda e^t} \qquad\qquad \text{since } \sum_{k=0}^\infty \frac{z^k}{k!} = e^z \\
&= e^{-\lambda + \lambda e^t}.
\end{aligned}
$$

EXERCISE (7.60). If X has the normal distribution with mean μ and variance σ^2, find $\mathbb{E}(X^3)$.

SOLUTION. Since X has the normal distribution with mean μ and variance σ^2, the moment generating function of X is

$$M_X(t) = \int_{-\infty}^{\infty} e^{tx} \frac{1}{\sqrt{2\pi\sigma^2}} e^{-\frac{1}{2\sigma^2}(x-\mu)^2} \, dx$$

$$= \int_{-\infty}^{\infty} \frac{1}{\sqrt{2\pi\sigma^2}} e^{-\frac{1}{2}[\frac{(x-\mu)^2}{\sigma^2} - 2tx]} \, dx$$

$$= \int_{-\infty}^{\infty} \frac{1}{\sqrt{2\pi\sigma^2}} e^{-\frac{1}{2\sigma^2}(x^2 - 2\mu x + \mu^2 - 2t\sigma^2 x)} \, dx$$

$$= \int_{-\infty}^{\infty} \frac{1}{\sqrt{2\pi\sigma^2}} e^{-\frac{1}{2\sigma^2}[x^2 - 2(\mu+t\sigma^2)x + (\mu+t\sigma^2)^2 - \frac{2\mu t\sigma^2 - t^2\sigma^4}{2}]} \, dx$$

$$= \int_{-\infty}^{\infty} \frac{1}{\sqrt{2\pi\sigma^2}} e^{-\frac{1}{2\sigma^2}[x-(\mu+t\sigma^2)]^2} e^{\frac{1}{2\sigma^2}(2\mu t\sigma^2 + t^2\sigma^4)} \, dx$$

$$= e^{\frac{1}{2\sigma^2}(2\mu t\sigma^2 + t^2\sigma^4)} \int_{-\infty}^{\infty} \frac{1}{\sqrt{2\pi\sigma^2}} e^{-\frac{1}{2\sigma^2}[x-(\mu+t\sigma^2)]^2} \, dx.$$

Note the completion of the square in the exponent. The function within the final integral is the density function of the normal distribution with mean $\mu + t\sigma^2$ and variance σ^2, and therefore this final integral equals 1, giving that

$$M_X(t) = e^{\frac{1}{2\sigma^2}(2\mu t\sigma^2 + t^2\sigma^4)}$$

$$= e^{\mu t + \frac{1}{2}\sigma^2 t^2}.$$

The derivatives of $M_X(t)$ are

$$\frac{d}{dx} M_X(t) = (\mu + \sigma^2 t) e^{\mu t + \frac{1}{2}\sigma^2 t^2}$$

$$\frac{d^2}{dx^2} M_X(t) = \sigma^2 e^{\mu t + \frac{1}{2}\sigma^2 t^2} + (\mu + \sigma^2 t)^2 e^{\mu t + \frac{1}{2}\sigma^2 t^2} = [\sigma^2 + (\mu + \sigma^2 t)^2] e^{\mu t + \frac{1}{2}\sigma^2 t^2}$$

$$\frac{d^3}{dx^3} M_X(t) = 2(\mu + \sigma^2 t)\sigma^2 e^{\mu t + \frac{1}{2}\sigma^2 t^2} + [\sigma^2 + (\mu + \sigma^2 t)^2](\mu + \sigma^2 t) e^{\mu t + \frac{1}{2}\sigma^2 t^2}.$$

Hence

$$\mathbb{E}(X^3) = \frac{d^3}{dx^3} M_X(t)|_{t=0}$$

$$= 2\mu\sigma^2 + (\sigma^2 + \mu^2)\mu$$

$$= \mu(\sigma^2 + \mu^2 + 2\sigma^2)$$

$$= \mu^3 + 3\mu\sigma^2.$$

EXERCISE (7.61). Show that, if X has a normal distribution, then so does $aX + b$, for any $a, b \in \mathbb{R}$ with $a \neq 0$. You may use Theorem 7.55 together with (7.51) and (7.58).

SOLUTION. Let X be a random variable having the normal distribution with parameters μ and σ^2. The moment generating function of $aX + b$ is

$$
\begin{aligned}
M_{aX+b}(t) &= \int_{-\infty}^{\infty} e^{t(ax+b)} \frac{1}{\sqrt{2\pi\sigma^2}} e^{-\frac{1}{2\sigma^2}(x-\mu)^2} \, dx \\
&= e^{tb} \int_{-\infty}^{\infty} e^{tax} \frac{1}{\sqrt{2\pi\sigma^2}} e^{-\frac{1}{2\sigma^2}(x-\mu)^2} \, dx \\
&= e^{tb} \int_{-\infty}^{\infty} \frac{1}{\sqrt{2\pi\sigma^2}} e^{-\frac{1}{2\sigma^2}\{[x-(\mu+\sigma^2 at)]^2 - 2\mu\sigma^2 at - \sigma^4 a^2 t^2\}} \, dx \\
&= e^{tb+\mu at+\frac{1}{2}\sigma^2 a^2 t^2} \int_{-\infty}^{\infty} \frac{1}{\sqrt{2\pi\sigma^2}} e^{-\frac{1}{2\sigma^2}[x-(\mu+\sigma^2 at)]^2} \, du \\
&= e^{tb+\mu at+\frac{1}{2}\sigma^2 a^2 t^2} \\
&= e^{(a\mu+b)t+\frac{1}{2}(a\sigma)^2 t^2},
\end{aligned}
$$

since the integrand in the latter integral is the density function of the normal distribution with mean $\mu + \sigma^2 at$ and variance σ^2, and thus has integral 1. The only distribution with moment generating function of the form above is the normal distribution with mean $a\mu + b$ and variance $(a\sigma)^2$. We deduce that $aX + b$ has this distribution by appealing to Theorem 7.55. Alternatively, we consider the linear function $aX + b$ of the random variable X. If $a, b \in \mathbb{R}$,

$$
M_X(t) = e^{\mu t + \frac{1}{2}\sigma^2 t^2}
$$

and

$$
\begin{aligned}
M_{aX+b}(t) &= \mathbb{E}(e^{t(aX+b)}) \\
&= \mathbb{E}(e^{atX} e^{tb}) \\
&= e^{tb} \mathbb{E}(e^{(at)X}) \qquad\qquad \text{by (6.63)} \\
&= e^{tb} M_X(at) \\
&= e^{tb} e^{\mu(at)+\frac{1}{2}\sigma^2(at)^2} \\
&= e^{(b+a\mu)t+\frac{1}{2}(a\sigma)^2 t^2},
\end{aligned}
$$

which we recognize by (7.58) as the moment generating function of the normal distribution with mean $a\mu + b$ and variance $(a\sigma)^2$. We deduce that $ax + b$ has this distribution by appealing to Theorem 7.55.

EXERCISE (7.62). Let $X_1, X_2, \ldots$ be identically distributed[1] random variables with common moment generating function M. Let N be a random variable taking non-negative integer values with probability generating function G, and suppose N is independent of the sequence (X_i). Show that the random sum $S = X_1 + X_2 + \cdots + X_N$ has moment generating function $M_S(t) = G(M(t))$.

SOLUTION. The moment generating function of S is

$$
\begin{aligned}
M_S(t) &= \mathbb{E}(e^{tS}) \\
&= \mathbb{E}(e^{t \sum_{i=1}^{N} X_i}) \\
&= \sum_{k=0}^{\infty} \mathbb{E}(e^{t \sum_{i=1}^{N} X_i} \mid N = k)\mathbb{P}(N = k) \qquad \text{by Theorem 2.42} \\
&= \sum_{k=0}^{\infty} (\mathbb{E}(e^{t \sum_{i=1}^{N} X_i}))^k \mathbb{P}(N = k) \\
&= \sum_{k=0}^{\infty} (\mathbb{E}(e^{t \sum_{i=1}^{N} X_i}))^k \mathbb{P}(N = k) \\
&= \sum_{k=0}^{\infty} (M(t))^k \mathbb{P}(N = k) \\
&= G(M(t))
\end{aligned}
$$

since

$$
\begin{aligned}
\mathbb{E}(e^{t \sum_{i=1}^{N} X_i}) &= \mathbb{E}(e^{tX_1} e^{tX_2} \cdots e^{tX_k}) \\
&= \prod_{i=1}^{k} \mathbb{E}(e^{tX_i}) \\
&= (\mathbb{E}(e^{tX_1}))^k \\
&= (M(t))^k,
\end{aligned}
$$

giving that

$$
M_S(t) = G(M(t)).
$$

7.5. Two inequalities

EXERCISE (7.72). Determine which distributions on the non-negative reals, if any, with mean μ are such that 2μ is a median.

---

[1]Errata from solution writer: be independent, identically distributed

SOLUTION. Let X be a random variable. The real number m is called a median of X if

$$\mathbb{P}(X < m) \le \frac{1}{2} \le \mathbb{P}(X \le m).$$

Exercise 5.14 was to show that every random variable possesses at least one median m. Since X is non-negative, it follows that

$$\frac{1}{2} \le \mathbb{P}(X \ge m) \le \frac{\mathbb{E}(X)}{m} = \frac{\mu}{m}$$

by Markov's inequality. Therefore, any median m satisfies $m \le 2\mu$. Here we shall determine whether or not equality can hold. Let $A = \{\omega \in \Omega \colon X(\omega) \ge m\}$. The equality can hold if and only if $\mathbb{P}(X \ge m) = \frac{1}{2}$ and $A = \Omega \backslash \{\omega \in \Omega \colon X(\omega) = 0\}$. Thus

$$\mathbb{P}(X < m) = 1 - \mathbb{P}(X \ge m)$$
$$= \frac{1}{2}.$$

Consider the discrete distribution X that places probability $\frac{1}{2}$ on the each value 0 and 2μ. Then $\mathbb{E}(X) = \mu$ and $m = 2\mu$, as required.

EXERCISE (7.73). Let I be an interval of the real line, and let $f \colon I \to \mathbb{R}$ be twice differentiable with $f''(x) > 0$ for $x \in I$. Show that f is convex on I.

SOLUTION. By Taylor's theorem,

$$f(t) = f(x_0) + f'(x_0)(t - x_0) + \frac{f''(\xi)}{2!}(t - x_0)^2.$$

Hence

$$f(t) \ge f(x_0) + f'(x_0)(t - x_0)$$

since $f''(\xi) > 0$ for $\xi \in I$. Thus

$$f(x_0) \le f(t) - f'(x_0)(t - x_0). \qquad (1)$$

Taking $x_0 = \alpha x + (1 - \alpha y)$ and $t = x$ for $\alpha \in [0,1]$ and $x, y \in I$. Then

$$f(\alpha x + (1 - \alpha)y) \le f(x) - f'(\alpha x + (1 - \alpha y))(1 - \alpha)(x - y). \qquad (2)$$

Taking $x_0 = \alpha x + (1 - \alpha)$ and $t = y$. Then (1) becomes

$$f(\alpha x + (1-\alpha)y) \le f(y) + f'(\alpha x + (1-\alpha)y)\alpha(x-y). \qquad (3)$$

Multiply throughout (2) by α, multiply throughout (3) by $1-\alpha$ and add together to obtain

$$f(\alpha x + (1-\alpha)y) \le \alpha f(x) + (1-\alpha)f(y).$$

Therefore f is convex on I.

EXERCISE (7.74). Show by Jensen's inequality that $\mathbb{E}(X^2) \ge \mathbb{E}(X)^2$.

SOLUTION. The function $g(x) = x^2$ is convex on the interval $(-\infty, \infty)$. By Jensen's inequality applied to a random variable X with finite mean,

$$\begin{aligned}
\mathbb{E}(g(X)) &= \mathbb{E}(X^2) \\
&\ge g(\mathbb{E}(X)) \\
&= [\mathbb{E}(X)]^2,
\end{aligned}$$

so that

$$\mathbb{E}(X^2) \ge \mathbb{E}(X)^2.$$

EXERCISE (7.75). The harmonic mean η of the positive reals $x_1, x_2, \ldots, x_n$ is given by

$$\frac{1}{\eta} = \frac{1}{n}\sum_{i=1}^{n}\frac{1}{x_i}.$$

Show that η is no greater than the geometric mean of the x_i.

SOLUTION. By Arithmetic/geometric mean inequality applied to positive reals $\frac{1}{x_1}, \frac{1}{x_2}, \ldots, \frac{1}{x_n}$,

$$\begin{aligned}
\frac{1}{\eta} &= \frac{1}{n}\sum_{i=1}^{n}\frac{1}{x_i} \\
&\ge \sqrt[n]{\frac{1}{x_1}\cdot\frac{1}{x_2}\cdot\ldots\cdot\frac{1}{x_n}} \\
&= \frac{1}{\sqrt[n]{x_1 x_2 \cdots x_n}}.
\end{aligned}$$

Thus

$$\eta = \frac{1}{\frac{1}{n}\sum_{i=1}^{n}\frac{1}{x_i}}$$
$$\leq \sqrt[n]{x_1 x_2 \cdots x_n}.$$

Therefore η is no greater than the geometric mean of the x_i.

7.6. Characteristic functions

EXERCISE (7.95). Show that the characteristic function of a random variable having the binomial distribution with parameters n and p is

$$\phi(t) = (q + pe^{it})^n,$$

where $q = 1 - p$.

SOLUTION. If X having the binomial distribution with parameters n and p, then

$$\phi_X(t) = \sum_{k=0}^{n} e^{itk}\binom{n}{k}p^k q^{n-k}$$

$$= \sum_{k=0}^{n}\binom{n}{k}(pe^{it})^k q^{n-k}$$

$$= (q + pe^{it})^n \qquad\qquad \text{by binomial expansion}$$

where $q = 1 - p$.

EXERCISE (7.96). Let X be uniformly distributed on (a, b). Show that

$$\phi_X(t) = \frac{e^{itb} - e^{ita}}{it(b - a)}.$$

If X is uniformly distributed on $(-b, b)$, show that

$$\phi_X(t) = \frac{1}{bt}\sin bt.$$

SOLUTION. Since X is uniformly distributed on (a, b), it follows that

$$\phi_X(t) = \int_a^b e^{itx}\frac{1}{b - a}\,dx$$

$$= [\frac{1}{it(b - a)}e^{itx}]_a^b$$

$$= \frac{e^{itb} - e^{ita}}{it(b - a)},$$

as required. By applying the result above to X being uniformly distributed on $(-b, b)$, we obtain

$$
\begin{aligned}
\phi_X(t) &= \frac{e^{itb} - e^{-itb}}{it(2b)} \\
&= \frac{(\cos(tb) + i\sin(tb)) - (\cos(tb) - i\sin(tb))}{2itb} \\
&= \frac{2i\sin(tb)}{2itb} \\
&= \frac{1}{bt}\sin bt,
\end{aligned}
$$

as required.

EXERCISE (7.97). Find the characteristic function of a random variable having
(a) the gamma distribution with parameters w and λ,
(b) the Poisson distribution with parameter λ.

SOLUTION. Since X has the gamma distribution with parameters w and λ, it follows that

$$
\begin{aligned}
\phi_X(t) &= \int_0^\infty e^{itx} \frac{1}{\Gamma(w)} \lambda^w x^{w-1} e^{-\lambda x}\, dx \\
&= \frac{\lambda^w}{\Gamma(w)} \int_0^\infty x^{w-1} e^{-(\lambda - it)x}\, dx \\
&= \frac{\lambda^w}{\Gamma(w)} \int_0^\infty \left(\frac{u}{\lambda - it}\right)^{w-1} e^{-u} \frac{1}{(\lambda - it)}\, du \quad \text{by the subsitition } u = (\lambda - it)x \\
&= \frac{\lambda^w}{\Gamma(w)} \frac{1}{(\lambda - it)^w} \int_0^\infty u^{w-1} e^{-u}\, du \\
&= \frac{\lambda^w}{\Gamma(w)} \frac{1}{(\lambda - it)^w} \Gamma(w) \\
&= \left(\frac{\lambda}{\lambda - it}\right)^w.
\end{aligned}
$$

Sicne X has the Poisson distribution with parameter λ, it follows that

$$\phi_X(t) = \sum_{k=0}^{\infty} e^{itk} \frac{1}{k!} \lambda^k e^{-\lambda}$$

$$= e^{-\lambda} \sum_{k=0}^{\infty} \frac{(\lambda e^{it})^k}{k!}$$

$$= e^{-\lambda} e^{\lambda e^{it}} \qquad \text{since } \sum_{k=0}^{\infty} \frac{z^k}{k!} = e^z$$

$$= e^{-\lambda + \lambda e^{it}}.$$

EXERCISE (7.98). If X and Y are independent and identically distributed random variables, show that

$$\phi_{X-Y}(t) = |\phi_X(t)|^2.$$

SOLUTION. We have that

$$\phi_{-Y}(t) = \mathbb{E}(e^{it(-Y)})$$

$$= \mathbb{E}(\overline{e^{itY}})$$

$$= \overline{\mathbb{E}(e^{itY})}$$

$$= \overline{\phi_Y(t)}$$

$$= \overline{\phi_X(t)} \qquad \text{since } X \text{ and } Y \text{ are identically distributed random variables.}$$

Note that X and Y are independent, so are X and $-Y$. By independence and Theorem 7.87,

$$\phi_{X-Y}(t) = \phi_{X+(-Y)}(t)$$

$$= \phi_X(t)\phi_{-Y}(t)$$

$$= \phi_X(t)\overline{\phi_X(t)}$$

$$= |\phi_X(t)|^2,$$

as required.

7.7. Problems

PROBLEM (7.7.1). Let X and Y be random variables with equal variance. Show that $U = X - Y$ and $V = X + Y$ are uncorrelated. Give an example to show that U and V need not be independent even if, further, X and Y are independent.

SOLUTION. We have that

$$
\begin{aligned}
\operatorname{cov}(U,V) &= \mathbb{E}(UV) - \mathbb{E}(U)E(V) \\
&= \mathbb{E}((X-Y)(X+Y)) - \mathbb{E}(X-Y)\mathbb{E}(X+Y) \\
&= \mathbb{E}(X^2 - Y^2) - (\mathbb{E}(X) - \mathbb{E}(Y))(\mathbb{E}(X) + \mathbb{E}(Y)) \\
&= \mathbb{E}(X^2) - \mathbb{E}(Y^2) - (\mathbb{E}(X))^2 + (\mathbb{E}(Y))^2 \\
&= 0,
\end{aligned}
$$

so that U and V are uncorrelated.

Let X and Y be independent random variables, each being uniformly distributed on $(-1,1)$. Then the chracteristic function of $U = X - Y$ is

$$
\begin{aligned}
\phi_{X-Y}(t) &= |\phi_X(t)|^2 \\
&= \left| \frac{1}{t} \sin t \right|^2 \\
&= \frac{1}{t^2} \sin^2 t,
\end{aligned}
$$

and the chracteristic function of $V = X + Y$ is

$$
\begin{aligned}
\phi_{X+Y}(t) &= [\phi_X(t)]^2 \\
&= (\frac{1}{t} \sin t)^2 \\
&= \frac{1}{t^2} \sin^2 t.
\end{aligned}
$$

Thus U and V have the same distribution by Thereom 7.88. Therefore

$$
\begin{aligned}
\phi_{U+V}(t) &= \phi_{2X}(t) \\
&= \phi_X(2t) \\
&= \frac{\sin(2t)}{2t} \\
&\neq \frac{1}{t^2} \sin^2 t \cdot \frac{1}{t^2} \sin^2 t \\
&= \phi_U(t)\phi_V(t),
\end{aligned}
$$

giving that U and V are dependent.

PROBLEM (7.7.2). Let $X_1, X_2, \ldots$ be uncorrelated random variables, each having mean μ and variance σ^2. If $X = n^{-1}(X_1 + X_2 + \cdots + X_n)$, show that

$$\mathbb{E}(\frac{1}{n-1}\sum_{i=1}^{n}(X_i - \overline{X})^2) = \sigma^2.$$

This fact is of importance in statistics and is used when estimating the population variance from knowledge of a random sample.

SOLUTION. We have that

$$\mathbb{E}(\frac{1}{n-1}\sum_{i=1}^{n}(X_i - \overline{X})^2) = \frac{1}{n-1}\mathbb{E}(\sum_{i=1}^{n}(X_i - \overline{X})^2)$$

$$= \frac{1}{n-1}\mathbb{E}(\sum_{i=1}^{n}(X_i^2 - 2X_i\overline{X} + \overline{X}^2)),$$

$$= \frac{1}{n-1}\mathbb{E}(\sum_{i=1}^{n}X_i^2 - 2\overline{X}\sum_{i=1}^{n}X_i + n\overline{X}^2)$$

$$= \frac{1}{n-1}\mathbb{E}(\sum_{i=1}^{n}X_i^2 - 2n\overline{X}^2 + n\overline{X}^2) \qquad \text{since } \frac{1}{n}\sum_{i=1}^{n}X_i = \overline{X}$$

$$= \frac{1}{n-1}(\sum_{i=1}^{n}\mathbb{E}(X_i^2) - 2n\mathbb{E}(\overline{X}^2) + n\mathbb{E}(\overline{X}^2))$$

$$= \frac{1}{n-1}(\sum_{i=1}^{n}\mathbb{E}(X_i^2) - n\mathbb{E}(\overline{X}^2)).$$

Note that

$$\sum_{i=1}^{n}\mathbb{E}(X_i^2) = \sum_{i=1}^{n}[\text{var}(X_i) + (\mathbb{E}(X_i))^2]$$

$$= n(\sigma^2 + \mu^2) \qquad\qquad \text{by symmetry,}$$

and

$$\mathbb{E}(\overline{X}^2) = \mathbb{E}(\frac{1}{n^2}(\sum_{i=1}^{n} X_i)^2)$$

$$= \frac{1}{n^2}\mathbb{E}(\sum_{i=1}^{n} X_i^2 + 2 \sum_{\substack{i < j \\ i = 1,2,\ldots,n-1}} X_i X_j)$$

$$= \frac{1}{n^2}\sum_{i=1}^{n}\mathbb{E}(X_i^2) + 2 \sum_{\substack{i < j \\ i = 1,2,\ldots,n-1}} \mathbb{E}(X_i X_j)$$

$$= \frac{1}{n^2}\sum_{i=1}^{n}\mathbb{E}(X_i^2) + 2 \sum_{\substack{i < j \\ i = 1,2,\ldots,n-1}} \mathbb{E}(X_i)\mathbb{E}(X_j) \quad \text{by uncorrelatedness}$$

$$= \frac{1}{n^2}n(\sigma^2 + \mu^2) + 2\frac{(n-1)n}{2n^2}\mu^2$$

$$= \frac{1}{n}(\sigma^2 + \mu^2) + \frac{(n-1)}{n}\mu^2.$$

Thus

$$\mathbb{E}(\frac{1}{n-1}\sum_{i=1}^{n}(X_i - \overline{X})^2) = \frac{1}{n-1}\{n(\sigma^2 + \mu^2) - n[\frac{1}{n}(\sigma^2 + \mu^2) + \frac{(n-1)}{n}\mu^2]\}$$

$$= \frac{n}{n-1}(\sigma^2 + \mu^2) - \frac{1}{n-1}(\sigma^2 + \mu^2) - \frac{n}{n-1}\frac{(n-1)}{n}\mu^2$$

$$= \sigma^2,$$

as required.

PROBLEM (7.7.3). Let $X_1, X_2, \ldots$ be identically distributed, independent random variables and let $S_n = X_1 + X_2 + \cdots + X_n$. Show that

$$\mathbb{E}(\frac{S_m}{S_n}) = \frac{m}{n} \qquad\qquad \text{for } m \leq n,$$

provided that all the necessary expectations exist. Is the same true if $m > n$?

SOLUTION. For $m < n$,

$$\mathbb{E}(\frac{S_m}{S_n}) = \mathbb{E}(\frac{X_1 + X_2 + \cdots + X_m}{S_n})$$

$$= \mathbb{E}(\frac{X_1}{S_n}) + \mathbb{E}(\frac{X_2}{S_n}) + \cdots + \mathbb{E}(\frac{X_m}{S_n})$$

$$= m\mathbb{E}(\frac{X_1}{S_n}) \qquad \text{by symmetry.}$$

Note that

$$1 = \mathbb{E}(\frac{S_n}{S_n})$$

$$= n\mathbb{E}(\frac{X_1}{S_n}),$$

giving that

$$\mathbb{E}(\frac{X_1}{S_n}) = \frac{1}{n}.$$

Hence

$$\mathbb{E}(\frac{S_m}{S_n}) = \frac{m}{n} \qquad \text{for } m \leq n,$$

as required. The result is generally false when $m > n$. See also Problem 3.6.8.

PROBLEM (7.7.4). Show that every distribution function has only a countable set of points of discontinuity.

SOLUTION. We prove that $\{x\colon F(x) - \lim_{y\uparrow x} F(y) > 1/n\} < n$ for all n by contradiction. Assume that there is some positive integer n such that there are m points $x_1 < x_2 < \cdots < x_m$ satisfying $F(x) - \lim_{y\uparrow x} F(y) > 1/n$ and $m \geq n$. Then there exists $y_1, y_2, \ldots, y_m$ such that $F(x_i) - F(y_1) > 1/n$ and $x_{i-1} < y_1 < x_i$. The fact that $F(x_i) - F(y_i) > 1/n$ is equivalent to the fact that $\mathbb{P}(X \in (y_i, x_i)) > 1/n$. Hence

$$\mathbb{P}(X \in \bigcup_{i=1}^{m}(y_i, x_i)) > m\frac{1}{n} \geq 1,$$

which contradicts the fact that $\mathbb{P}(A) \leq 1$ for any event A. Therefore, $\{x\colon F(x) - \lim_{y\uparrow x} F(y) > 1/n\} < n$ for all n, so that every distribution function has only a countable set of points of discontinuity

PROBLEM (7.7.5). Let X and Y be independent random variables, X having the gamma distribution with parameters s and λ, and Y having the gamma distribution with parameters t and λ. Use moment generating functions to show that $X + Y$ has the gamma distribution with parameters $s + t$ and λ.

SOLUTION. By Theorem 7.52,

$$M_{X+Y}(t) = M_X(t) M_Y(t)$$

$$= (\frac{\lambda}{\lambda - t})^s (\frac{\lambda}{\lambda - t})^t$$

$$= (\frac{\lambda}{\lambda - t})^{s+t} \qquad \text{if } t < \lambda,$$

which we recognize by Exercise 7.59(a) as the moment generating function of the gamma distribution with parameters $s + t$ and λ. We deduce that $X + Y$ has this distribution by appealing to Theorem 7.55.

PROBLEM (7.7.6). Let $X_1, X_2, \ldots, X_n$ be independent random variables with the exponential distribution, parameter λ. Show that $X_1 + X_2 + \cdots + X_n$ has the gamma distribution with parameters n and λ.

PROBLEM. By Theorem 7.52, the sum $S = X_1 + \cdots + X_n$ of n independent random variables has moment generating function

$$M_S(t) = M_{X_1}(t) M_{X_2}(t) \cdots M_{X_n}(t)$$

$$= \begin{cases} (\dfrac{\lambda}{\lambda - t})^n & \text{if } t < \lambda, \\ \infty & \text{if } t \geq \lambda. \end{cases}$$

The only distribution with density function of the form above is the gamma distribution with parameters n and λ.

PROBLEM (7.7.7). Show from the result of Problem 7.7.5 that the χ^2 distribution with n degrees of freedom has moment generating function

$$M(t) = (1 - 2t)^{-\frac{1}{2}n} \qquad \text{if } t < \frac{1}{2}.$$

Deduce that, if $X_1, X_2, \ldots, X_n$ are independent random variables having the normal distribution with mean 0 and variance 1, then

$$Z = X_1^2 + X_2^2 + \cdots + X_n^2$$

has the χ^2 distribution with n degrees of freedom. Hence or otherwise show that the sum of two independent random variables, having the χ^2 distribution with m

and n degrees of freedom, respectively, has the χ^2 distribution with $m+n$ degrees of freedom.

SOLUTION. For the first part, we note that if X has the gamma distribution with parameters w and λ, then the moment generating function of X is

$$M_X(t) = (\frac{\lambda}{\lambda - t})^w,$$

and note that the χ^2 distribution is the same as the gamma distribution with parameters $w = \frac{1}{2}n$ and $\lambda = \frac{1}{2}$. It follows that the χ^2 distribution with n degrees of freedom has moment generating function

$$
\begin{aligned}
M(t) &= (\frac{\frac{1}{2}}{\frac{1}{2} - t})^{\frac{1}{2}n} \\
&= (\frac{1}{2})^{\frac{1}{2}n} (\frac{1 - 2t}{2})^{-\frac{1}{2}n} \\
&= (\frac{1}{2})^{\frac{1}{2}n} (\frac{1}{2})^{-\frac{1}{2}n} (1 - 2t)^{-\frac{1}{2}} \\
&= (1 - 2t)^{-\frac{1}{2}n} \qquad\qquad\qquad \text{if } t < \frac{1}{2}.
\end{aligned}
$$

For the middle part, we shall find the moment generating function of X_1^2 and use Theorem 7.52. The moment generating function of X_1^2 is

$$
\begin{aligned}
M_{X_1^2}(t) &= \mathbb{E}(e^{tX_1^2}) \\
&= \int_{-\infty}^{\infty} e^{tx^2} \frac{1}{\sqrt{2\pi}} e^{-\frac{1}{2}x^2} \, dx \\
&= \int_{-\infty}^{\infty} \frac{1}{\sqrt{2\pi}} e^{(t-\frac{1}{2})x^2} \, dx \\
&= \int_{-\infty}^{\infty} \frac{1}{\sqrt{2\pi}} e^{-\frac{1}{2}(1-2t)x^2} \, dx \\
&= \int_{-\infty}^{\infty} \frac{1}{\sqrt{2\pi}} e^{-\frac{1}{2}u^2} \frac{1}{\sqrt{1 - 2t}} \, du \qquad \text{by the substitution } u = \sqrt{1 - 2t}x \\
&= \frac{1}{\sqrt{1 - 2t}} \int_{-\infty}^{\infty} \frac{1}{\sqrt{2\pi}} e^{-\frac{1}{2}u^2} \, du \\
&= \frac{1}{\sqrt{1 - 2t}} \\
&= (1 - 2t)^{-\frac{1}{2}} \qquad\qquad\qquad \text{if } t < \frac{1}{2}.
\end{aligned}
$$

The only distribution with moment generating function of the form above is the χ^2 distribution with 1 degrees of freedom. By Theorem 7.52, the sum $Z = X_1^2 + X_2^2 + \cdots + X_n^2$ of n independent random variables has moment generating function

$$M_Z(t) = M_{X_1^2} M_{X_2^2} \cdots M_{X_n^2}$$
$$= (1 - 2t)^{-\frac{1}{2}n} \qquad\qquad \text{if } t < \frac{1}{2}.$$

The only distribution with density function of the form above is the χ^2 distribution with n degrees of freedom.

PROBLEM (7.7.8). Let $X_1, X_2, \ldots$ be independent, identically distributed random variables and let N be a random variable which takes values in the positive integers and is independent of the X_i. Find the moment generating function of $S = X_1 + X_2 + \cdots + X_N$ in terms of the moment generating functions of N and X_1, when these exist.

SOLUTION. We use the partition theorem, Theorem 2.42, with the events $B_n = \{N = n\}$ to find that

$$
\begin{aligned}
M_S(t) &= \mathbb{E}(e^{t(X_1 + \cdots + X_N)}) \\
&= \sum_{n=0}^{\infty} \mathbb{E}(e^{t(X_1 + \cdots + X_N)} \mid N = n) \mathbb{P}(N = n) \qquad \text{by Theorem 2.42} \\
&= \sum_{n=0}^{\infty} \mathbb{E}(e^{t(X_1 + \cdots + X_N)}) \mathbb{P}(N = n) \\
&= \sum_{n=0}^{\infty} (M_{X_1}(t))^n \mathbb{P}(N = n) \qquad\qquad \text{by (7.54)} \\
&= G_N(M_{X_1}(t))
\end{aligned}
$$

by the definition of G_N.

PROBLEM (7.7.9). Random variables $X_1, X_2, \ldots, X_N$ have zero expectations, and

$$\mathbb{E}(X_m X_n) = v_{mn} \qquad\qquad \text{for } m, n = 1, 2, \ldots, N.$$

Calculate the variance of the random variable

$$Z = \sum_{n=1}^{N} a_n X_n,$$

and deduce that the symmetric matrix $V = (v_{mn})$ is non-negative definite. It is desired to find an $N \times N$ matrix A such that the random variables

$$Y_n = \sum_{r=1}^{N} a_{nr} X_r \qquad \text{for } n = 1, 2, \ldots, N$$

are uncorrelated and have unit variance. Show that this will be the case if and only if

$$AVA' = I,$$

and show that A can be chosen to satisfy this equation if and only if V is non-singular. (Any standard results from matrix theory may, if clearly stated, be used without proof. A' denotes the transpose of A.) (Oxford 1971F).

SOLUTION. For the first part, we have that

$$\mathbb{E}(Z) = \mathbb{E}(\sum_{n=1}^{N} a_n X_n)$$
$$= \sum_{n=1}^{N} a\mathbb{E}(X_n)$$
$$= 0$$

since random variables $X_1, X_2, \ldots, X_N$ have zero expectations, and

$$\mathbb{E}(Z^2) = \mathbb{E}((\sum_{n=1}^{N} a_n X_n)^2)$$
$$= \sum_{n=1}^{N} a_n^2 \mathbb{E}(X_n^2) + 2 \sum_{\substack{n < m \\ 1 \le n \le n-1}} a_n a_m \mathbb{E}(X_n X_m)$$
$$= \sum_{n=1}^{N} a_n^2 v_{nn}^2 + 2 \sum_{\substack{n < m \\ 1 \le n \le n-1}} a_n a_m v_{nm}.$$

Hence

$$\text{var}(Z) = \mathbb{E}(Z^2) - (\mathbb{E}(Z))^2$$

$$= \sum_{n=1}^{N} a_n^2 v_{nn}^2 + 2 \sum_{\substack{n < m \\ 1 \le n \le n-1}} a_n a_m v_{nm}.$$

Let

$$V = \begin{pmatrix} v_{11} & v_{12} & \cdots & v_{1N} \\ v_{21} & v_{22} & \cdots & v_{2N} \\ \vdots & \vdots & \ddots & \vdots \\ v_{N1} & v_{N2} & \cdots & v_{NN} \end{pmatrix},$$

$$a = \begin{pmatrix} a_1 & a_2 & \cdots & a_N \end{pmatrix}.$$

Then

$$Va' = \begin{pmatrix} v_{11} & v_{12} & \cdots & v_{1N} \\ v_{21} & v_{22} & \cdots & v_{2N} \\ \vdots & \vdots & \ddots & \vdots \\ v_{N1} & v_{N2} & \cdots & v_{NN} \end{pmatrix} \begin{pmatrix} a_1 \\ a_2 \\ \vdots \\ a_N \end{pmatrix}$$

$$= \begin{pmatrix} \sum_{i=1}^{N} a_i v_{1i} \\ \sum_{i=1}^{N} a_i v_{2i} \\ \vdots \\ \sum_{i=1}^{N} a_i v_{Ni} \end{pmatrix},$$

so that

$$aVa' = \begin{pmatrix} a_1 & a_2 & \cdots & a_N \end{pmatrix} \begin{pmatrix} \sum_{i=1}^{N} a_i v_{1i} \\ \sum_{i=1}^{N} a_i v_{2i} \\ \vdots \\ \sum_{i=1}^{N} a_i v_{Ni} \end{pmatrix}$$

$$= \sum_{1 \le i,j \le N} a_i v_{ij} a_j$$

$$= \operatorname{var}(Z) \ge 0.$$

Thus $aVa' \ge 0$ for all the vector $a = \begin{pmatrix} a_1 & a_2 & \cdots & a_N \end{pmatrix}$, so that the symmetric matrix $V = (v_{mn})$ is non-negative definite.

For the second part, let

$$A = \begin{pmatrix} a_{11} & a_{12} & \cdots & a_{1N} \\ a_{21} & a_{22} & \cdots & a_{2N} \\ \vdots & \vdots & \ddots & \vdots \\ a_{N1} & a_{N2} & \cdots & a_{NN} \end{pmatrix},$$

$$X = \begin{pmatrix} X_1 & X_2 & \cdots & X_N \end{pmatrix}.$$

Then

$$AX' = \begin{pmatrix} a_{11} & a_{12} & \cdots & a_{1N} \\ a_{21} & a_{22} & \cdots & a_{2N} \\ \vdots & \vdots & \ddots & \vdots \\ a_{N1} & a_{N2} & \cdots & a_{NN} \end{pmatrix} \begin{pmatrix} X_1 \\ X_2 \\ \vdots \\ X_N \end{pmatrix}$$

$$= \begin{pmatrix} \sum_{i=1}^{N} a_{1i} X_i \\ \sum_{i=1}^{N} a_{2i} X_i \\ \vdots \\ \sum_{i=1}^{N} a_{Ni} X_i \end{pmatrix}$$

$$= \begin{pmatrix} Y_1 \\ Y_2 \\ \vdots \\ Y_N \end{pmatrix}.$$

Suppose that Y_i's are uncorrelated and have unit variance. Since $\mathbb{E}(Y_i) = 0$ for all i, it follows that $\mathbb{E}(X_i Y_j) = 0$ for $i \neq j$ and $\mathbb{E}(Y_i^2) = 1$. By the first part,

$$W = (\mathbb{E}(Y_i Y_j))_{1 \leq i,j \leq N}$$

$$= \begin{pmatrix} 1 & 0 & \cdots & 0 \\ 0 & 1 & \cdots & 0 \\ \vdots & \vdots & \ddots & \vdots \\ 0 & 0 & \cdots & 1 \end{pmatrix}$$

$$= I,$$

where I is the identity matrix. But

$$\mathbb{E}(Y_i Y_j) = E((\sum_{t=1}^{N} a_{it} X_t)(\sum_{k=1}^{N} a_{jk} X_k))$$

$$= \sum_{1 \leq t,k \leq N} a_{it} a_{jk} \mathbb{E}(X_t X_k)$$

$$= \sum_{1 \leq t,k \leq N} a_{it} a_{jk} v_{tk}$$

$$= \bar{a}_i V \bar{a}_j',$$

where $\bar{a}_i = \begin{pmatrix} a_{i1} & a_{i2} & \cdots & a_{iN} \end{pmatrix}$. Note that $\bar{a}_i V \bar{a}_j'$ is the element at the ith row and jth column of AVA'. Therefore $AVA' = W = I$.

Conversely, if $AVA' = I$, then

$$\mathbb{E}(Y_i Y_j) = \begin{cases} 1 & \text{if } i = j, \\ 0 & \text{if } i \neq j, \end{cases}$$

$$\mathrm{var}(Y_i) = \mathbb{E}(Y_i^2) - (\mathbb{E}(Y_i))^2$$
$$= 1,$$

and

$$\mathbb{E}(Y_i Y_j) = \mathbb{E}(Y_i)\mathbb{E}(Y_j)$$
$$= 0,$$

for $i \neq j$. Thus Y_i's are are uncorrelated and have unit variance.

PROBLEM (7.7.10). Prove that if $X = X_1 + \cdots + X_n$ and $Y = Y_1 + \cdots + Y_n$, where X_i and Y_j are independent whenever $i \neq j$, then $\mathrm{cov}(X,Y) = \sum_{i=1}^{n} \mathrm{cov}(X_i, Y_i)$. (Assume that all series involved are absolutely convergent.)

Two players A and B play a series of independent games. The probability that A wins any particular game is p^2, that B wins is q^2, and that the game is a draw is $2pq$, where $p + q = 1$. The winner of a game scores 2 points, the loser none; if a game is drawn, each player scores 1 point. Let X and Y be the number of points scored by A and B, respectively, in a series of n games. Prove that $\mathrm{cov}(X,Y) = -2npq$. (Oxford 1982M)

SOLUTION. For the first part, we have that

$$\mathrm{cov}(X,Y) = \mathbb{E}(XY) - \mathbb{E}(X)\mathbb{E}(Y).$$

Note that

$$
\begin{aligned}
\mathbb{E}(XY) &= \mathbb{E}((X_1 + \cdots X_n)(Y_1 + \cdots + Y_n)) \\
&= \mathbb{E}(\sum_{1 \le i,j \le n} X_i Y_j) \\
&= \sum_{1 \le i,j \le n} \mathbb{E}(X_i Y_j) \\
&= \sum_{i=1}^{n} \mathbb{E}(X_i Y_i) + \sum_{i \ne j} \mathbb{E}(X_i Y_j) \\
&= \sum_{i=1}^{n} \mathbb{E}(X_i Y_i) + \sum_{i \ne j} \mathbb{E}(X_i)\mathbb{E}(Y_j) \qquad \text{by independence}
\end{aligned}
$$

and

$$
\begin{aligned}
\mathbb{E}(X)\mathbb{E}(Y) &= \mathbb{E}(X_1 + \cdots + X_n)\mathbb{E}(Y_1 + \cdots + Y_n) \\
&= \mathbb{E}(\sum_{i=1}^{n} X_i)\mathbb{E}(\sum_{j=1}^{n} Y_j) \\
&= (\sum_{i=1}^{n} \mathbb{E}(X_i))(\sum_{j=1}^{n} \mathbb{E}(Y_j)) \qquad \text{by independence} \\
&= \sum_{i=1}^{n} \mathbb{E}(X_i)\mathbb{E}(Y_i) + \sum_{i \ne j} \mathbb{E}(X_i)\mathbb{E}(Y_j).
\end{aligned}
$$

Hence

$$
\begin{aligned}
\mathrm{cov}(X,Y) &= \sum_{i=1}^{n} \mathbb{E}(X_i Y_i) + \sum_{i \ne j} \mathbb{E}(X_i)\mathbb{E}(Y_j) - (\sum_{i=1}^{n} \mathbb{E}(X_i)\mathbb{E}(Y_i) + \sum_{i \ne j} \mathbb{E}(X_i)\mathbb{E}(Y_j)) \\
&= \sum_{i=1}^{n} \mathbb{E}(X_i Y_i) - \sum_{i=1}^{n} \mathbb{E}(X_i)\mathbb{E}(Y_i) \\
&= \sum_{i=1}^{n} (\mathbb{E}(X_i Y_i) - \mathbb{E}(X_i)\mathbb{E}(Y_i)) \\
&= \sum_{i=1}^{n} \mathrm{cov}(X_i, Y_i),
\end{aligned}
$$

as required.

For the second part, let X_i and Y_i be the number of points scored by A and B, respectively, in ith game. Then $X = X_1 + \cdots + X_n$ and $Y = Y_1 + \cdots + Y_n$, where X_i and Y_j are independent whenever $i \neq j$. By the first part,

$$\mathrm{cov}(X, Y) = \sum_{i=1}^{n} \mathrm{cov}(X_i, Y_i).$$

In order to find $\mathrm{cov}(X_i, Y_i)$, we should calculate $\mathbb{E}(X_i)$, $\mathbb{E}(Y_i)$ and $\mathbb{E}(X_i Y_i)$. We have that

$$\mathbb{P}(X_i) = \begin{cases} p^2 & \text{if } X_i = 2, \\ 2pq & \text{if } X_i = 1, \\ 0 & \text{if } X_i = 0, \end{cases}$$

$$\mathbb{P}(Y_i) = \begin{cases} q^2 & \text{if } X_i = 2, \\ 2pq & \text{if } X_i = 1, \\ 1 - q^2 - 2pq & \text{if } X_i = 0, \end{cases}$$

and

$$\mathbb{P}(X_i Y_i) = \begin{cases} 0 & \text{if } X_i Y_i = 2, \\ \mathbb{P}(X_i = Y_i) & \text{if } X_i Y_i = 1, \\ \mathbb{P}(X_i = 0) + \mathbb{P}(Y_i = 0) & \text{if } X_i Y_i = 0, \end{cases}$$

$$= \begin{cases} 0 & \text{if } X_i Y_i = 2, \\ 2pq & \text{if } X_i Y_i = 1, \\ 2 - p^2 - q^2 - 4pq & \text{if } X_i Y_i = 0. \end{cases}$$

$$= \begin{cases} 0 & \text{if } X_i Y_i = 2, \\ 2pq & \text{if } X_i Y_i = 1, \\ 1 - 2pq & \text{if } X_i Y_i = 0. \end{cases}$$

Hence

$$\mathbb{E}(X_i) = 2p^2 + 2pq$$
$$= 2p,$$

$$\mathbb{E}(Y_i) = 2q^2 + 2pq$$
$$= 2q(q + p)$$
$$= 2q,$$

$$\mathbb{E}(X_i Y_i) = 2pq,$$

$$\mathrm{cov}(X_i, Y_i) = \mathbb{E}(X_i Y_i) - \mathbb{E}(X_i)\mathbb{E}(Y_i)$$
$$= 2pq - 4pq$$
$$= -2pq,$$

so that

$$\mathrm{cov}(X, Y) = \sum_{i=1}^{n} \mathrm{cov}(X_i, Y_i) = -2npq.$$

PROBLEM (7.7.11). The *joint moment generating function* of two random variables X and Y is defined to be the function $M(s, t)$ of two real variables defined by

$$M(s, t) = \mathbb{E}^{(sX + tY)}$$

for all values of s and t for which this expectation exists. Show that the joint moment generating function of a pair of random variables having the standard bivariate normal distribution (6.73) is

$$M(s, t) = \exp[\frac{1}{2}(s^2 + 2\rho st + t^2)].$$

Deduce the joint moment generating function of a pair of random variables having the bivariate normal distribution (6.76) with parameters μ_1, μ_2, σ_1, σ_2, ρ.

SOLUTION. For the first part, we shall first find the joint density function of $U = X$ and $V = sX + tY$ by the method of change of variables, and then find the marginal density function of V.

We consider first the case $t \neq 0$. The mapping T of this case is given by $T(x, y) = (u, v)$, where

$$u = x, \qquad\qquad v = sx + ty,$$

and T is a bijection from $D = \{(x, y) : x, y \in \mathbb{R}\}$ to $S = \{(u, v) : u, v \in \mathbb{R}\}$. It has inverse $T^{-1}(u, v) = (x, y)$, where

$$x = u, \qquad\qquad y = -\frac{s}{t}u + \frac{1}{t}v.$$

The Jacobian of T^{-1} is

$$\begin{vmatrix} \dfrac{\partial x}{\partial u} & \dfrac{\partial x}{\partial v} \\[2mm] \dfrac{\partial y}{\partial u} & \dfrac{\partial y}{\partial v} \end{vmatrix} = \begin{vmatrix} 1 & 0 \\[2mm] -\dfrac{s}{t} & \dfrac{1}{b} \end{vmatrix} = \frac{1}{t},$$

giving by Jacobian formula, (6.51) that U and V have joint density function

$$\begin{aligned}
f_{U,V}(u, v) &= f_{X,Y}(x(u, v), y(u, v)) \, |J(u, v)| \\
&= \frac{1}{2\pi |t| \sqrt{1 - \rho^2}} e^{-\frac{1}{2(1-\rho^2)}[u^2 - 2\rho u(-\frac{s}{t}u + \frac{1}{t}v) + (-\frac{s}{t}u + \frac{1}{t}v)^2]} \\
&= \frac{1}{2\pi |t| \sqrt{1 - \rho^2}} e^{-\frac{1}{2(1-\rho^2)}[(1 + 2\rho \frac{a}{b} + \frac{s^2}{t^2})u^2 - \frac{2}{t^2}(\rho t + s)uv + \frac{1}{t^2}v^2]}.
\end{aligned}$$

For $m > 0$, then

$$\begin{aligned}
\int_{-\infty}^{\infty} e^{-\frac{1}{2}(mu^2 + fu + g)} \, du &= \int_{-\infty}^{\infty} e^{-\frac{1}{2}[(\sqrt{m} + \frac{f}{2\sqrt{m}})^2 + g - \frac{f^2}{4m}]} \, du \\
&= e^{-\frac{1}{2}(g - \frac{f^2}{4m})} \int_{-\infty}^{\infty} \frac{1}{\sqrt{m}} e^{-\frac{1}{2}t^2} \, dt \\
&= \frac{\sqrt{2\pi}}{\sqrt{m}} e^{-\frac{1}{2}(g - \frac{f^2}{4m})}.
\end{aligned}$$

The marginal density function fo V is

$$\begin{aligned}
f_V(v) &= \int_{-\infty}^{\infty} f_{U,V}(u, v) \, du \\
&= \frac{1}{2\pi |t| \sqrt{1 - \rho^2}} \cdot \frac{\sqrt{2\pi}}{\dfrac{\sqrt{s^2 + 2\rho st + t^2}}{|t|\sqrt{1-\rho^2}}} e^{-\frac{1}{2(1-\rho^2)}[\frac{v^2}{t^2} - \frac{4(\rho t + s)^2}{4t^4(1 + 2\rho\frac{s}{t} + \frac{s^2}{t^2})}v^2]} \\
&= \frac{1}{\sqrt{2\pi}\sqrt{s^2 + 2\rho st + t^2}} e^{-\frac{1}{2(1-\rho^2)t^2}(1 - \frac{\rho^2 t^2 + 2\rho st + s^2}{t^2 + 2\rho st + s^2})v^2} \\
&= \frac{1}{\sqrt{2\pi}\sqrt{s^2 + 2\rho st + t^2}} e^{-\frac{1}{2(1-\rho^2)t^2} \cdot \frac{(1-\rho^2)t^2}{t^2 + 2\rho st + s^2}v^2} \\
&= \frac{1}{\sqrt{2\pi(s^2 + 2\rho st + t^2)}} e^{-\frac{1}{2(s^2 + 2\rho st + t^2)}v^2},
\end{aligned}$$

so that $V = sX + tY$, where $t \neq 0$, has the normal distribution with mean 0 and variance $s^2 + 2\rho st + t^2$. Thu

$$\mathbb{E}(e^{sX+tY}) = \mathbb{E}(e^V)$$

$$= \int_{v=-\infty}^{\infty} e^v \frac{1}{\sqrt{2\pi(s^2+2\rho st+t^2)}} e^{-\frac{1}{2(s^2+2\rho st+t^2)}v^2} \, dv$$

$$= \frac{1}{\sqrt{2\pi(s^2+2\rho st+t^2)}} \int_{v=-\infty}^{\infty} e^{-\frac{1}{2}\left(\frac{1}{s^2+2\rho st+t^2}v^2-2v\right)} \, dv$$

$$= \frac{1}{\sqrt{2\pi(s^2+2\rho st+t^2)}} \sqrt{2\pi}\sqrt{s^2+2\rho st+t^2} e^{-\frac{1}{2}\left[\frac{-4(s^2+2\rho st+t^2)}{4}\right]}$$

$$= e^{\frac{1}{2}(s^2+2\rho st+t^2)}.$$

We consider next the case $t = 0$. The moment generating function of V is

$$M_V(\xi) = \mathbb{E}(e^{sX\xi})$$
$$= \mathbb{E}(e^{(s\xi)X})$$
$$= M_X(s\xi),$$

where

$$M_X(\xi) = e^{-\frac{1}{2}\xi^2},$$

giving that

$$M_V(\xi) = e^{\frac{1}{2}s^2\xi^2},$$

which we recognize by (7.58) as the moment generating function of the normal distribution with mean 0 and variance s^2. The marginal density function of V is

$$f_V(v) = \frac{1}{\sqrt{2\pi s^2}} e^{-\frac{1}{2s^2}v^2},$$

so that

$$\mathbb{E}(e^V) = \frac{1}{\sqrt{2\pi s^2}} \int_{-\infty}^{\infty} e^v e^{-\frac{1}{2s^2}v^2} \, dv$$

$$= \frac{1}{\sqrt{2\pi s^2}} \int_{-\infty}^{\infty} e^{-\frac{1}{2}\left(\frac{v^2}{s^2}+2v\right)} \, dv$$

$$= \frac{1}{\sqrt{2\pi s^2}} \sqrt{2\pi}s e^{-\frac{1}{2}\cdot\frac{4s^2}{4}}$$

$$= e^{\frac{1}{2}s^2}.$$

Therefore, in both case, the moment generating function of the pair (X, Y) is

$$M(s,t) = e^{\frac{1}{2}(s^2+2\rho st+t^2)}.$$

For the second part, let the pair (X, Y) have the bivariate normal density function of (6.76), and let U and V be given by (6.78). Then U and V have the standard bivariate normal distribution. By the result of the first part, the moment generating function of the pair (U, V) is

$$M_{U,V}(s, t) = M(s, t)$$
$$= e^{\frac{1}{2}(s^2 + 2\rho st + t^2)}.$$

Thus

$$M_{X,Y}(s, t) = \mathbb{E}(e^{sX + tY})$$
$$= \mathbb{E}(e^{s(\sigma_1 U + \mu_1) + t(\sigma_2 V + \mu_2)})$$
$$= e^{s\mu_1 + t\mu_2} \mathbb{E}(e^{s\sigma_1 U + t\sigma_2 V})$$
$$= e^{s\mu_1 + t\mu_2} M_{U,V}(s\sigma_1, t\sigma_2)$$
$$= e^{s\mu_1 + t\mu_2} M(s\sigma_1, t\sigma_2).$$

PROBLEM (*7.7.12). Let X and Y be independent random variables, each having mean 0, variance 1, and finite moment generating function $M(t)$. If $X + Y$ and $X - Y$ are independent, show that

$$M(2t) = M(t)^3 M(-t)$$

and deduce that X and Y have the normal distribution with mean 0 and variance 1.

SOLUTION (1). For the first part, note that X and Y are indpendence, so are X and $-Y$. We have that

$$M(2t) = M_X(2t)$$

$$\qquad = M_{2X}(t) \qquad\qquad\qquad\qquad \text{by (7.51)}$$
$$\qquad = M_{(X+Y)+(X-Y)}(t)$$
$$\qquad = M_{X+Y}(t) M_{X-Y}(t) \qquad\qquad \text{by independence and Theorem 7.52}$$
$$\qquad = M_X(t) M_Y(t) M_X(t) M_{-Y}(t) \quad \text{by independence and Theorem 7.52}$$
$$\qquad = M^3(t) M_{-Y}(t) \qquad\qquad\qquad \text{since } X \text{ and } Y \text{ have the same finite mgf } M(t)$$
$$\qquad = M^3(t) M_Y(-t) \qquad\qquad\qquad \text{by (7.51)}$$
$$\qquad = M(t)^3 M(-t),$$

as required.

For the last part, let $\psi(t) = M(t)/M(-t)$. Then

$$\psi(2t) = \frac{M(2t)}{M(-2t)}$$

$$= \frac{M^3(t)M(-t)}{M^3(-t)M(t)}$$

$$= [\frac{M(t)}{M(-t)}]^2$$

$$= \psi^2(t).$$

Thus $\psi(2t) = \psi^2(t)$. This implies that

$$\psi(t) = [\psi(\frac{t}{2})]^2 > 0$$

for all t. Repeat the procedure to obtain

$$\psi(t) = (\psi(\frac{t}{2^n}))^{2^n}$$

for all $n \in \mathbb{N}$. As $t = 0$ and $n = 1$, then $\psi(0) = (\psi(0))^2$. This implies that

$$\psi(0) = 0 \qquad\qquad \text{or} \qquad\qquad \psi(0) = 1.$$

But $\psi(t) > 0$ for all t, it follows that $\psi(0) = 1$. We note that

$$\psi'(0) = \frac{M'(0)M(0 + M'(0)M(0)}{(M(0))^2}$$

$$= 2\mathbb{E}(X)$$

$$= 0.$$

By Taylor's theorem, we have

$$\psi(t) = \psi(0) - \frac{t^2}{2}\psi''(c)$$

$$= 1 + \frac{t^2}{2}\psi''(c).$$

But

$$\psi'(t) = \frac{d}{dt}[(\psi(t))^2] = \psi'(\frac{t}{2})\psi(\frac{t}{2})$$

$$\psi''(t) = \frac{d}{dt}[\psi'(\frac{t}{2})\psi(\frac{t}{2})] = \frac{1}{2}\psi''(\frac{t}{2})\psi(\frac{t}{2}) + \frac{1}{2}(\psi'(\frac{t}{2}))^2,$$

giving that

$$\psi''(0) = \frac{1}{2}\psi''(0),$$

since $\psi'(0) = 0$. Hence

$$\psi''(0) = 0.,$$

so that $\psi(t) = 1 + o(t^2)$ as $t \to 0$. It follows from

$$\psi(t) = (\psi(\frac{t}{2^n}))^{2^n}$$

that

$$\begin{aligned}
\psi'(t) &= \psi(\frac{t}{2^n})\psi'(\frac{t}{2^n})\\
&= \lim_{n\to\infty} \psi(\frac{t}{2^n})\psi'(\frac{t}{2^n})\\
&= 0
\end{aligned}$$

for all $n \in \mathbb{N}$. Thus $\psi'(t) = 0$, but $\psi(0) = 1$, so $\psi(t) = 1$. Therefore, $M(t) = M(-t)$ since $\psi(t) = M(t)/M(-t)$. The equation $M(2t) = M^3(t)M(-t)$ becomes

$$M(t) = (M(\frac{t}{2}))^4. \qquad\qquad (1)$$

Let $h(t) = \ln M(t)$. We deduce from (1) that

$$\ln M(t) = 4\ln M(\frac{t}{2}),$$

giving that

$$h(t) = 4h(\frac{t}{2}).$$

Let

$$g(t) = \frac{h(t)}{t}$$
$$= \frac{4h(\frac{t}{2})}{t}$$
$$= 2\frac{h(\frac{t}{2})}{\frac{t}{2}}$$
$$= 2g(\frac{t}{2})$$

and

$$k(t) = \frac{g(t)}{t}$$
$$= \frac{2g(\frac{t}{2})}{t}$$
$$= \frac{g(\frac{t}{2})}{\frac{t}{2}}$$
$$= k(\frac{t}{2}).$$

We deduce from $k(t) = k(\frac{t}{2})$ that

$$k(t) = k(\frac{t}{2^n})$$
$$= \lim_{n \to \infty} k(\frac{t}{2^n})$$
$$= a$$

for some a. Hence

$$h(t) = at^2,$$

so that

$$M(t) = e^{at^2}.$$

But

$$M''(0) = \mathbb{E}(X^2)$$
$$= 1$$

since $\mathbb{E}(X) = 0$ and $\text{var}(X) = 1$. And, $M'(t) = 2ae^{at^2} + (2at)^2 e^{at^2}$. So $2a = 1$, giving that $a = 1/2$, and hence

$$M(t) = e^{\frac{1}{2}t^2}.$$

SOLUTION (2). Let $\psi(t) = M(t)/M(-t)$. Then

$$\psi(2t) = \frac{M(2t)}{M(-2t)}$$
$$= \frac{M^3(t)M(-t)}{M^3(-t)M(t)}$$
$$= [\frac{M(t)}{M(-t)}]^2$$
$$= \psi^2(t).$$

Thus $\psi(2t) = \psi^2(t)$. This implies that

$$\psi(t) = [\psi(\frac{t}{2})]^2 > 0$$

for all t. Repeat the procedure to obtain

$$\psi(t) = (\psi(\frac{t}{2^n}))^{2^n}$$

for all $n \in \mathbb{N}$. As $t = 0$ and $n = 1$, then $\psi(0) = (\psi(0))^2$. This implies that

$$\psi(0) = 0 \qquad \text{or} \qquad \psi(0) = 1.$$

But $\psi(t) > 0$ for all t, it follows that $\psi(0) = 1$. We note that

$$\psi'(0) = \frac{M'(0)M(0 + M'(0)M(0)}{(M(0))^2}$$
$$= 2\mathbb{E}(X)$$
$$= 0.$$

By Taylor's theorem, we have

$$\psi(t) = \psi(0) - \frac{t^2}{2}\psi''(c)$$
$$= 1 + \frac{t^2}{2}\psi''(c).$$

But

$$\psi'(t) = \frac{d}{dt}[(\psi(t))^2] = \psi'(\frac{t}{2})\psi(\frac{t}{2})$$

$$\psi''(t) = \frac{d}{dt}[\psi'(\frac{t}{2})\psi(\frac{t}{2})] = \frac{1}{2}\psi''(\frac{t}{2})\psi(\frac{t}{2}) + \frac{1}{2}(\psi'(\frac{t}{2}))^2,$$

giving that

$$\psi''(0) = \frac{1}{2}\psi''(0),$$

since $\psi'(0) = 0$. Hence

$$\psi''(0) = 0.,$$

so that $\psi(t) = 1 + o(t^2)$ as $t \to 0$. It follows from

$$\psi(t) = (\psi(\frac{t}{2^n}))^{2^n}$$

that

$$\psi'(t) = \psi(\frac{t}{2^n})\psi'(\frac{t}{2^n})$$

$$= \lim_{n \to \infty} \psi(\frac{t}{2^n})\psi'(\frac{t}{2^n})$$

$$= 0$$

for all $n \in \mathbb{N}$. Thus $\psi'(t) = 0$, but $\psi(0) = 1$, so $\psi(t) = 1$. Therefore, $M(t) = M(-t)$ since $\psi(t) = M(t)/M(-t)$. The equation $M(2t) = M^3(t)M(-t)$ becomes

$$M(t) = (M(\frac{t}{2}))^4,$$

giving that

$$M(t) = (M(\frac{t}{2^n}))^{4^n}.$$

Note that

$$M(t) = M(0) + M'(0) \cdot t + \frac{1}{2}M''(0) \cdot t^2 + \frac{1}{6}M'''(c)t^3.$$

But

$$M(0) = 1, \qquad M'(0) = \mathbb{E}(X) = 0, \qquad M''(0) = \mathbb{E}(X^2) = var(X) = 1.$$

So

$$M(t) = 1 + \frac{1}{2}t^2 + o(t^2),$$

giving that

$$M(\frac{t}{2^n}) = 1 + \frac{1}{2} \cdot \frac{t^2}{4^n} + o(\frac{t^2}{4^n}).$$

Hence

$$M(t) = \lim_{n \to \infty} (M(\frac{t}{2^n}))^{4^n}$$
$$= \lim_{n \to \infty} (1 + \frac{1}{2} \cdot \frac{t^2}{4^n} + o(\frac{t^2}{4^n}))^{4^n}$$
$$= e^{\frac{1}{2}t^2}.$$

PROBLEM (7.7.13). Let X have moment generating function $M(t)$.

(a) Show that $M(t)M(-t)$ is the moment generating function of $X - Y$, where Y is independent of X but has the same distribution.

(b) In a similar way, describe random variables which have moment generating functions

$$\frac{1}{2 - M(t)}, \qquad\qquad \int_0^\infty M(ut)e^{-u}\, du.$$

SOLUTION. For part (a), note that X and Y are independent, so are X and $-Y$. We have that

$$M_{X-Y}(t) = M_X(t)M_{-Y}(t) \qquad \text{by independence and Theorem 7.52}$$
$$= M_X(t)M_Y(-t) \qquad \text{by (7.51)}$$
$$= M(t)M(-t),$$

since X and Y have the same moment generating function $M(t)$ as they have the same distribution by appealing to Theorem 7.55.

For the first part of part (b), let $X_0, X_1, X_2, \ldots$ be independent, identically distributed random variables and let N be a random variable which takes values in the non-negative integers and is independent of the X_i. Then the moment generating function of $S = X_0 + X_1 + X_2 + \cdots + X_N$ is $M_S(t) = G(M(t))$ (see Problem 7.7.8), where $G(s)$ is the probability generating function of N. Consider

$$G(t) = \frac{1}{2 - t}.$$

We have that

$$G(t) = \frac{1}{2} \cdot \frac{1}{1 - \frac{t}{2}}$$
$$= \frac{1}{2}(1 + \frac{1}{2}t + \frac{1}{2^2}t^2 + \cdots)$$
$$= \frac{1}{2}\sum_{k=0}^{\infty}(\frac{1}{2})^k t^k,$$

giving that $G(t)$ is the probability generating function of the random variable N that having the mass function

$$p_k = \frac{1}{2^{k+1}} \qquad\qquad \text{for } k = 0, 1, 2, \ldots.$$

Thus the moment generating function of S is

$$M_S(t) = G(M(t)) = \frac{1}{2 - M(t)}.$$

For the last part of part (b), Let Y be the random variable that has the density function $f_Y(y) = e^{-x}$ for $x > 0$, that is, Y has the exponential distribution with parameter $\lambda = 1$. Thus

$$G_S(t) = \int_0^{\infty} M(ut)e^{-u}\,du$$
$$= \mathbb{E}(M(tY))$$
$$= \mathbb{E}(\mathbb{E}(e^{tYX}))$$
$$= \mathbb{E}(e^{t(XY)})$$
$$= M_{XY}(t).$$

Therefore the function $G_S(t) = \int_0^{\infty} M(ut)e^{-u}\,du$ is the moment generating function of $U = XY$.

PROBLEM (7.7.14). *Coupon-collecting problem.* There are c different types of coupon, and each coupon obtained is equally likely to be any one of the c types. Find the moment generating function of the total number N of coupons which you must collect in order to obtain a complete set.

SOLUTION. Let Y_i for $i = 1, 2, \ldots, c-1$ be the additional number of coupons collected, after obtaining i distinct types, before a new type is collected. Then each Y_i has the geometric distribution with parameter $(c - i)/c$ (see Problem 3.6.12), and moment generating function of Y_i is

$$M_{Y_i}(t) = \sum_{k=1}^{\infty} e^{tk} \frac{c-i}{c} (1 - \frac{c-i}{c})^{k-1}$$

$$= \frac{c-i}{c} \cdot \frac{c}{i} \sum_{k=1}^{\infty} (\frac{i}{c})^{k-1} e^{tk} \frac{c-i}{c}$$

$$= \frac{c-i}{c} \cdot \frac{c}{i} \sum_{k=1}^{\infty} (\frac{ie^t}{c})^{k}$$

$$= \frac{c-i}{i} \cdot \frac{\frac{ie^t}{c}}{1 - \frac{ie^t}{c}}$$

$$= \frac{(c-i)e^t}{c - ie^t}.$$

It is not difficult to show that the moment generating function of $Y_0 = 1$, $M_{Y_0}(t) = \mathbb{E}(e^{tY_0}) = e^t$, also satisfies the formula given above, so long as one allows $i = 0$. Since Y_i are independent, we conclude from (7.54) that the total number $N = Y_0 + Y_1 + \cdots + X_{c-1}$ of coupons which we must collect in order to obtain a complete set has moment generating function

$$M_N(t) = M_{Y_0}(t) M_{Y_1}(t) \cdots M_{Y_{c-1}}(t).$$

$$= \prod_{i=0}^{c-1} \frac{(c-i)e^t}{c - ie^t}.$$

PROBLEM (7.7.15). Prove that if ϕ_1 and ϕ_2 are characteristic functions, then so is $\phi = \alpha\phi_1 + (1 - \alpha)\phi_2$ for any $\alpha \in \mathbb{R}$ satisfying $0 \leq \alpha \leq 1$.

SOLUTION. If $\phi_1(t)$ and $\phi_2(t)$ are the chractereistic function of the discrete random variables X and Y with the mass funtions $p_k = \mathbb{P}(X = k)$ and $q_k = \mathbb{P}(Y = k)$, respectively. Then

$$\alpha\phi_1(t) + (1 - \alpha)\phi_2(t) = \alpha \sum_{k=0}^{\infty} e^{it_k} p_k + (1 - \alpha) \sum_{k=0}^{\infty} e^{itk} q_k$$

$$= \sum_{k=0}^{\infty} e^{itk} [\alpha p_k + (1 - \alpha) q_k].$$

Let Z be the discrete random variable with the mass function $s_k = \mathbb{P}(Z = k) = \alpha p_k + (1-\alpha)q_k$ for $k = 0, 1, 2, \ldots$ $(\alpha p_k + (1-\alpha)q_k \in [0,1]$ and $\sum_{k=0}^{\infty}[\alpha p_k + (1-\alpha)q_k] = 1)$. Then $\alpha\phi_1(t) + (1-\alpha)\phi_2(t) = \sum_{k=0}^{\infty} e^{itk} s_k = \mathbb{E}(e^{itz}) = \phi_Z(t)$, where $\phi_Z(t)$ is the chracteristic function of Z. Hence $\alpha\phi_1(t) + (1-\alpha)\phi_2(t)$ is a characteristic function.

If $\phi_1(t)$ and $\phi_2(t)$ are the chractereistic function of the continuous random variables X and Y with the density funtions $f_X(x)$ and $f_Y(y)$, respectively. Then

$$\alpha\phi_1(t) + (1-\alpha)\phi_2(t) = \alpha \int_{-\infty}^{\infty} e^{itx} f_X(x)\, dx + (1-\alpha) \int_{-\infty}^{\infty} e^{itx} f_Y(x)\, dx$$
$$= \int_{-\infty}^{\infty} e^{itx}[\alpha f_X(x) + (1-\alpha)f_Y(x)]\, dx.$$

Let Z be the continuous random variable with the density function $f_Z(x) = \alpha f_X(x) + (1-\alpha)f_Y(x)$ $(\alpha f_X(x) + (1-\alpha)f_Y(x) \geq 0$ and $\int_{-\infty}^{\infty} [\alpha f_X(x) + (1-\alpha)f_Y(x)]\, dx = 1)$. Then $\alpha\phi_1(t) + (1-\alpha)\phi_2(t) = \int_{-\infty}^{\infty} e^{itx} f_Z(x)\, dx = \mathbb{E}(e^{itZ}) = \phi_Z(t)$, where $\phi_Z(t)$ is the chracteristic function of Z. Hence $\alpha\phi_1(t) + (1-\alpha)\phi_2(t)$ is a characteristic function.

PROBLEM (7.7.16). Show that X and $-X$ have the same distribution if and only if ϕ_X is a purely real-valued function.

SOLUTION. X and $-X$ have the same distribution if and only if X and $-X$ have the same chracteristic function by appealing to Theorem 7.88. This is equivalent to

$$\phi_X(t) = \phi_X(-t)$$
$$\Longleftrightarrow \quad \mathbb{E}(e^{itX}) = \mathbb{E}(e^{-itX})$$
$$\Longleftrightarrow \quad \mathbb{E}(\cos tX + i\sin tX) = \mathbb{E}(\cos(-tX) + i\sin(-tX))$$
$$\Longleftrightarrow \quad 2i\mathbb{E}(\sin(tX)) = 0 \qquad \text{since } \cos(-tx) = \cos tX \text{ and } \sin(-tX) = -\sin tX$$
$$\Longleftrightarrow \quad \mathbb{E}(\sin tX) = 0.$$

This is equivalent to $\phi_X(t)$ is a purely real-valued function.

PROBLEM (7.7.17). Find the characteristic function of a random variable with density function

$$f(x) = \frac{1}{2} e^{-|x|} \qquad \text{for } x \in \mathbb{R}.$$

PROBLEM (7.7.18). Let $X_1, X_2, \ldots$ be independent random variables each having the Cauchy distribution, and let

$$A_n = \frac{1}{n}(X_1 + X_2 + \cdots + X_n).$$

Show that A_n has the Cauchy distribution regardless of the value of n.

SOLUTION. Each X_i has the Cauchy distribution with characteristic function

$$\phi_X(t) = e^{-|t|} \qquad \text{for } t \in \mathbb{R}.$$

Since Y_i are independent, we conclude from (7.54) that $B_n = X_1 + X_2 + \cdots + X_n$ has moment generating function

$$\phi_{B_n}(t) = \phi_{X_1}(t)\phi_{X_2}(t)\cdots\phi_{X_n}(t)$$
$$= e^{-n|t|},$$

giving that $A_n = \frac{1}{n}(X_1 + X_2 + \cdots + X_n) = \frac{1}{n}B_n$ has moment generating function

$$\phi_{A_n}(t) = \phi_{\frac{1}{n}B_n}(t)$$
$$= \phi_{B_n}\left(\frac{1}{n}t\right) \qquad \text{by (7.51)}$$
$$= e^{-n\left|\frac{1}{n}t\right|}$$
$$= e^{-|t|},$$

which we recognize by Exercise 7.80 as the characteristic function of the Cauchy distribution. We deduce that A_n has this distribution by appealing to Theorem 7.88.

PROBLEM (7.7.21). Let $X_1, X_2, \ldots, X_n$ be independent random variables, each with characteristic function $\phi(t)$. Obtain the characteristic function of

$$Y_n = a_n + b_n(X_1 + X_2 + \cdots + X_n),$$

where a_n and b_n are arbitrary real numbers.
Suppose that $\phi(t) = e^{-|t|^\alpha}$, where $0 < \alpha \le 2$. Determine a_n and b_n such that Y_n has the same distribution as X_1 for $n = 1, 2, \ldots$. Find the probability density functions of X_1 when $\alpha = 1$ and when $\alpha = 2$. (Oxford 1980F)

SOLUTION. By Theorem 7.87, the characteristic function of $Y_n = a_n + b_n(X_1 + X_2 + \cdots + X_n)$ is given by

$$\phi_{Y_n}(t) = e^{ita_n}(\phi(b_n t))^n,$$

where ϕ is the common characteristic function of the X_i.

If $\phi(t) = e^{-|t|^\alpha}$, where $0 < \alpha \le 2$, then the characteristic function of Y_n becomes

$$\phi_{Y_n}(t) = e^{ita_n}(e^{-|b_n t|^\alpha})^n.$$

Now, Y_n has the same distribution as X_1 for $n = 1, 2, \ldots$ if and only if they have the same characteristic function, i.e.,

$$
\begin{aligned}
& e^{ita_n}(e^{-|b_n t|^\alpha})^n = e^{-|t|^\alpha} && \text{for all } t \in \mathbb{R} \\
\Longleftrightarrow \quad & e^{ita_n}e^{-n|b_n t|^\alpha} = e^{-|t|^\alpha} && \text{for all } t \in \mathbb{R} \\
\Longleftrightarrow \quad & e^{ita_n}e^{-n|b_n t|^\alpha + |t|^\alpha} = 1 && \text{for all } t \in \mathbb{R} \\
\Longleftrightarrow \quad & e^{ita_n + (1 - n|b_n|^\alpha)|t|^\alpha} = 1 && \text{for all } t \in \mathbb{R} \\
\Longleftrightarrow \quad & ita_n + (1 - n|b_n|^\alpha)|t|^\alpha = 0 && \text{for all } t \in \mathbb{R}
\end{aligned}
$$

this is equivalent to (since the real part and the imaginary part in the above equation must equal to zeros)

$$
\begin{cases}
a_n & = 0, \\
(1 - n|b_n|^\alpha)|t|^\alpha & = 0,
\end{cases}
$$

$$
\Longleftrightarrow
\begin{cases}
a_n & = 0, \\
1 - n|b_n|^\alpha & = 0, \qquad \text{since } t \text{ is arbitrary}
\end{cases}
$$

$$
\Longleftrightarrow
\begin{cases}
a_n & = 0, \\
|b_n| & = (\dfrac{1}{n})^{1/\alpha},
\end{cases}
$$

$$
\Longleftrightarrow
\begin{cases}
a_n & = 0, \\
b_n & = \pm(\dfrac{1}{n})^{1/\alpha}.
\end{cases}
$$

If $\alpha = 1$, then the characteristic function of X_1 becomes

$$\phi(t) = e^{-|t|},$$

which we recognize by Example 7.80 as the characteristic function of the Cauchy distribution. We deduce that X_1 has this distribution by appealing to Theorem 7.88. Thus, the probability density functions of X_1 is

$$f_{X_1}(x) = \frac{1}{\pi(1+x^2)} \qquad \text{for } x \in \mathbb{R}.$$

If $\alpha = 2$, then the characteristic function of X_1 becomes

$$\phi(t) = e^{-t^2},$$

which we recognize by Example 7.82 as the characteristic function of the normal distribution with mean $\mu = 0$ and variance $\sigma^2 = 2$. We deduce that X_1 has this distribution by appealing to Theorem 7.88. Thus, the probability density function of X_1 is

$$f_{X_1}(x) = \frac{1}{\sqrt{4\pi}} \exp(-\frac{1}{4}x^2) \qquad \text{for } x \in \mathbb{R}.$$

CHAPTER 8

The main limit theorems

8.1. The law of averages

EXERCISE (8.8). Let Z_n be a discrete random variable with mass function

$$\mathbb{P}(Z_n = n^\alpha) = \frac{1}{n}, \qquad\qquad \mathbb{P}(Z_n = 0) = 1 - \frac{1}{n}. \qquad\qquad ,$$

Show that Z_n converges to 0 in mean square if and only if $\alpha < \frac{1}{2}$.

SOLUTION. Z_n converges to 0 in mean square as $n \to \infty$ if and only if $\mathbb{E}(Z_n^2) \to 0$ as $n \to \infty$. But

$$\mathbb{E}(Z_n^2) = 0^2(1 - \frac{1}{n}) + (n^\alpha)(1 - \frac{1}{n}).$$
$$= \frac{1}{n^{1-2\alpha}}.$$

Thus $\mathbb{E}(Z_n^2) \to 0$ as $n \to \infty$ if and only if $\dfrac{1}{n^{1-2\alpha}} \to 0$ as $n \to \infty$. This is equivalent to $1 - 2\alpha > 0$, giving that $\alpha < \dfrac{1}{2}$.

EXERCISE (8.9). Let $Z_1, Z_2 \ldots$ be a sequence of random variables which converges to the random variable Z in mean square. Show that $aZ_n + b \to aZ + b$ in mean square as $n \to \infty$, for any real numbers a and b.

SOLUTION. For any real numbers a and b,

$$\mathbb{E}([(aZ_n + b) - (aZ + b)]^2) = \mathbb{E}([a(z_n - z)]^2)$$
$$= a^2\mathbb{E}([z_n - z]^2) \to 0 \qquad \text{as } n \to \infty,$$

since $\mathbb{E}([z_n - z]^2) \to 0$ as $n \to 0$. Hence, $aZ_n + b \to aZ + b$ in mean square as $n \to \infty$, for any real numbers a and b.

EXERCISE (8.10). Let N_n be the number of occurrences of 5 or 6 in n throws of a fair die. Use Theorem 8.6 to show that, as $n \to \infty$,

$$\frac{1}{n}N_n \to \frac{1}{3} \qquad\qquad \text{in mean square.}$$

SOLUTION. We have that

$$\mathbb{P}(N_n = k) = \binom{n}{k}(\frac{2}{3})^{n-k}(\frac{1}{3})^k \qquad\qquad \text{for } k = 1, 2, \ldots, n.$$

The binomial theorem states that

$$(a + x)^n = \sum_{k=0}^{n} \binom{n}{k} a^{n-k} x^k.$$

Take derivative of this differentiate this equation with respect to x to obtain

$$n(a + x)^{n-1} = \sum_{k=1}^{n} k \binom{n}{k} a^{n-k} x^{k-1} \qquad\qquad (1)$$

Multiply both sides of this equation by x to obtain

$$n(a + x)^{n-1} x = \sum_{k=1}^{n} k \binom{n}{k} a^{n-k} x^k.$$

Take derivative of this equation with respect to x to obtain

$$\sum_{k=1}^{n} k^2 \binom{n}{k} a^{n-k} x^{k-1} = n(a + x)^{n-1} + n(n-1)x(a+x)^{n-2}. \qquad (2)$$

Thus

$$\begin{aligned}
\mathbb{E}(\frac{1}{n}N_n) &= \frac{1}{n}\mathbb{E}(N_n) \\
&= \frac{1}{n}\sum_{k=0}^{n} k \binom{n}{k}(\frac{2}{3})^{n-k}(\frac{1}{3})^k \\
&= \frac{1}{3n}\sum_{k=0}^{n} k \binom{n}{k}(\frac{2}{3})^{n-k}(\frac{1}{3})^{k-1} \\
&= \frac{1}{3n}n(\frac{2}{3} + \frac{1}{3})^{n-1} \\
&= \frac{1}{3} \qquad\qquad\qquad\qquad \text{by (1),}
\end{aligned}$$

and

$$\mathbb{E}(\frac{1}{n^2} N_n^2) = \frac{1}{n^2} \sum_{k=0}^{n} k^2 \binom{n}{k} (\frac{2}{3})^{n-k} (\frac{1}{3})^k$$

$$= \frac{1}{3n^2} \sum_{k=0}^{n} k^2 \binom{n}{k} (\frac{2}{3})^{n-k} (\frac{1}{3})^{k-1}$$

$$=$$

$$= \frac{n + n(n-2)\frac{1}{3}}{3n^2} \qquad \text{by (2).}$$

Then

$$\mathbb{E}(\frac{1}{n} N_n - \frac{1}{3})^2 = E(\frac{1}{n^2} N_n^2 - \frac{2}{3n} N_n + \frac{1}{9})$$

$$= E(\frac{1}{n^2} N_n^2) - \frac{2}{3} E(\frac{1}{n} N_n) + \frac{1}{9}$$

$$= \frac{n + n(n-1)\frac{1}{3}}{3n^2} - \frac{2}{9} + \frac{1}{9} \to 0 \qquad \text{as } n \to \infty.$$

Hence, as $n \to \infty$,

$$\frac{1}{n} N_n \to \frac{1}{3} \qquad \text{in mean square.}$$

EXERCISE. Show that the conclusion of the mean-square law of large numbers, Theorem 8.6, remains valid if the assumption that the X_i are independent is replaced by the weaker assumption that they are uncorrelated.

SOLUTION. This is a straightforward calculation. We write

$$S_n = X_1 + X_2 + \cdots + X_n$$

8.2. Chebyshev's inequality and the weak law

EXERCISE (8.20). Prove the following alternative form of Chebyshev's inequality: if X is a random variable with finite variance and $a > 0$, then

$$\mathbb{P}(|X - \mathbb{E}(X)| > a) \leq \frac{1}{a^2} \mathrm{var}(X).$$

SOLUTION (1). By Markov's inequality, Theorem 7.63, applied to the positive random variable $(X - \mathbb{E}(X))^2$,

$$\mathbb{P}(|X - \mathbb{E}(X)| > a) = \mathbb{P}((X - \mathbb{E}(X))^2 > a^2) \leq \frac{\mathbb{E}((X - \mathbb{E}(X))^2)}{a^2} = \frac{1}{a^2} \mathrm{var}(X),$$

308   8. THE MAIN LIMIT THEOREMS

as required.

SOLUTION (2). We have that

$$\mathbb{P}(|X - \mathbb{E}(X)| > a) = \int_{|x - \mathbb{E}(x)| \geq a} dF_X(x)$$

$$\leq \int_{|x - \mathbb{E}(x)| \geq a} \frac{[x - \mathbb{E}(X)]^2}{a^2} dF_X(x) \quad \text{since if } |x - \mathbb{E}(x)| \geq a, \text{ then } \frac{[x - \mathbb{E}(X)]^2}{a^2} \geq 1$$

$$\leq \frac{1}{a^2} \int_{-\infty}^{\infty} [x - \mathbb{E}(X)]^2 dF_X(x)$$

$$= \frac{1}{a^2} \text{var}(X) \qquad \text{recall that } \text{var}(X) = \int_{-\infty}^{\infty} [x - \mathbb{E}(X)]^2 dF_X(x).$$

This method can also be applied to prove Markov's inequality. Recall Markov's inequality, Theorem 7.63: For any non-negative random variable X,

$$\mathbb{P}(X \geq t) \leq \frac{\mathbb{E}(X)}{t} \qquad \text{for } t > 0.$$

Indeed, for $t > 0$,

$$\mathbb{P}(X \geq t) = \int_{x \geq t} dF_X(x)$$

$$\leq \int_{x \geq t} \frac{x}{t} dF_X(x) \qquad \text{since if } x \geq t, \text{ then } \frac{x}{t} \geq 1$$

$$\leq \frac{1}{t} \int_0^{\infty} x\, dF_X(x) \qquad \text{since } X \geq 0$$

$$= \frac{\mathbb{E}(X)}{t} \qquad \text{recall that } \mathbb{E}(X) = \int_0^{\infty} x\, dF_X(x)$$

EXERCISE (8.21). Use Chebyshev's inequality to show that the probability that in n throws of a fair die the number of sixes lies between $\frac{1}{6}n - \sqrt{n}$ and $\frac{1}{6}n + \sqrt{n}$ is at least $\frac{31}{36}$.

SOLUTION. Let X_n be the number of sixes in n throws of a fair die. Then

$$\frac{1}{6}n - \sqrt{n} < X_n < \frac{1}{6}n + \sqrt{n}$$

if and only if

$$\left| X_n - \frac{n}{6} \right| < \sqrt{n}.$$

We apply Chebyshev's inequality to the random variable $Y = X_n - \frac{n}{6}$, to find that

$$\mathbb{P}\left(\left|X_n - \frac{n}{6}\right| \geq \sqrt{n}\right) \leq \frac{1}{n}\mathbb{E}\left(\left(X_n - \frac{n}{6}\right)^2\right)$$

Note that

$$\mathbb{P}(X_n = k) = \binom{n}{k}\left(\frac{5}{6}\right)^{n-k}\left(\frac{1}{6}\right)^k \qquad \text{for } k = 0, 1, 2, \ldots, n.$$

Hence

$$\mathbb{E}(X_n) = \sum_{k=0}^{n} k\binom{n}{k}\left(\frac{5}{6}\right)^{n-k}\left(\frac{1}{6}\right)^k.$$

The binomial theorem states that

$$(a + x)^n = \sum_{k=0}^{n}\binom{n}{k}a^{n-k}x^k.$$

Take derivative of this equation in x to obtain

$$n(a + x)^{n-1} = \sum_{k=1}^{n} k\binom{n}{k}a^{n-k}x^{k-1}$$

Multiply both sides of this equation by x to obtain

$$n(a + x)^{n-1}x = \sum_{k=1}^{n} k\binom{n}{k}a^{n-k}x^k. \tag{1}$$

We apply this with $a = \dfrac{5}{6}$ and $x = \dfrac{1}{6}$ to obtain

$$\mathbb{E}(X_n) = \frac{n}{6}.$$

Take derivative of (1) in x to obtain

$$n(a + x)^{n-1} + n(n - 1)(a + x)^{n-2} = \sum_{k=1}^{n} k^2\binom{n}{k}a^{n-k}x^{n-k}.$$

Multiply both sides of this equation by x to obtain

$$n(a + x)^{n-1}x + n(n - 1)(a + x)^{n-2}x^2 = \sum_{k=1}^{n} k^2\binom{n}{k}a^{n-k}x^{n-k}.$$

We apply this with $a = \dfrac{5}{6}$ and $x = \dfrac{1}{6}$ to obtain

$$E(X_n^2) = \sum_{n=0}^{n} k^2 \binom{n}{k} (\frac{5}{6})^{n-k} (\frac{1}{6})^k$$
$$= \frac{n}{6} + \frac{n(n-1)}{36}$$
$$= \frac{n^2 + 5n}{36}.$$

Alternatively, we note that X has the binomial distribution with parameters n and $p = \dfrac{1}{6}$, hence $\mathbb{E}(X) = np = \dfrac{1}{6}n$ and $\mathbb{E}(X^2) = npq + n^2 p^2 = \dfrac{n^2 + 5n}{36}$ (see Exersice 2.37). Thus

$$\mathbb{E}((X_n - \frac{1}{6}n)^2) = \mathbb{E}(X_n^2) - \frac{1}{3}n\mathbb{E}(X_n) + \frac{n^2}{36}$$
$$= \frac{n^2 + 5n}{36} - \frac{n^2}{18} + \frac{n^2}{36}$$
$$= \frac{5n}{36},$$

giving that

$$\mathbb{P}(\left|X_n - \frac{n}{6}\right| \geq \sqrt{n}) \leq \frac{1}{n}\mathbb{E}((X_n - \frac{n}{6})^2)$$
$$= \frac{1}{n} \cdot \frac{5n}{36}$$
$$= \frac{5}{36}.$$

Therefore

$$\mathbb{P}(\left|X_n - \frac{n}{6}\right| < \sqrt{n}) = 1 - \mathbb{P}(\left|X_n - \frac{n}{6}\right| \geq \sqrt{n})$$
$$\geq 1 - \frac{5}{36}$$
$$= \frac{31}{36},$$

as required.

EXERCISE (8.22). Show that if $Z_n \to Z$ in probability then, as $n \to \infty$,

$$aZ_n + b \to aZ + b \qquad \text{in probability,}$$

for any real numbers a and b.

SOLUTION. If $a = 0$, then the result is trivial. If $a \neq 0$, then, for $\epsilon > 0$ be given,

$$P(|(aZ_n + b) - (aZ + b)| > \epsilon) = \mathbb{P}(|a|\,|(Z_n - Z| > \epsilon)$$
$$= \mathbb{P}(|(Z_n - Z| > \frac{\epsilon}{|a|}) \to 0 \qquad \text{as } n \to \infty,$$

since $Z_n \to Z$ in probability. Thus, as $n \to \infty$,

$$aZ_n + b \to aZ + b \qquad\qquad \text{in probability,}$$

for any real numbers a and b.

8.3. The central limit theorem

EXAMPLE (8.30). (**Statistical sampling**) The central limit theorem has many applications in statistics, and here is one such. An unknown fraction p of the population are jedi knights. It is desired to estimate p with error not exceeding 0.005 by asking a sample of individuals (it is assumed they answer truthfully). How large a sample is needed?

SOLUTION. Suppose a sample of n individuals is chosen. Let X_i be the indicator function of the event that the ith such person admits to being a jedi knight, and assume the X_i are independent, Bernoulli random variables with parameter p. Write

$$S_n = \sum_{i=1}^{n} X_i.$$

Then S_n has the binomial distribution with parameters n and p (see Exercise 3.31).

EXERCISE (8.32). A fair die is thrown $12,000$ times. Use the central limit theorem to find values of a and b such that

$$\mathbb{P}(1900 < S < 2200) \approx \int_a^b \frac{1}{\sqrt{2\pi}} e^{-\frac{1}{2}x^2}\, dx,$$

where S is the total number of sixes thrown.

SOLUTION. Let X_i be the indicator function of the event that the ith throw is a six, and assume the X_i are independent, Bernoulli random variables with parameter $p = \dfrac{1}{6}$ with mean and variance given by

$$\mu = \mathbb{E}(X_i) = 1 \cdot \frac{1}{6} = \frac{1}{6},$$

$$\sigma^2 = \mathrm{var}(X_i)$$
$$= \mathbb{E}(X_i^2) - (\mathbb{E}(X_i))^2$$
$$= \frac{1}{6} - (\frac{1}{6})^2$$
$$= \frac{5}{36}.$$

Write

$$S = \sum_{i=1}^{12,000} X_i.$$

The standardized version of S is

$$Z_n = \frac{S - n\mu}{\sigma\sqrt{n}}$$
$$= \frac{S - 12,000 \cdot \frac{1}{6}}{\sqrt{12,000 \cdot \frac{5}{36}}}.$$

By the central limit theorem,

$$\mathbb{P}(1900 < S < 2200) = \mathbb{P}(\frac{1900 - 12,000 \cdot \frac{1}{6}}{\sqrt{12,000 \cdot \frac{5}{36}}} < \frac{S - 12,000 \cdot \frac{1}{6}}{\sqrt{12,000 \cdot \frac{5}{36}}} < \frac{2200 - 12,000 \cdot \frac{1}{6}}{\sqrt{12,000 \cdot \frac{5}{36}}})$$

$$= \mathbb{P}(\frac{-100}{\sqrt{12,000 \cdot \frac{5}{36}}} < \frac{S - 12,000 \cdot \frac{1}{6}}{\sqrt{12,000 \cdot \frac{5}{36}}} < \frac{200}{\sqrt{12,000 \cdot \frac{5}{36}}})$$

$$= \mathbb{P}(-\sqrt{6} < \frac{(S - 2000)\sqrt{6}}{100} < 2\sqrt{6}),$$

$$\approx \int_{-\sqrt{6}}^{2\sqrt{6}} \frac{1}{\sqrt{2\pi}} e^{-\frac{1}{2}x^2}\, dx$$

Thus $a = -\sqrt{6}$ and $b = 2\sqrt{6}$.

EXERCISE (8.33). For $n = 1, 2, \ldots$, let X_n be a random variable having the gamma distribution with parameters n and 1. Show that the moment generating function of $Z_n = (X_n - n)/\sqrt{n}$ is

$$M_n(t) = e^{-t\sqrt{n}}(1 - \frac{t}{\sqrt{n}})^{-n},$$

and deduce that, as $n \to \infty$,

$$\mathbb{P}(Z_n \le x) \to \int_{-\infty}^{x} \frac{1}{\sqrt{2\pi}} e^{-\frac{1}{2}u^2}\, du \qquad\qquad \text{for } x \in \mathbb{R}.$$

SOLUTION. For the first part, the density function of X_n is

$$f_{X_n}(x) \begin{cases} \dfrac{1}{\Gamma(n)} x^{n-1} e^{-x} & \text{if } x > 0, \\ 0 & \text{if } x \le 0. \end{cases}$$

The moment generating function of X_n is

$$
\begin{aligned}
M_{X_n}(t) &= \int_0^\infty e^{tx} \frac{1}{\Gamma(n)} x^{n-1} e^{-x}\, dx \\
&= \frac{1}{\Gamma(n)} \int_0^\infty x^{n-1} e^{-(1-t)x}\, dx \\
&= \frac{1}{\Gamma(n)} \int_0^\infty (\frac{u}{1-t})^{n-1} e^{-u} \frac{1}{1-t}\, du \quad \text{by the substitution } u = (1-t)x \\
&= \frac{1}{\Gamma(n)(1-t)^n} \int_0^\infty u^{n-1} e^{-u}\, du \\
&= \frac{1}{\Gamma(n)(1-t)^n} \Gamma(n) \qquad\qquad \text{since } \int_0^\infty x^{n-1} e^{-x}\, dx = \Gamma(n) \\
&= (\frac{1}{1-t})^n \qquad\qquad \text{if } t < 1.
\end{aligned}
$$

The moment generating function of $Z_n = (X_n - n)/\sqrt{n}$ is

$$
\begin{aligned}
M_n(t) &= M_{Z_n}(t) \\
&= M_{\frac{1}{\sqrt{n}} X_n - \sqrt{n}}(t) \\
&= e^{t(-\sqrt{n})} M_{X_n}(\frac{1}{\sqrt{n}}t) \qquad\qquad \text{by (7.51)} \\
&= e^{-t\sqrt{n}} (\frac{1}{1 - \frac{t}{\sqrt{n}}})^n \\
&= e^{-t\sqrt{n}} (1 - \frac{t}{\sqrt{n}})^{-n},
\end{aligned}
$$

as required.

For the last part, we rewrite $M_n(t)$ in the form

$$M_n(t) = [\frac{e^{-t}}{(1 - \frac{t}{\sqrt{n}})^{\sqrt{n}}}]^{\sqrt{n}}.$$

Taking logarithms, we have

$$\log M_n(t) = \sqrt{n}(-t - \sqrt{n}\log(1 - \frac{t}{\sqrt{n}})) \qquad\qquad \text{since } \log e^{-t} = -t$$

$$= \sqrt{n}[-t - \sqrt{n}(-\frac{t}{\sqrt{n}} - \frac{t^2}{2n} - \frac{t^3}{3n\sqrt{n}} + o(\frac{1}{n}))] \qquad \text{use Taylor's theorem to expand } \log(1 - \frac{t}{\sqrt{n}})$$

$$= n[\frac{t^2}{2n} + \frac{t^3}{3n\sqrt{n}} + o(\frac{1}{n})] \to \frac{1}{2}t^2 \qquad\qquad \text{as } n \to \infty,$$

giving that

$$M_n(t) \to e^{\frac{1}{2}t^2} \qquad\qquad\qquad \text{as } n \to \infty,$$

and the result follows from Theorem 8.27. That is, as $n \to \infty$,

$$\mathbb{P}(Z_n \leq x) \to \int_{-\infty}^{x} \frac{1}{\sqrt{2\pi}} e^{-\frac{1}{2}u^2} \, du \qquad\qquad \text{for } x \in \mathbb{R}.$$

8.4. Large deviations and Cramér's theorem

8.5. Convergence in distribution, and characteristic functions

8.6. Problems

PROBLEM (8.6.1). Let $X_1, X_2, \ldots$ be independent random variables, each having the uniform distribution on the interval $(0, a)$, and let $Z_n = \max\{X_1, X_2, \ldots, X_n\}$ Show that
   (a) $Z_n \to a$ in probability as $n \to \infty$.
   (b) $\sqrt{Z_n} \to \sqrt{a}$ in probability as $n \to \infty$.
   (c) if $U_n = n(1 - Z_n)$ and $a = 1$, then

$$\mathbb{P}(U_n \leq x) = \begin{cases} 1 - e^{-x} & \text{if } x > 0, \\ 0 & \text{otherwise,} \end{cases}$$

so that U_n converges in distribution to the exponential distribution as $n \to \infty$.

SOLUTION. (a) The distribution function of Z_n is

$$F_{Z_n}(x) = \mathbb{P}(Z_n < x)$$
$$= \mathbb{P}(X_i < x, i = 1, 2, \ldots, n)$$
$$= \prod_{i=1}^{n} \mathbb{P}(X_i < x) \qquad \text{by independence}$$
$$= \prod_{i=1}^{n} F_{X_i}(x)$$
$$= \begin{cases} 0 & \text{if } x < 0, \\ \dfrac{x^n}{a^n} & \text{if } 0 \le x \le a, \\ 1 & \text{if } x > a, \end{cases} \qquad \text{since } F_{X_i}(x) = \begin{cases} 0 & \text{if } x < 0, \\ \dfrac{x}{a} & \text{if } 0 \le x \le a, \\ 1 & \text{if } x > a. \end{cases}$$

For $\epsilon > 0$,

$$\mathbb{P}(|Z_n - a| > \epsilon) = \mathbb{P}(Z_n - a > \epsilon \text{ or } Z_n - a < -\epsilon)$$
$$= \mathbb{P}(Z_n - a < -\epsilon) \qquad \text{since the event } Z_n - a > \epsilon \text{ does not happen}$$
$$= \mathbb{P}(Z_n < a - \epsilon)$$
$$= \begin{cases} 0 & \text{if } a - \epsilon < 0, \\ \dfrac{(a - \epsilon)^n}{a^n} & \text{if } 0 \le a - \epsilon < a. \end{cases}$$

Since $\dfrac{a - \epsilon}{a} < 1$ if $0 \le a - \epsilon < a$, it follows that $\dfrac{(a - \epsilon)^n}{a^n} \to 0$ as $n \to \infty$ if $0 \le a - \epsilon < a$. Thus $\mathbb{P}(|Z_n - a| > \epsilon) \to 0$ as $n \to \infty$. Hence $Z_n \to a$ in probability as $n \to \infty$.

(b) For $\epsilon > 0$,

$$\mathbb{P}\left(\left|\sqrt{Z_n} - \sqrt{a}\right| > \epsilon\right) = \mathbb{P}(\sqrt{Z_n} - \sqrt{a} > \epsilon \text{ or } \sqrt{Z_n} - \sqrt{a} < -\epsilon)$$
$$= \mathbb{P}(\sqrt{Z_n} - \sqrt{a} < -\epsilon)$$
$$= \mathbb{P}(\sqrt{Z_n} < \sqrt{a} - \epsilon)$$
$$= \begin{cases} 0 & \text{if } \sqrt{a} - \epsilon < 0, \\ \mathbb{P}(Z_n < (\sqrt{a} - \epsilon)^2) & \text{if } 0 \le \sqrt{a} - \epsilon < \sqrt{a}, \end{cases}$$
$$= \begin{cases} 0 & \text{if } \sqrt{a} - \epsilon < 0, \\ \dfrac{[(\sqrt{a} - \epsilon)^2]^n}{a^n} & \text{if } 0 \le \sqrt{a} - \epsilon < \sqrt{a}. \end{cases}$$

Since $0 \leq \sqrt{a} - \epsilon < \sqrt{a}$, so $0 \leq (\sqrt{a} - \epsilon)^2 < a$, implying $0 < \dfrac{[(\sqrt{a} - \epsilon)^2]^n}{a^n} < 1$ if $0 \leq \sqrt{a} - \epsilon < \sqrt{a}$. It follows that $\dfrac{[(\sqrt{a} - \epsilon)^2]^n}{a^n} \to 0$ as $n \to \infty$ if $0 \leq \sqrt{a} - \epsilon < \sqrt{a}$. Thus $\mathbb{P}(\left| \sqrt{Z_n} - \sqrt{a} \right| > \epsilon) \to 0$ as $n \to \infty$. Hence $\sqrt{Z_n} \to \sqrt{a}$ in probability as $n \to \infty$.

(c) We have that

$$\mathbb{P}(U_n \leq x) = \mathbb{P}(n(1 - Z_n) \leq x)$$

$$= \mathbb{P}(Z_n \geq \frac{n - x}{n})$$

$$= 1 - \mathbb{P}(Z_n < \frac{n - x}{n})$$

$$= \begin{cases} 1 & \text{if } \dfrac{n - x}{n} < 0, \\ 1 - \dfrac{(\frac{n-x}{n})^n}{1} & \text{if } 0 \leq \dfrac{n - x}{n} \leq 1, \\ 0 & \text{if } \dfrac{n - x}{n} > 1. \end{cases}$$

If $x \leq 0$, then $\dfrac{n - x}{n} > 1$, so $\mathbb{P}(U_n \leq 0) = 0$. If $x > 0$ and $n > x$, then $0 < \dfrac{n - x}{n} < 1$, so

$$\mathbb{P}(U_n \leq x) = 1 - (\frac{n - x}{n})$$

$$= 1 - (1 - \frac{x}{n})^n \to 1 - e^{-x} \qquad \text{as } n \to \infty.$$

Thus

$$\mathbb{P}(U_n \leq x) = \begin{cases} 1 - e^{-x} & \text{if } x > 0, \\ 0 & \text{otherwise,} \end{cases}$$

so that U_n converges in distribution to the exponential distribution as $n \to \infty$.

PROBLEM (8.6.2). By applying the central limit theorem to a sequence of random variables with the Bernoulli distribution, or otherwise, prove the following result in analysis. If $0 < p = 1 - q < 1$ and $x > 0$, then

$$\sum \binom{n}{k} p^k q^{n-k} \to 2 \int_0^x \frac{1}{\sqrt{2\pi}} e^{-\frac{1}{2}u^2} \, du \qquad \text{as } n \to \infty,$$

where the summation is over all values of k satisfying $np - x\sqrt{npq} \leq k \leq np + x\sqrt{npq}$

SOLUTION. Let $X_1, X_2, \ldots$ be independent, Bernoulli random variables with parameter p, each with mean $\mu = p$ and non-zero variance $\sigma^2 = p(1-p)$
. Write

$$S_n = \sum_{i=1}^{n} X_i$$

and so

$$Z_n = \frac{S_n - n\mu}{\sigma\sqrt{n}}$$
$$= \frac{S_n - np}{\sqrt{np(1-p)}}.$$

By the central limit theorem, Theorem 8.25,

$$\mathbb{P}(Z_n \leq x) \to \int_{-\infty}^{x} \frac{1}{\sqrt{2\pi}} e^{-\frac{1}{2}i^2} \, du \qquad\qquad \text{for } x \in \mathbb{R}.$$

Thus

$$\mathbb{P}(|Z_n| \leq x) \to \int_{-x}^{x} \frac{1}{\sqrt{2\pi}} e^{-\frac{1}{2}i^2} \, du \qquad\qquad \text{as } n \to \infty,$$

and so

$$\mathbb{P}(|Z_n| \leq x) \to 2 \int_{0}^{x} \frac{1}{\sqrt{2\pi}} e^{-\frac{1}{2}i^2} \, du \qquad\qquad \text{as } n \to \infty, \qquad (1)$$

since $\int_{-x}^{x} \frac{1}{\sqrt{2\pi}} e^{-\frac{1}{2}i^2} \, du = 2 \int_{0}^{x} \frac{1}{\sqrt{2\pi}} e^{-\frac{1}{2}i^2} \, du$. On the other hand

$$\mathbb{P}(|Z_n| \leq x) = \mathbb{P}(-x \leq Z_n \leq x)$$
$$= \mathbb{P}\left(-x \leq \frac{S_n - np}{\sqrt{np(1-p)}} \leq x\right)$$
$$= \mathbb{P}(np - x\sqrt{npq} \leq S_n \leq np + x\sqrt{npq}). \qquad (2)$$

The moment generating function of X_i is

$$M_{X_i}(t) = \mathbb{E}(e^{iX_i})$$
$$= e^{t \cdot 0}(1-p) + e^{t \cdot 1}p$$
$$= pe^t + 1 - p,$$

giving that S_n has moment generating function

$$M_{S_n}(t) = \prod_{k=1}^{n} X_k$$
$$= (pe^t + 1 - p)^n$$

Let Y be the random variable that has the binomial distribution with parameters p and n. Then Y has moment generating function

$$M_Y(t) = \mathbb{E}(e^{tY})$$
$$= \sum_{k=0}^{n} e^{tk} \binom{n}{k} p^k (1-p)^{n-k}$$
$$= \sum_{k=0}^{n} \binom{n}{k} (pe^t)^k (1-p)^{n-k}$$
$$= (pe^t + 1 - p)^n \qquad\qquad \text{by the binomial formula}$$

Thus $M_{S_n}(t) = M_Y(t)$. By the uniqueness theorem for the moment generating function

$$F_{S_n}(x) = F_Y(x),$$

where $F_{S_n}(x)$ and $F_Y(x)$ are the probability distribution function of S_n and Y, respectively. Hence

$$\mathbb{P}(np - x\sqrt{npq} \le S_n \le np + x\sqrt{npq}) = \mathbb{P}(np - x\sqrt{npq} \le Y \le np + x\sqrt{npq})$$
$$= \sum \binom{n}{k} p^k q^{n-k} \qquad (3)$$

where the summation is over all values of k satisfying $np - x\sqrt{npq} \le k \le np + x\sqrt{npq}$. From (1), (2), (3) we obtain

$$\sum \binom{n}{k} p^k q^{n-k} \to 2 \int_0^x \frac{1}{\sqrt{2\pi}} e^{-\frac{1}{2}u^2}\, du \qquad\qquad \text{as } n \to \infty,$$

where the summation is over all values of k satisfying $np - x\sqrt{npq} \le k \le np + x\sqrt{npq}$.

PROBLEM (8.6.3). Let X_n be a discrete random variable with the binomial distribution, parameters n and p. Show that $n^{-1}X_n$ converges to p in probability as $n \to \infty$.

SOLUTION. Since X_n has the binomial distribution with parameters n and p, it follows that

$$M_{X_n}(t) = (pe^t + 1 - p)^n,$$

and so

$$E(X_n) = M_n'(0)$$
$$= np,$$
$$E(X_n^2) = M_n''(0)$$
$$= np(1 - p) + n^2 p^2.$$

Since

$$E([n^{-1}X_n - p]^2) = E(n^{-2}X_n^2 - 2pn^{-1}X_n + p^2)$$
$$= \frac{1}{n^2}E(X_n^2) - \frac{2p}{n}E(X_n) + p^2$$
$$= \frac{1}{n^2}[np(1-p) + n^2 p^2] - \frac{2p}{n}np + p^2$$
$$= \frac{p(1-p)}{n} + p^2 - 2p^2 + p^2$$
$$= \frac{p(1-p)}{n}$$
$$\leq \frac{1}{4n} \to 0 \qquad \text{as } n \to \infty \quad \text{since } p(1-p) \leq \frac{1}{4},$$

$n^{-1}X_n$ converges to p in mean square as $n \to \infty$. By Theorem 8.14, $n^{-1}X_n$ converges to p in probability as $n \to \infty$.

PROBLEM (8.6.5). By applying the central limit theorem to a sequence of random variables with the Poisson distribution, or otherwise, prove that

$$e^{-n}(1 + n + \frac{n^2}{2!} + \cdots + \frac{n^n}{n!}) \to \frac{1}{2} \qquad \text{as } n \to \infty.$$

SOLUTION. Let $X_1, X_2, \ldots, X_n$ be independent random variables, each having the Poisson distribution with parameter 1 with probability generating function

$$G_{X_i}(s) = E(s^{X_i}) = \sum_{k=0}^{\infty} s^k \frac{e^{-1}}{k!} = e^{s-1}.$$

Let $S_n = X_1 + X_2 + \cdots X_n$. Then S_n has the probability generating function

$$G_{S_n}(s) = \prod_{i=1}^{\infty} G_{X_i}(s) \qquad\qquad \text{by independence}$$

$$= e^{n(s-n)},$$

so that S_n has the Poisson distribution with parameter n. Hence mean and variance of S_n are given by $\mathbb{E}(S_n) = 0$ and $\text{var}(S_n) = 1$. Now,

$$Z_n = \frac{S_n - n}{\sqrt{n}},$$

giving by the central limit theorem, Theorem 8.25, that the limiting distribution of Z_n is the normal distribution with mean 0 and variance 1, giving that

$$\mathbb{P}(S_n \le n) = e^{-n}\left(1 + n + \frac{n^2}{2!} + \cdots + \frac{n^n}{n!}\right)$$

$$= \mathbb{P}(Z_n \le 0) \to \int_{-\infty}^{0} \frac{1}{\sqrt{2\pi}} e^{-\frac{1}{2}x^2} \, dx = \frac{1}{2} \qquad \text{as } n \to \infty$$

since $\displaystyle\int_{-\infty}^{\infty} \frac{1}{\sqrt{2\pi}} e^{-\frac{1}{2}x^2} \, dx = 1$. Hence

$$e^{-n}\left(1 + n + \frac{n^2}{2!} + \cdots + \frac{n^n}{n!}\right) \to \frac{1}{2} \qquad \text{as } n \to \infty.$$

PROBLEM (8.6.7). Use the Cauchy–Schwarz inequality to prove that if $X_n \to X$ in mean square and $Y_n \to Y$ in mean square, then $X_n + Y_n \to X + Y$ in mean square.

SOLUTION. We have that

$$\mathbb{E}([(X_n + Y_n) - (X + Y)]^2)$$
$$= \mathbb{E}([(X_n - X) + (Y_n - Y)]^2)$$
$$= \mathbb{E}((X_n - X)^2) + \mathbb{E}((Y_n - Y)^2)$$
$$\qquad + 2\mathbb{E}((X_n - X)(Y_n - Y))$$
$$\le \mathbb{E}((X_n - X)^2) + \mathbb{E}((Y_n - Y)^2)$$
$$\qquad + 2\sqrt{\mathbb{E}((X_n - X)^2)\mathbb{E}((Y_n - Y)^2)} \qquad \text{by the Cauchy–Schwarz inequality, Theorem 7.30.}$$

But $X_n \to X$ in mean square and $Y_n \to Y$ in mean square, i.e,

$$\mathbb{E}([X_n - X]^2) \to 0 \qquad\qquad \text{as } n \to \infty$$
$$\mathbb{E}([Y_n - Y]^2) \to 0 \qquad\qquad \text{as } n \to \infty,$$

and so $\mathbb{E}((X_n - X)^2) + 2\sqrt{\mathbb{E}((X_n - X)^2)\mathbb{E}((Y_n - Y)^2)} + \mathbb{E}((Y_n - Y)^2) \to 0$ as $n \to \infty$. Thereofore, $\mathbb{E}([(X_n + Y_n) - (X + Y)]^2) \to 0$ as $n \to \infty$, i.e, $X_n + Y_n \to X + Y$ in mean square.

PROBLEM 8.6.1. Use the Cauchy–Schwarz inequality to prove that if $X_n \to X$ in mean square, then $\mathbb{E}(X_n) \to \mathbb{E}(X)$. Give an example of a sequence $X_1, X_2, \ldots$ such that $X_n \to X$ in probability but $\mathbb{E}(X_n)$ does not converge to $\mathbb{E}(X)$.

SOLUTION. $X_n \to X$ in mean square, i.e,

$$\mathbb{E}([X_n - X]^2) \to 0 \qquad\qquad \text{as } n \to \infty$$

For every $n \in \mathbb{N}$, let Y_n be the random variable that $\mathbb{P}(Y_n = 1)$, then $\mathbb{E}(Y_n) = 1$, $\mathbb{E}(Y_n) = 1$. Applying the Cauchy–Schwarz inequality to obtain

$$\mathbb{E}((X_n - X)Y_n) \le \sqrt{\mathbb{E}((X_n - X)^2)\mathbb{E}(Y_n^2)}$$
$$= \sqrt{\mathbb{E}((X_n - X)^2)} \to 0 \qquad\qquad \text{as } n \to \infty.$$

But $\mathbb{E}((X_n - X)Y_n) = \mathbb{E}(X_n - X) = \mathbb{E}(X_n) - \mathbb{E}(X)$. So $\mathbb{E}(X_n) - \mathbb{E}(X) \to 0$ as $n \to \infty$. Thus $\mathbb{E}(X_n) \to \mathbb{E}(X)$.

Example 8.19 is an example of a sequence $X_1, X_2, \ldots$ such that $X_n \to X$ in probability but $\mathbb{E}(X_n)$ does not converge to $\mathbb{E}(X)$.

PROBLEM 8.6.2 (8.6.11). Adapt the proof of Chebyshev's inequality to show that, if X is a random variable and $a > 0$, then

$$\mathbb{P}(\lfloor X \rfloor \ge a) \le \frac{1}{g(a)}\mathbb{E}(g(X)),$$

for any function $g \colon \mathbb{R} \to \mathbb{R}$ which satisfies
   (a) $g(x) = g(-x)$ for $x \in \mathbb{R}$,
   (b) $g(x) > 0$ for $x \ne 0$,
   (c) g is increasing on $[0, \infty)$.

SOLUTION. If $|X| > a > 0$, then $|X| \ne 0$ and so $g(|X|) > 0$ by condition (b). Since g is increasing on $[0, \infty)$ and by applying Markov's inequality, Theorem 7.63, we have

$$\mathbb{P}(\lfloor X \rfloor \ge a) = \mathbb{P}(g(|X|) \ge g(a)) \le \frac{1}{g(a)}\mathbb{E}(g(|X|)). \qquad (1)$$

If $X \ge 0$, then $|X| = X$, so $g(|X|) = g(X)$. If $X < 0$, then $|X| = -X$, so $g(|X|) = g(-X) = g(X)$ by condition (a). Therefore, in all cases we obtain

$$g(|X|) = g(X) \qquad\qquad\qquad (2)$$

Combine (1) and (2) to obtain

$$\mathbb{P}(\lfloor X \rfloor \geq a) \leq \frac{1}{g(a)} \mathbb{E}(g(X)),$$

as required.

PROBLEM (8.6.14). Let $(X_n \colon n \geq 1)$ be a sequence of random variables which converges in mean square. Show that $\mathbb{E}([X_n - X_m])^2 \to 0$ as $m, n \to \infty$.
If $\mathbb{E}(X_n) = \mu$ and $\mathrm{var}(X_n) = \sigma^2$ for all n, show that the correlation between X_n and X_m converges to 1 as $m, n \to \infty$.

SOLUTION. For the fist part, suppose $X_n \to X$ in mean square as $n \to \infty$. We have that

$$\begin{aligned}
(X_n - X_m)^2 &= [(X_n - X) + (X - X_m)]^2 \\
&= (X_n - X)^2 + 2(X_n - X)(X - X_m) + (X_m - X)^2,
\end{aligned}$$

and so

$$\begin{aligned}
0 \leq \mathbb{E}((X_n - X_m)^2) &= \mathbb{E}((X_n - X)^2) + \mathbb{E}((X_m - X)^2) \\
&\quad + 2\mathbb{E}((X_n - X)(X - X_m)) \\
&\leq \mathbb{E}((X_n - X)^2) + \mathbb{E}((X_m - X)^2) \\
&\quad + 2\sqrt{\mathbb{E}((X_n - X)^2)\mathbb{E}((X - X_m)^2)} \quad \text{by the Cauchy–Schwarz inequality.}
\end{aligned}$$

Thus

$$0 \leq \mathbb{E}((X_n - X_m)^2) \leq \mathbb{E}((X_n - X)^2) + 2\sqrt{\mathbb{E}((X_n - X)^2)\mathbb{E}((X - X_m)^2)} + \mathbb{E}((X_m - X)^2) \quad (1)$$

Since $X_n \to X$ in mean square as $n \to \infty$, so $\mathbb{E}((X_n - X)^2) \to 0$ and $\mathbb{E}((X_m - X)^2)$ as $n \to \infty$. Therefore

$$\mathbb{E}((X_n - X)^2) + 2\sqrt{\mathbb{E}((X_n - X)^2)\mathbb{E}((X - X_m)^2)} + \mathbb{E}((X_m - X)^2) \to 0 \quad \text{as } m, n \to \infty. \quad (2)$$

Combine (1) and (2) to obtain $\mathbb{E}([X_n - X_m])^2 \to 0$ as $m, n \to \infty$.

For the second part, recall that the correlation of the random variables X_n and X_m is

$$\rho(X_n, X_m) = \frac{\mathbb{E}((X_n - \mu)(X_m - \mu))}{\sqrt{\operatorname{var}(X_n)\operatorname{var}(X_m)}}$$

$$= \frac{\mathbb{E}((X_n - \mu)(X_m - \mu))}{\sigma^2}$$

$$= \frac{\mathbb{E}(X_n X_m - \mu(X_n + X_m) + \mu^2)}{\sigma^2}$$

$$= \frac{\mathbb{E}(X_n X_m) - \mu(\mathbb{E}(X_n) + \mathbb{E}(X_m)) + \mu^2}{\sigma^2}$$

$$= \frac{\mathbb{E}(X_n X_m) - \mu^2}{\sigma^2} \qquad \text{since } E(X_n) = E(X_m) = \mu$$

Thus

$$\rho(X_n, X_m) = \frac{\mathbb{E}(X_n X_m) - \mu^2}{\sigma^2} \qquad (1)$$

We also have

$$0 \leq |\mathbb{E}(X_n X_m) - E(X_n^2)| = |\mathbb{E}(X_n(X_m - X_n))|$$

$$\leq \sqrt{\mathbb{E}(X_n^2)E((X_m - X_n)^2)} \qquad \text{by the Cauchy–Schwarz inequality}$$

$$= \sqrt{\mu^2 + \sigma^2}\sqrt{\mathbb{E}((X_m - X_n)^2)} \to 0$$

since $\mathbb{E}(X_n^2) = \mu^2 + \sigma^2$ and by the first part. Therefore

$$\lim_{n,m\to\infty} \mathbb{E}(X_n X_m) = \lim_{n\to\infty} \mathbb{E}(X_n^2) = \mu^2 + \sigma^2 \qquad (2)$$

since $\sigma^2 = \operatorname{var}(X_n) = \mathbb{E}(X_n^2) - \mu^2$, so $\mathbb{E}(X_n^2) = \mu^2 + \sigma^2$ for all n.

Combine (1) and (2), we have

$$\lim_{m,n\to\infty} \rho(X_n, X_m) = \lim_{m,n\to\infty} \frac{\mathbb{E}(X_n X_m) - \mu^2}{\sigma^2}$$

$$= \frac{\lim_{m,n\to\infty} \mathbb{E}(X_n X_m) - \mu^2}{\sigma^2}$$

$$= \frac{\mu^2 + \sigma^2 - \mu^2}{\sigma^2}$$

$$= 1.$$

Printed in Great Britain
by Amazon

79737062R00183